Praise for *The Definitive Book of Handwriting Analysis*

"For over 20 years I have made it my self-appointed task to scan the graphological landscape to document and report on significant researchers and events. Marc Seifer has consistently hit my radar with his research and sharing of knowledge. His *Definitive Book of Handwriting Analysis* is a fine example of a work that is both a point of reference and a suitable book for teaching. He has fused modern thinking on the subject from many different nations. For the beginner this is a perfect starting point and even the most knowledgeable graphologist will find something new."

—Nigel Bradley, University of Westminster,
Graphology commentator

"This is a book that covers it all—graphology, questioned documents examination, and the brain—a lofty aim, and well done. There are many high quality handwriting samples, made interesting, both by their qualities and the celebrity of the writers.... Further, we find detailed discussions of the handwritings of some very bad people including Osama bin Laden, whose bizarre signature has puzzled many graphologists. If you are serious [about graphology], this....volume is worth putting on your shelf."

—Sheila Lowe, editor of *The Vanguard* (a graphology
newsletter), author of
Handwritings of the Famous and Infamous

Praise for Marc Seifer's Past Work:

"Tinged with pathos, this meticulously researched biography deserves attention from all who would understand the human tragedies played out in the shadows of our neon culture."

—*Booklist*

"Seifer's vivid, revelatory, exhaustively researched biography rescues pioneer inventor Nikola Tesla from cult status and restores him to his rightful place as a principal architect of the modern age. Seifer provides the fullest account yet of Tesla as an entrepreneur, experimental physicist and inventor."

—*Publisher's Weekly*

"The depth of Marc Seifer's scholarship and the clarity of his thinking make this book a worthwhile read for anyone interested in the frontiers of consciousness research."

—Jeffrey Mishlove, PhD, Dean of Consciousness
Studies Research, University of Philosophical Research

THE DEFINITIVE BOOK OF

HANDWRITING ANALYSIS

The Complete Guide to
Interpreting Personalities, Detecting Forgeries,
and Revealing Brain Activity Through
the Science of Graphology

Marc Seifer, PhD

NEW PAGE BOOKS
A division of The Career Press, Inc.

THE DEFINITIVE BOOK OF HANDWRITING ANALYSIS
EDITED BY GINA TALUCCI
TYPESET BY EILEEN DOW MUNSON
Cover design by Howard Grossman / 12E Design
Printed in the U.S.A.

To order this title, please call toll-free 1-800-CAREER-1 (NJ and Canada: 201-848-0310) to order using VISA or MasterCard, or for further information on books from Career Press.

The Career Press, Inc., 220 west Parkway, Unit 12
Pompton Plains, NJ 07444
www.careerpress.com
www.newpagebooks.com

Library of Congress Cataloging-in-Publication Data

Seifer, Marc J.
    The definitive book of handwriting analysis : the complete guide to interpreting personalities, detecting forgeries, and revealing brain activity through the science of graphology / by Marc Seifer.
        p. cm.
    Include bibliographical references (p.   ) and index.
    ISBN 978-1-60163-025-4
    1. Graphology. I. Title.

BF891.S375 2009
155.2' 82--dc22
                                                                            2008020685

For my mother

Thelma Imber Seifer

who began this quest with me

in Graphology at the New School

for Social Research in New York City

37 years ago.

Photo credit: Stanley Seifer

**Thelma Seifer with her son at the National
Society for Graphology, circa 1992.**

Acknowledgments

This book began in 1970 after I read an article by Dan Anthony on handwriting analysis. Shortly thereafter, I enrolled in his handwriting investigation courses at the New School for Social Research in New York City. This program was also attended by my mother Thelma Imber Seifer, who has been my colleague in this endeavor since that time. I would like to thank Dan Anthony and his wife, Florence, for their superb guidance in this complex field. The breadth of this work has been inspired and guided by Dan Anthony.

In 1972, I began a master's program at the University of Chicago. I would like to thank my professors; my mentor, Daniel G. Freedman; Bruno Bettelheim, for his guidance and work in psychoanalysis; and Herbert Meltzer, MD and David Goode, MD, the two medical doctors with whom I worked at Billings Hospital when I studied the handwritings of schizophrenic patients.

In 1974 I began my apprenticeship as a QD expert at the Crime Laboratory at the University of Rhode Island. I would like to thank David DeFanti, PhD, for all his support during that time.

In 1990, I began my work as a handwriting expert for the fraud units of the Department of Human Services and the attorney general's office in Rhode Island. In particular, I would like to thank George Moriarty, head investigator.

I would also like to thank the following people, for providing MRIs, handwriting samples, and counsel: handwriting experts Alan Levine, MD; Pat Siegel; Iris Holmes Hatfield; Ruth Holmes; Sarah Holmes; Roger Rubin; Heidi Harrelson; Nigel Bradley; Dafna Yalon; Robert O'Block; Kathie Koppenhaver; Thelma Imber Seifer; Felix Klein; Marge Westergaard; Thea Stein Lewinson; and Sheila Lowe. Also Stanley Krippner, my mentor for my doctorate who edited my Tesla treatise; Warren TenHouten, PhD; and Joseph Bogen, MD, who provided the handwriting samples of the epileptic split-brain patients; editors Walter Donway and Cynthia Read of the Dana Foundation, who edited my article on brain damage and handwriting for *Cerebrum*; the editors at *Rhode Island Monthly* who did a feature article on me; and two doctors from the Department of Neurology, School of Medicine, Brown University, Syed Risvi, MD, specialist in multiple sclerosis and neuro-immunology, and Lorcan O'Tuama, MD, neuroradiology. Also, Randy and Rena Tyson, Clifford Irving, and Harold Rhoden for various Howard Hughes papers, Kate Wolff and Beverly Canin for Werner Wolff material, and the archives of Bancroft Library at the University of California at Berkeley, Stanford White papers, and Butler Library at Columbia University for the handwritings of R.U. Johnson and Nikola Tesla. Also a special thanks to Bob Eaton of R&R Enterprises for the many handwriting samples of numerous VIPs and celebrities they provided.

Other individuals who helped in this project include Lynn Sevigny for her beautiful drawings, particularly the frontispiece, Nigel Bradley, Uri Geller, Nelson DeMille, Sanford Neuschatz, Elliott Shriftman, Howard Smukler, John White, Carl, Esther and Stephen Rosati, and the many lawyers for whom I have worked; also my brother Bruce Seifer, sister Meri Keithley and her husband, John, and my understanding wife, Lois Mary Pazienza.

Most importantly I would like to thank editors Michael Pye and Adam Schwartz; the publisher, Ronald Fry, and the rest of the staff at Career Press; also Roger Williams University, Dean Ruth Koelle, Don Whitworth, PhD, Garrett Berman, Matt Zaitchik, Laura Turner, Charles Trimbach, Frank DiCataldo, and the rest of the psychology department for having the foresight to break new ground in allowing the study of handwriting to take its proper place in the fields of forensic and neuropsychology in America.

Marc J. Seifer, PhD

Narragansett, Rhode Island

Photo Acknowledgements:

R&R Auction House: Neil Armstrong, Fred Astaire, Tallulah Bankhead, Theta Bara, James Belushi, Peter Benchley, Sarah Bernhardt, Marlon Brando, Martin Buber, Joseph Conrad, Jean Cocteau, Agatha Cristie, Salvador Dali, Jack Dempsy, Marlene Dietrich, Tom Edison, Dakota Fanning, Anna Freud, Sigmund Freud, Robet Fulton, Terry Gilliam, Alfred Hitchcock, Billie Holiday, Michael Jackson, Jackie Kenedy, Martin Luther King, Hedi Lemarr, Jerry Lewis, Liberace, Jayne Mansfield, Grandma Moses, Paul Newman, Jack Nicklaus, Jesse Owen, Ignace Paderewski, Pele, Erwin Rommel, General Sherman, Buce Springsteen, Harold Takata, Lowell Thomas, Hunter Thompson, Sidney Toler, Kurt Vonnegut, Count Zeppelin.

MetaScience Archives: Robert Adsit, Buzz Aldrin, Dan Anthony, Fred Allen, Lloyd Boucher, Noel Coward, Nelson DeMille, Jimmy Durante, Elizabeth Edwards, Ira Einhorn, Anthony Fokker, Uri Geller, Rene Haynes, Felix Klein, Thea Stein Lewinson, Marjorie Main, J. Pierpont Morgan, Paul Scofield, Lynn Sevigny, Lawrence Stevens, Herry Teltscher, Arturo Tuscanini, Werner Wolff

Contents

Part I: Behavioral Profiling

Part II: Handwriting and Brain Organization

Part III. Questioned Documents

Part

I

Behavioral Profiling

Figure 1.1. Edgar Allan Poe

In April 1841, *Graham Magazine* published *Murders of the Rue Morgue*, the famous detective story by Edgar Allan Poe. The introduction to the tale contained passages adapted from Poe's work on "autography" or handwriting analysis, which first appeared in the *Southern Literary Messenger*:

> The analyst…glories…in that moral activity which disentangles. He derives pleasure from even the most trivial occupations bringing his talents into play. He is fond of enigmas, of conundrums, of hieroglyphics; exhibiting in his solutions of each a degree of acumen which appears to the ordinary apprehension preternatural. His results, brought about by the very soul and essence of method, have in truth, the whole aim of intuition.

Poe makes it clear that there are systemized procedures to "autography." The true handwriting analyst must be able to distinguish the differences between calculation and analysis by a "host of observations and inferences…. It is in matters beyond the limits of mere rule that the skill of the analyst is evinced" (164).

Although questioned document experts assure us that "handwriting exhibits identifying characteristics…which enable it to be identified beyond a reasonable doubt" (Harrison, 288–291), mainstream psychologists have rarely studied graphology in America.

European Heritage

Graphology is a required or available course for graduate studies in a number of European psychology curriculums. Centers of learning that have offered or still offer courses in graphology include universities in England, Spain, France, Germany, Switzerland, and Italy. Consequently, most of the major developments in the field are European in origin. Trained handwriting analysts with advanced degrees in Europe can testify in court, although this practice was more prevalent before World War II. Klara Roman, a research associate to psychologist Kurt Lewin, had written her doctorate on graphology in 1928. Soon after, she became the authorized handwriting expert to the Royal Hungarian Criminal Court (Wolfson, in Roman, xiii). In the 1930s and 1940s, Rhoda Weiser, authority on the handwriting of criminals, became the "handwriting expert to the courts and police of Austria," and Max Pulver, who taught handwriting at the University of Zurich, worked in a similar capacity in Switzerland (Roman, 1962, 446). During this same era, Dr. Hans Schneikert held the chair in criminalistic graphology at Berlin University, and Captain Arthur J. Quirke, who was both graphologist and questioned documents examiner, was the handwriting expert to the Department of Justice in Ireland (Quirke, xi).

Today, important centers for graphology include the Moretti Graphology Institute at Urbino University in Italy, Leipzig University in Germany, the University of Barcelona in Spain, and graphology institutes in Zurich and Paris. Dr. Helmut Ploog, editor of *Angewandte Graphologie und Personlichkeits Diagnostik,* teaches graphology at the University of Munich. Ursula Avé-Lallemant, creator of the Star Wave test, has developed a grapho-diagnostic technique for children and adolescents that she has implemented in Switzerland, England, Norway, and Germany having been supported with a grant from the Bavarian Ministry of Education (1999, 120). Pierre Faideau, president of *Groupement des graphologues-conseils de France*, has edited the comprehensive textbook called *La Graphologie*. In England, Nigel Bradley has played a key role organizing conferences, editing proceedings, reprinting out-of-print classics, and helping to translate other works into English. In America, Patricia Siegel, president of the American Society of Professional Graphologists has brought many European graphologists to America to lecture, and Carole Schuler of the National Society for Graphology has condensed and transcribed every lecture given at that society for more than a quarter century.

The term *graphology* was coined by French clergyman Abbé Jean Hippolyte Michon, student of Abbé Louis J.E. Flandrin, who in the 1830s founded a school of handwriting interpretations with the Archbishop of Cambrai; this school became the source of modern graphology. After 30 years of empirical study comparing hundreds of known characteristics with various graphological signs, Michon wrote *System de Graphologie*, which is considered to be the first modern major treatise on the subject. Arthur Quirke once said of Michon:

> Michon owes his status as the pioneer of graphology to the fact that he had an insatiable penchant for research. As a result, the amount of material amassed by him [has provided ample data...] for a generation of subsequent investigators.

Each specific "element of the handwriting" or "sign" corresponded to a specific character trait, "and the absence of a specific sign indicated the lack of its matching trait." It was Michon who coined the word *graphology* from the Greek *grapho* meaning "to write" or "draw," and *logos*, which stands for "word" or "reason" (Saudek, 13). Paul de St. Colombe stated:

> Ancient Egyptians held handwriting sacred, that as early as 1,000 B.C. in China and Japan, a rudimentary handwriting analysis was practiced. Japanese scholars of the time judged that character conformed to the way a man traced his bars according to thickness, length, rigidity or suppleness.

The science of handwriting analysis can trace its roots to antiquity. In ancient China, Confucius (551–479 BC) warned, "Beware of a man whose writing sways like a reed in the wind" (Rockwell, 4). "King Jo-Hau (1060–1180 AD) a philosopher and painter of the Sung Period declared that 'handwriting infallibly shows whether the scribe comes from a vulgar or a noble-minded person'" (Hatfield Holmes, 2006; Dolch, 2006). The Greeks also had graphologists. C. Suetonius Tranquillus wrote of Caesar in 120 AD, "He does not hyphen words and continue on to the following line...but simply squeezes them in and curves the end of the line downward" (Jacoby, 17). Nevertheless, a full-bodied work on the science did not appear until 1622, when the Italian physician and professor of Theoretical Medicine from the University of Bologna, Camillo Baldi, wrote his treatise *Method to Recognize the Nature and Quality of a Writer from his Letters*. In this study, Baldi stated, "it is obvious that all persons write in their own peculiar way.... Characteristic forms...cannot be truly imitated by anybody else" (Jacoby, 18). He also pointed out the necessity of careful observation to mark down characteristics that tend to recur and to distinguish artificial from natural tendencies.

A century later, in the 1770s, Lavater wrote *Physiognomic Fragments*, which continued to expand the theory of handwriting interpretation. This was followed by the 1816 French text *The Art of Judging the Soul and Character of Man by Studying His Handwriting* by Edouard Hocquart. In 1820, Hocquart and Lavatar's colleague, Goethe, concurred by stating, "There can be no doubt that the handwriting of a person has some relation to his mind and character" (Jacoby, 20). Other early notables who practiced the art included Charles Dickens, Emile Zola, the Brownings, Disraeli, Sir Walter Scott, Ernst Mach, Baudelair, Balzaq, and Sir Arthur Conan Doyle.

Jean Crépieux-Jamin

It was Michon's student, Jean Crépieux-Jamin (1858–1940), son of a watchmaker and himself a dental surgeon who treated French and Belgian troops during World War I, who synthesized the work of his predecessors. Crépieux-Jamin abandoned the restrictive tradition of correlating each graphic sign to a specific character trait and the simplistic notion that if a graphological sign was missing, the corresponding character trait must be missing as well. Robert Saudek once said of him: "All knowledge of graphology is either based on...or is derived from adaptions, imitations and plagiarisms of [Crépieux-Jamin's] works."

In 1888, Crépieux-Jamin published *L'ecriture et le caractère (Handwriting and Character)*, in which he emphasized that handwriting must be analyzed as a totality with each trait contributing to the whole. In this way, he laid the groundwork for the Gestalt approach to graphological interpretation. "No modern graphologist would claim that any one graphic feature or 'sign' has in itself any fixed meaning" (Roman, 444). Credited as the discoverer of the theory of resultants that enabled the graphologist to deduce secondary qualities from the combination of known primary

Figure 1.2. Crépieux-Jamin

characteristics, Crépieux-Jamin created the framework for modern-day graphology, with his books as a primary source of all that was to follow. "The study of elements," Crépieux-Jamin wrote, "is to graphology as the study of the alphabet is to the reading of prose."

Writing about such related topics as the psychology of movement and sex in handwriting, Crépieux-Jamin founded the *Societe Francais de Graphologie*, and had his works translated into English as far back as 1892. A charismatic figure, Crépieux-Jamin remained the dominant French theoretician for more than half a century. A well-known figure at international European congresses, which were held until the outbreak of WWII, Crépieux-Jamin influenced Nobel Prize–winner/philosopher Henri Bergson; Pierre Janet; Alfred Binet, designer of the Stanford Binet IQ test; Jean Piaget, the well-known child psychologist; and Henri Pieron, who, working with Binet, conducted research on the topics of graphology and personality at the Sorbonne in Paris. Crépieux-Jamin's American translation also became the standard from which all other turn-of-the-century graphology textbooks had to be compared.

Criticism of Crépieux-Jamin

The Germans were initially sparked by the work of the French, who were their predecessors, but the Germans were more attuned to finding psycho-physiological correlates to graphic signs found in the handwriting. Robert Saudek, a Czech who moved to England in the 1920s, in part to bring graphology to the English-speaking world, notes that although Crépieux-Jamin was "unsurpassed as a practical worker… endowed with that faculty of sharp observation…he reared a new edifice of crooked construction" (Saudek, 16–17). Crépieux-Jamin's methods were "inexact," because they were based on intuition and empirical study rather than on scientific analysis or biological premises. Further, Crépieux-Jamin saw the signature as an "autonomous product" unrelated to the handwriting, "a method quite suitable for graphological entertainment at a tea-party, but which renders impossible a scientific treatment of the subject…. But in spite of this, pupils with an innate talent for psychology and graphology will learn more quickly from him than from the more thorough, more scientific… but more cumbersome German authors" (16–17).

The German School

Adolf Henze, a contemporary of Michon's, caught the attention of the public when he published articles on graphology in a Leipzig periodical and published the book *Chirogrammatomantie*, which referred to teaching the characteristics and abilities of humans from the handwriting. Henze, who in 1855, was the first to introduce the word *garland* to refer to u-like movements in such letters as m's and n's, was followed by E. Schweidland, later professor of economics, who translated some of the work of the French for a number of pupils, particularly Wilhelm Langenbruch, who founded the first German graphology journal in 1895. The most famous contributor was Dr. William Preyer, a full professor of medicine from the University of Jena, who was well known for his work on the neuropsychology of language acquisition.

However, Langenbruch was soon eclipsed by Hans Busse, editor of the competing and more prestigious graphological periodical, *Monthly Journal*. Busse also translated much of the French work into German, and he also compiled an extensive bibliography of international literature on the subject, which helped Germany become the leader in theoretical and experimental graphology.

In 1879 came two important works, Albreacht Erlenmeye's *Handwriting: Main Characteristics of its Psychology and Pathology*, and Wilhelm Preyer's (1895) *On the Physiology of Writing*. These books established that handwriting was actually brain writing. By having writers perform with their opposite hand, their foot, and even their mouth, crucial similarities were displayed, which conclusively established that writing was centrally organized. Other German psychologists who studied handwriting for personality traits and psychopathology included Magdalene Ivanovic, who is credited with being the first to discuss the air stroke. Wilhelm Wundt, the father of modern-day psychology, and his associate Emil Kraepelin, "who attempted to measure pressure and speed in normal and mentally disturbed persons with his Kraepelin Scale" (Roman, 1962, 437). Kraepelin invented a method of measure that became the basis for psychiatry's *Diagnostic Statistical Manual*, the standard bearer for cataloging all mental disorders. Unfortunately, Preyer passed away at the age of 56 in 1897.

Ludwig Klages

Busse continued to edit *Monthly Journal* throughout the early 1900s. Two new writers of note emerged: Dr. George Meyer and Dr. Erwin Axel. Meyer's 1901 treatise, *The Scientific Basis of Graphology*, expanded on the Gestalt approach while noticing that "the intention of the writer is always manifest at the beginning of words, lines or sentences, whereas further text or ends of lines show the real nature of the unconscious of the writer" (Saudek, 22). On the other hand, Axel, who was unknown at the time, attacked Michon's work on fixed signs and Crépieux-Jamin's doctrine of harmony. He called for an end to unscientific suppositions and stated his belief that graphology should be based solely upon what can be proven. His premise sowed the seed for a scientific theory of expressive behavior. Notable proponents of this line of investigation include Robert Saudek, Gordon Allport, Werner Wolff, Thea Stein Lewinson, and Klara Roman.

Saudek (1926) informs the reader that it was not until a full decade later, in 1910, that Axel revealed his true identity: Ludwig Klages (23). A graduate from the University of Munich with training in physics, chemistry, and philosophy, Klages (1872–1956) was a brilliant characterologist who attempted to link the mystery of human existence and its psychophysical character to natural forces, and thus to the very pulsation of life itself. Klages realized that the dynamic

Figure 1.3. Ludwig Klages

relationship between contraction and release in handwriting, the interplay of up and down strokes, is manifested in its *rhythm*. Mentally healthy writers would display a natural balance between contraction (movements toward the body) and release (movements away from the body), whereas mentally disturbed individuals would display impaired rhythm.

Criticism of Klages

Eric Singer (1949/69), doctor of law from the University of Vienna and popular author of graphology books, both praises and criticizes Klages. Singer credits Klages as being "the first to create a complete and systematic theory of graphology." Klages was also the first to realize the link between rhythm, or movements of contraction and release, with theories of expressive behavior and characterology. However, according to Singer, Klages was unable to realize that opposite traits can exist in the same person. "Secondly, Klages' intellectualism, and his tendency to supercilious condescension in appreciating the achievements of the French" thwarted further development of the field. Klages only knew German script, and this was also a hampering factor, as was his inability to appreciate the work of Freud and psychodynamic theory, "and so he missed the connection between graphology and the modern psychology of the unconscious" (36).

Robert Saudek

Born in Kolin, Czechoslovakia, the graphologist Robert Saudek was also a diplomat for the Czech government. A playwright and novelist as well, his books include *A Child's Conscience* and *Jewish Youths*. Having studied graphology at universities in Prague, Leipzig, and at the Sorbonne, one of his life's goals was to bring scientific graphology to the English-speaking world. "During the First World War, Saudek maintained an Intelligence Unit in The Hague and at the end of the War in 1918 he entered the diplomatic service for the Czechoslovakian Government, serving in Holland before finally settling in London" (Senate House Library archives, University of London). In 1930, Saudek founded *Character and Personality: An International Quarterly for Psychodiagnostics*, the first major English language journal that routinely published articles on graphology. After he died, the periodical was taken over by Charles Spearman, a student of Wilhelm Wundt's, who was made famous for his groundbreaking work on human intelligence. Spearman, in turn, was the teacher of Raymond Cattell, who worked with E.L. Thorndike on theories of personality, and David Wechsler, designer of the widely used Wechsler Intelligence Test.

Lecturing on experimental graphology in Amsterdam, Berlin, Brussels, and Prague, Saudek used motion picture equipment to record and measure

Figure 1.4. Robert Saudek

handwriting and conducted extensive studies on the handwriting and corresponding mental abilities of twins. His two texts *Psychology of Handwriting* (1926) and *Experiments in Handwriting* (1928) are essential works in the field. In the former, Saudek discusses the concept of the "counterdominant." Whereas the dominant feature in a writing is one single characteristic that "prevails over the others by the marked frequency of its occurrence, the counterdominant is a contradiction" (143)—that is, a feature that somehow seems out of place. An example would be a small signature in an otherwise large handwriting. This contradiction, if and when it appears, becomes a focal point from which the "real source of personality" can be uncovered.

Saudek is seen as the first graphologist to explore "the differences between national characters and national copy-book writing" (Singer, 36). The handwriting model in Germany is more angular than French, Italian, or English writings, and this reflects a difference between, for instance, the more regimented Germanic nature and the more easygoing Italian disposition.

Max Pulver

Eric Singer credits Max Pulver as being the first to "abandon" some of Klages's more abstruse ideas and link graphology to psychodynamic theory (36–37). An associate of Carl Jung, and lecturer at the University of Zurich, Swiss psychologist Max Pulver (1890–1953) discusses symbolic characteristics of the writing field and its movement in three dimensions, vertical, horizontal, and depth (or pressure).

On handwriting, Pulver once said, "In order to grasp expression in an adequate way, it is absolutely necessary to know the unconscious images that act upon graphic action. The man who writes unconsciously portrays his inner nature."

Figure 1.5. Pulver

Using ideas from projection theory and psychoanalysis, Pulver was the first to introduce the concept of the three zones in the writing space. "We take as a point of departure for our orientation the line, real or ideal. It is bounded between above and below; it is the horizon the demarcation between day and night. Spontaneous imagination looks above, the sky, the sun, the day, the light, the powers, and spirits on high.

Below the line, it is the opposite realm: the night, the darkness, the abyss, the depths" (12). The area *on* the line represents terra firma or everyday world. From this, Pulver formulated his trizonal symbology:

Upper zone	Head	Heaven	Mental Ideas	Superego
Middle Zone	Body	Earth	Everyday World	Ego
Lower zone	Genitals	Hades	Libidinal Drives	Id

Carl Jung added his thoughts to Pulver's ideas when he said:

The unconscious knows more than consciousness does; but it is knowledge of a special sort, knowledge in eternity, usually without reference to the here and now, not couched in language of the intellect. Only when we let its statements amplify themselves…does it come within the range of our understanding; only then does a new aspect become perceptible to us.

As a technique for gaining insight, as told to me many years ago by a Swiss émigré who met Pulver, the graphologue would project handwritings onto a wall to study them. "It is not the meaning of the written communication, but the symbolic significance borne by the play of the movements of the graphic image that reaches the organs of perception." Leaving the handwriting up for days on end, new insights began to emerge. In this way, Pulver was allowing unconscious perception or intuition to play a role (Pulver, 1953/80, 3–4). In one instance, after looking at the writing, he reached to his neck and then guessed that the writer wore a bow-tie, and he was right.

This kind of analysis was influenced by Rafael Schermann. A celebrity psychic of Polish origin who made his mark between the two world wars, Schermann displayed numerous astounding insights that were based more on his pronounced intuitive abilities then on precepts derived from scientific graphology. For instance, Schermann had the ability, upon meeting a per-

Figure 1.6. Handwriting that looks like ocean liner

son, to simulate that person's signature. Assuming his abilities to be genuine, thought transference apparently played a role, Freud himself took an interest in this unusual individual (*NY Freudian.org*). However, there was some crossover to known tenets from graphology. For instance, after looking at handwriting on an envelope that resembled an ocean liner, Schermann speculated that the writer was planning a cruise, and he was right (Bagger, 1924). In this instance, the writer's own subconscious presented clues concerning an upcoming event.

It is well known that writers sometimes place symbols in their handwriting that correlate to their profession or to physical features. For example, the baseball player Ted Williams often makes a t-bar that resembles a bat; the first man on the moon, Neil Armstrong, has a signature that resembles a rocket ship; Marlene Dietrich's signature resembles a lady in repose.

"One can refine intuitive sensitiveness," Klara Roman writes, "but the scientific mind feels the need for objective principles by which to check subjective perceptions and clarify their vague, hit-or-miss impressions" (1962) For Roman, handwriting as an expressive behavior reveals the "dynamic interplay of purposive and unconscious factors" (442). She sums up the process in her book *Encyclopedia of the Written Word*:

> Viewing the writing pattern as a whole in order to grasp its essential overall expression; closer scrutiny of...its individual features and correlating them with the personality factors they stand for; then ordering them all into related groups and synthesizing them in the context of the whole...[will serve to create an] integrated, dynamic personality picture. It should be emphasized that it is never the form of single letters alone, or on any particular characteristic, but the combination and interaction of all parts of the writing pattern that reveal the personality of the writer.

Figure 1.7. Robert Walsh signature

19th-Century Graphology in America

> The handwriting is bold, large, sprawling, and irregular. It is rather rotund than angular, and is by no means illegible. One would suppose it was written in a violent hurry. The t's are crossed with a sweeping scratch of the pen, giving the whole letter an odd appearance if held upside down, or in any position other than the proper one. A dictatorial air pervades the whole...betraying a blustering self-conceit.

> —Edgar Allan Poe's analysis of the signature of journalist Robert Walsh, *Southern Literary Messenger*, February 1836

The first American autographer of note is none other than Edgar Allan Poe, who analyzed the signatures of more than 100 notables in a running column that ran in *Graham Magazine* and *The Southern Literary Messenger* from 1836 until 1842. Elizabeth Barrett Browning and Lord Baconsfield were also intrigued by the study of handwriting, says R.D. Stocker (1901) who credits Miss Rosa Baughan as "the first modern English writer to compile a serious treatise on graphology," which she published in 1875. Her forbearers included two other British authors: Thomas Byerley, editor of *The Literary Chronicle and Weekly Review*, who devoted a chapter on signatures in 1823, and Isaac D'Israeli, father of the prime minister of England who added a chapter on the topic in his popular book, *Curiosities of Literature*, in 1824 (Backman, 2006).

> I am prejudiced in favor of he who, without impudence, can ask boldly. He has faith in humanity, and faith in himself. No one who is not accustomed to giving grandly can ask nobly and with boldness.
>
> —Johann Kaspar Lavater

All of these individuals ultimately trace their initial interest in the topic to the work of the Swiss pastor, Johan Kasper Lavater (1741–1801), physiognomist and handwriting analyst. "I have remarked a perfect analogy in the language, movement of the body of a person and his handwriting," Lavater wrote, predating Harvard educated psychologist Gordon Allport and his assertion of the same observation by 150 years. "The more I compare different handwritings," Lavater reflected, "the more I am convinced that handwriting is the expression of the character of him who writes" (Stocker, 1901, p. vi). The Internet lists many quotes from the astute Lavater, including the following, which aptly predates the work of Max Pulver and the Gestalt psychologists: "Intuition is the clear conception of the whole at once."

> The finest delineations are made by combining characteristics. In fact, that is imperative if the student desires absolute accuracy. The most incompatible traits are sometimes indicated, and he must remember that human nature often exhibits curious anomalies. If two traits seem to be opposed, he must find their relative strength, and from that deduce the resultant characteristic. Any sign in a specimen may be strong or weak, plentiful or scarce.
>
> —John Rexford

Other 19th-century American autographers include *The Scarlet Letter* author Nathaniel Hawthorne, who wrote a chapter on signatures stating, "The original manuscript has always something which print itself must inevitably lose. An erasure, even a blot, a casual irregularity of execution, bring us close to the writer and perhaps convey some of those subtle intimations or which language has no shape.... The writer's character," Hawthorne concludes, "is revealed in the autograph" (DeSalamanca, 3–4). However, similar to Poe and most other early-19th-century handwriting analysts, Hawthorne's work was based almost purely on intuition with no scientific counterpart. Thus, these early graphologists were often wrong in their personality assessments, because they had no theoretical or scientific basis for the assumptions that they made. In a nutshell, handwriting analysis in the early and mid-19th century was no more than a hobby.

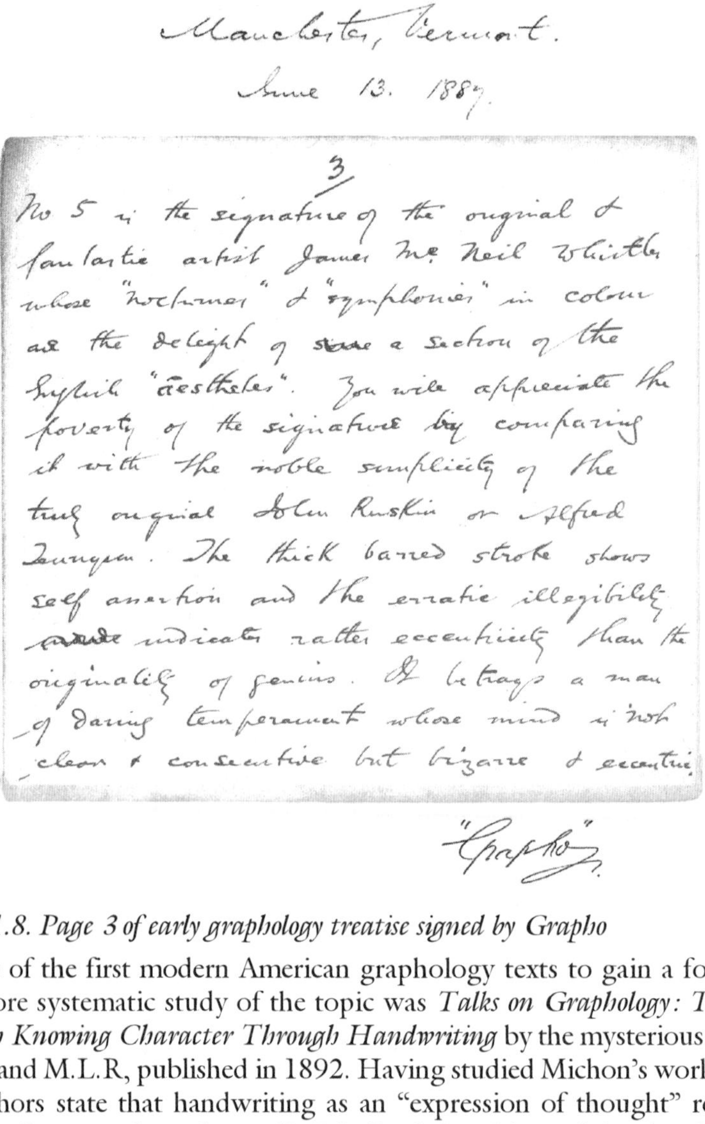
Manchester, Vermont.
June 13. 1887.

3

No 5 is the signature of the original & fantastic artist James McNeil Whistler whose "nocturnes" & "symphonies" in colour are the delight of a section of the English "aesthetes". You will appreciate the poverty of the signature by comparing it with the noble simplicity of the truly original John Ruskin or Alfred Tennyson. The thick barred stroke shows self assertion and the erratic illegibility indicates rather eccentricity than the originality of genius. It betrays a man of daring temperament whose mind is not clear & consecutive but bizarre & eccentric.

"Grapho"

Figure 1.8. Page 3 of early graphology treatise signed by Grapho

One of the first modern American graphology texts to gain a foothold for a more systematic study of the topic was *Talks on Graphology: The Art Through Knowing Character Through Handwriting* by the mysterious couple H.L.R. and M.L.R, published in 1892. Having studied Michon's work, these two authors state that handwriting as an "expression of thought" revealed traits that "emanate from the soul" (16). Predating this work is a handwritten manuscript, "The Principles and Practice of Graphology or Character Reading from Handwriting," by J. Harrington Keene, given to a student in 1887. Under the pen name Grapho, Keene, who was also a sports fisherman, came to publish the well-illustrated and popular text *Mystery of Handwriting* in 1896, which displayed the signatures of many famous people of the day. Using a typology system that broke down writers into four general types—sanguine, bilious, nervous, and lymphatic—Keene would write that "handwriting was a gesture of the mind."

Figure 1.9. Keene and Von Hagen

Stocker, Von Hagen, and Rexford

Other major treatises from the late 1890s and early 1900s include *The Language of Handwriting* by Richard Dimsdale Stocker, *Reading Character from Handwriting* by Hugo von Hagen, PhD, *Graphology* by Clifford Howard, and Crépieux-Jamin's masterwork, *Handwriting & Expression*, which, translated from the French, was published in America in 1892. Aside from Crépieux-Jamin, whose resultant theory will be discussed in a later chapter, Stocker's book strikes the reader as perhaps the most sophisticated.

Attempting to create a science of graphology, Stocker, an expert on will power and the science of mind, wrote that "thought has form," and this "form is preserved" in handwriting. Stocker explains that sexuality is not necessarily revealed in a writing because "men and women both possess the same faculties, modified by development" (15). He also notes that heredity plays a role in style, but also that handwriting is influenced by momentary feelings. "It has been proved by experiment that it is almost impossible for anyone to simulate any passion (either physiogomically or graphologically) and at the same time free himself from the feeling therewith" (6). In other words, handwriting by its nature has to reflect the mind, mood, and even the momentary temperament of the writer. When analyzing a writing, Stocker says to consider the "style as a whole as well the size of the letters, their shape, slope, position on the paper and texture" (25). The book also contains an impressive bibliography.

Having studied at the Paris Graphology Society, Hugo Von Hagen moved to Boston where he started the first American Graphology Society in 1892. With more than 100 clear examples, von Hagen (1902) created an exhaustive chart of graphic signs with their corresponding personality characteristics. Some examples are shown here.

Sign	Indicates
Writing is simple and plain	Modesty, naturalness, simplicity
Perpendicular slant	Mind controls, lack of feeling, coldness
Large	Enterprise, desire to do great things, pride
Small	Observation, criticism, narrow-mindedness
Writing close together	Moderation, thriftiness, carefulness
Writing is very close together	Meanness, avarice, stinginess
Heavy pressure	Resoluteness, will power, obstinate
Harmonious	Clear and level-headed
Unharmonious	Weak character, hard work to keep himself under control
Lines ascending	Activity, enterprise, ambition, optimism
Lines descending	Pessimism, inactivity, laziness, melancholy, discouragement
Round loop on end of words to left	Selfishness, flattery
T-bars made after t	Enterprise, enthusiasm, curiosity, ambition
Large loop underneath first word	Vanity, conceit, pride
Wide margin	Desire for originality
Uneven margin	Careless in spending money, little order, lively

The last author of note from this early period is John Rexford, who writes in his book *Analytic Graphology* that "every act of a man's life bears the stamp of his personality.... Hence, if an act or a series of acts, could be recorded and studied, a clear idea of the character of the person could be obtained." Of all the American authors from this period, it was Rexford who constructed a well organized, succinct, yet comprehensive text

Figure 1.10. The Mystery of Handwriting *book cover*

with chapters on the rules of analysis, size, slope, shape, thickness of the writing trail, spacing, connections, finals, punctuation, speed, flourishes, general style, individual letters, and the signature. Rexford also has two appendices, one with an exhaustive list of traits and corresponding graphic patterns, and another devoted to deviant handwritings and questioned documents. In his section on the final analysis, Rexford recommends making a list of various traits noted, weighing each of them for emphasis or lack thereof, and then combining them all together into one cohesive summary.

Pen Names

Handwriting analysis has always been linked to fortune telling, and such related topics as phrenology, astrology, and palm reading. In fact, it was Adolphe Desbarrolles, one of the fathers of modern palmistry, who, in 1872, wrote the introduction to Abbé Michon's first major treatise on graphology. Ten years earlier, Samuel Wells, a phrenologist and partner of the publishing firm Fowler & Wells, published a book on physiognomy that devoted a chapter to "graphomancy," which was the term Wells used before the word *graphology* came into vogue (Backman, 2001). No wonder many authors of books on graphology, particularly ones who had a penchant for questioned documents examination, tended to use pseudonyms. H.L.R. and M.L.R. wrote perhaps the first important American book on the subject; Harrington Keene wrote under the name Grapho; J.A. Adams called himself Graphique; Ludwig Klages used the pseudonym Dr. Erwin Axel; Clifford Howard wrote under the name Simon Arke; and Elijah Prentiss Bailey wrote under the name John Rexford.

Figure 1.11. Bailey

Klages eventually revealed his name, but Bailey never did. Born in 1834 in upstate New York, and a graduate of Colgate University and Fordham, Bailey was the son of a prominent member of the New York State Anti-Slavery Society and was editor of *The Liberty Press*. In 1853, Bailey began to work for the *Utica Observer* where he became a telegraph operator and journalist. Through time, editor-in-chief and owner of the newspaper. A member of the Masonic fraternity for more than 30 years and manager of the Utica Homeopathic Hospital, Bailey was also elected school commissioner of Utica, commissioner for the Northern Pacific Railroad, president of the New York Associated Press, and also appointed by Presidents Harrison and Cleveland to be postmaster of Utica and President of the New York State Civil Service Commission.

Emigration of European Graphologists

As Hitler moved his country closer to war, a number of key graphologists emigrated, such as Eric Singer, who went to England; Robert Saudek, who was already there; Arie Naftali, who moved to Israel; and Klara Roman, Werner Wolff, Ulrich Sonnemann, Rudolf Arnheim, Wladimir Eliasberg, Herry Teltscher, Alfred Kanfer, and Felix Klein, who all came to New York. Clearly, European graphology suffered because of the war, but at the same time Great Britain and the United States gained a number of prominent practitioners.

Eric Singer

Figure 1.12. Singer illustrations I

Born at the turn of the century in Vienna, Eric Singer studied law at Vienna University and graphology with Ludwig Klages. Of Jewish descent, Singer was also drawn to the ideas of Sigmund Freud, who was living not far from Singer's home. Thus, Singer (1969) began to look beyond the limiting aspects of Klages's teaching. In the mid-1930s he traveled to Switzerland to continue his studies, where he probably took courses at the University of Zurich with Max Pulver. Singer was able to tolerate Hitler until Crystal Night, and so in 1938 he fled to England. There he "worked as a consulting gra-phologist," and at the same time looked to fashion books on the topic that would appeal to a widespread audience. After the war, having been influ-enced by Pulver's ideas on symbology, Singer began to sketch out drawings that would help portray well-accepted graphological features with correspond-ing personality characteristics. In the late 1940s he met with artist Gertrude Elias who translated his ideas into the amusing and insightful illustrations that adorn his many books. Enclosed are several of drawings done by Lynn Sevigny to give the reader an idea of the power of Singer's contribution to the field. After he died, in 1969, his wife, E.A. Singer, republished his works in England and America.

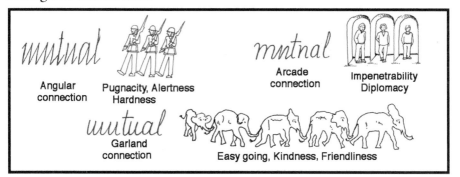

Figure 1.13. Singer illustrations II

Thea Stein Lewinson

Figure 1.14. Thea Stein Lewinson signature

Thea Stein, daughter of a wealthy Jewish businessman from Berlin, was sent by her mother to work in a household for a family in Paris. Born in 1907, and quite spoiled, Thea was fond of reminiscing that she never brushed her own hair until the age of 18! Thus, it was not surprising that she failed as a servant. Already trained in graphology, having studied with Martha Goldberg in Berlin, and now out on her own, she met Gus Lewinson, who helped her get a quick visa for America, and she married him shortly thereafter. During the war, Thea worked for the U.S. government in the censorship department reading German correspondence. This led to the capture of a German spy who she knew personally (Keehner, James, 2004). Later, she would also do a graphological profiling of job applicants for the CIA, as well as enemies of the state such as Lee Harvey Oswald and Saddam Hussein. In 1942, Thea worked with the American statistician Joseph Zubin to cowrite *Handwriting Analysis*, a methodological treatise that contained a series of numerical scales for evaluating four dynamic aspects of handwriting, its form, vertical and horizontal components, and its depth. Combining the findings of Pulver and Klages, Thea attempted to establish an objective basis for measuring rhythm in handwriting. By a minute analysis of individual letters and even parts of letters, Thea created a continuum scale from very contracted motor movements to very released movement. Normal writings, she stated, should gravitate toward the central point of the scale (14). Isolated graphics measured such variables as contour, vertical, and horizontal strokes and pressure.

Well into her 80s, Thea Stein-Lewinson founded the American Society of Professional Graphologists. At that time, she appointed the author, Marc J. Seifer, editor-in-chief of their publication, the only academic journal about graphology in the United States at the turn of the 21st century. At one of our meetings at Swarthmore College in 1993, she recalled a conference she attended in 1937. There, many of the originators of the field could be found, including Max Pulver, Ludwig Klages, Hans Jacoby, Otto Fanta, Jean Crépieux-Jamin, Werner Wolff, and Klara Roman. The conference was essentially split into two camps, the so-called intuitive camp headed by Crepieux-Jamin, and the German camp, who saw themselves as more scientific, headed by Klages. Speaking for the German contingency, Thea recalled a half-century later, "We did not think much of the French." But even within the German camp there was dissension. Never one to hold back opinions, Thea remembered that her taste for "that little man" Werner Wolff was not her cup of tea, because his ideas were too amorphous.

An elitist who for 50 years eschewed most American graphology societies, only to lecture in Europe, Thea went on, "Max Pulver, of course, was most impressive. He was very imaginative and fascinating. But of course," she huffed conspiratorially, "there was tremendous animosity between Klages and Pulver."

"Did you ever meet Carl Jung?"

"Only at a lecture in New York. When I saw him I was disappointed. He was a little fat man and not as mythical [as I expected]," she added with a chuckle.

"How did Pulver get along with Klages?"

"Not at all. When a Pulver man spoke at the Congress, the Klages group got up and walked out. He and Pulver were on a collision course. Pulver said he never read Klages, but Klages wrote 10 volumes and I read them all."

"And Klages's talk?"

"Klages gave a ridiculous lecture on voluntary movement which he had published in 1910. However, he was a charismatic and terrific presence. He was the one who put graphology on the map, and the basis of my book *Handwriting Analysis* rests on his 'science of expressive movement' (that is, on the interplay of muscle contraction [downstrokes—movements towards the body], and release [upstrokes—movements away from the body], as revealed in the rhythm of the writing). Klages wrote complex German, but his own philosophy was close to the Nazi philosophy."

According to Klages, "Every volitional movement is also influenced by its personal 'guiding image' *(Leitbild)*.... Expression, as an aspect of impulse …[or] volitional movement, represents the essence of personality." For Klages, handwriting is "a permanent and measurable record of volitional movement… [combining] intellectual, emotional and physical tendencies…. Klages science of expression is his system of graphology." It lies in what Klages calls *Formniveau*, or form level, where it can be seen in the originality, aesthetic appeal, organization, harmony, rhythm, and strength of the form. Because of Klages's work and "leadership in the field of characterology and the science of expression, graphology has been used as a psychodiagnostic method in Europe for the last three decades and has found practical application in the fields of child and vocational guidance…personality adjustment, for various legal and business purposes and for personality studies of patients suffering from certain chronic diseases" (Lewinson,1938, 163–76).

"Was Klages really an anti-Semite?"

"Oh, yes, of course. He was very anti-Semitic," Thea stated matter-of-factly. She then explained that a number of years earlier (most likely in the early 1930s), Klages had gotten into a fight with a Jewish journalist, and had become anti-Semitic ever since. "Klages assumed a science of expression that postulates two forces within man: 'mind,' which binds and inhibits him; and 'soul,' which frees and develops him creatively. According to Klages, these two forces, always dynamically at variance, influence all of man's behavior and are most crystallized in his *expressive movements*" (Roman, 437). "The mind for Klages was representative of the Jew, and the soul representative of the German. Klages claimed that the mind suddenly tore into the soul and destroyed the soul, so the Jew destroyed the German soul. Klages had an obnoxious personality, but he was very good looking," Thea concluded (Seifer, 1993, 3–4).

The European/American analyst Erika Karohs stated at the 1992 AAHA/AHAF Denver conference that "when Hitler came to power, Klages positioned himself so that only his system came in. Klages used the Fortune Telling Law to put 90 percent of the graphologists out of business (so that only his school would remain)" (Seifer, 4). Thus, the rise of Nazi Germany drove many well-known graphologists to the United States. Klages stayed on as a supporter of the Third Reich, but eventually moved to Switzerland.

In the case of Klara Roman, she lost her husband to the Nazis and had to hide in a friend's cellar before her escape. Rudolf Arnheim, whose doctorate was on handwriting and facial expression, would come to teach at Harvard and gain prominence for his book *Art & Visual Perception*. Werner Wolff fled to Spain and taught at the University of Barcelona, but he got caught in their civil war, and so he immigrated to America and found a job at Bard College. Three other graphologists located themselves in New York City. Ulrich Sonnemann would be one of the rare few major graphologists to teach his craft at the university level, which was at the New School for Social Research. The other two, Alfred Kanfer and Felix Klein, were released from Third Reich concentration camps before America entered the fray. Kanfer, as the discoverer of minute neuromuscular spasms in the writing of cancer patients, would collect thousands of handwritings and work at the Strang Clinic. Felix Klein, founder of the National Society for Graphology in New York City, would make his living as a watchmaker before his graphology skills really took hold.

Felix Klein

Figure 1.15. Felix Klein signature

No doubt, the most popular graphologist of European descent in America in the 1970s, 1980s and 1990s was Felix Klein (1911–1994), who was aptly named the "dean of American graphologists." By his nature, Felix helped unify diverse handwriting groups, and was a well-known fixture at national and international conferences for half a century.

Felix Klein had been in Dachau and Buchenwald. At a conference in Chicago in the 1980s, he recalled to me that part of the reason he was able to survive in the concentration camps was because he would use graphology to analyze the handwriting of the girlfriends of some of the Nazi guards. In this way, he kept himself protected and occasionally got extra food, such as the core of an apple or small loaf of bread, which he cut into little pieces and shared with his fellow prisoners. Felix was able to emigrate to England right before WWII erupted, and from there he made his way to America and New York City. There, he founded the National Society for Graphology and their accompanying newsletter, which has run continuously from the 1970s until the present day. For many years, the newsletter was edited by Carole Schuler, who also wrote up the lecture of every speaker at NSG for more than a quarter century.

> The guiding image is accordingly a very strong reflection of the writer's taste, background, even his eidetic faculty—the complex of forms he likes and therefore remembers and imitates, as well as those he dislikes, wishes to forget, and therefore excludes from his writing.
>
> —Ludwig Klages

Felix Klein's contributions included his development of Klages's idea of the "guiding image" (or *Leitbild* in German) and its Gestalt pattern, which corresponds to Robert Saudek's concept of the "dominant" and "counterdominant" characteristics in a handwriting. Klein (1986) tells us that "any trait can be the guiding image, but also, any combination of related traits or any contradictory indicators can establish the basis for the guiding image. In fact, the contradictory" because this can cause a tension, can "impel the individual to overcome, balance out or compensate in his or her attempts to regain harmony." Two key factors that often reveal the guiding image are the **trend,** which is seen as "directional pressure" stemming from the left (the past) or right (the future), and the **form**. "Whatever the guiding image is, it is the core of the personality" (51–60). With Felix Klein's death, the mantle has been passed to Roger Rubin, who, following in Felix's footsteps, has become one of the most respected handwriting analysts in America.

Figure 1.16. Felix Klein and the author, NYC, 1992.

Rubin (2007) discusses the influence of the mother and father in the handwriting trail. The father shows up positively in movement to the right (the future) and the upper zone (aspirations, ambition), and negatively when authoritarian issues become prevalent, seen as rigidity and over-control. The mother shows up generally in left trend, linked psychoanalytically to a person's beginnings, and in the lower zone, the unconscious more linked to the mother than the father. "Take the normal lower zone loop," Rubin says. "It comes down with a slight movement to the right, easily curves to the left and loops back up to the baseline. Psychologically, we see here the *integration* of the masculine and feminine influences released naturally into the middle zone, the plane of reality. In a normal right-slanted writing, opposition to the father can be seen in a lower zone extension which moves, contrarily, to the right. Aggression towards the mother could be seen in sharp triangles in the lower zone, and sexual confusion can be seen in counterstrokes in the lower zone and when a lower loop is made as a straight line down with an arcade ending to the left."

Klara Roman

Klara Roman (1881–1962), a Hungarian already into her 60s, arrived in New York City in the early 1940s. She had worked as a handwriting expert for the Royal Hungarian Criminal Courts. Seeking to objectify graphological research, Roman (1931) invented the graphodyne, a mechanical pen that recorded "quantitative and qualitative measurements of the dynamic components of the writing movement such as pressure and speed, interruptions of flow and variations of emphasis [all which] constituted parts of the supposedly intangible phenomena labeled rhythm" (1952/70).

Figure 1.17.
Klara Roman

Work at the New School for Social Research

A dynamic woman who could not understand the indifference to graphology by the American psychological community, Roman was able to establish an accredited college course at the New School for Social Research in New York City, now New School University, which remains, a half-century later, the only major American university to offer college courses on the topic.

Roman, who would come to write two important texts, *Handwriting: A Key to Personality* and *Encyclopedia of the Written Word*, followed in the footsteps of another important graphologist, Ulrich Sonnemann, who taught at the New School from 1949to 1951.

The Psychogram

In 1955, with the assistance of later-day art gallery owner, George Staemphli, Klara Roman developed the Graphological Psychogram, a diagnostic checklist that organized 40 variables such as organization, I emphasis, angularity, rhythm, and spontaneity into eight major categories. These included creativity, ego strength, drives, and inhibitions. The advantage of this system is that the handwritings can be broken down into 40 separate subcomponents with eight categories that can be converted to a numerical system. In this way, different kinds of handwritings can be separated out, compared, and studied from a statistical standpoint. The Klara Roman Psychogram allows for handwriting to be studied in a rigorous scientific manner.

> When Klara Roman introduced the Psychogram, she defined it as a "pictorially rendered profile" in a circle of the writers' personality projected as a dynamic whole.
>
> —Charlie Cole

Ulrich Sonnemann

> The first and most general dichotomy of all components of the graphic [trend]...divides them into movements of contraction and movements of release. With the single exception of the level of form quality, there is no graphic characteristic...which cannot be classified in either of both groups.... Psychologically, emphasis on contraction [movements towards the body] relates to ego emphasis with its possible implications of relative increases in volitional, emotional, and concept control; emphasis on release [movements away from the body] relates to object emphasis with its possible implications of relative increases in spontaneity, impulsivity, and fantasy life.
>
> —Ulrich Sonnemann

Author of the essential text *Handwriting Analysis*, Ulrich Sonnemann (1912–1993) presented to the English-speaking world a superb exposé on the work of Ludwig Klages (whose books were never translated into English). Born in Berlin, Sonnemann obtained a doctorate from the University of Basel in 1934. His topic was the social thinking of H.G. Wells. With an interest in graphology stemming from boyhood, Sonnemann eluded the Nazis by escaping an internment in Brussels in 1941, moving to Zurich and

Figure 1.18. Ulrich Sonnemann

then to the United States. After working with the Veterans' Administration and Fairfield State Hospital in the mid-1940s, he came to the New School and then returned to Germany in 1955 to teach in Munich and also lecture internationally. In 1982, he returned to the United States for a brief period to teach at the University of Missouri before returning to Europe and founding an organization in his name.

Alex Parley remembers his course with Sonnemann at The New School in the early 1950s:

> Sonnemann would put the handwritings up on an overhead and point things out. He was warm and understanding. If you asked a question in class, some teachers might see it as an affront. But I'm the type of guy who would ask. Sonnemann would put a hand on my shoulder and he gave me an A. He had an almost 6th sense about things.

Dan Anthony

Q. How would you describe yourself?

A. Arrogant, imperious and two unprintables.

—Ellen Bowers interviewing
Dan Anthony, 1989

Grand-nephew of Susan B. Anthony, Dan (1912–1997) was born in Easton, Pennsylvania, six years after the famous suffragette passed away. He graduated from Brown University with a master's degree in 1935. After college, he worked as a salesman for Vicks Medications, but he hated selling, and soon after enlisted in the service, spending six years as a U.S. Army classification specialist. He then moved to Muncie, Indiana, where he directed the Middletown Project "educating the middle and upper classes about the trade union movement. In 1948, he became the New Jersey director of the National Conference of Christians and Jews...coached high school swimming and won many medals in master's swimming events" (*Brown Alumni Magazine*). A Ford Foundation research fellow at Rutgers, director of the Newark Human Rights Commission, and budding graphoanalyst (part of his history he certainly did not advertise!), Dan also studied with Margaret Drake, who was a student of Louise Rice.

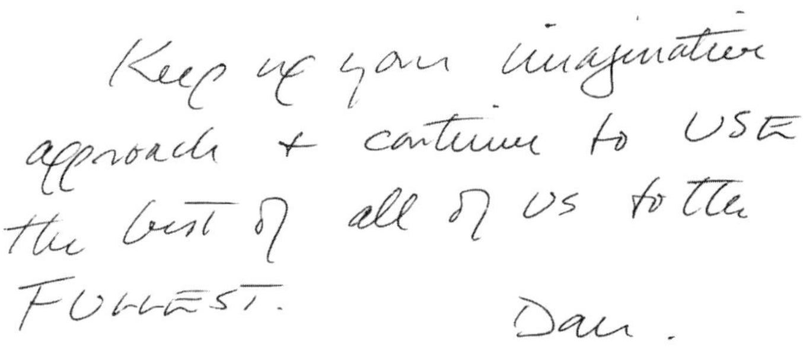

Figure 1.19. Handwriting of Dan Anthony commenting on an early version of part of this manuscript.

> Keep up your imagination approach + continue to USE the best of all of us to the FULLEST.   Dan.

In 1989, Anthony explained in an interview with Ellen Bowers, "I then spent the next 13 years reading, searching and absorbing everything about graphology I could find, even paying for German translations." And then Dan's life took a very positive and fateful turn when he enrolled in Klara Roman's graphology courses at the New School. It was at that time he befriended Gordon Allport, who had studied graphology in Germany before becoming a Harvard professor, and Rudolf Arnheim, who was also teaching at the New School at that time, which was the late 1940s.

Dan's most important contribution is his *Psychogram Workbook*, which amplified the meaning of each of Roman's 40 indicators, and made slight modifications to them, replacing two, "monotony" and "sharpness," with "firmness of ductus" and "linear/pictorial." Dan also figured out a mathematical scale to add up certain indicators to obtain "Form Level" and "Functional Productivity" scores. This was crucial for creating an objective scientific assessment scale that could be applied to any kind of handwriting. It also was helpful in the corporate world, in the field of personnel selection, which was his main profession. For instance, if a person had a high functional productivity score and a low form level score, this would suggest that this individual would tend to be an achiever in the workplace, but would not excel in social graces.

Q. What advice would you share with beginning graphologists?

A. Never read any book on psychology, number one. Go to every art museum possible and read *Education Through Art* by Herbert Read and *Art & Visual Perception* by Rudolf Arnheim. These two books would do more for graphology than any books on psychology or graphology except for Klara Roman's *Handwriting: A Key to Personality* and Werner Wolff's *Diagrams of the Unconscious*.

In this author's opinion, who studied with Dan and Florence for five semesters from 1970 to 1972, and reflecting more than 35 years, Dan Anthony remains the most astute graphologist I have come in contact with. It is unfortunate that he rarely spoke before other American graphology societies, because he taught so many valuable techniques. These included how to study print script, the relationship between touchpoint analysis and the creativity of the writer (which was an extension of the work of Werner Wolff), the relationship between the physical act of writing as an expressive gesture to the writer's personality, how to analyze job applications for personnel selection, the link between handwriting and neuronal organization (which stemmed from the work of Alexander Luria), the importance of doodles, left-handed writers, the handwriting of children, and also such ideas as taking a pen and actually tracing over the writing of the sample being analyzed, so that the actual motor movements involved could be better understood by the analyst. As a rule, Dan did not assign any writing in class if he didn't have access to biographical information about the subject. The student needed to see, as much as possible, the link between the handwriting trail and the life of the person. Dan also introduced the student, of which he had hundreds, to Rudolf Arnheim's book *Art & Visual Perception* and Rhoda Kellogg's work on the psychology of children's art.

An expert's expert, Dan was quoted in *Newsweek* and the *Wall Street Journal*, he had articles in *Psychology Today* and other periodicals, and he also worked on a number of high-profile cases, such as the Son of Sam assassin, and also the blood writing on the wall from the Sharon Tate murder. When it came to questioned documents, Dan stressed the importance of obtaining enough exemplars to compare, how to guard against pitfalls, and how to use a light-box. Although he could be elusive at times, whenever this author asked him how he came to his conclusion, he always could point out the reason. Similar to Sherlock Holmes, working with a magnifying glass, compass, and ruler, Dan Anthony based his astute analyses on the evidence. He taught a full eight-semester program with his wife, Florence, throughout the 1960s and 1970s, having designed the only full-bodied accredited university program in graphology to be taught in the United States.

In the same interview with Ellen Bowers, Anthony also said, "Both Klara Roman and I considered it a horrible mistake to have gone to California and shared our work. The nice gal/guy ethos of shared work to promote graphology was transformed into something totally foreign to that which we had intended. And now that unfortunate legacy follows…. It's a little tough to make that assessment, but, throughout the country, I'm known for my candor."

In 1959, Klara Roman flew out to California to lecture at the American Handwriting Analysis Foundation, which was run by Charlie Cole. The following year, Dan Anthony also lectured there. Charlie had first become interested in graphology in 1941, after meeting with the German refugee and graphologist Hans Swartz. After working with Roman and Anthony, Charlie readapted the Psychogram and set up an important school in California, which spawned many new graphologists on the West Coast. Charlie also brought in other top speakers, most notably Irene Marcuse (*Handwritingfoundation.org*). Granddaughter of social philosopher Herbert Marcuse, Irene was European educated. With a doctorate in psychology from the University of Florence, and lectures at universities in Rome, Bologna, and Milan, Irene had studied with Max Pulver in Zurich before emigrating to the United States. Author of *Guide to Personality* and *Guide to the Disturbed Personality Through Handwriting*, Dr. Marcuse was an important graphologist in the 1950s and 60s, bringing the topic to the attention of the American psychological community through her research, writings, and public appearances, such as on the popular David Susskind TV show.

After Dan and Florence Anthony retired, their courses at the New School were taken over by Patricia Siegel, a graduate of Cornell University, who later became president of the American Society of Professional Graphologists, and her colleague Lois Vaisman, a graduate of Columbia University, psychotherapist and vice president of ASPG.

Other Contributors

Other noteworthy graphologists from Europe include Alfred Mendel, H.J. Jacoby, Anita Muhl, Nadya Olyanova, René LaSenne, Ania Teillard, Girolamo Moretti, Ursula Ave-Lallemant, Christian Dettweiler, Erika Karohs, Wladimir Eliasberg, Herry O. Teltscher, and Paul de Sainte Colombe. Well-known American analysts include June Downey, Gordon Allport, M.N. Bunker, Frank Victor, Dorothy Sara, Huntington Hartford, Roger Rubin, Marc Seifer, Patricia Siegel, Ruth Holmes, Iris Hatfield Holmes, Sheila Lowe, Marcel Matley, Suzy Ward, Jeanette Farmer, and Jane Nugent Green.

In his 1947 book, *Personality in Handwriting*, Alfred Mendel describes the concept of the stable and mobile axes. The downstroke, which he calls the stable axis, is the backbone of the writer's character (216). Changing slants, Mendel correlates to mixed feelings toward the parents, especially the father. The mobile axis, on the other hand, is associated with the horizontal stroke. It depicts "our attitude towards the future and our fellow man" and the exteriorization of libidinal drives" (235). Undue pressure in the mobile axis reveals displaced energy and/or neglect of the self due to desire for future goals or because of the expectation of others. The horizontal axis generally moves away from the writer, whereas the stable axis comes toward the writer. Mendel's text, along with Roman (1970), Jacoby (1938), Saudek (1926/28), Sonnemann (1950), and Wolff (1948/60), remain the key books in the field, along with Huntington Hartford's (1973) compendium, which is essentially a compilation of these and related works.

Forensic Profiling

Robert Saudek was, perhaps, the first major graphologist to create a list of common traits associated with dishonesty. These include covering strokes, abrupt stops above the line, twisted loops, breaks and mends, slowness, ovals open at the bottom, and counterstrokes—that is, strokes that go in a direction opposite to what is expected. Using such a list, a general profile of the criminal mind can be created; however, there are numerous exceptions to the rule, and people commit crimes for many different reasons. Other graphologists who have studied signs of dishonesty include Anita Muhl, MD (1939), who studied hundreds of juvenile delinquents and criminals, Max Pulver (1940), Alfred Mendel (1940), Paul de St. Colombe (1967), and most recently, Iris Holmes Hatfield (1988/1997), who did her research in the prison system of Kentucky. In her books *History of Graphology* and *A Question of Honesty*, Hatfield notes that people become dishonest for varying reasons including "greed, fear, laziness, selfishness, shame, sensuality, ignorance and rebellion." On the other hand, such factors as "guilt, procrastination, repression and fear of being caught" prevent many people from becoming dishonest. Ideally, people should act honestly, because they have a "well defined and balanced moral code of ethics" (8). The CIA, ever interested in the criminal mind, has referred to Hatfield's text and also has used such graphologists as Thea Stein Lewinson, who created personality profiles of potential spies and foreign potential enemies of the state.

Beginning hook

Counterstroke

Figure 1.20. Evolution of a counterstroke in the same subject

Psychodiagnostics

Frank Victor (1952) a psychotherapist from Kew Gardens, New York, urged graphologists to base their analyses on attempts to reconstruct the actual movement pattern of the writer in a purely objective way. This helps greatly in the analysis. He noted, for instance, that some handwritings that appear disconnected really have connections that occur in the air. The pen has been lifted off the paper, but the movement continues. This is called an air-stroke. Irene Marcuse (1969) studied the handwritings of suicides. Although no single graphic feature could be isolated as evidence for self-destruction, depression can be seen in connecting strokes, which continually droop below the baseline and downward-sloping handwritings, often seen in many samples of Ernest Hemingway. Nadya Olyanova, having worked with psychiatrists, suggests that graphology can be used as an alternative to psychological tests when the therapist requires insight of a patient.

Wladimir Eliasberg, MD, a psychiatrist from Germany, arrived in New York in the early 1940s. He published a number of graphology articles in medical journals including "Methods in Graphologic Diagnostics" in *The Psychiatric Quarterly* (1944). With Herry O. Teltscher, a Viennese graphologist and psychologist, he furthered research in the fields of neuropsychiatry and graphology in order to study the onset of disease, especially Parkinson's.

Coining the term *graphodiagnostics*, these studies produced several papers and Teltscher's popular text *Handwriting: Revelation of Self* (1971).

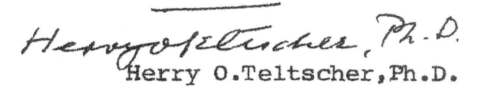

Herry O.Teltscher,Ph.D.

Figure 1.21. Teltscher signature

In the early 1950s, Teltscher conducted a research project at Essex Country Overbrook Hospital in New Jersey. The object was to determine to what extent "blind" psycho-graphological analyses could be matched with clinical specimens. Teltscher prepared detailed analyses plus psychiatric diagnoses where indicated. The judges were able to match the analyses with their own observations. The results proved to be statistically significant on the 0.5 percent level.

More recently, Suzy Ward, past president of the Rocky Mountain chapter of the American Handwriting Analysis Foundation, did a study of the handwriting of 76 survivors of sexual abuse. California graphologist Marilyn Martin had studied 2,000 prisoners who were alleged to have been sexually abused as children, and she identified 34 common graphic characteristics. Ward (1995), who attended a Martin lecture, expanded the list to 43. These include rigid initial strokes, confusing an "a" for an "o," broad arcades, an uneven baseline, crowded spacing, covering strokes, drooping garlands, flames (upper loops that resemble a flame), extra loops in letters that create figure 8's, distorted letters in all three zones (for example, twisted upper loops, sharp angle-arcade and pinched "m" and "n," unusual or distorted forms in lower zone letters such as the "p" and "g"), left trend, unbalanced margins, looped and double-looped ovals, excessive or inconsistent slant, loops that hook down, foreshortened or "nonexistent" upper and lower zone, closing of letters that should be open (closed "c" and "u"), neglected letter forms, patching, letters with rockers, and circular letters with insertions in them. Aware of the problem of linking the parts to the whole, Ward's study paves the way for the creation of a profile of individuals who have been sexually abused.

Typologies

There have been a number of typology systems that graphologists have referred to. Ania Teillard (1966) applied Jung's four personality types to handwriting analysis in *The Soul of Handwriting*. In *Traité de caractérologie* René LaSenne used the four humours from the ancient Greco/Roman system and added four more:

> The advantages of typologies is the host of personality traits readily associated with a distinct type, while the danger is the stock characterization which results when the analyst fails to modify a pure type sufficiently to differentiate specific writers.
>
> —Carole Schuler

Unstable

Tense

Nervous   Choleric

Introverted Melancholic   Sanguine **Extroverted**

Phlegmatic   Self-indulgent

Prudent

Stable

He then correlated the eight types with specific graphic variables and measured each for [+E-] (**emotional** response or lack thereof); [+A-] (ability to **act** or stay passive); and [P] (immediacy of **reaction** time), or [S] (for delayed response).

Graphotherapeutics

The last European writer from this group of émigrés is Paul de Sainte Colombe (1967), a Hollywood film writer, author of *Grapho-Therapeutics*, and protégé of Pierre Janet, professor of psychiatry at the College de France, "the country's highest institute of learning" (4). Janet, whose superlative theories on the unconscious predates Freud's, referred to handwriting analysis as "the science of the future." One of the reasons Janet said this was because he himself had tested graphotherapeutics in clinical trials at the Sorbonne from 1929 to 1931. Working with Professor Charles Henry, Janet was following the theories of Dr. Edgar Bérillon, who in 1908 introduced the technique as a way to treat mental disease.

Graphotherapeutics is based on the "psychological principle that a character flaw expresses itself exteriorly in bad habits," for example, laziness. De St. Colombe suggests that, under the guidance of a psycho-graphologist, if one is taught to change poor qualities in the handwriting through repetitious exercise of desirable graphic traits, such as writing the G.D Boardman quote repetitively in a clear, harmonious fashion, a corresponding change in the personality will also take place. The success of the technique, similar to any other form of therapy, depends on the will of the patient and the skill of the therapist (16). De Sainte Colombe's work correlates with Teltscher's findings and those of Jeanette Farmer in her 1997 book, *Can Handwriting Exercises Be The Unrecognized Road to Developing Literacy?* During the process of psychotherapy, Teltscher was able to pinpoint significant changes in the handwriting with major psychological transformations. Farmer, on the other hand, worked in reverse. By assigning **rhythmic handwriting exercises** to students with poor reading skills, the idea is that in a corresponding manner, as the student became more proficient in writing, his brain would be retrained as well. An analogous example would be how the TV personality Barbara Walters, through speech therapy, learned to no longer say Baba Wawa.

> The law of the harvest is to reap more than you sow. Sow a thought and you reap an act; sow an act, and you reap a habit; sow a habit and you reap a character; sow a character and you reap a destiny.
>
> —G.D. Boardman, 19th century American missionary in Burma

Perhaps the most exciting new development in the field of graphology and projective techniques is the star wave test (SWT) conceived by Ursula Ave-Lallemant. In her book *The Star-Wave Test* she writes that the SWT "can bridge the gap between them" (7). She has used the SWT in conjunction with other projective measures, which could include the Draw A Family or Tree Test, the Rorschach, and the Wartegg Drawing Test. To administer the SWT, the diagnostician simply asks the child or older subject to "draw a starry sky over ocean waves." The range of responses is truly remarkable. After studying it and applying graphological and related principles such as those found in dream interpretation, and/or when trying to decipher symbols, the diagnostician can soon discover rhythmic expressions from disturbed ones, fantasy life, inhibitions, and creativity. "An additional bonus is the fact that the universal use of the symbols of sky, stars, and ocean has proved to be helpful when dealing with a multi-cultural population" (Vaisman and DiLeo, 51).

Star Wave Test

Troubled Child   Creative Child

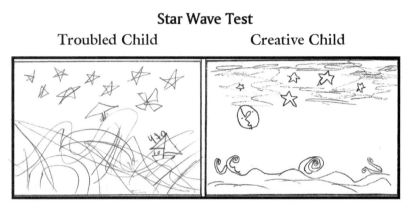

Figure 1.22. Star Wave drawings

The above illustrations were taken with permission from Dafna Yalon's excellent book *The Star Wave Test Across the Life Span* (2004). Yalan states that the drawing on the left is made with "infantile and intense crude strokes." Its "erratic elements," stemming from being abused as a child reflects "uncontrolled aggression and impulsive behavior." What looks like a doorway made with parallel lines (bottom left) "is very important." These are arcades suggesting a need for protection. The boats drawn are in a stormy sea reflective of the dangerous and self-destructive impulses with which this individual is wrestling. The drawing on the right, on the other hand, is clear and creative, and the seas are much calmer. This was the Star Wave Test of an excellent fourth-grade student who got high marks from her teacher in social behavior, as well as her academics.

Italian Graphology

Giorlamo Moretti (1879–1963), a friar and founder of the Graphology Institute in Urbino, has had an enormous impact on the practice of graphology in Italy. Emphasizing the Gestalt approach, Moretti, much like Crépieux-Jamin, created a system that gave energy to different graphic traits and set up well-thought-out rules on how to combine them to understand the dynamic and structural aspects of personality (Fogarolo, 2006). Moretti emphasized the idea that every personality is unique. S. Deranga (1994) used Moretti's temperament scale "to define a personality structure within which suspected 'sine cause' patients may be classified" in her 1994 article "Search For a Hypothesis For Personality Structure Using Moretti's Graphology Method." In other words, in cases of illnesses without physical causes, graphology becomes an excellent tool in the hands of competent practitioners. Specifically, in analyzing the handwriting of an individual who suffered from psychosomatic sterility, Derana, et al., were thereby able to compile an idiographic portrait that outlined key personality factors, which may have contributed to the malady.

Israeli Graphology

A place where handwriting analysis enjoys a position of prestige is in Israel, where many corporations employ graphologists. Israeli graphologists of note include Richard Pokorny, who, in 1952, was the first to publish a book on how to analyze Hebrew writing; Arie Naftali, MD, a student of Pophal's who was a documents expert for the Israeli Police and studied how stress affected the writing stroke; Anna Koren, who is perhaps the most successful Israeli graphologist in the field of personnel selection; Dafna Yalon, who has integrated graphological principles with the Star Wave test; and Israel Odem, Israel's essential father of graphology. Odem, an adept in the field for more than 50 years, stressed the importance of the angle of writing, correlating the slant with a typology of nine major personality types (for example, indolent, integrative, impulsive, narcissistic, and anarchic-instinctual).

Graphology in America

On the American scene, June Downey, a graduate of the University of Wyoming and the University of Chicago, stands out as one of the first experimentalists. In 1919, she performed a study examining handwriting as an example of the expressive behavior exhibited by individuals. Rating 12 writers on such bipolar characteristics such as fluent or jerky, and impulsive or deliberate, her scores correspond 10 percent above chance with 11 judges who rated the same individuals basing their observations on the gait, carriage, and gestures of the subjects. This line of investigation was supported in the 1930s by intelligence theorist Phillip Vernon and his colleague, and one of the giants in the field of psychology, Harvard professor Gordon Allport (1933/67), who wrote: "From our results it appears that a man's gestures and handwriting reflect an essentially stable and constant style.... Furthermore, the evidence indicates that there is a congruence between expressive movements and the attitudes, traits, values and other dispositions of the inner personality" (Allporr, Vernon 247–8).

M.N. Bunker and Graphoanalysis

On the poplar front, Dorothy Sara (1968) and Huntington Hartford (1963) have both written graphology books with widespread appeal. But the most important mid-20th-century American figure in terms of capturing the imagination of the people and in training large numbers of handwriting analysts has to be Milton N. Bunker (1892–1961), father of graphoanalysis. His teachings provide step-by-step correspondence courses, which delineate an atomistic approach to handwriting interpretation. From the 1930s through the

1980s, graphoanalysis had been, by far, the most popular approach to American graphology, although it differentiates itself from the studies mentioned previously.

Having taken correspondence courses in short hand at the turn of the 20th century, Bunker soon became interested in handwriting analysis. He became a student of DeWitt B. Lucas through the mail, and, according to graphology historian Bob Backman, purchased a German rendition of Crépieux-Jamin's text on resultants, which had been "unmercifully condensed, omitting much critical information." In the 1920s, while "a regional sales manager" for International Correspondence Schools, Bunker continued his studies with Louise Rice, who, similar to Lucas, had written an excellent book in the field, and who had also founded the highly regarded American Graphological Society (AGS). "They became personal friends, yet also were enemies, graphologically speaking. In 1928, Bunker gave radio broadcasts on graphology. He ran for the office of President of the AGS, but was roundly defeated by Rice. He smarted from the defeat and it motivated him to begin a [correspondence course] in graphology to compete with Rice" (Backman, 2001). Thus, Bunker's "Graphoanalysis" was born.

Criticisms of Graphoanalysis

The problem with graphoanalysis was twofold. First of all it was cult-like. Graphoanalysts were taught many yardsticks, which enabled them to compile impressive handwriting analyses, but these yardsticks were too rigid and reductionistic. Harking back to the work of Michon, this graphic sign = trait approach ignored the relationship of the sign to the total pattern, and also to the idea that a similar symbol in two different handwritings could have different meanings. Also, graphoanalysts were *forbidden* from reading any books on graphology! Further, students of graphoanalysis were banned from interacting with graphologists, and this was a practice that was strictly enforced for decades. Thus, many graphoanalysts lived in an isolated community, an essentially artificial world that was unable to expand into the more comprehensive field of graphology. How would it be possible for a true student of handwriting analysis to ignore the works of Roman, Saudek, Mendel, Wolff, and others? Yet this was one of the rules that graphoanalysts were forced to obey. The only solution for many in this predicament was to break their bonds with the Bunker school, so they could attend regional and international conferences and interact with the so-called graphology crowd. In this manner, many graduates of the Bunker method have gone on to become respected and highly successful professionals in the field.

Jane Nugent Green

World War II greatly impacted the development of the field of graphology, disrupting the lives of many practitioners, forcing some to come to England or America, where graphology was much less accepted. In terms of textbooks in the field, there has been little advance in nearly half a century. One recent book that stands out is *You and Your Private I* (1975/88), by Jane Nugent Green. Coming from the Adlerian ideas of psychology and influenced by Felix Klein and Dan Anthony, Green has devoted an entire text to discussing the variations of the personal pronoun "I," which is the written symbol of the ego. Differentiating from the signature that becomes a consciously produced trademark, "the 'I' may be compared to the man asleep, unconsciously experiencing himself…. It is written much more naturally and is much less subject to deliberate tampering" (141–2).

Figure 1.23. Graphology for All *book cover*

> [For] those who have carefully studied the subject, there is no truer or surer guide to character than the handwriting.
>
> —Graphique

To be truly versed in the complexity of personality, it is important for psychologists to be knowledgeable about the history of graphology. Many highly respected psychologists have studied and produced research papers on the topic. Advances by experimental and theoretical graphology has continued not only in the psychology of expressive behavior and depth psychology, but also in business, self-exploration, forensic psychology, criminal profiling, neurophysiological research, graphotherapeutics, and cancer detection. Unlike any other projective measure, handwriting, as uninhibited self-expression, provides a valuable and tangible road map to that mysterious borderland between the brain and the mind.

Chapter 2
How to Analyze a Handwriting ———————

There are many ways to analyze handwriting. In an ideal situation, one would have an original page or series of pages of writing to look at along with one or more signatures. In general, all originals should be protected; a good way is to file them in plastic sheets. I would also suggest making several copies of the original, and to do all measurements from these copies. The tools of the trade include a magnifying glass, a compass, a protractor, a ruler, a notebook, good lighting, and a toothpick. The age and sex of the writer should be known. In general, one cannot tell the sex of a writer from the handwriting for a variety of reasons. Handwriting will reflect the archetypal manifestations of masculinity and femininity, as well as aesthetic factors common to both sexes. One can make a good guess, but, as a rule, graphology cannot be used to ascertain the sex of a writer. Again, concerning the age, graphology cannot be used to ascertain to any degree of certainty the physical age of the writer, but rather his or her mental age. I have samples of writing for the same person 40 years apart, and the two samples are quite similar.

Look at the writing as a whole. Turn it upside down, place it near your eye, and check alignment control. Sit with it a while. Compare it to several other handwritings, particularly ones that, at first glance, might appear to be similar. Find out what makes it different. Every person is unique. Do not prejudge any sample. Each represents a complex and multi-leveled being. Look at the capitals and the beginnings of words and lines, and compare them to their ends. Does the writing look spontaneous or inhibited, fast or slow, connected or disconnected? What are your first impressions? Jot them down. Which zone predominates? What is the thrust of the writing and its overall impression? Make a list of all dominant traits, symbols, usual or unusual forms, and placement on the page. See if there are any contradictory features, which Saudek called the counterdominants or dominating contradictions. Sometimes, there may not be any. Does the signature match the writing? Does the first name of the signature match the last name? Take the toothpick, or a pen with the point protected, and *trace* the letters as if you were writing them yourself. Can you begin to feel how this person moves his or her pen across the page?

One of the biggest problems is the relationship of the parts to the whole. No one sign or single graphic should be used as an earmark for a particular character trait. Try to find several signs that support of the suggestion of that single sign. Look at each sign or symbol in a multi-dimensional way. For instance, if a t-bar does not cross through the stem, the simplistic cookbook graphology text may say such a sign means procrastination. Think about it more deeply. If this is a consistent pattern, start with what you know, what is **irrefutable**—that is, the objective overt physical characteristics. In this case, the lateral movement of the t-bar has not crossed the vertical stem.

This is, perhaps, the best way to begin an analysis. *Simply describe the graphics without jumping to what a particular sign means.* If all i-dots are high, just write down "all i-dots are high." If only the capital K is printed, but the others are cursive, state that. In this **first stage** of analysis, the analyst simply writes down what he notices.

An Illustration

I recently was asked to analyze the writing of a lady who sat before me. I gave her a sheet of paper and asked her to "write a sentence and sign your name." She wrote, "Today is October 10," and the year, and signed it. Its placement on the page was very high, way near the top. I pointed the placement position out to her, and she asked me what it meant. I said that I didn't know yet. I needed to think about it. Interpretation comes later.

It certainly occurred to me that she purposely chose a sentence that she thought revealed absolutely no information about herself, but, in this instance, one can see that the choice of sentence and the placement of the sentence way at the top supported the hypothesis that she was fearful, afraid to use too much space on the paper, and afraid to say anything that might give herself away. Does she live a guarded life? Does she count her pennies? The position of the line on the page suggested that her nature was the opposite of being extravagant. That's how my thinking began even before I looked at the actual graphics of letter formation.

Major Criteria

Extrapolating from de St. Colombe, Wolff, Saudek, and Mendel, we come up with 12 key factors:

Graphic	Defines
Arrangement	Organizational Abilities—Margins, zone emphasis, aesthetic sense.
Pattern	Abstract Thought—Repetitive use of symbolic or particular graphic.
Form	Cultural or Inborn Tendencies—Tasteful, original, or crude.
Slant	Emotion—Relation to others, left, upright, right or extreme right.
Axes	Self or Object—Emphasis on vertical or horizontal or both.
Speed	Orientation to Time—Rhythm of physical and mental activity.
Rhythm	Spontaneity—Dynamic, static or tense, harmonious or disharmonious.
Size	Opinion of Self—Vanity, pragmatism, seriousness of purpose.
Continuity	Coherence of Thought—Sociability, connected or disconnected.
Baseline	Mood, Control—Discipline or lack thereof, optimism or pessimism.
Pressure	Vitality, Appetites, Drive—Heavy, light, consistent or inconsistent.
Trend	Orientation to Past and Future—Rightward or leftward.

Now list the:

Dominants	⇒	Physical characteristics that dominate, zonal emphasis
Counterdominants	⇒	Contradictions, puzzling features
Symbolic aspects	⇒	Favored movement patterns or abstract symbols that recur

Connecting Strokes

In his book *Diagrams of the Unconscious*, Werner Wolff describes an experiment involving the different kinds of connecting strokes, and what they represented.

I asked thirty students to describe their feelings when writing thready, waved lines. Seventy-five percent of the subjects described their feeling as "nice," "free," "easy going," "relaxed," while 25 percent describe it as "disagreeable," "awkward," "sloppy." The feelings when making angular lines were in 85 percent of the cases "harsh," "sharp," "abrupt," "aggressive," and in 15 percent "forceful," "domineering." The feelings when making arcades were in 55 percent related to "effort," "obstacle," "insecurity," and in 45 percent to concepts like "systematic," "precise," "co-ordinated." The feelings when making garlands were in 50 percent of the cases described as "gay," "natural," "simple," "enjoyable," and in the other 50 percent as "difficult," "sinking," "retreating," "unpleasant."

—Werner Wolff

Arcade ⇒ Arch-like m's and n's. Similar to a picket fence, the arcades reveal the tendency for protection and self-preservation.

Angle ⇒ Either up or down shows lack of compromise, aggressive, sharp, and decisive.

Garland ⇒ U-like m's and n's. Openness, ease of movement.

Thread ⇒ Amorphous, difficult to pin down, in a rush.

Keep in mind that many particular features have both positive and negative facets. For instance, a speedy writer may be a fast thinker, but he might also be haphazard. Signs of caution may indicate sober thinking but also inhibition. Write down all the possibilities for each sign, and cull through the list when more information is gleaned. This is achieved by constantly linking these individual parts to a whole composite view.

If a true dominant emerges, how does this feature color all others? Take, as an analogy, a beef stew. If there's too much salt, how does that affect the carrots, celery, beef, or tomato? Does the pepper in the soup off-set or counterbalance the salt? Are there features in the handwriting that remain under the surface, or unconscious to the writer? Suppose there are inconsistencies to the lower zone length. Why would a person always foreshorten a g-loop but not a y-loop? For some reason, the letter g may have some symbolic meaning to the writer. Maybe the family name begins with the letter G, and this would suggest an inhibitory factor associated with the father, who carried the name. One way or another, there appears here to be an unconscious aspect to the personality affecting, and probably in conflict with, the conscious side. You see how complicated it all can become.

The Relationship of the Part to the Whole

At some point, you may want to refer to a list of character traits or a typology system that appears to fit (see trait list on pages 126–129). Once this is done, you can refer to Crépieux-Jamin's *Theory of Resultants* (1895–2002) or Gordon Allport's trait theory, which essentially are ways to synthesize the list that you have created to create personality clusters, and hopefully take the analysis to the next level, one goal being the ascertaining or inferring of additional traits after the first level has been catalogued. See Crépieux-Jamin's book *Handwriting & Expression* or any major text on theories of personality for a discussion of the interrelationship between central, dominant, supporting and secondary traits. Here are a few of Crépieux-Jamin's examples concerning the trait "imagination," which could be seen in the graphics as emphasis on the upper zone with original and abstract forms.

Trait Combinations	Resultant
Imagination + Animation (dynamic speed)	Enthusiasm
Imagination + Thoughtlessness (missing diacritics)	Frivolity
Imagination + Hesitation (abruptions, ill-formed letters)	Perplexity
Imagination + Feeble will (e.g., uncrossed t-bars)	Indecision
Imagination + Untruth (serpentine lines)	Swindling
Imagination + Liberality (spaced out letters and words)	Extravagance

Other resultants Crépieux-Jamin lists are:

❯ Agitation + hastiness = irritability

❯ Hastiness + force = anger

❯ Grace + liveliness = gaiety

Allport discusses **common, individual,** and **unique** traits, as well as cardinal, central, and secondary traits.

The **cardinal trait** corresponds to Saudek's dominant trait. It is a trait that is "so pervasive that it dominates just about everything that a person does. It is the eminent trait, the ruling passion, the master-sentiment, or the radix [fulcrum, basis] of a life" (Allport, 1937, Cloninger, 2004, p. 205). Some people are known for this single trait (for example, Machiavellian, Jeffersonian, the Goracle, Christ-like, chauvinistic, goofy, quixotic, sadistic).

The **central traits** are a group of traits, up to about a half dozen, "that best describes a person" (217).

Secondary traits are "less conspicuous, less consistent," and less important than central traits. Examples given include a person's preference for decaffeinated coffee, or a color preference for "mauve" (204–5).

In discussing Allport, Monte (1987) uses as an example with the trait of "gregariousness." If this is a central or cardinal trait, we can hypothesize the following cluster:

SOCIAL SITUATIONS		PERSONAL STYLE
Theater going		Invites friends
Church going	GREGARIOUSNESS	Devotion, concern
Letter writing		Sharing confidence
Family gatherings		Making others comfortable

Naturally, these trait theories should be taken with a grain of salt, and need to be used cautiously. In general, when referring to graphology, typology, and personality books for the "answers," be flexible in your thinking. Always consider that a finding located is a *possibility*, no more, no less. Analyzing handwriting is a very difficult task and one needs to be humble in the endeavor. Allow for a multidimensional perspective that recognizes that oftentimes people are in conflict, and therefore it is quite possible that they may indeed have graphic traits that are incompatible with each other. Crépieux-Jamin's and Allport's theories do point the analyst in the right direction, and that is to get beyond the surface level to create a more complete portrait of the person being studied.

Extrapolating from a chapter from Werner Wolff's *Diagrams of the Unconscious* (1948/63) about personality traits and trait clusters, we come up with the following (304–5):

> In comparison to reading: "Prose is not treated alphabetically, but knowledge of the alphabet is essential. It is not the sum of the letters, but their interplay which forms the meaning of the word. Just as the same sign forms many words, the same graphic indicators form many meanings. There are as many 'resultants' as there are human beings."
>
> Concerning resultants: "A 'resultant' depends on two variables: on the intensity and the relationship of its factors." Wolff gives as an example the trait "activity." "The activity of an artist is so different from the activity of a businessman that these *two relationships* of the same trait change the value of the trait."

On Gestalt patterns of the "form" of writing and its "expression," Wolff says that "principles of organization" are involved in grouping particular traits. This explains why certain traits tend to cluster, for example, caution and control. Some trait pairing combines an emotional trait, for example, "happiness" with an expressive trait, and "outgoing." Wolff goes on to say that trait clustering could involve traits associated with **emotion, thought,** and **socialization** (for example, (E) anxious + (T) timid + (S) isolated). Thus, we see how complicated trait clustering can become.

The Contradictory Nature of People

We have to also keep in mind that humans, by their nature, are **contradictory**. Thus, it is quite possible that an anxious, timid, and isolated person could become a Hollywood star. As a simplistic example, Woody Allen comes to mind. In his case, there were other traits that compelled him to overcome this particular burdensome trait cluster.

Masculinity and Femininity

As a rule, one cannot determine the sex of a writer from his handwriting because what one is measuring is not the individual's sex, but rather one's masculinity or femininity. Determining sexual orientation based on determining masculine or feminine features is also a recipe for disaster. Just as there are many women with masculine traits that are heterosexual, there are also many men with feminine traits that are also heterosexual. In general, women tend to have more well-defined fine motor control. In comparison, many men's handwritings can often appear more crudely written or haphazard. Thus, a qualified graphologist will oftentimes be able to tell the sex of a writer at a much higher percentage than chance would predict. However, the higher the form level, the harder it is to determine the sex. Obviously, to be a full-rounded person, one should have both masculine and feminine traits. Sexual orientation is an entirely different ball of wax. The actor Rock Hudson, for instance, was quite masculine, but at the same time he was homosexual. Because there are so many exceptions to the rule, it is best to refrain from guessing the sex of the writer unless absolutely necessary—for instance, in a forensic case. Always ask for the sex of the writer and *insist* on knowing it before undertaking an analysis.

The following discussion has been adapted from Mel Szochet's article "Determination of Male and Female in Handwriting." **Masculine traits** include bold, logical, tenacious, aggressive, rigid or stubborn, controlled, disciplined, willful, extroverted, future oriented, confident, and nonconforming. **Feminine traits** include adaptable, receptive, delicate, passive, intuitive, emotional, yielding, dependent, giving, sensuous, narcissistic, past-oriented, and conforming.

Masculine Graphics: angles, heavy pressure, individualized letter-forms, simplified, linear, sharp, firm, thrusting t-bars, lack of fine motor control.

Feminine Graphics: garlands, pictorial, intuitive breaks, light pressure, neat, rounded forms, right slant, signs of extroversion, lower zone loops, fine motor control.

Symbolic Features

Humans are symbolic creatures. More often than not, when a person writes, whether through conscious or unconscious action, symbolic features will appear. Symbols are multidimensional. To complicate matters, the same symbol might mean different things to different people. Sometimes symbols will reveal a person's occupation, a physical feature, interest, sexual orientation, influence of ego, superego or id, and conscious or unconscious proclivities.

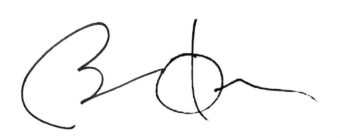

Figure 2.1. Barack Obama's signature

Senator Barack Obama's signature obviously has symbolic features. Because he has to sign his name so many times, perhaps as much as a hundred or more times a day, the presidential candidate has come up with an abbreviated signature that nevertheless suggests his full name. The capital B resembles a heart. I think it is fair to say that the good senator gives heartfelt speeches. The most interesting symbol, however, is the bisected capital O. The downward vertical has evolved from the letter b, the second letter of his last name. One can see how important it is to know something about the writer when conducting an analysis. A mistake would be made to see this sign as a negative, for instance as a split personality. Rather, in Obama's case, it is quite the opposite. Half black and half white, Barack Obama seeks to *recognize* and *unify* the polarity of his heritage in the same way Carl Jung suggests when he uses the term **individuation**—that is, to reconcile the opposites. Obama has done this not only in his self-image, but also in his actions as he tries to unify a country divided in so many ways. As he has said in his speeches, we are not a country of red states (Republican) and blue states (Democrat), but rather, we are the United States. Had the graphologist not known the meaning of this symbol because of knowledge of the writer's background, a quite different analysis could have emerged. It is very important to stay humble when analyzing the complexity of symbols in handwriting, and it is also important, whenever possible, to learn as much as you can about the history and background of the writer.

The In-Depth Analysis

First level: List the graphics without interpretation. This will enable the analyst to see idiosyncratic patterns, particularly when some handwritings, at first glance, appear to be highly similar. Try to refrain from drawing conclusions. At this stage, you are simply describing objectively what you see in the graphics, what is irrefutable, large or small writing, consistent or changing slant, short or tall capital letters, wide or narrow right margin, fast or slow writing, i's dotted or not, pressure or not at the ends of words, and so on. Do not draw conclusions. Just list the particular and idiosyncratic graphic patterns that you see.

Second level: List dominant and counterdominant characteristics. Look for guiding image and any contradictions or curiosities. Consider the meaning of various symbolic features on their own and in relation to the body of the text. Look at the signature and compare it to the capital I. Refer to a trait list to try and capture the right words to describe what you see. Link graphic patterns to character traits.

Third level: See where this takes you. The final analysis comes after putting all the pieces of the puzzle together to come up with a more in-depth picture. The goal, which sometimes is never reached, is to get to the "a-ha!" stage whereby true insights are revealed—when the analyst feels that he or she has really captured the essence of the writer. Referring back to lessons from Dan Anthony, ultimately, any conclusion drawn must be derived from the evidence—the graphic pattern, and the relationship of the parts to the whole.

"If I have been able to see further, it was only because I stood on the shoulders of giants."
Sir Isaac Newton

Figure 3.1. Newton Postage stamp and handwriting

Saudek (1926) writes that Isaac Newton has the very highest of Form Levels.
This document dates from 1682. Note the excellent spacing, organization on the
page, simplification, and high aesthetic value, and how modern the style is.

Form Level

The life of handwriting lies in the strength of its form.

—Ludwig Klages

The Form Level, or global quality of the handwriting, takes into account such variables as overall style, rhythm of movement, structure of the letters, left and right trend, connection vs. disconnection, traditionalism vs. originality, negation of form vs. elaboration, aesthetic concerns, volitional and unconscious symbolic features (the guiding image), and arrangement on the page.

Historical Review

The "key to unlocking a person's overall personality," according to Ludwig Klages, is in the evaluation of the "style value," *formnwo*, "or Form Level of a handwriting. Klages generalized by classifying handwritings into either "positive" or "negative" categories. A Form Level score was arrived at by looking at the Gestalt first, and then considering the rhythm, arrangement of space, and originality. Six divisions were created ranging from very high, to slightly above and below average, to very low Form Level.

Klages linked a person's Form Level in handwriting to other natural processes, such as the "perfect expression" of form as seen in the "purely natural form of an organism." There is a relationship, he maintains, between the shapes of plants and animals to the shapes created by humans through the movements and forms of handwriting. The key difference is that man is influenced by an extra component, the mind, which is "non-physical," as opposed to physical forces that create the physical forms of life.

To what extent, Klages asks, does man's mind influence or control the rhythm of life, and to what extent does the rhythm of life affect man's mind? We note here a reciprocal arrangement. How has man overcome, incorporated, and integrated this life rhythm?

Manifesting from the writing's Gestalt, the concept of originality, or lack thereof, is a key factor. The opposite of originality, which he lists as "negation of forms," include "banality of form, stereotypical forms, and school type forms."

Excessive features reduce Form Level, whereas harmonious features enhance it. High Form Level can be seen in the fluid, simplified script of a New York City artist (Figure 3.2), whereas low Form Level can be seen in the artificially enhanced writing of a college student in Figure 3.3. Low *forminwo* can be seen in crude and neglected forms, changing slant, poor baseline, and arrhythmic connections, whereas high *forminwo* can be seen in aesthetic forms, easy flow, good organization, trizonal dynamics, and overall clarity. All trait and trait clusters are modified by the Form Level, and every trait has within it ambivalent and/or antithetical components. Thus, even positive traits may

also have negative aspects. Each trait should be seen as a multifaceted poten-
tiality. One's strength can at the same time be one's weakness. For instance, if
a so-called Democrat is liberal, he may also be lax; if a leader is strong, he
may also be stubborn. In both cases, the same trait may be responsible for
different response patterns to different situations.

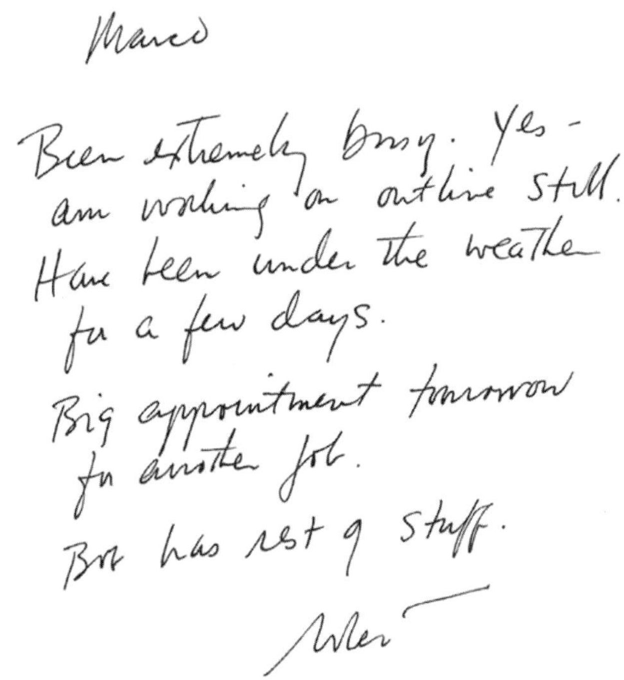

Figure 3.2. Robert Adsit. An example of harmonious writing and high Form Level in the handwriting of an artist. Note the extreme creativity and flow to the Robert signature. See also Figures 11.7, 13.22, and 13.23 for additional samples and example of Robert's work.

Forminwo can often be ascertained quickly at a glance, even though the component of what makes up a form level are rather complex. These components can be analyzed from at least four separate perspectives. We could consider the graphic components, corresponding neurophysiological elements, and cognitive and psychoanalytic aspects. Klages measures Form Level in three ways: rhythm of movement, spatial arrangement, and original-ity. Based on Klages, we can come up with eight different types. To correlate with Psychogram scores (discussed below) we will place the different types on a 100-point scale, with 50 (or "C") as an average Form Level:

A+ = Superior Form Level, scored a 90 to 100.

A = Excellent, scored 80 to 89.

B = Well above average, 70 to 79.

C+ = Above average, 59–69.

C = Average, 48–58.

C– = Below average, 40–48.

D = Poor, 30–40.

F = Abysmal, 0–29.

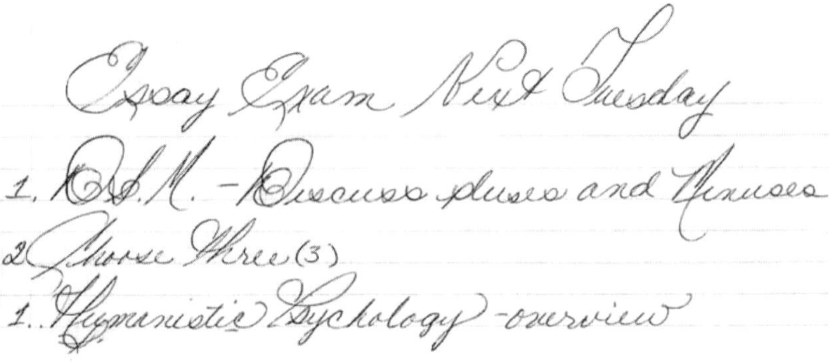

Figure 3.3. Low Form Level. Excessive features or secondary elaboration reduces Form Level in the student's handwriting. Note the general artificiality to the writing, slightly wavy baseline, and lack of control over size in the word pluses *[sic] line 2. All of this serves to lower FL score.*

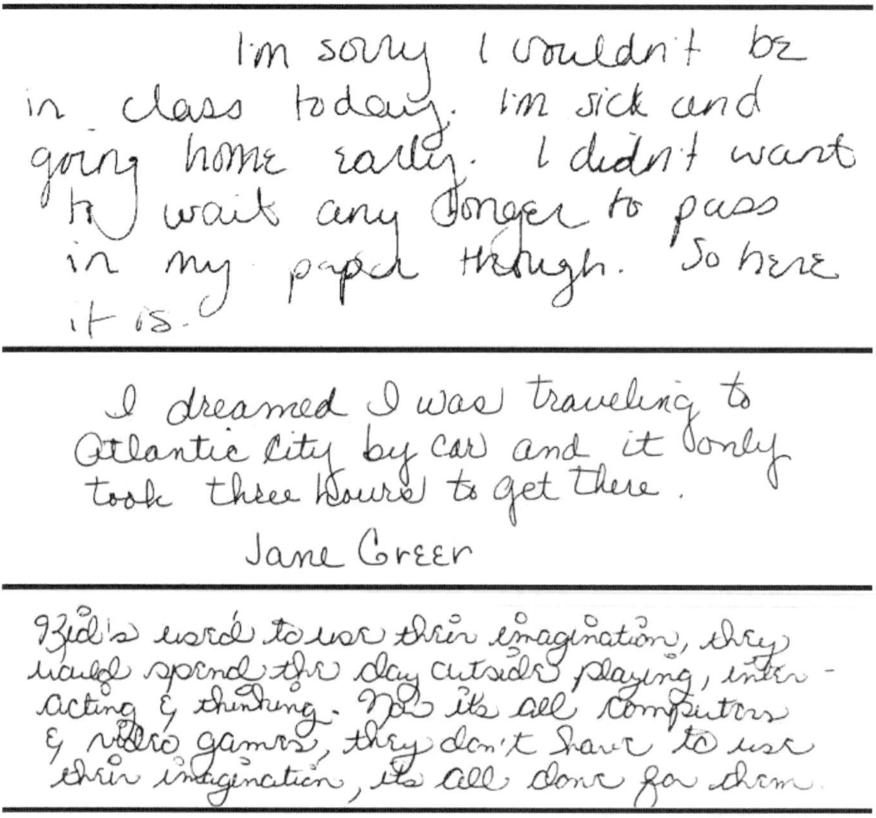

Figure 3.4. The Greek ε appearing in three female handwritings. From an aesthetic point of view, the top writing best integrates this graphic. Its use is completely artificial in the middle writing and distorted in the bottom sample. All three individuals are attempting to add a measure of distinction to their self-image.

Sonnemann (1950) notes that Form Level is the "overriding factor" that modifies each trait in handwriting. For example, the use of a Greek ∈ in a handwriting that has low Form Level would have a different meaning than when it is found in a high form level writing. The same could be said for flourishes, wavy baselines, use of print script, and use of thread. Mendel modifies this statement to say that Form Level is the "yardstick" that allows for differentiation of the same characteristic between two writers. The question then arises as to whether or not it really is the "same characteristic."

Figure 3.4 contains the handwritings of three females who all make use of this Greek ∈. The top writing is that of a college student who dresses in a provocative fashion and who has a tongue ring. (At this current time, tongue rings are common, found as frequently as one or two per class of 30.) The writing is slack and has a disturbed rhythm, sometimes with ample letters, and at other times with neglected forms (for example, the g-loop of the second g in "going," line 3, and in the o of "to," line 4). Nevertheless, the letter is well organized, and the Greek ∈ is fairly well integrated into the body of the script.

The middle writing contains a conventional style offset by a deep need to stand out. This writer is seeking to establish a separate identity, but, so far, the attempt remains superficial.

The bottom script is the most disturbing. The writing is distorted, and there is a tortured feeling to the forms. The Greek ∈, for some reason, has an important symbolic aspect for the writer. Due to the lack of the structure of the vertical axis, one would guess that there was a good amount of dishonesty in the household that she grew up in. One also suspects sexual abuse in childhood, although this is unconfirmed.

The overall arrangement can be analyzed in terms of the handwriting's general layout on the page. Does it appear orderly or disorderly? Crowded or dispersed? Form Level, according to Mendel's interpretation of Klages, can be broken down into four major components:

- **Rhythm**: harmony in forms and spaces, richness and variety of organization.
- **Symmetry**: inner balance, a person's fit in society.
- **Simplification**: does a person try to improve himself—that is, modify beyond convention?
- **Legibility/Fluency**: purposefulness mixed with social cooperation.

Time is a key factor. How much time does the writer allow himself in the act of writing? Graphologically, this is linked not only to speed, but also to simplification and rhythm. A disturbed rhythm may be due to the person's general inability or unwillingness to spend the time necessary to execute the letters in a completely clear and well-paced fashion. Roman (1970) writes that Klages breaks rhythm down into three divisions:

- **Rhythm of Movement**: the periodicity or repeating element in the writing: extensions into the vertical and horizontal dimensions, smooth or jerky nature of the stroke, and the quality of the speed.

- **Rhythm of Form**: the construction of the letters and interrelationship of the parts: simplification or elaboration, originality of letters, types of connections, naturalness, linearity, or pictorialness of style.

- **Rhythm of Arrangement**: the spatial distribution of the graphic pattern as a whole: the margins, figure/ground relationship, spacing, and trizonal components.

This last area is what Mendel calls "rhythm of space," which measures space within letters, between words and lines, and relationship to margins. Is the spatial arrangement harmonious or disharmonious? Werner Wolff links this last area to the "principle of configuration" and to his "diagrams of the unconscious," which will be discussed further.

In the area called "rhythm of form," Mendel discusses the concept of symmetry. Is one zone overdeveloped at the expense of another? Or are there harmonious proportions between height, width, pressure, slant, use of loops, bars, dots, and flourishes? Saudek's concept of "dominants" and "counterdominants" could be integrated here as well.

Originality and creativity are also key factors, and Mendel differentiates between the two:

- **Original** is individual.
- **Creative** adds something new.

Creative people are always original, but the reverse is not always true. "To invent and use new and better characters or connections of characters is a feat perhaps only a genius can achieve," he notes. Creation in writing "must facilitate the writing." It must be easy to do, and be written in such a way as to not impair legibility. Mendel notes that "only a person who does a great deal of writing who is daily confronted with the need to create more easily executed characters" will develop (or tend to develop) his handwriting in this way. Creativity could also be measured in life as well as in handwriting. For instance, a carpenter who does no writing may have a crude penmanship, but be highly creative. I personally knew such a man who, although in his 20s, happened to be illiterate. Obviously, there would be no way to measure his Form Level, because he could not write, but, in terms of his carpentry skills, I would have rated him at a very high level.

This brings us to one of the greatest difficulties there is in analyzing handwriting: comparing the handwriting of one who writes a lot, such as a professor, with one who does not write at all, such as a builder. Certainly, in nine times out of 10, the professor will have a higher Form Level. Highly educated people may have extremely high Form Levels, and yet they may also have psychological problems, which are more easily masked because they are so glib with the actual act of writing. Simultaneously, well-educated people and glib writers who do not make much effort to alter their handwriting from the learned standard (for example, the Palmer method) may at the same time be creative individuals, but their creativity simply does not show up in any conventional way in their handwriting (for example, in the creation of unusual or original forms).

Usually, in these instances, the creativity shows up in the Rhythm of Form and Rhythm of Spatial Arrangement. For example, organization on the page will play a key factor. This type of creative person may have what

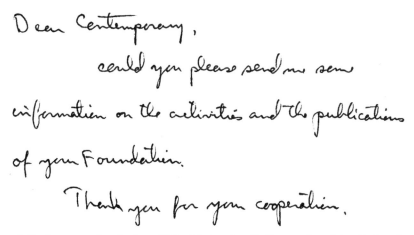

Figure 3.5. An example of what Gille-Maisani calls "aerated writing" whereby the space between lines and words has deep significance for the writer

Dan Anthony calls touch-points, yet, at the same time, original letter forms or original connections may not appear. Touch-points are found by using a compass, ruler, and pen to connect the tops of letters and diacritics that tend to line up rhythmically in exacting fashion even though letter heights and baselines may vary. For instance, in these types of writings it is not uncommon to find three or four i-dots lining up with exact precision diagonally down a page.

Professor Jean-Charles Gille-Maisani (1991) discusses this concept of the Rhythm of Spatial Arrangement, more in terms of the overall placement of the words than in the link between the letters. "What a man does not say is as important as what he does say," says Gille-Maisani. Harmony can be perceived in the "distribution of the masses." A person who leaves a significant amount of blank spaces often portrays a "need for mental clarity." Gille-Maisani calls these kinds of handwritings "aerated writings." See Figure 3.5, which is the handwriting of a college professor of chemistry. These writers tend to be "reflective in thought and judgment." They are also objective, as they can "stand back" and perceive. They may be "steady and critical, capable of restraint," yet, at the same time, suffer from feelings of "isolation and distancing." In the opposite situation, a person who "entangles lines" may be one who "compensates by a debased extraversion," and thus might be "excessively open to change." Writers who "squeeze" letters together oftentimes are close with relatives, but "reserved with strangers."

If we look at the structure of handwriting and its relationship to the concept of Form Level from the neurophysiological perspective, we note that the writing could be understood from a left brain vs. right brain point of view, or as a manifestation of an integrated process involving the brain as a whole.

The higher the Form Level, the greater the use of advanced centers of the brain. In Dan Anthony's *Psychogram* book, he links the Form Level score to such variables as:

| Organization | Rhythm | Alignment control | Lower zone |
| Simplification | Spontaneity | Pressure | Speed |

There is also emphasis in the connecting strokes of the arcades, angles, and garlands. Graphologically, this translates into dynamic handwritings that display excellent rhythm, good use of trizonal dynamics, harmonic use of pressure, sound organization, and a rightward trend. What the Psychogram has attempted to do is break down the Gestalt into its parts and then reconstruct the whole in a mathematical and pictorial way through the use of a mandala-shaped chart.

Rhythm: The Balance Between Contraction and Release

This brings us to the dual nature of handwriting analysis, analyzing a writing by looking at the whole, and breaking down the process into its constituent parts. Both Sonnemann and Mendel discuss the concepts of the vertical and horizontal axes. Up and down movements, or the vertical dimension, relate to a person's "self-orientation and available values." Its downstroke is called the "stable axis," and portrays, according to Mendel, the "backbone" of the writer. The horizontal or mobile axis expresses our "attitude towards the future and our fellow man" and also the exteriorization of libidinal drives. Sonnemann calls this the person's "orientation to reality."

These two processes, the up and down movement and the one from left to right, occur in time, and thus, this would also relate to what Klages calls the Rhythm of Movement. A periodicity or a repeating element should appear in a natural way, displaying the Rhythm of Space, or the Principle of Configuration that Wolff discusses.

Other processes to be considered in the creation of these two axes are cognitive and emotional factors, a homeostatic quality that seeks to control or integrate these two diametrically opposed criteria, and pressures erupting from past, present, and future considerations. For example, emotional baggage from childhood, present day-to-day pressures, and goals for one's future. How does the brain control all of these processes? What is happening psycho-motorically—that is, in terms of muscle groups used in the expression of fine motor control needed to write? What is the link between the rhythm of contraction (downstroke) and release (upstroke), and for the right-handed writer, movement to the right, release, and movement to the left, contraction.

The Problem of the Left-Handed Writer

Things are much more complex for the left-handed writer for this dynamic, because a releasing movement away from the body for a lefty is to the left, and this movement opposes the natural rightward progression of the writing. Further, if the base of the palm remains on the page, the left-hand writer also runs the risk of smudging his writing as he writes! The lefty must therefore come upon a strategy that eases the difficulty of trying to write toward the body in a smooth or rapid fashion.

Simplistically stated, left-trend in a right-handed writer generally serves to lower Form Level, but the same movement in a lefty should not affect Form Level to the same extent or even in the same way. In other words, a left-tending movement that would have a negative connotation for a righty could have a positive connotation for a lefty, for the simple reason that it is a contractual or restrictive movement for a righty and an expansive releasing movement for a lefty. That said, the lefty still needs to curb his natural releasing movement to the left, because it opposes the goal of progressing to the right when he writes. He therefore must find release in a movement to the right, which is generally a contractual movement for him, because it is a movement toward the body. Release will therefore be found in a different set of muscle groups in the arm and wrist for the lefty as compared to the musculature release in a righty. The end result is that right-trend will still be seen in a positive light for a lefty even though it is more difficult for him to execute than right-trend for a righty.

Figure 3.6, a signature of President Bill Clinton, is an excellent example of unusual rightward trend in the handwriting of a lefty. The natural way for a righty to make the letter *l* is to swing back to the left to create the loop. This movement would be even easier for a lefty to execute, so for a lefty to come up with this tent-like *l* is even more extraordinary, and it can be seen as a sign of brilliance. This movement is also is a form of primary thread, which is a thread in the vertical axis. Secondary thread can be seen at the end of the signature. Symbolically, on the positive side, the rightward trend reflects a forward thinker. On the negative side, it may also symbolize a wish to escape the past. Note the tight capital I's. Here we see the dual nature of Bill Clinton, out there shaking hands and enjoying the limelight, as seen in the open signature, and also hiding something, as seen in the restricted left-leaning capital I's.

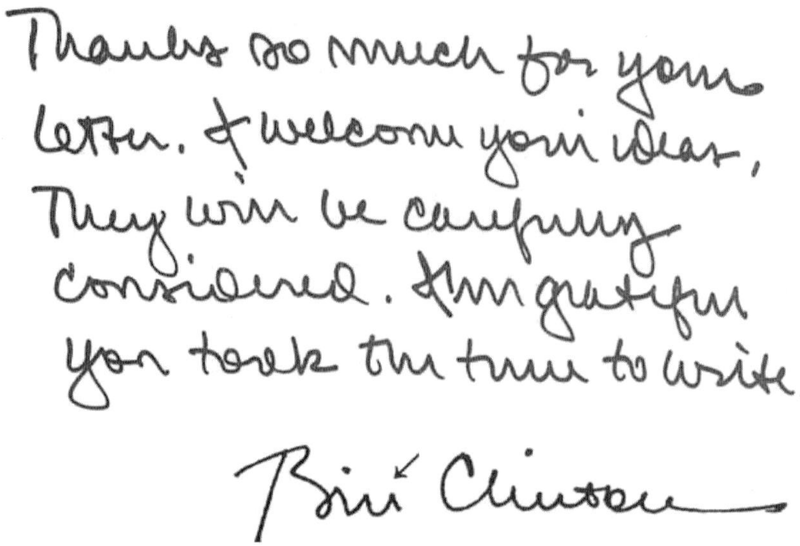

Figure 3.6. Note left slant, yet extreme rightward trend in President Bill Clinton's handwriting. For a lefty, this move to the right is exceptional, particularly in the I's of the first name. This is an example of primary thread.

Upstrokes and Downstrokes

Sonnemann and Jacoby begin to clue us in on the relationship between contraction and release and conscious and unconscious processes. Rightward trend involves the process of externalization, whereas leftward trend involves contact avoidance. The first is future-oriented, the second, past-oriented. During the act of writing, complex letter forms are created. At the same time, thoughts, words, sentences, and paragraphs are being formed in the mind of the writer as individualized letter forms are created. If handwriting were not a predominantly preconscious, automatized process, thinking and writing simultaneously would not be possible. Handwriting is thus a mainly preconscious activity.

Nevertheless, handwriting is not one continuous smooth operation. Sonnemann discusses that, by its nature, handwriting is a discontinuous process involving changes in direction, separation of words, alterations in size and speed, and continuous shifting from contractual movements to ones of release. Here is where the concept of Form Level enters. Handwriting variables fall essentially into one of two categories:

1. Contraction/Release.

2. Overall pattern (for example, form quality).

The connecting of letters with upstrokes involves an integrated contiguous movement to the right, which Jacoby associates not only to the ability of the writer to see how things are linked, but also to the writer's "intellectual, emotional and practical adaptability." The term *spontaneity* is associated here. Connection suggests spontaneity and disconnection, but its element of inhibition suggests the opposite.

From a mechanical point of view, disconnection involves the elimination of upstrokes, which, Jacoby tells us, "are the very lines of the connection of bridges between the ego and the world." Thus, connectivity measures the

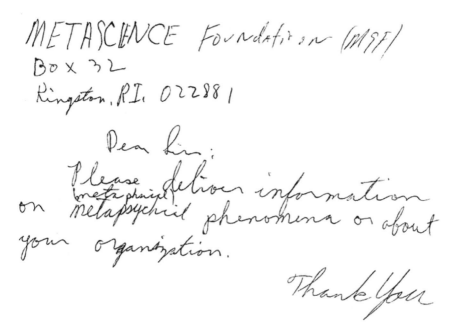

Figure 3.7. This writer has much difficulty controlling the impulse pattern. The distortion in size and spatial arrangement served to greatly lower FL score.

degree of connection between the person and the world, the degree of social adaption, self-coordination, and spiritual connection. Too much connection, on the other hand, can be associated with too much adaptability, an overexcited nature, one who is obsessed, or one who has uncontrollable thoughts.

Arrhythmic disconnections reflect a schism within the self, such as people who have been adopted, people who have never connected emotionally with the mother, people who feel isolated, schizophrenic individuals, and the epileptic split-brain writers all display this graphic variable. Thus, a lack of rhythmic connections shows a lack of natural ability to access the unconscious, and corresponding right hemispheric structures of the brain. Obviously, Form Level will be affected in a negative way if there are arrhythmic disconnections.

There is much disturbance in the rhythm of spatial arrangement in Figure 3.7. Great lack of emotional control is revealed in this low Form Level sample. Contrast this sample with Figure 3.8. Although there are some significant size and slant fluctuations, overall, the Gestalt pattern is evolved. This is a high-level thinker who has excellent organizational skills. Her great emotional range is offset by keen intellectual insight.

Conscious, Preconscious, and Unconscious Determinants

Werner Wolff (1948/61) notes that the general direction of writing is conscious; the automatized steps involved in creating the numerous letter forms as in the hand gliding across the page is preconscious, and the overall pattern, probably the slant, and the placement of such things as diacritics is unconscious. Wolff differentiates between movements that are learned—that start out as being conscious and, through time, after practice, become preconscious on movements that are unconscious—not learned, inborn. This is the form and quality of the writing (for example, why we emphasize a curve, why we choose a linear or pictorial graphic pattern, and so on).

Wolff's landmark text, *Diagrams of the Unconscious*, could be looked at from the Form Level point of view as really being an attempt to analyze the rhythm of spatial arrangement. It is also an attempt to find a meeting ground between inborn primeval processes and those learned after birth. These are combined into what he calls the **principle of configuration**: how the words and preconscious patterns lay out across the page.

In Thelma Seifer's (1991) article, "A Right Brain Approach to Handwriting Analysis," she attempts to discuss how one goes about measuring this configuring principle. It is her contention that this overall pattern is directly linked to unconscious factors in the writer. Certain symbols could be highlighted in different-colored pens to help reveal the pattern, or a ruler

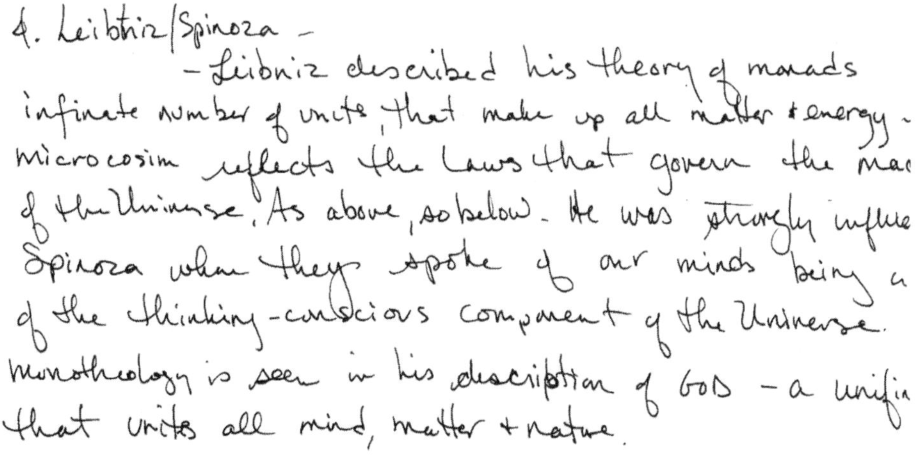

4. Leibniz/Spinoza –
  – Leibniz described his theory of monads
infinite number of units, that make up all matter + energy.
Microcosim reflects the Laws that govern the mac[ro]
of the Universe. As above, so below. He was strongly influe[nced]
Spinoza when they spoke of our minds being a
of the thinking-conscious component of the Universe.
Monotheology is seen in his description of God – a unifi[er]
that unites all mind, matter + nature.

Figure 3.8. Although there is some entanglement of lines, size distortion (long lower zone), and changing slant (g leaning back in word "being" line 5) overall, this is a very positive handwriting of a 26-year-old university student. The legibility, rhythm of spatial arrangement, simplification, and aesthetic value all contribute to a high FL score.

could be used to connect touch-points either within words or even between words horizontally or diagonally down a page. This unconscious symbolic patterning represents an integrative function, an aesthetic Gestalt that is a global factor, which affects Form Level in a positive way.

The question remains: What are we really looking at when we look at Form Level? Graphologically, this chapter has attempted to say that we are looking at rhythms in the movement, form, and distribution. Form Level is that quality of the Gestalt that modifies the individual parts, that colorizes different graphic clusters and their psychological counterparts to give the handwriting analyst a clearer picture of the writer's level of integration and uniqueness of personality.

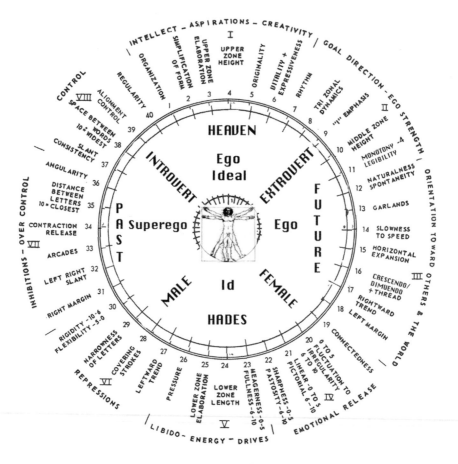

Roman-Staempfli Psychogram
1955 - Revised by Dan Anthony 1964
Revised by Marc J. Seifer © Copyright 2007

Figure 4.1.

In the 1950s Klara Roman crystallized her idea as to how to objectify handwriting. Working with her student George Staemphli, she compiled 40 graphic variables, such as organization, simplification, lower zone length, narrowness, angles, and garlands, which she organized into eight psychological sectors such as Intellect, Emotional Release, and Inhibitions. Each variable was graded on a 1 to 10 scale. For instance, if a handwriting was well organized, it might get a rating of 8, if poorly organized, a 3, and so on. Roman also cleverly placed the indicators and psychological sectors into a circular arrangement, so that the resulting mandala-like bar chart of the handwriting graded would be able to express in pictorial fashion the various orientations, strengths, and weaknesses of the person.

The Roman psychogram was slightly modified by Dan Anthony in the early 1960s, changing two criteria. At the same time, he created a workbook that discussed each of the 40 indicators and formulated mathematical equations to establish Functional Productivity and Form Level scores from the various indicators. The advantages of the psychogram are many. For one, it forces the budding graphologist to study at least 40 different graphic features and grade each on a 1 to 10 scale. This alone helps greatly in comprising an analysis. Further, each of the indicators is grouped into global personality clusters. It thus becomes a somewhat objective process to begin to grade a person for his or her goal orientation, drives, inhibitions, and so on. Most importantly, a numerical scale has been constructed that allows the complex psychophysiological act of inner speech transformed into *handwriting to be transformed into a numerical scale*. This is Klara Roman's monumental accomplishment: the creation of an objective procedure that allows the scientific method to be applied to handwriting analysis.

The present author has used the psychogram or aspects thereof to study with medical doctors (1) the handwritings of schizophrenics and measure their muscle tension output as compared to normals (Seifer and Goode, 1975); and (2) the psychomotor functioning of epileptic split-brain writers as compared to normals (Tenhouten, Seifer, and Siegel 1988).

With specifics to the 40 indicators, Dan Anthony removed the indicators "monotony" and also "sharpness" from Roman's original psychogram, and replaced them with "firmness of ductus" and "linear/pictorial." Having worked with the Psychogram it occurred to the present author that the variable "thread," which was placed in the 16th position, often had a low score in people who were extraverted. In other words, it was not a good indicator for all handwritings because most people do not thread their writing. Also, Anthony's addition of "firmness of ductus" was somewhat redundant, as the quality of the stroke is judged in "sharpness/pastosity" and also in "pressure."

For these reasons, the variable "thread" was combined with "crescendo and dimuendo," and Anthony's "firmness of ductus" was replaced with "monotony/legibility." The Anthony *Graphological Psychogram* book is an excellent reference. To maintain its integrity, I have, for the most part, refrained from referring to it in the following discussion of the 40 indicators. The references for most of the information on these 40 indicators, particularly the trait lists, derives from the works of Sonnemann (1950), Karoh's, (1981) and Felix Klein's (1983) translations of Klages as well as Saudek (1926); Quirke (1930); Jacoby (1939); Mendel (1947); Wolff (1948/60); de St. Colombe (1967); and Roman (1963, 1970). The idea for the + and – lists of traits stems from Klages's (1926) masterwork *Handschrift und Charakter*, of which I have a copy.

Referring back to Max Pulver, he realized that (1) the baseline or *middle zone* of a writing related to **ego**, the realm of the earth, the body, social existence and the everyday world; (2) the **upper zone** correlated to the **superego**, the heavens, spirituality, and God; and 3) the **lower zone** to the **id**, the instincts, the genitals, material world, underworld, sex, and Hades. The Roman/Anthony psychogram, slightly modified once again by me, also reflects this kind of symbology. **Above** is the heavens and spirituality, **Below** is Hades and the libido, **Left** is the past and repression, and **Right** is the social world and the future.

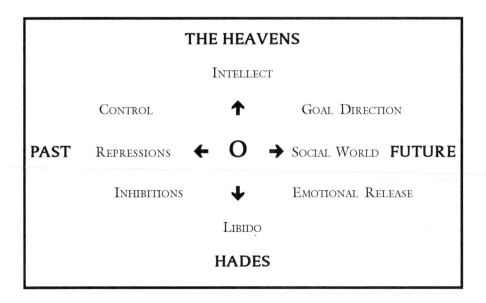

8 Personality Clusters and Their Graphic Indicators

I: Intellect, Aspirations, and Creativity

    (1) Organization   (3) Upper zone elaboration

    (2) Simplification   (4) Upper zone height

    (5) Originality

II: Goal Direction and Ego Strength

    (6) Expressiveness and vitality   (8) Trizonal dynamics

    (7) Rhythm   (9) "I" emphasis

    (10) Middle zone height

III: Orientation Toward Others and the World

    (11) Crescendo, diminuendo,   (14) Slowness to speed
         and thread   (15) Horizontal expansion

    (12) Naturalness/Spontaneity   (16) Monotony

    (13) Garlands   (17) Rightward trend

IV: Emotional Release

    (18) Left Margin   (20) Fluctuation to irregularity

    (19) Connectedness   (21) Linear/Pictorial

    (22) Line quality: Sharpness and Pastosity

V: Libido, Energy Drives

    (23) Meagerness/Fullness   (25) Lower zone elaboration

    (24) Lower zone Length   (26) Pressure

VI: Repressions

    (27) Leftward trend   (29) Narrowness of letters

    (28) Covering strokes   (30) Rigidity/Flexibility

VII: Inhibitions and Over Control

    (31) Right margin   (34) Contraction/Release

    (32) Left-right slant   (35) Distance between letters

    (33) Arcades   (36) Angularity

VIII: Control

    (37) Slant consistency   (38) Space between words

    (39) Alignment control   (40) Regularity

I: Intellect, Aspirations, and Creativity

We are looking at the overall Form Level of the writing, its aesthetic value, simplification of form, and expression of individuality. Such a writing will be well organized and aesthetically placed on the page, it will have original forms, and the sense of a driving interest in the idea of growth and even spiritual development. Symbolically, we should see abstract qualities and emphasis on the upper zone, with a certain clarity, maturity, and ease of movement.

(1) Organization

Overall arrangement. We are starting off with the total pattern, the Gestalt. Does the page of writing resemble a framed painting with a sense that the writer knew ahead of time the amount of space he or she had to work with, or are adjustments made along the way? Is there a heading and proper spacing for a salutation? If you are dealing with more than a one-page letter, what can you tell about the plan the subject had when he began to write? Do the lines get more crowded toward the bottom, or are words squeezed in at the ends of lines? How does this person utilize the available space? Order vs. disorder; neat vs. sloppy; emphasis on margins vs. margin neglect; crowded vs. well spaced between letters and between words. Is there a sense of dynamic fluctuation vs. either irregularity or monotony? If the writing is poorly organized, give the writer a 2 or a 3. If the organization seems adequate, give him a 5 or 6; if exceptional, a 7 or 8. In general, save extreme grades at both ends of the spectrum for highly unusual writings.

Good organization is a sign of intelligence. It is one of the best measures. It also shows the ability to plan, to keep things in order. It is a measure of intellect over emotion. **Poor organization** is *not* a sign for lack of intelligence. There are many highly intelligent people who are not well organized. It is a sign of lack of discipline, possibly lack of training or indication that emotions rule.

(2) Simplification

What changes has the writer made off the standard model, which in America is usually the Palmer model? This is one of the biggest keys to unlocking the secret of the subject's personality. What changes has that person made from what he was taught? If you list the differences and answer that question, you will really begin to hone in on what makes that writer different from all other writers, and what makes that person unique.

Become familiar with the standard model and see what types of changes, if any, have been made. Make sure you can recognize the difference between true simplification and neglect. Simplification is a sign of maturity, a form of streamlining that does not impair legibility, and it allows the writer to move at a faster pace. Examples would include the removal of beginning strokes and return loops, such as a y made with only the downstroke, connecting a diacritic such as a t-bar to the next letter. Many people write the word "the" whereby the t-bar becomes or leads into the h; a shortened form for the "ing" ending, or other creative shortcuts. Time is precious, and the person who simplifies his writing has reduced the amount of time necessary to put the message down on paper so that time can be used elsewhere.

Neglect involves the dropping of letters or parts of letters because of laziness, avoidance of certain issues, nervousness, being caught in a rat race, and having to dash off a note too quickly. It could also be a sign of dishonesty or some type of character flaw.

Positive Signs	Negative Signs	Neglect
pragmatic	Machiavellian	inability to see things through
simplicity	lack of empathy	shoddiness
purposefulness	coldness	inaccuracy
ability to see essentials	abruptness	unfaithful
objectivity	ambiguity	deceptive, cunning
humbleness	dismissal of social graces	deceitful, dishonest
grace	too casual a manner	
deal with fundamentals		
determination		

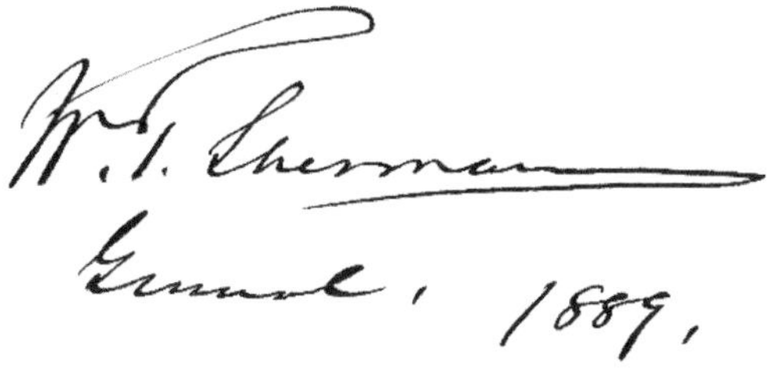

Figure 4.2. General Sherman, Union Army, Civil War

(3) Upper Zone Elaboration

We are looking here at emphasis on the upper zone particularly through the use of symbols as seen in high i-dots, flying t-bars, and other letters that appear to shoot up to or are drawn into the upper zone. The great overstroke of the T in Tom Edison's famous signature is a magnificent manifestation of upper zone elaboration. Walt Disney also greatly emphases the upper zone with large circular movements.

+	−
idealism	flighty, unrealistic, a dreamer
imaginative	affected, vain
spiritual	paranoid
enthusiastic	pretentious
ambitious	wants to impress others
abstract ability	avoidance of self

The key is to understand the difference between **primary elaboration**, which is a direct manifestation from unconscious/primal forces, and **secondary elaboration**, which has artificiality to it (the last two traits on the negative side of the list). Primary elaboration will be associated with high Form Level writing. It is a sign of the essence of creativity and connection to the inner self, or an expression of the soul, if you will. Secondary elaboration would be in writings that have evidence of an overactive filter or censor. The person wants to make a good impression, so he or she consciously tries to enhance the writing. The circle i-dot is a case in point. Clearly, the person is striving to be creative and wants others, as well as himself, to think that he is creative, but it is artificial.

Secondary elaboration reminds me of some of Steven Spielberg's movies. For instance, early on in *Jurassic Park* (1993) we see the crew of travelers near a fenced enclosure where the dinosaurs lurk and you hear a rumbling. Having seen so many movies, it seemed to me that he copied that scene from someplace, essentially from Hitchcock, who would create terror by *not* showing the violence, but having the viewer imagine it instead. There's a surrealistic circus scene in *Empire From the Sun* (1987), which looks like it was lifted from Michelangelo Antonioni's (1966) masterpiece *Blowup*. This would be equivalent to secondary elaboration: wanting to be creative, but having to resort to copying someone else to try and achieve the creative effect. It comes off as artificial. Evidence of primary elaboration, if we stay with the analogy, would be *Schindler's List* (1993), which clearly came from a deeper region of Spielberg's creative brain, perhaps really from his heart. *ET* (1982) of course, would also be on that level. Primary elaboration is a pure expression from the wellspring, unconscious forces that are also revealed in great art. The true power in handwriting analysis as a crystallized portrait of the dynamic invisible process of soul → mind → brain interaction is revealed in primary elaboration.

(4) Upper Zone Height

We are not just talking about the actual height of the upper zone, but its relationship to the other zones. The analyst needs to establish a foundation that appears to be an average height, which is essentially twice the height of the middle zone. If it is higher than that, give it a 6 or 7. If upper zone letters are exceedingly tall, give it an 8. A 9 is rare. Save this score for a very extreme case. Most often upper zone height will correlate with upper zone elaboration. However, there are cases whereby upper zone letters are short or relatively short, and, if so, grade them a 4 or even a 3, but there may still be upper zone elaboration, such as high or circle i-dots or flying t-bars way above a short stem.

Vertical Axis

Upper zone height is related to the vertical axis, what Mendel calls the **stable axis**, the up and downstrokes. This movement refers to the very backbone of the writer. Mendel, Sonnemann, and Klages all point out that, if one removes all the upstrokes, most words are still legible, but if all downstrokes are removed, the word becomes unintelligible. Thus, one can see that upstrokes, movements away from the body, are less conscious than the defining downstroke toward the body: up and down, away and toward, release and contraction, relaxation and tension, unconscious and conscious.

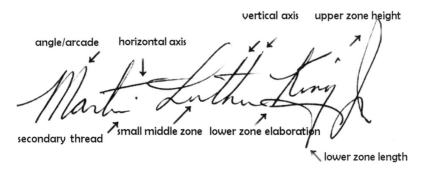

Figure 4.3. Note Martin Luther King's reach up into the spiritual zone in the J of Jr.

◐ **Downstrokes (toward the body)**: self-assertion, ego-centric, definitive, a "me first" attitude.

◐ **Upstrokes (away from the body)**: away from self, toward the intellect, toward high ideals, lofty ambitions, the heavens, or God. This is generally evidence of the influence of the superego type personality, one ruled by the conscience, and the censor, a moralist. If it is paired with covered strokes (for example, retraced upper loops), it is a sign of great repression and secrets. The person may appear to be moral, but in fact hides the very opposite tendency.

Directional Pressure

If the downstroke is bowed in a way so that it bulges toward the left, this would be the influence of a decisive impact from the past, what Felix Klein called a "kick in the gut" (Seifer, 2006). If the bulge is bowed on the right side, then it can be seen as a sail on a sailboat gaining a gust of wind. It is a boost from the future impelling the writer forward. If the downstroke has an s-like kink in it, this has been called the "broken back" stroke. It is a sign of a fundamental weakness in the character, either a sign of severe early trauma and/or a sign of potential dishonesty (see Figure 8.1). One way or another is it someone who has difficulty telling the truth either to themselves or to others.

Tall Capitals		Short Capitals	
+	–	+	–
intelligence	haughtiness	humble	inferiority
ambitious	presumptuous	modest	dull
dignified	dreamer	unassuming	docile
pride	dominating	lacks ambition	outgoing
hides inferiority	repressed	well-bred	false modesty, a ruse

(5) Originality

Look for unexpected, original and creative letter formations, odd patterns, and unusual but skillful interconnections. In a positive handwriting, these forms should be combined with a sense of pacing, playfulness, aesthetic balance, and rhythmical distribution. You should try to ascertain the difference between a form that looks original, but was probably copied from some other writing, such as a Greek $\in$ or circle i-dot, as compared to a unique form that has truly sprung from a spontaneous expression stemming from the unconscious. Is the overall effect natural or artificial, unprompted or inhibited, aesthetically balanced or crooked?

Figure 4.4.
Joseph Conrad, author of Heart of Darkness.

Creative Forms		Conventional Forms	
+	–	+	–
nonconforming	eccentric	traditional	conformist
creative, ingenious	affected	conservative	rigid
in touch w/inner self	prone to fantasy	realistic	unimaginative

II: Goal Direction and Ego Strength

This second global cluster will chart graphics involved in, on the positive side, self-confidence and self-actualization. A person who has had positive support through his or her upbringing has a better chance of developing a strong ego and a strong sense of self. There is the implication that such a person has been loved and encouraged as a child. This kind of person will be propelled to make his mark on the world. On the other hand, there is another category of people I call the "in spite of" types, for example, Jerry Lewis, (see Figure 4.12). They could be extremely goal-directed, but have a sense of inferiority. In fact, it could be this very chink in their armor that gives them the impetus to better themselves. One way or another, we are looking here at graphics that involve the inner strength of the person, the development of his or her ego, and related factors associated with the drive to impel one toward success.

Figure 4.5.
The
enthusiastic
print script of
Jackie Kennedy.
The left slant
and

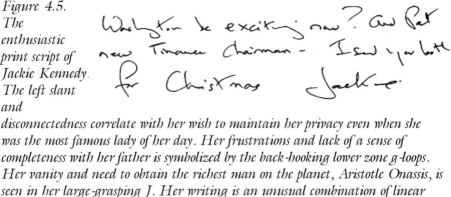

disconnectedness correlate with her wish to maintain her privacy even when she was the most famous lady of her day. Her frustrations and lack of a sense of completeness with her father is symbolized by the back-hooking lower zone g-loops. Her vanity and need to obtain the richest man on the planet, Aristotle Onassis, is seen in her large-grasping J. Her writing is an unusual combination of linear aspects seen in the concise middle zone (which relates to her expertise as an editor) and pictorial aspects seen in the large caps. There are extra frills (for example, the f of for) and an overall sense of aesthetic design.

(6) Expressiveness and Vitality

> Expression involves a discharge of emotional and mental phenomena…. For their investigation we must know how a majority of people express themselves and how the individual modifies the general expressive principle.
>
> —Werner Wolff, 1948/63, p. 177

Max Pulver (1980) points out that the very act of writing is an expression from "I" to "you" from the inner self to the outer world. But what is it that is being expressed? And which handwritings are more expressive and which are not? Sonnemann (1950) emphasizes two aspects of the movement pattern: a "purposive goal" and an "expressive gesture." One aspect involves volitional properties, exertion of the will, the very decision to write and to move one's hand across the page to achieve that end, and to a great extent, an expression of unconscious factors, including one's mood, temperament, genetic, and symbolic features. Artificial aspects will take away from expression, as will slowness, narrowness, and other signs of inhibition. The writing's spontaneity, vitality, and color (texture to the stroke) will add to its expressive value.

Handwriting is but one expressive behavior; hand gestures and facial expressions are two others. Some people and some cultures are more prone to talk with their hands. Consider all the hand gestures that exist; for example, thumb's up for success, calling for a waiter with the first finger raised, pointing someone out with the first finger in the horizontal, giving someone the middle finger as a way of cursing them, the sign of the cuckold (first and fourth finger up, middle two fingers curled down by thumb), sign of peace (first two fingers apart), Spock's sign of the Vulcan (creating a "V" by separating the four fingers, two by two), Austin Powers's Dr. Evil's biting of his pinky as a sign of (semi) serious contemplation.

Sonnemann gives but one example of a facial expression: that of "fright" to explain what he means by the expressive quality of writing. Look at the writing's Gestalt pattern; what expression is revealed? This expression will be closely tied to its vitality. Is it hurried, slow, chaotic, animated, abstract, conforming, sharp, angry, agitated, staid, or friendly? In Rudolf Arnheim's (1954) book *Art and Visual Perception* he introduces the word *Isomorphism*—that is "the structural kinship between the stimulus pattern and the expression it conveys" (450). Quoting Goethe on expression, Arnheim goes on to say, "One may use metaphorically the differences pointed up in the physical theory of cohesion…to express the diversities of character: strong, firm, dense, elastic, flexible, agile, rigid, tough, fluid, and who knows what other characters" (452). Allport and Vernon (1933) have compiled a list of expressive features and their opposites, which include the following:

adroit	⇔	inept	fluent	⇔	jerky
artistic	⇔	crude	forceful	⇔	ineffectual
confident	⇔	tremulous	frank	⇔	reserved
conspicuous	⇔	colorless	free	⇔	inhibited
dainty	⇔	clumsy	majestic	⇔	common
defiant	⇔	cringing	mature	⇔	childish
eager	⇔	apathetic	military	⇔	listless
eccentric	⇔	wholesome	naïve	⇔	affected
explosive	⇔	stolid	precise	⇔	sloppy
extravagant	⇔	unassuming	restless	⇔	calm

If the handwriting looks alive and conveys animation, creativity and vitality, score the writing a 7 or 8. If the writing appears restricted, guarded, narrow, monotonous, and slow, score a 3 or 4.

(7) Rhythm

> Klages describes the meaning of rhythm as the expression of the strength of an individual's inner life force. Graphologically, he considers it the most important component of the *forminwo*. He states that rhythm never has a double meaning as do other graphic indicators, but rather provides the key for the classification of all other characteristics as either "positive" or "negative."
>
> —Erika Karohs

Rhythm is the balance between contraction and release, the muscular movements away and toward the body. Klages seeks to place the rhythm of the writing in a larger context, the lap of the oceans, the turning of the seasons, night and day, the very pulsation of life. Graphologically, rhythm is measured in three areas of rhythm:

1. **Movement**—the pulse of the driving impetus forward.

2. **Form**—symbolic features and the shape of the letters.

3. **Arrangement**—the pattern on the page.

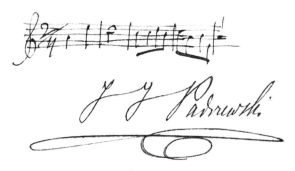

Figure 4.6. Pianist Ignace Paderewski, the highest paid performer of the Gay Nineties, and a future prime minister of Poland. Note how the d becomes the e in his signature, and the rhythmic placement of what looks like two y's.

Klages compares the rhythm of the writing to a musical score, and notes that there is a difference between the beat, which is unchanging, and the rhythm, which is dynamic. Some handwritings look rhythmical at first glance, but really are repetitious beats. A true rhythmic writing will pulsate. "Jackhammers and pendulum clocks run according to beat…. Poetry and prose show rhythm. Once one learns to play the piano with the help of a metronome, the next step is to discard this external crutch so that one's music dos not sound 'mechanical' and 'dead'" (Klein, 1983). One's beat corresponds to, according to Klages, one's **mind,** which is inhibiting and influenced by restrictions from culture, whereas rhythm reflects a dynamic expression from one's **soul**.

Lack of rhythm would give the writing a static pattern, whereas a highly rhythmic writing would be syncopated, a dynamic alteration between volitional downstrokes, contraction and emphasis on self, and unconscious upstrokes, except for the first stroke, the beginning upstroke, which would display volitional properties. The following chart pairs the positive and negative sides of **contraction** (left side) and **release** of rhythm of the form of the letters.

Regulated (Control)		Released (Emotion)	
+	−	+	−
self-denial	constriction	relaxed	lack of purpose
self-protected	obedient	free	unruly
resolution	coldness	impulsive	fickle
concentration	boring	creative	weak-willed

Mendel (1947) discusses the rhythm of spatial arrangement between letters, words, and lines, as well as the margins (42). Draw your eye to the total pattern to look at the "space rhythm." Measure rhythm for letter formation, sense of movement forward, and also for the entire pattern. If the handwriting appears alive and rhythmic, mark it a 7 or 8. If the writing appears static or overly regulated, give it a 3 or 4.

(8) Trizonal Dynamics

Here we are considering symmetry or lack thereof between all three zones: upper, middle, and lower. Western writing begins on the left and goes to the right, from self to other, but along the way, there are up and down movements. As the pen moves along the horizontal axis, it must accommodate the vertical. As we have learned earlier, the upper zone relates to the sky, heaven, the head, and the superego; the middle zone represents the baseline, the plane of reality, the earth, the torso, and the ego; the lower zone represents the genitals, the underworld, and the id. The letter f is the only letter that covers all three zones, starting in the middle, the ego, proceeding to the upper zone of superego, plunging down to the lower zone of the id, and back up to ego. The "gh" combination, as in the word *enough* is a trizonal movement; and in the reverse, words that end in "ty" or "ly" for example, "party" or "Billy" show movement from the upper to middle to lower zone in one action.

Does one zone predominate over the others? Does the writer have difficulty moving into one zone or another? Is there easy access from the lower zone of the unconscious to the upper zone of imagination? This is what is being considered.

Make a little chart that catalogs the writer's preferences with regard to the zones. In some instances, a deficit in a particular zone may relate to a physical malady. A paralyzed person may have foreshortened lower zones a heart attack patient may show trouble in the middle or upper zone; a stroke victim may show a kink in the upper zone. The following chart was adapted from Sonnemann (1950, 60–63).

Predominates

Middle Zone		Upper Zone		Lower Zone	
+	−	+	−	+	−
orderly	envy	intellectual	elusive	earthy	voracious
realistic	inferiority	enthusiastic	flighty	erotic	greedy
leadership	lacks fiber	ambitious	paranoid	athletic	obtrusive

Klages considers here whether the writing is symmetrical or asymmetrical. High symmetry is found in rhythmic handwritings, whereas lack of symmetry shows a disturbance and uneven discharge of energy. The following chart is adapted from Klein translating Klages (1983).

Symmetry		Lack of Symmetry	
+	−	+	−
depth	dullness of character	impressionable	shallow
composed	unreceptive	receptive	affectation
calmness	rigid	tender	irritable
cheerful	indifferent	sensitive	agitated
harmonious	apathetic	creative	restless, moody

If the writer moves easily from the lower zone to the upper zone, and has symmetry with all three zones, score the writer a 7 or 8. If a zone is truly neglected, give the writer a 4 or even a 3.

(9) "I" Emphasis

"I" emphasis is a broad area because the "I," or sense of self, shows up in a number of different ways. Here is a chance to include the signature. Does the signature show self-confidence, or is something crossed out, neglected, or missing? It always seemed telling to me that John F. Kennedy missed the upper loop of the *d* in his last name (see Figure 4.13). This relates to ideals. Kennedy was a man of opposites, idealistic yet he often cheated on his wife. The missing upper loop of his d is symbolic of a neglect or deficit in the realm of his ideals.

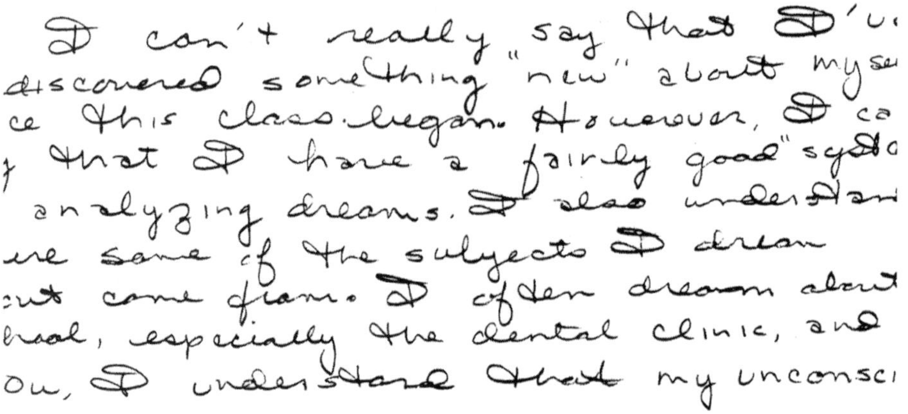

Figure 4.7. 18-year-old female. Note D-like capital I's dominating the page.

In general, "I" emphasis will be seen in the size of the middle zone; it should be large and clear, and in the capitals. They should stand proud and tall. But also, there is the personal pronoun I, known in graphology as the PPI. For a full account of this letter, I would suggest Jane Nugent Green's book *You & Your Private I* (1976). Where the signature is an obvious form of self-identity, the capital I is an unconscious manifestation of self. Compare the two. Oftentimes they will be different. The signature reveals the impression of self that the individual wants to or is willing to release to the world; the capital I is part of his identity that he himself is unaware of.

Similar to any letter, Green splits the capital I into three zones: upper, middle, and lower, and the analysis of the PPI should follow the traditional route. If the upper zone is emphasized, this relates to traits associated with the upper zone, for example, ambition, spiritual inclinations, pride, or someone who seeks power. Look for confirming signs in the rest of the script. However, Green also suggests that in the traditional Palmer capital I, the upper loop is the first loop written, and thus it relates to the mother, and the second loop, which swings back and then angles forward, relates to the father. She gives in one instance, the capital I with a shrunken first upper zone loop, and a second loop, which, instead of moving laterally, swings into the upper zone. This, Green suggests, is the mark of a man who wants to dominate women; the father is above the mother.

In the case of the block cap print script I, which is made with one vertical and two horizontal strokes, again, the mother is the top lateral, and the father is the bottom lateral, the one that lies on the baseline. Green gives as an example of an I whereby the bottom lateral is much longer than the top lateral. This, she says, suggests that the writer, a female, is "daddy's girl." Green is an excellent graphologist, and would be the first to tell the budding analyst that this hypothesis that the mother is the top loop and the father is the second lower loop is simply that, a hypothesis, a possibility, a good guess. Sometimes this theory will be right, and she supports her theory with a number of examples; sometimes the theory will be wrong. So, if there is a hint in the capital I that the writer, if it's a man, seeks to dominate women, look for other supporting evidence through the rest of the script. One sign does not stand alone.

Sometimes the capital I will lean back, while the rest of the writing leans forward. Sometimes the capital I will be small in comparison with the other capital letters. In both cases, there is a problem with the identity. Consider how a person gains his identity. It must link back to the upbringing, the relationship between the writer and his parents. Clearly the PPI will reflect this relationship. Here would be a good place for scientific graphologists to do research either as Green has done, through the idiosyncratic approach, or more globally by getting great numbers of people to write their capital I's, and, for example, giving them a questionnaire that inquires about their relationships to their father and mother.

(10) Middle Zone Height

> This zone corresponds to the place in life where the essential and most real actions and reactions are inconspicuously centered: the sphere of everyday life in which the adaptation of a person to everyday reality and his sociability is manifested. In this zone of handwriting, a person's likes and dislikes, sympathies and antipathies, his habits, his personal and emotional attitude towards the ever-recurring everyday events are expressed. What is psychologically understood by the word "character" is principally materialized with this inconspicuous zone of handwriting.
>
> —H.J. Jacoby

Closely linked to "I emphasis" is middle zone height. If these two graphics do not correlate, this would be evidence of a counter-dominant—a dominating contradiction. If the capital I is tall and strong, one would expect a middle zone with heft. Middle-zone height would be measured two ways: its actual size in millimeters, and its relationship to upper and lower zones. See trizonal dynamics on page 82, for a chart relating to the middle zone. In general, if the middle zone is large, this is a people person. Oftentimes, the middle zone will be so dominant that upper and lower zone letters are truncated. This would suggest a social bug who has put more emphasis on her relationship to the world of people, to the detriment of her aspirations and libidinal needs.

Together, middle zone height and I emphasis relate to the **size** of the writing, whether it be **large** or **small**. In general, common sense rules. A large writing portrays self-confidence and an extraverted nature, but it could also be a neurotic need for attention, or for artificially building up one's own self-image and bravado. Small writing portrays the ability to concentrate; it indicates the sign of the introvert and suggests, in some writings, a sense of inferiority and unworthiness. However, an understatement sometimes is a roundabout way to draw attention to the self. Robert F. Kennedy had very small writing, yet he did not shy away from taking center stage, particularly after his brother John was killed.

Klages introduces the word *pathos* in relationship to the size of the writing. He is referring to the "emotional," "passionate," and "impulsive" energy the writer brings to the table in order to "realize" a goal. Pathos is divided into three realms: **emotions, will power,** and **pathos of self,** or **confidence.** The rule is, the larger the handwriting, the greater the pathos or élan. The chart following is adapted from the Felix Klein translation.

Large Writing		Small Writing	
Emotional Realm			
+	**−**	**+**	**−**
enthusiastic	unrealistic	realistic	unenthusiastic
ability to admire	living in illusion	objective	sober
eager	uncritical	impartial	obsessive
Realm of Willpower			
+	**−**	**+**	**−**
enterprising	hasty, careless	concentration	narrow-minded
bold, energetic	thoughtless	dutiful, petty,	pedantic
independent	preoccupied	concise, precise	doubtful, meek
Realm of Self-Confidence			
+	**−**	**+**	**−**
prideful, earnest	conceited	humble	faint-hearted
dignified, earnest	arrogant, haughty	modest, content	self-doubt
magnanimous	dictatorial	pious, tolerant	anxiety
aristocratic	megalomania	loyal	anxious

Many times the writer uses a print script, which essentially should be analyzed the same way as cursive writing. It is harder to analyze printing because, by its nature, there is more control, more breaks between letters, and less emphasis on upper and lower zones. Find out if the writer has a cursive style as well, or get them to write in cursive, if at all possible. The cursive will usually provide additional information for the analyst. Many block cap printers are involved in the world of art, such as graphic designers, and this can mask some of the real self. Even so, many of the 40 indicators will help bring forth insights not seen at first glance. If it is a big middle zone writer, such as a block cap writer, mark it a 7 or 8. An average size will be 4, 5, or 6, depending on its relationship to a normal size, which would be about 2 millimeters.

III: Orientation Toward Others and the World

Closely linked to Part II (Goal Direction and Ego Strength) is Cluster III. In general, if a person has a good sense of self and a modicum of ambition, he or she will also show signs of extraversion and interest in the outside world. Variables 12 through 18 are all linked to how the writer deals with and plans for the future, which for Mendel (1947) is the **mobile axis**, the horizontal. Mendel suggests locating where the rightward trend is emphasized in the **upper**, **middle**, or **lower zone**. Sometimes the writing itself may appear stagnant, but the t-bars are long. This is the sign of the dreamer (239).

Concerning the **middle** zone, look at word endings. Does the writer continue on naturally with an air stroke to the next word (a sign of dynamic integration, spontaneity)? Does she stop abruptly with resting points (self-satisfaction or perhaps fear to go on)? Do her words rise up (optimism, spirituality), or turn down (defiance, self-determination, wanting to make a big impression or pessimism)? Or does the writer end with a lateral stroke of pressure? This is a sign of displaced libido, the Peggy Lee syndrome urging someone onward so that he or she will not acquiesce to "is that all there is?" Look for other signs to confirm where the evidence leads.

Mendel isolates two kind of lateral rightward trending strokes in the **lower** zone—ones with and without pressure. In either case, by underlining a word, the person is drawing attention to it. If a word or series of words is underlined in a page of writing, this may indicate a person "who insists on his own opinions" (244). If the writer tends to place an underline without pressure with a short underline, Mendel suggest that such a writer may be one who wishes to dominate—the "domestic tyrant or crank." Such a sign should be associated with supporting graphics, such as pinched letters and sharp angles. On the other hand, if the **signature** is underlined, there is "an unconscious desire for greatness, importance, fame, immortality" (243).

In general, we are looking at movements away from the body, releasing movements that display an active impetus for the writer to plunge into the future, to partake of the next day.

(11) Crescendo, Diminuendo, and Thread

We are looking here at the dynamic forward progression of the writing along the **mobile axis** as the writer must accommodate the rhythmic up and down movements along the **vertical axis**. Think of a taut string that is plucked. That kind of reverberation seems to also occur in writing. Use a pencil and ruler with your copy of the writing and see if the letters that are getting larger or smaller truly triangulate. These are called touch points, which Dan Anthony links to a high measure of creativity. By playing with a ruler this way, global configuration patterns of the writing also begin to emerge. Crescendo involves an unconscious tendency to enlarge the middle zone letters as the word progresses. Diminuendo is the opposite: The letters progressively get smaller. **Remember:** Crescendo and diminuendo in this psychogram section are concerned *only* with the **middle-zone letters**, not the capitals that are listed separately below.

Crescendo <		Dimuendo >	
+	–	+	–
naivety	self-conscious	diplomatic	elusive
creative	sense of inferiority	perceptive	fatigued
artistic	frustrated (w/ pressure)	insightful	
ending w/energy		needs to make big impression	

In the Capitals (Particularly the M)

(First determine whether the capitals are natural or artificial.)

ambitious	defers to others	pride	haughtiness
looking up to others	inferiority	aristocratic	arrogant

The last choice is the thread that is called the filiform connections, of which there are three types: the primary thread, the secondary thread, and the double thread, which is a winding snake-like trail that is the combination of rounded garlands (u's) and arcades (n's). It is distinguished from diminuendo because the middle zone height maintains a sameness. This is an amorphous trail that suggests feigned sincerity or lack of commitment. Ulrich Sonnemann (1950) has created a chart of great insight on the difference between primary and secondary thread, and the chart on the following page is based on Sonnemann's work (91) along with that of Dan Anthony.

Primary thread involves the **vertical axis**. The writer ignores the horizontal, or what Mendel calls the mobile axis, so that his thread incorporates almost all up an down movements. This is a sign of extremely high intelligence and brilliance, but also rebellion. The reason for this is that primary thread is the ultimate form of simplification. Architect Stanford White of

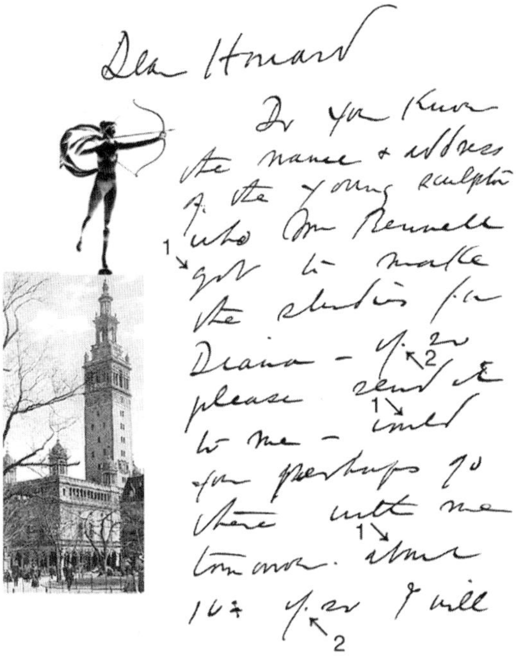

Stanford White, architect from the Gilded Age murdered in his own Madison Square Garden in a love triangle over Gibson girl Evelyn Nesbit in 1906. This is the handwriting of a genius, seen in the great simplification, speed and 1) primary thread. Note also the 2) compulsive erotically linked dot after every f; the 3) wonderful architectural arcades; and 4) highly inventive way he connects his t-bar to the f in his aesthetically pleasing signature.

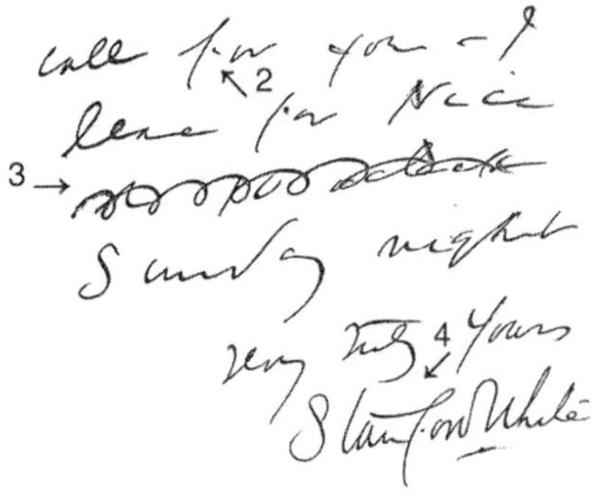

Figure 4.8.

McKim, Mead & White (Figure 4.8) has primary thread. Here was a man who set up his own rules in life. A lothario who spent time with 16-year-old girls, White was also a rebel, forging his own style in the architectural world, resurrecting, in a sense, the drama and majesty of the great Roman and Greek architectural triumphs in White's many brilliant designs (for example, Tennis Hall of Fame and Rosecliffe in Newport, Rhode Island, the Capitol in Providence, Rhode Island, the original Madison Square Garden in New York City, the Tesla Wardenclyffe Laboratory and wireless tower, churches, municipal buildings, and private homes), many of which are still standing as wonderful landmarks and tributes to White's genius more than 100 years after they were built.

+	−
the essence of impulsivity coupled with intensity	ruthless, Machiavellian
original	refusal to conform to society's rules
spur-of-the-moment	anti-social
genius	decadent
talented, a prodigy	destructive
ability to get to the heart of the matter	"demonic"
non-conformist	"evil genius" (Sonnemann, p. 91)
prophetic	

Figure 4.9.
Rumsfeld and
Bernhardt.
Two very
different
secondary
thread writers.
Both, however,
use the thread
as a practical
way to get
things done
quickly. In
Rumsfeld's
case he wanted

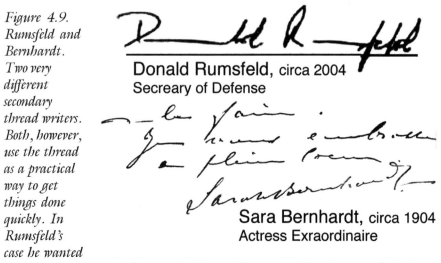

Donald Rumsfeld, circa 2004
Secreary of Defense

Sara Bernhardt, circa 1904
Actress Exraordinaire

a swift win to a war in Iraq, and this was illusory thinking because of the deep ethnic hatred that existed there. In Bernhardt's case the thread gives the writing an ethereal yet hypersensitive effect.

Secondary thread involves the **mobile axis** and is essentially the opposite of primary thread, because all vertical strokes are eliminated and replaced by a wavy horizontal thread. Quoting Porkony (1949, 1973), Karohs (1980) writes that thread "indicates weakness, lack of discipline and inner laxity. It also signals lack of respect for the reader...and intentional vagueness and indistinctness" (p. 47). Thread can be the sign of genius or high intelligence, because, if done correctly, it reflects the essence of simplicity. It can be used as a shortcut, such as a way to simplify the "ing" ending. The key in both cases is **legibility**. If the writing can be read, even though threaded, this adds greatly to the positive use of this graphic. In a speedy, high-form level handwriting, thread can indicate "special aptitudes, above average intelligence, adaptability, diplomacy and a multiplicity of talents" (Karohs, 47).

+	−
adaptable, versatile	evasive
prolific	ambiguous
flexible	avoidance of commitments
rapid thinker	too hasty
eclectic	non-committal
efficient use of time	"pathological susceptibility"
deals with essentials	"femininity in men" (Sonnemann, p. 91)
diplomatic	

In grading for the psychogram, if there are natural bursts of crescendos or diminuendos or a fair amount of thread, give the writing a 6, 7, or 8.

(12) Naturalness and Spontaneity

The ability to be truly spontaneous is the ability to access unconscious forces in an unfettered manner. The aesthetic quality of the Gestalt pattern will give the analyst an understanding of the nature of the writer to be spontaneous, thus the word *natural*, which implies an underlying kindness or sense of social grace. As the ego develops, it is hampered or checked by the censor or superego. What types of brakes are placed on the writer's nature? How are the id, the sexual and aggressive tendencies, or primitive nature expressed?

One of the greatest keys to creative expression, ego strength, and self-actualization is the ability for the writer to be spontaneous, to let go, and express the true self. Freud (1938) and Rapaport (1956) use the term *hypercathexis* to explain a positive release of unconscious forces. The term is made up of two parts: cathexis, which is energy, and hyper, and refers to expression or release. The opposite is *countercathexis*, which is a repressing or checking force. As the child grows and develops, if he is loved and encouraged and given affection, his ego will develop in such a way that will grow and express itself naturally, spontaneously. If, on the other hand, the upbringing has involved great restriction and punishment when the child tries to sow his oats, spontaneity will be checked. The handwriting will appear affected, over-regulated, conforming, and have narrow or pinched aspects. It will also be tense and restricted.

If the writing is spontaneous, it will be written in a speedy manner without affectation. Mark it a 7 or 8. Save a 9 or 10 for the highly unusual. Use those two grades sparingly. If the writing appears over-regulated, give it a 3 or 4.

(13) Garlands

Garlands are u-like movements that can occur in a few places, such as between letters as taught in the Palmer method, but also in the normally arcaded

Figure 4.10. Sam Clemens/Mark Twain

m's, n's, and h's. The garland is easier to write than an arcade and appears in mature handwriting with high-form level. Picture a happy line of dancers holding hands with their arms raised. It is a gesture of welcoming, in handwriting, of openness. The following chart is adapted from Sonnemann (1950) and Roman (1970). Remember, garlands are predominantly measured on m's and n's.

Garlands are usually positive signs. However, there are other types of garlands, known as **pseudo-garlands**, which are not generally seen in a positive light; for example, looped garlands which have been associated with "emotional timidity, an inhibition to express genuine feelings or calculated amiableness" (Jacoby, 1938). The low-slung u-like garlands involve retraced strokes. This, too, is a sign of fake sincerity, the social gadfly who can put up a good front, but may in fact be mean spirited and jealous underneath.

+	−
responsive, open	too easy-going
receptivity	avoidance of commitments
sincerity, frankness	lack of firm attitudes
adaptability, social ease	dependency
warmth, empathy	easily influenced, fickle
desire to give	lack of discipline, weakness of will
devotion	moody
womanliness in female	femininity in men

If m's and n's are made with graceful garlands, mark the psychogram with a 6, 7, or 8.

(14) Slowness to Speed

Signs For

Speed	Slowness
smooth unbroken strokes	wavering forms and broken strokes
rounded forms	frequent left-tending strokes
rightward trend	precision
uncertainty of aim	too much certainty of aim
increasing width between	narrowness
letters and words	retracing and restriction
great difference between	little difference between shading
shading of up and downstrokes	of up and downstrokes
widening of left-hand margin	straight left margin
increasing angle of slant	constant angle of slant
extended endstrokes	pressure on endstrokes
increased connectedness	arrhythmic disconnections
wide writing	artificial flourishes
i-dots & t-bars flying to the right	precise placement of diacritics

There are many ways to tell if writing is fast or slow. Robert Saudek has devoted almost half of his book *Experiments With Handwriting* to ascertaining the speed of writing, which include primary and secondary signs of speed and slowness. He even includes signs of slowness in a rapid writing so he is not just measuring fast and slow writings, but also different gradations and variations thereof. The list above is adapted from Saudek (1928) and Klages (Klein, 1983).

Klages splits up the measure of speed in relationship to separate spheres for willpower and for emotions. The following chart is adapted from Klein's translation of Klages's *Handschrift und Charakter* (1917/26; 1983).

Willpower

Fast		Slow	
+	**−**	**+**	**−**
active	unrest	calm	inactive
industrious	hasty	composed	indecisive
diligent	rash	cautious	weak-willed
eager	inconsistent	steady	idle
energetic	unreliable	reliable	fearful
agile	superficial	factual	sluggish
intelligent	loose thinker	careful	lazy

Emotional Sphere

Fast		Slow	
+	**−**	**+**	**−**
liveliness	easily excited	equanimity	dullness
impulsive	careless	patient	apathetic
flexible	irritable	contemplative	rigid
vivacious	unsteadiness	composed	timid

(15) Horizontal Expansion

Horizontal expansion is closely associated with rightward trend and spontaneity, what Mendel calls the **mobile axis**. Writing proceeds from left to right, the right linked to the future. How is the writer moving toward his goals? Is he inhibited, does he move forward courageously, or is it in a dangerous madcap fashion? There are two types of horizontal expansion: **primary width**, which is within the letters—are letters broad, narrow, or pinched?—and **secondary width**, which is between the letters. If secondary width is great, this positively suggests zeal, an enterprising spirit, and impatience to achieve the next goal. On the negative side, it suggests someone running away from or avoiding the past. Mendel (1947) suggests that space between lines is more consciously planned, whereas space between letters and words is not planned (64).

Prolific 1930's Hollywood producer Carl Laemmle.

Figure 4.11. Prolific 1930s Hollywood filmmaker and founder of Universal Pictures, Carle Laemmle, who produced more than 100 movies including Tarzan, Show Boat, *and* The Hunchback of Notre Dame.

Primary width should be in proportion to the rest of the script. Good primary width is associated with middle zone height, I emphasis, and legibility.

+		−	
spontaneous	natural	uncontrolled	tactless
impulsive	enterprising	rash	negligent
has drive	intrepid	careless	forgetful
zeal	spirited	impatient	impetuous
courageous	traveler	inexact	heedless
goal directed	fresh	inconsiderate	social gadfly
social	frank	incautious	talkative
expressive	generous	madcap	elusive
extroverted	hearty		spendthrift
	high-spirited		

(16) Monotony and Legibility

Sometimes, however, legibility is nothing but a cloak which is used to produce the definite appearance of clarity and sincerity. In this group we find first of all the paranoiac person, and also the swindler and deceiver, the "wolf in sheep's clothing" who tries to hide his real nature behind conventional smooth and expressionless forms.

—H.J. Jacoby

The purpose of handwriting is as a means of communication. Looking at it from an evolutionary perspective, the act of writing, as a form of inner speech, is considerably more advanced than language.

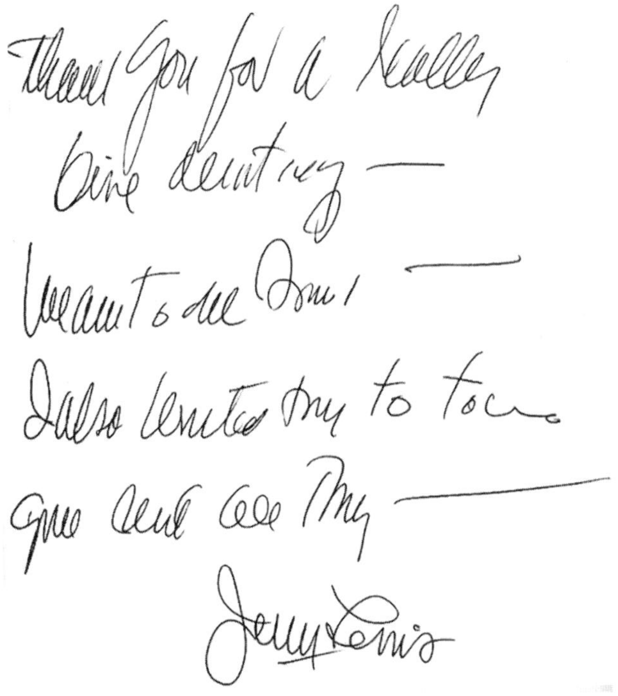

Figure 4.12. Comedian/filmmaker/philanthropist Jerry Lewis, 1967. This letter, although written in large hand, is illegible. Note also the peculiar lower zone elaboration with very long lower loops in the top line, bizarre curl-back through the loop symbol in the y of dentistry, line 2, and cut-off of the y in the signature. Obviously, Jerry Lewis's whacky sense of humor is linked to an outlandish, even off-the-wall, id fantasy life. He is hiding a lot, for example, anger toward a father who was incapable of praising him, feelings of sexual inadequacy, and yet also egocentric and demanding at the same time. A complex, contradictory comedic genius with many demons inside. Note the diminuendo on the first word, third line. This trait is linked to his astuteness and ability to introspect.

It is true that some writings are not meant to convey information to another. Because I myself am a writer, I often scribble notes and rewrites on early drafts in such a way that I know that only I would be able to read it. The purpose is not to convey information to another. It is to jot down my own ideas that I will soon be transcribing into type. If we are marking legibility, we must make allowances for the kind of sample being analyzed. In general, we are considering handwriting that was set forth with the object that another would, in fact, be reading it—for instance, a letter to a friend or colleague.

Jacoby (1939) sees writing as an extroverted act, because it is a way for one person to communicate with another. "Its very purpose demands a certain degree of legibility." Yet, there is a difference between writing that is "legible" and "decipherable." In the latter case, it takes a trained eye to figure out what is being written, and so the writing would not be considered "legible" (70).

However, this does *not* equate to the fact that if it is legible, it's positive. First off, a writing can be legible, but certain letters remain illegible. Why is the *m* or *h* always squinched in a particular writing? Why that letter and not another? Clearly if a writer is having difficulty writing a particular letter, that letter must have some type of symbolic meaning. Yet, still the writing could be completely legible.

In general, if the writing is produced naturally and spontaneously, and is legible, the person has a "clearness of expression" and "wants to be understood. This is positively indicative of the clear, sincere, and transparent character of a person who does not think it necessary to conceal certain traits to himself or others, to twist, to distort, to veil facts" (71). And so, Jacoby is implying here that a legible handwriting reveals a positive character. However, he also suggests that such a person may have, on some level, given up the fight. There is no nagging passion lurking underneath, prompting such a writer. Such a person may have become a conformist.

Concerning illegible writing, Jacoby challenges the analyst to figure out why. Is the writing illegible through conscious design or because of unconscious factors? If the writing is purposely illegible, on the positive side, it could be the sign of a person who marches to his own beat, a positive counterculture figure. On the negative side, it indicates a secretive nature, self-deception, possible dishonesty and neglect, and also Machievellian tendencies. Jacoby also wants the analyst to figure out *where* in the writing is it illegible, in the upper or lower zone, in the connections, alignment control, and so on. Make a note.

Speed is also a key factor. There is a trade-off involved. The longer it takes to write, the less time the writer has for other activities. So legibility has to be seen in relationship to the speed of writing, and if it is a speedy writing and still pretty much legible, that has positive connotations. The following list assumes a normal or rapid pace to the writing. Slow writing greatly magnifies the negative side of both variables. The list is adapted from Jacoby (69–79) and Nevos (1992, 40, 108).

Legibility		Illegibility	
+	**–**	**+**	**–**
sincere	conventional	original	imprecise
communicative	inner barrenness	speedy thinker	secretive
transparent	lack of creativity	dynamic (w/ speed)	careless
clarity of thinking	mediocre	abstract ability	dishonest, cunning
noble	persona writing	non-conformist	selfish
logical	boring		irresponsible
			fatigue, depression
			inhibition

When scoring for legibility, take into account the speed and flexibility of the script. If the writing comes across as monotonous, you should subtract as much as 4 or even 5 points from your scale. So, if the writing is very legible, but it appears slow, measured, monotonous, or artificial, score such a writing, as say, 7 − 4 = 3.

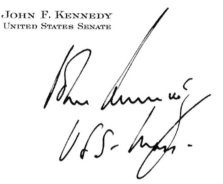

JOHN F. KENNEDY
UNITED STATES SENATE

Figure 4.13. Note the tall K, rapidity of writing, and general threading in John Kennedy's signature. One curious feature is the neglected d in his last name. As a rule, Kennedy rarely completes the upper loop. From a symbolic standpoint, one sees a contradiction in terms of his moral code. The tall K reflects his idealistic trend, whereas the missing upper zone to the d compares well with his tendency to philander. Creativity, ambition, and foresight are noted in the upper zone elaboration of the oh combination.

(17) Rightward Trend

> Viewed in its broader aspects, directional trend also provides evidence as to fixation; a leftward trend indicates withdrawal or regression, a yearning for the protection of the mother, for the shelter of the womb, while a rightward trend is a move toward the father's world, towards activity and adventure.
>
> —Klara Roman

Writing involves movement in all directions. Movement, for Klara Roman (1970), "represents an instant unmediated instant projection from the deepest strata of being." She goes on to say "it is the leading clue as to what kind of basic substance the personality is."

Rightward trend clearly involves the writer's relationship to the future. It can be measured in movement, form, and arrangement, in diacritics (i-dot and t-bars), in their lengths and placements, in the capitals, within and between letters, and, most importantly, at the ends of words (1970).

As a form of communication, the directional trend of the writing reveals a lot about the relationship the writer has to himself and to the outside world. If there is much **rightward trend**, then there is emphasis on proceeding out into the world, thus **extroversion**; and if there is **leftward trend**, there is more swingback movement toward the self, and thus it is a measure of **introversion**. Because we are measuring rightward trend in this sector, look at which zone shows the trend. If it is the upper zone, for example,

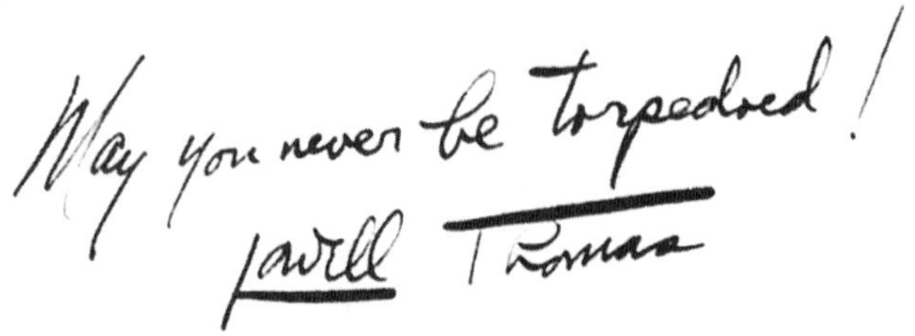

Figure 4.14. Lowell Thomas, one of the most famous radio news broadcasters of the 1940s.

high-flying t-bars to the right of the stem, this suggests ambition and interest in ideas; in the middle zone, there would be expansion in the social world. The lower zone is tricky, because in the case of f's, y's, and g's, the required movement is to the left to complete the loop. Should the writer abandon this required left-tending movement in favor of a v-like swing back to the baseline to complete the next letter or word, the movement suggests moving forward instead of backward, moving toward others instead of the self. This is why such a movement is noted as a sign of altruism. The following chart is adapted from Sonnemann (1950).

+		–	
future-oriented	empathy	wasteful	forgetful
adventuresome	helpfulness	easily influenced	too impulsive
adaptability	unselfish	dependency	unthinking
enterprising	goodness	weakness	suggestibility
dexterity	desire to give	fickle	spreading oneself too thin

IV: Emotional Release

Emotional release bundles connectedness/disconnectedness, fluctuation to irregularity, and linear/pictorial and sharpness/pastosity together. Ultimately, the ability to *connect* stems from the very first stage of development is what Erikson calls Trust versus Mistrust. Has the child bonded with the mother? If so, he is able to naturally release hormones that are associated with the very bonding process. Think about being hugged and how good it feels. Has the child been hugged? Can he connect to others and thus to himself? If not, what is called **fluctuation** in graphology, the natural dynamic process of living and adapting, has been interrupted, and the child will have an irregular dispersion of energy. The next two variables are closely linked to **temperament**, right brain/left brain, and Jung's four personality types of Thinking, Feeling, Intuitive, and Emotional. In general, a linear/technical thinker, will most often have a sharp handwriting. Neurologically, this suggests more the left-brain logical/intellectual thinker. The person who thinks in pictures and has a broad pastose, sensual handwriting is someone who is more right-brain-oriented. They are more in touch with their unconscious and emotional energies. If this global cluster averages a 6, 7, or 8, it shows that the writer is able to express emotions. If the average is 4 or 3, clearly these energies are blocked.

(18) Left Margin

There are four margins: top, left, right, and bottom. Look at the entire page as if it were a picture in a frame. How well placed is this picture? Does it start too high on the page? Are there small margins or wide margins? What is happening at the end of the page? Does the writer shift gears so he can try and squeeze in a few more lines? The use of margins corresponds to a number of variables including a person's sense of economy, how he handles his wallet, and whether he is generous or a miser. And how this is balanced against aesthetic concerns and respect for the reader's sense of space? Some writings simply blanket the page with little or no margins, and they are jarring to look at. Clearly such a writer has not thought about the concerns of the reader. Is the writer selfish, uncultured, or obtuse?

Sonnemann (1950) suggests that margins reflect the person's sense of economy; is he a saver or a spender of time, space, and money?

The top margin, in general, relates to respect for others. The left margin, how this person wants to appear to the outside world. The right margin indicates how he really feels in relationship to his goals, and the bottom margin indicates economy, planning, and even his sense of mortality. De St. Colombe (1967) states that the left margin reveals "the front he puts up for the public.... A wide left margin wishes that the writer appears distant to other people; a narrow left margin, that he wants to seem close. The right margin shows how he actually feels on the question" (113). A wide left margin, according to de St. Colombe, means shyness, stubbornness, or pride. A very wide left margin suggest that writer "seeks to be original and be noticed." If the left margin narrows, it suggest depression (115), but it may also signify a form of self-checking. As the writer writes, if he is moving along at a rapid rate, the left margin tends to widen. The writer may become aware of this tendency, and thus moves to correct himself; this would indicate self-observation.

If the left margin increases, this suggests that the writer is so absorbed in his writing that he is unaware that the margin has drifted to the right, and thus it is a sign of rightward trend. It also suggests that as the writer proceeds "he demands more space" because of "goal absorption." If the left hand margin shrinks, this is a "contractual movement...the writer is returning to the security of the self" (Sonnemann, 1950).

Note also whether or not there is a line down the page to indicate where the margin should be. If one is present, does the writer adhere to it or ignore it? If he adheres to it, this shows some form of conventional thinking or subconscious acceptance of the status quo. If the writer bursts through the line, it means that he sets up his own parameters. It would be the sign of the non-conformist.

If the left margin is wide, mark it with a 7 or 8.

(19) Connectedness

We are looking here at connectedness and disconnectedness. In terms of the psychogram, connectedness would be linked to the sector it is in, Emotional Release, whereas disconnectedness relates to the sector of Inhibition. Sonnemann (1950) uses a logical approach to explain the difference between the two:

1. **Connectedness:** tendency to "bind, mix, bring together, arrange, tackle, organize, compromise, advance, continue, attack, conquer, drive on" (52).

2. **Disconnectedness:** tendency to "isolate, enclose, collect, conserve, fence off, secure, rest, wait, contemplate, ponder, accumulate" (52).

Connectedness involves an integration of up and down movements, conscious and unconscious, left- and right-brain activities. It takes coordination to connect if the writing is spontaneous, and thus it would be an indication of functional integration of all personality components, ego ideal, super-ego, ego, id, conscious, preconscious, and unconscious. The key is if the writing is written rapidly and with fluidity. This is a measure of high-form level and direct access to unconscious forces, seen graphologically as good trizonal dynamics (see Figure 3.2).

The following chart is adapted from Sonnemann (1950).

Connected		Disconnected	
+	−	+	−
reach out	copycat	intuitive	jumpy
deductive	poor observer	inductive	inhibited
logical	lack of creativity	observer	illogical
steadiness	fear (of lifting pen)	witty	unpredictable
a planner	stereotypy	inventive	cold, schizotypal
adventuresome	superficial	caution	lacks adaptability
abstract thinker in a speedy HW	pedestrian	wait, ponder	lack of bonding with the mother schizophrenia

At the extremes we have complete connectedness on the one side, and total disconnection and fragmentation on the other side. However, the analyst must also be able to ascertain pseudo-connected writings as well. If the writing is slow or cleverly patched, it may appear to be connected, but is really not. Such a writer wants to be seen as sociable, integrated, and in the world of people, but actually he feels isolated and is fearful because of this.

Certain connected handwritings have occasional well-placed disconnections within words. These are meaningful pauses associated physically with the difficult act of writing and connecting certain letter combinations that rhythmically are easier to disconnect. In rapid, high-form level writings, this is a measure of, in Sonnemann's words, the "creative and avant-garde" writers (54). On the other hand, arrhythmic disconnections are seen in the handwritings where there was, most likely, great discord, or lack of bonding in the upbringing of the child. It is a sign of isolation, cold spots, or, possibly, evidence of adoption.

(20) Fluctuation to Irregularity

All irregularities reveal emotions. The smaller and the more
often they appear, the deeper and stronger the emotions
they represent; the bigger the irregularities the more superficial are the emotions they represent, e.g., between jerky
writing and bubbling (effervescent) writing there is nuanced
writing which, with its constant but discreet irregularities,
shows a perfect harmony of the mind and the heart.

—Renna Nevos

Regularity, according to Klages, is measured by heights and widths of the middle zone letters—they should be somewhat even—and the parallelism or lack thereof of the downstrokes. A regular handwriting should have a consistency in "dimension, slant, spacing, form and pressure." In general, Nevos (1992) states that regular handwritings reflect a "strong libido, stability and regularity in action" (120–121). On the other hand, irregular fluctuation, as opposed to a natural fluctuation, displays "predominance of emotion over reason, weak will, easily influenced, instability, indecision, unhappiness and uncertainty" (160).

Fluctuation		Irregular	
+		**–**	
sensitive	inventive	easily distracted	lack of discipline
imaginative	versatile	unstable, moody	vacillating, aimless
intuitive	passionate	contradictory	insecure
dynamic	warm	anxious	conflicted
creative			argumentative (pressure)

(21) Linear/Pictoral

Movement is a projection of unconscious forces, whereas form is more conscious, as the person has not been taught how fast to write, but has been taught to create letters in particular ways. Arrangement combines the two. "Therefore, it shows us the writer's capacity for integrating inner promptings with outer reality" (Roman, 1970). If the pattern is lin-

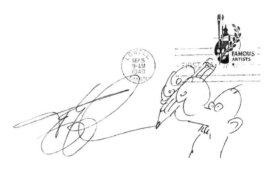

Figure 4.15. Surreal filmmaker, Terry Gilliam.

ear, this bespeaks a more technical, austere, and pragmatic type. If the arrangement is colorful, well-framed, and pastose, it reflects an artistic temperament with a rich inner life. One must look carefully at the linear writing in its gestalt pattern to see how truly dry the arrangement is. Here is where Werner Wolff's and Dan Anthony's "diagrams of the unconscious" come in. A writing may appear lackluster in terms of individual letter forms, but the overall pattern may, in fact, portray a more pictorial inclination. While using a ruler and pencil to plot out touch-points as Dan Anthony taught, Thelma Seifer (1993) suggests using colored pencils to fill in loops and curious letterforms in different colors to give the analyst a better idea of the underlying overall pattern. If the handwriting is more linear, grade it a 4 or 3. If it is pictorial, give it a 6, 7, or 8.

(22) Line Quality: Sharpness and Pastosity

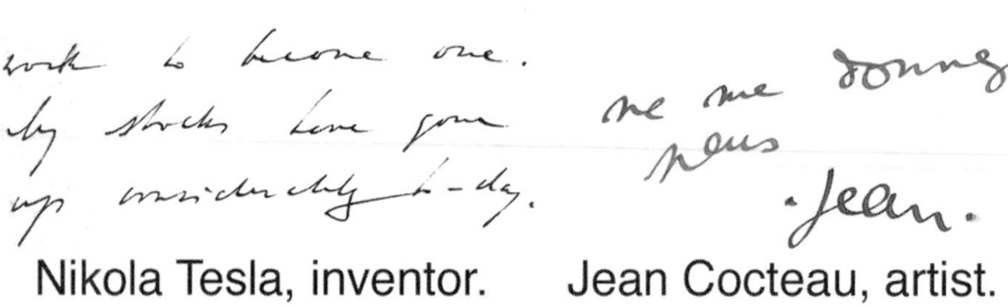

Nikola Tesla, inventor.   Jean Cocteau, artist.

Figure 4.16. The sharp, ascetic, and linear handwriting of inventor Nikola Tesla as compared to the sensuous and pastose writing of the French Jean Cocteau.

We are looking here at the actual type of ink dispersion on the page. This, of course, is linked to the choice of pen, but also the hold of the pen as well. In general, the pastose stroke is broad, such as that produced with a paintbrush.

People who choose broad felt-tipped pens are more likely to produce pastose strokes. They choose such a pen because it reflects an inner wish to create this more colorful pen stroke, which, by its nature, reduces the polarity between the pressure pattern of the contractual downstroke and the releasing upstroke. Said in another way, more release can be achieved with a curved pastose stroke as compared to a sharp tense downstroke. The pastose stroke is more diffuse and achieved by the angle of the pen on the paper and a looser grip. Technical writers and those who eschew close contact may prefer an extremely fine pen-point. Thus, they will produce a much more narrow stroke, which graphologically is called sharp and concentrated.

Pophal has identified three kinds of qualities to the edges of the stroke, which must be seen with either a high-powered magnifying glass or microscope: homogeneous, which is a clean even stroke associated with inner firmness, reliability, and inner clarity; granulated, which is a loose, porous stroke that he associates with lack of inner firmness and lack of harmony; and amorphous, which is a lifeless, uniform, monotonous stroke found mostly in slow handwritings associated with indifference, weakness of character, and a boring undeveloped nature. In general, the sharp stroke will tend to be homogeneous and the pastose stroke may also be homogeneous or granulated (Levine, 1993). If there is a predominance of sharp or very sharp straight lines, this would indicate decisiveness. The following chart is adapted from Sonnemann (1950).

Pastose		Sharp	
+	–	+	–
sensual	libidinal	logical	cold
in the moment	crude	purposeful	unimaginative
artistic	easily tempted	reserved	remote
colorful	overindulgent	nuanced	driven
thinks in images	addictive personality	spiritual	resentful

V: Libido, Energy Drives

Sector 5 concerns itself with the available energy of the writer and thus his or her libido, which, for Freud, mainly expressed itself in sexual and aggressive ways. From the psychogram point of view, we are concerned here with the lower zone and expression of vital energy. If the person has a good sense of self and is active physically, sexually, and in the work environment, he will display a bold, energetic, good-sized writing with a well-developed lower zone. His pressure will be vigorous and the writing will appear lively. Blocked libido will be seen in uneven pressure, truncated lower zone graphics, and meager, pinched, or neglected middle zone letters.

(23) Meagerness/Fullness

This variable is closely associated with #10, middle zone height, but here we are looking at its breadth and curvedness. A **meager** handwriting is exactly that. It will have diminished letterforms that will be narrow, tight, re-traced, extremely small, or missing al-together. When missing, this is called neglect, and it is a sign of a deficit in the nature, a character flaw. Meager, ne-glected handwritings are associated with an

Figure 4.17. Tallulah Bankhead, actress; Grand Ma Moses, artist.

avoidance issue in the personality, either through early trauma or repression, or because of a Machievellian aspect whereby the person would rather not ad-dress certain responsibilities or superego protocols. It is important for the analyst to be able to differentiate between neglect, where letters are greatly diminished or missing for psychological reasons, and simplification, where they are missing because they are not necessary for the legibility of the word. The negative character traits associated with meagerness and neglect are greatly magnified in slow handwritings.

Fullness, on the other hand, is seen in warm, generous, caring, and social people. Fullness is a lot more common. Graphologically, a full writing can be seen in moderately large, clear rhythmic writing, and it reflects solid ego development and a good sense of self. The following chart is adapted from Sonnemann (1950).

Meagerness		Fullness	
+	−	+	−
pragmatic	miserly	artistic	imposing
sharp	unimaginative	imaginative	clouded thinking
theoretical	dearth of imagery	rich inner life	uncritical of self
clarity	self-denial	warmth	daydreamer
sober	weak memory	excellent memory	unrealistic
concentrated	cold	remembers dreams	

(24) Lower Zone Length

The length of the lower zone should be measured in relationship to the other two zones. In general, we are looking for a sense of symmetry between upper and lower loops with a well-developed middle zone. If the lower zone is truncated, this relates to some type of "cutting off" of the libido. Sometimes writers truncate y-loops but not g-loops or visa versa. One would have to surmise that, when there is a difference between the length of one lower zone letter as compared to another, each of the letters symbolize something different for the writer, and this difference is unconsciously realized. If the p is truncated, it may relate to the word *penis*, which could stand for the father or for the person's sexual life. Sometimes the letter *p* is quite prominent in the writing of a female and this may relate to her identification with the animus, or male archetype. Thus, it would be a sign of ambition. The letter *p* may also stand for power.

A well-developed lower zone has been associated with biological and instinctual imperatives, earthiness, athleticism, interest in money, and sexuality. If the lower zone is exceptionally long, it may reflect an interest in the depths and the unconscious, and be a sign of a person who has powerful dreams and a strong memory of them. In general, a well-developed lower zone is a sign of a healthy libido. An average lower zone length gets a 5, longer 6, 7, or 8, shorter 4 or 3. Exceptionally long, a 9 or even 10, exceptionally short, a 2.

(25) Lower Zone Elaboration

From Pulver, we recognize that the lower zone relates to what is below the baseline, Hades, the underworld, the id, the Jungian shadow, libidinal concerns, egoistic/narcissistic proclivities, sexuality and orientation, the realm of the surreal, and creativity and fantasy life. One should look at such variables as increase or lack of pressure; the size, shape and trend of lower loops; angles and double loops; ending strokes; dashes and hooks; left and right trend; ending up or down; vertical or horizontal pressure; elimination of loops; underlinings and middle zone; or capital letters that also plunge into the lower zone. The following chart is adapted from de St. Colombe (1967).

Loops and Extensions

	Upper Loops	Lower Loops
Long	intellectual interests	physically active, vital, sexual
Short	realistic or inhibited ambition	weakness, sexual inhibition
Inflated	egotistical, boastful, paranoid	athletic, vain, lustful, avaricious
Squeezed	guilt ridden, inhibited	secretive
Broken	character flaw, dishonest	sexually troubled

As a movie fan, I have been quite attracted to the beautiful actress Carole Lombard. Her handwriting, however, paints a different picture, with a selfish mean-spirited aspect lying beneath or alongside a warm persona. The lower loops say one thing, the signature, quite

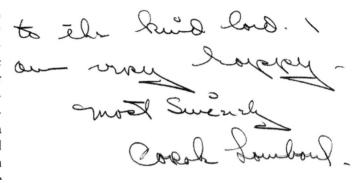

Figure 4.18. The handwriting of actress Carole Lombard.

another. Note the extremely sharp angles in the writing as compared to the garlands, circle-i-dots and overall pleasing design of her signature.

There are six letters that have lower loops. The following chart discusses the most common ones and should be seen as a list of possible traits associated with these lower zone elaborations. Look for confirmation in other graphics. Also, try to discern the difference between a random graphic and a deliberate symbol that the writer gravitates to over and over again. The following is adapted from Singer (1969).

f   This letter is the only one that goes into all three zones. For some writers, it may symbolize a four-letter word. If the bottom loop creates a figure 8, this is a left-tending extra loop in the lower zone and thus may relate to a reversal in sexual orientation. If it is knotted creating a third loop on the baseline (resembling a tied shoelace), this has been associated with fortitude. Written like a zig-zag vertical letter z, this is a form of primary thread Z. If the lower loop resembles a hangman's noose, this may indeed portend depression and self-destructive tendencies.

g and *y*   If the g-loop ends like a reverse *c* swinging back to the left, this suggests interest in the past and a poetic proclivity. If the lower loop looks (a) like a lateral figure 8, it can represent whimsical sexual fantasies; (b) inflated, it can mean large sexual appetites and/or interest in making a lot of money; (c) like a reverse loop, similar to the letter *p*, this is a counterstroke, and thus a sign of dishonesty either to the self or to others; (d) like a triangle that could represent anger, perhaps toward the mother. In this instance, the triangle is a female phallic symbol, and it is coupled with sharp angles; (e) like a long retraced or very tight loop, it can represent dark secrets and repression; (f) like it ends with a large curl, greed; (g) looped but not returning to the baseline, frustration; (h) like a straight downstroke, practicality.

p   If the p rises above the middle zone, thus entering the upper zone, this can be seen as a sign of ambition and enterprise.

(26) Pressure

Pressure has been divided into three areas: grip pressure, that is, how tightly the pen is held; primary pressure; and secondary pressure. Primary pressure deals with the rhythmic creation of downstrokes, which is done with movements toward the body. Secondary pressure can be seen in upward and lateral strokes. Primary pressure can actually be felt on the page by placing your fingers gently on the back side. The indentations that you feel are the pressure or depth component of the writing. It reflects vitality or available energy. "Good mental and physical health are indicated when a writing is executed with rhythmical alterations of pressure that is neither extremely heavy nor extremely light" (Karohs, 1980).

Here is a time to take out the magnifying glass and look at the stroke texture. If it wobbles, or has tremors, this is a sign of anxiety, conflict, or some type of physical malfunction. The location of the tremor, for example, in upper, middle, or lower zone, has also been linked to the possible location of the disability. For instance, heart trouble would be more likely to show up as a tremor in the top of the middle or upper zone, such as a kink in an upper loop.

Pophal and Klages recognized that "the pressure pattern is revealed solely through the difference in shading between up and downstrokes." This indicates the writer's vital energy. Moderate pressure is the most optimum expression of energy, as it implies that there is reserve energy available for emergencies. If the pressure is heavy, this indicates "wound up tension," and this is "no longer healthy." Pophal associates extremely light pressure with being highly sensitive, but also superficial, and is "a warning sign that the writer tires easily." It also indicates "anxiety or lack of energy" (32).

"Broad spotting" is a negative sign associated with the anal stage and suggests uncleanliness and disorderliness. Changing pressure portends anxiety. "Faint, wobbly lines" Wolff (1948/63) associates with "vagueness and passivity" (318).

Klages categorizes pressure with respect to will power and to emotional criteria. The following chart is adapted from Sonnemann's (1950) and Klein's translation of Klages *Handschrift und Charakter* (1917/26; 1983).

Active and Passive Will

Pressure		Lack of Pressure	
+	−	+	−
energetic	rigid, stubborn	adaptability	lack of initiative
determined	inconsiderate	sentimental	indecisive, yielding
resolute	inflexible, tense	flexible	hesitant
self-control	depression	active	aimless
persevering	clumsy	swift	line of least resistance
tenacious	conflicted		weak-willed

Emotional Sphere

Pressure		Lack of Pressure	
+	−	+	−
masculine	contentious	excitable	touchiness
virile, manly	aggressive	sensitive	faint-hearted
passionate	aggressive	intellectual	unstable
impulsive	argumentative	psychic, dreamy	selfish
depth of emotion	inhibited	easy adjustment	superficial

VI: Repressions

The next four variables, leftward trend, covering strokes, narrowness, and rigidity, shed light on the darkest part of the personality, the person's fears, holds from the past, secrets, relationships to the primordial instincts, inner conflicts, tensions, defenses, and relationship (or lack thereof) to the unconscious. If this sector averages 7 or greater, this is an indication that the writer is carrying a heavy weight, hiding it, and paying the price because of that. At the extreme, it can be a sign of dishonesty in all its forms, to himself or to others. This is the heaviest part of the psychogram, and the analyst must show empathy and be humble when dealing with this sector. Remember that graphology is a limited tool, so be cautious in analyzing this sector and remember that there is a great difference between a novice who has just learned a few tricks of handwriting analysis and a serious professional who understands how truly complex and contradictory the psyche can be.

Sector VI relates to what Carl Jung called the shadow, the dark side, the seemingly irrational, the unconscious, the unknowable—an ultimately unfathomable realm that all humans one way or another have to confront.

(27) Leftward Trend

Left trend involves a pull from the past. By necessity, a left-handed individual may display a good amount of left trend, but lefties are treated differently, so the negative connotations associated with left trend need to be softened when analyzing a lefty. Although there are many positives associated with interest in the past, graphologically, left trend generally has negative connotations. The following chart, adapted from Sonnemann (1950), does indeed discuss the positives along with the negatives for this variable.

Left Trend

+	−
self-reflective	self-centered
independent	selfish, narcissistic
determined	overemotional
contemplative	jealous, resentful
good memory	cruel, envious
poetic	secretive
lyrical	compulsive
interested in the past	repressed

(28) Covering Strokes

These are retraced strokes that can be short or long, and can be seen in fast or slow handwritings. There is very little that is positive about covering strokes. At best, it is a sign of reserve and caution. In general, it relates to secrets and dark hidden aspects. The writer creates a line and then covers over it with another line. The longer the retraced stroke, the more that is being kept hidden. This is magnified even more in slow and/or persona handwriting. An abundance of covering strokes is a sign of dishonesty, either with the self or with others. It is a sign of a defense structure that is well guarded.

(29) Narrowness of Letters

Like the other graphic indicators, width (and narrowness) too, have double meanings. The negative meaning of wide writing would be if he writer were to underestimate the obstacles in the path to achieving his aims; in this case, width would have to be interpreted as carelessness, lack of thoroughness and haste. Narrowness brakes motion towards the goal; in a positive sense, says Klages, this means self-control. Narrowness becomes negative when caution is due to selfish reasons... [which diverts energy and] weakens goal directedness.

—Erika Karohs on Klages

Narrowness is a sign of restriction, inhibition, concealment, tension, and repression. Narrowness can show up in many ways, such as in upper and lower loops, in **retraced strokes** (which are called **cover strokes**), in pinched letters, between letters and words, and, for this category, within lower case or middle-zone letters. If they appear narrow, mark the chart with a 6, 7, or 8. If the writing is pathologically narrow, give it a 9. If the writing is wide, mark it with a 3 or 4. The following chart is adapted from Karohs's translation of Klages (1980) and Nezos (1992).

Narrowness

+	−
self-control	lack of spontaneity
restrained	egotistically cautious
reserved	suspicious
poised	hesitant
concentration	meanness, petty
prudent	introverted, inhibited
orderly	trapped inside the self

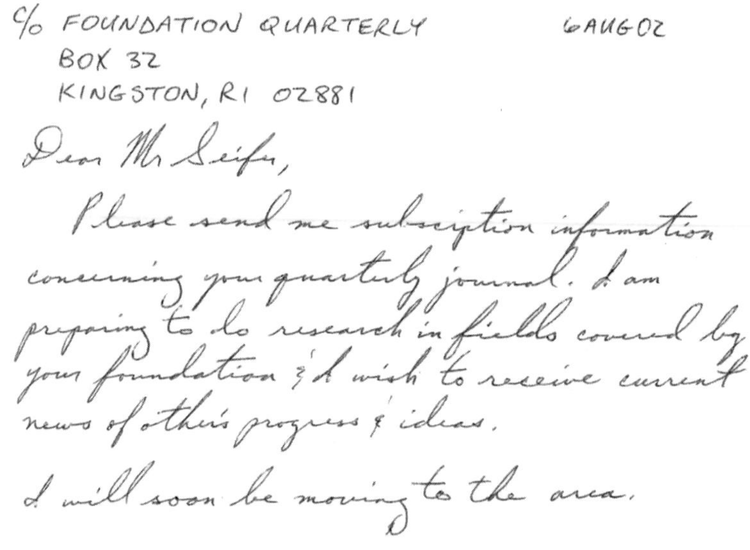

Figure 4.19. Military man, probably 20 to 24 years old.

In Figure 4.19, you can see a narrow, rigid writing, with a small middle zone and an upward thrust into the spiritual realm; thus we see the influence of the superego. The back-slanting g's suggest a rebellious spirit. This is a moralist who is ready to go to war. Note the sharp angles on the word *Mr.* The writing shows over-control, but also the possibility of exploding (back-slanted g's made with pressure). This is the writing of a young fellow who is strung a bit too tight. However, he is well organized and seeks to be honest (legible). There is also a sensitive, perhaps even feminine quality, which suggests the influence of the mother (small middle zone along with strong right slant). The retraced letters suggest that he has a hidden life as well.

(30) Rigidity/Flexibility
Look at the writing in its totality. If it appears brittle, over-controlled, and cautiously executed, these would be signs of rigidity and would be an indication of what Freud called the obsessive-compulsive personality. If the writing is rigid and over-regulated, it reflects fear of change, strong opinions, willfulness, close-mindedness, concentration, resoluteness, self-denial, constriction, coldness, inflexibility, and stubbornness.

The opposite is flexibility, which reflects dynamism, the ability to adapt to a variety of situations, aliveness, impulsivity, and spontaneity. If fluctuating too much, this would suggest instability, aimlessness, fickleness, at the mercy of emotions, and weakness of will (Sonnemann, 1950).

VII: Inhibitions and Over Control
The difference between Sector VI and this sector is one of degree. A person who is repressed is definitely inhibited, but a person who is inhibited may not be repressed. Being inhibited implies more conscious awareness of the stasis. When I analyze handwriting, I try to show the writer *where* in the writing the various traits that I am putting forth appear. The implication is that if the writer can become aware of where he is tense or why he fears the future, perhaps he can takes steps to make a change in his nature. I have always seen graphology as a tool to help people toward self-discovery with the thought that if they become more aware of the holds that are on them, they have more of a chance of making positive changes.

(31) Right Margin
The left margin reveals the beginning, whereas the right margin reveals the writer's relationship to the end. If the right margin is wide, this can show extravagance, aloofness, and wastefulness (de St. Colombe, 1967), or, on the negative side, hesitation, fear of the future, and fear of death. If the margin

has some narrowness in a natural pattern, this suggests a bold adventuresome writer, one who looks forward to the future. If it is a very tight, neat right margin, it suggests prudence on the positive side, or fussiness, obsessive neatness and stinginess on the negative side. If there are no margins, the person is overpowering and lacks respect for the reader.

Some lines tumble at the end, and this could be a sign of depression. I have seen this tendency in the handwriting of Nikola Tesla when he was writing from his wireless experimental station in Colorado Springs to his friends in New York City. Tesla did have a self-destructive side, but ultimately his failure in his wireless concern came down to a difficult relationship he had with his financial backer, J. Pierpont Morgan, who, at some point, insured the inventor's defeat by holding back additional funding.

The point I am making is that if Morgan had decided to "go the whole hog" in the enterprise, there is little doubt that Tesla would have had wireless radio and telephones at the turn of the century. This tumbling of the lines occurred two years before his meetings with Morgan at a time when he was at a high. Hindsight is 20/20. Perhaps he just wanted to squeeze as much as he could on the page. It brings to mind the main problem with handwriting: What does handwriting analysis show and what does it not show? There are limitations. It certainly cannot show everything. As you begin to look at handwritings, you will begin to see that many times your impressions of people upon meeting and knowing them is different than the portrait you see graphologically. The analyst must stay humble. That said, I think it is likely that the tumbling of the ends of lines in Tesla's handwriting, the squeezing of too much in at the ends (thereby eliminating margins) symbolically relates to his wish to jam too much into his wireless enterprise. And ultimately, that was the key reason why it failed. Had he set up a more modest goal with Morgan, such as sending simple wireless messages across the Atlantic, as opposed to trying also to send light, pictures, and power as well, he would have built a more modest enterprise, and thus would have had a much greater chance of success.

Sonnemann (1950) discusses dashes at the ends of lines. This corresponds to a neurotic or obsessive tendency toward the future, which become a form of magical thinking, whereby the writer wants to "avoid" or "touch the wall" as a way to ward off imagined threats (115).

If the margin is wide on the right, it is a sign of fear, apprehension, hesitation, and dread. Mark the psychogram with a 6, 7, or 8. On the other hand, a small right margin, in general, is a sign of buoyancy and self-assurance. If that is the case, mark it a 3 or 4.

(32) Left-Right Slant

The slant or slope of the writing correlates to one's sentiments toward the self in relationship to others. In Western writing, we are taught to slant to the right. This is for a variety of reasons. Most people are right handed, and it is simply more comfortable for a righty to slant to the right as his pen proceeds from left to right. Thus, the modest right slant is associated with a compliant nature, one who is sociable, and one who is able to feel comfortable and conform in society. The upright slant reflects the writer whose head dominates over the emotions, and the left slant (in a right-handed writer) reveals some type of non-compliance. Simply stated, we are taught to slant to the right, but the left-slanted writer has decided for one reason or another to buck convention. De St. Colombe (1967) states that the left-slanted writer expresses a "cold exterior that masks inhibited feelings" (85). Alfred Mendel (1947) has done extensive case studies of the writer who slants to the left and has found that in most cases there is evidence of the child being estranged from the father, either because the father is absent, difficult to get along with, or mean-spirited.

Karohs (1980) draws a parallel between slant and body posture, either leaning towards another, being cautious and upright, or leaning away from others. She points out that the right slant, according to Crépieux-Jamin, reveals a desire for "acceptance and submissiveness." According to Pophal, the extreme right slant portrays "loss of composure, and an indication of instability, impetuosity, recklessness, agitation, lack of resistance and yieldingness. With above average speed and straight baselines, he contends, we have the person who is driven" (27).

SLANT

Extreme Left	LEFT	UPRIGHT	RIGHT	Extreme Right
	\			/	

Defiant—Self-reliant—Compliant

The chart below is inspired by Karohs (1980) and Sonnemann (1950).

(33) Arcades (Particularly in M's and N's)

Figure 4.20. Philosopher/ existentialist Martin Buber. His handwriting supports the premise that much of his writing deals with the problem of spiritual survival in a difficult environment. He

appears to ward off the outside world so as to contain a rich, emotional, yet well-protected inner self.

Right Slant

+	−
social ease	lack of control
loving	undisciplined
altruistic	restless
optimistic	over-adaptable
curious	verbose
warm	aggressive
normally	mediocrity
sensitive	conformity

Extreme Right Slant

+	−
ardent	susceptible
affectionate	jealous
amiable	too passionate
very sensitive	reckless, hysterical
emotional	volcanic
easily offended	
driven	
dynamic	

Upright Slant

+	−
intellect rules	cold, unemotional
controlled	uncaring
foresight	indifferent,
prideful	ego-centric
unswerving	uncommunicative
cautious	overcontrolled

Extreme Left Slant

+	−
independent	difficult to get
mysterious	along with
detached	evasive
	ego dystonic
	reluctant, repressed
	negative identity

Left Slant

+	−	−
self conquest	rebellious	counterculture tendencies
self denial	self-coercion	plays Devil's advocate
introspective	artificial	arrogant
non-conforming	affected	fear of committing oneself
cool	stilted	repressed
	fearful	estranged from the father (Mendel)

Slant in a Lefty

Left	Right
in touch with self	conformity
following one's own rhythm in a right-handed world	willing to sacrifice some of self to be accepted
individualistic	careful, considerate
non-conforming	compliant
speedy	accepts rules too readily
conscientious	

In his 1939 book, *Analysis of Handwriting*, H.J. Jacoby says:

The opposite of the garland, namely, curves on the top with downward openings, are called *arcades*. Whereas the garland, performing a natural movement, opens itself to the right and upwards, the arcade closes itself on the top and to the right.... prescribing a vaultlike and covering form. Establish[ed] by this movement [is] the writer's relationship towards his fellow-beings, but at the same time, shutting himself in like an oyster against the outside world. Thus the person who writes in arcades adapts himself to the outside world, but never discloses his inner life.

Arcades are archlike movements. Think of the top of a picket fence. It is a movement of caution and self-protection, but also it is a curved movement, and thus encompasses an element of grace and warmth. Jacoby points out that, similar to the garland, the arcade has many different "nuances" such as the following (119–20):

- **Upright and tightly drawn**: sense of form, but egocentric and self-protective.

- **Flaccid creeping arcade, looped and open at the left**: "a sham adaptation bordering on hypocrisy, the sign of the swindler, the spy and the cheat."

- **Firmly shaped**: "self-control, suppression of personal emotions for the sake of formalism and ceremoniousness...[showing] a great reluctance to display personal feelings."

As we know, there are four main types of **connecting strokes**: the **garland,** the **thread**, the **arcade**, and the **angle**. Mendel (1947) points out that "thinking involves connecting," and the way a person connects and expresses his thoughts reveals a lot about that person. Mendel tells us that the arcade is, essentially, an upside-down garland, a u-like movement transformed into an arch. Thus, the arcade writer is connecting and expressing his thoughts in an opposite manner than the garland writer (165–168). Jacoby states that he has seen garland writers switch to using arcades when placed in more dangerous environments (1939). Yet, the arcade is complicated, its meaning almost a contradiction, particularly when it is realized that we are taught to use arcades, not garlands, when writing letters like m's and n's. Alfred Mendel's *Personality in Handwriting* describes arcades as this:

As a form of movement, the arcade is slower than the garland.... As a gesture, the arcade seems to serve two evident purposes: to hide something or to protect it; to shut out light and strangers, or to retire and contemplate and search within oneself; to erect a structure or edifice, such as a cathedral or dome, or barricade for defense and a trap for the unsuspecting.... The arcade writer's way of thinking and acting cannot be gauged by ordinary means.... He may be a sinister plotter or an artist who goes his own way.... The liar hides the truth, the plotter his scheme, the assassin his dagger, but the conscientious official hides important documents that are entrusted to his care, and shy, inhibited people hide themselves because they fear to be hurt and imposed on. Or take the builder [e.g., Count von Zeppelin]; his arcade is no hideout, but a symbol of his technical constructions.... In the interpretation of the arcade the style evaluation becomes of prime importance. Through it, we need never have any doubt whether a script belongs to a plotter or to an architect, to a thief or a technical genius... the more arched the arcade, the more prominent becomes its artistic qualities; the flatter it is, the more it reminds us of a lid to cover up something.

The following chart is adapted from Mendel (1947) and Sonnemann (1950).

+		−	
pensive	meditative	impenetrable	shut off
cautious	traditionalist	suspicious	pretentious
reserved	skeptical	artificial	distrustful
restrained	formal	conforming	mendacious

Tall Arcades		**Flat Arcades**	
self-sufficient	poised, profound	hypocrisy	scheming
architectural	artistic	distrustful	swindler

(34) Contraction/Release

Contractual movements are movements toward the body; thus they are seen in downstrokes. Releasing movements are away from the body and can be seen in up and lateral strokes. In terms of tension, muscles work in opposition to one another. A contractual downstroke, although it is linked to being tense, also involves the relaxation of opposing muscles. The same is true for upstrokes. They may be signs of release, but, in the releasing movement, other muscles are contracting. Thus we can see the nature of opposites in all movement patterns. In other words, a highly tense person is physically relaxing some muscles at the same time. That said, a predominance of downstrokes, movements toward the body, reflects tension in the person. A predominance of releasing strokes reflects a more relaxed and easygoing disposition. The contraction/release variable is most important in gaining a psychophysiological portrait of the writer, particularly in terms of whether they are **tense** or **relaxed**. The following chart is adapted from Sonnemann (1950).

Contraction		Release	
+	–	+	–
keyed up	too tense	warmth	undisciplined
resolute	constricted	vivacious	lazy
self-conquest	self-neglect	loose	easily influenced
concentrated	fearful	impulsive	irresponsible
self-directed	conflicted	carefree	uncommitted

(35) Distance Between Letters

> Graphologically, the distance between letters indicates the degree of spontaneity of self-expression including the extent of receptivity…and reciprocity between the individual and his environment…. Closely written letters are indicative of a contraction tendency while those spaced widely apart indicate tendencies towards release or expansion.
>
> —Dan Anthony

The connections between letters is called secondary width, as opposed to primary width, which is within the letter itself; for example, a broad or narrow *m* would be its primary width. Words are made up of letters and letter connections. Each letter represents a different step needed for the formation of the single word. If the letters are crowded together or even touching each other, mark the psychogram with a high number 7, 8, or 9. Crowded letters is a sign of constriction, dependency, inability to stand alone, and thus, possibly over-control. The opposite is great secondary width—great separation between letters. This graphic suggests zeal and enterprise, but also isolation and escape if seen in a speedy writing. The person may be attempting to flee into the future to avoid dealing with either the past or the present, or he may be trying rapidly to get to the next project, perhaps having not completed the last one. Wide spacing also indicates extraversion, but also the possible "squandering of resources" (Anthony, 1967). If the spacing is uneven, this suggests emotional disturbances.

Figure 4.21. Prince Philip and Queen Elizabeth of England. Note their precise, clear high i-dos suggesting an idealistic trend and impeccable attention to detail.

When discussing space between letters, another aspect is whether the letters are connected or disconnected. See #19 for a discussion of this topic. If there is significant space between letters, one should ascertain if this is due to feelings of isolation or the ability to stand apart, to be individualistic.

The i-dot

Another key is the i-dot. Is the dot close and over the i? This suggests a careful perfectionist streak and steadiness or patience. Oftentimes the dot flies to the right. This is an indication of a person in a hurry. If the dot has a little curl to it, this may be symbolic of a smile and is an indication of a sense of humor. If the i-dot is very high above the upper loops, this sign is linked to a writer who has unrealized dreams. There is ambition, but it is more in the unconscious plane. If the i-dot is connected to the next letter, it is a sign of integration and seen in the writings of abstract thinkers, artists, and states-man. The circle i-dot is found in the handwriting of people who want to be creative, but are not really in touch with their own wellspring, so they create this add-on instead.

Part of the following chart is adapted from Mendel (1947) and Anthony (1967):

- **Close spaces between letters**: dependency, stinginess, repression, selfishness, hostility, resentment, yet also possibly promiscuity.

- **Great distances between letters**: extraversion yet isolation, fleeing the present, enterprising in speedy writing, but also scattering of one's resources.

- **Uneven spacing between letters**: conflict, moodiness.

- **All letters connected**: logical and systematic.

- **Some letters connected**: intuitive, inventive, self-reliant.

- **Most letter disconnected**: isolated, egocentric, lack of integration.

- **Lack of end stroke**: abrupt in relationships or could be shy.

- **First letter stands apart**: cautious, procrastinator.

- **Last letter stands apart**: postpones signing documents, hesitant.

(36) Angularity

Figure 4.22. Marlon Brando likes angles so much, he adds an extra one in his first name! His last name contains primary thread, the mark of a genius, but one who could be ruthless at times, as his practical jokes suggest.

Unlike the arcade, garland, or thread, which all use curved connected strokes, the angle creates a stop. It is a movement with no compromise. Either it's up or it's down. There is no in-between. As an experiment in lectures and classes I ask the audience to get mean and angry and to write out mean and angry strokes. I make no movements with my hands. It is completely a verbal command. Invariably, many of the participants create sharp angles with a lot or pressure. Think of a wolf's teeth. Those are angles. Jacoby (1939) points out that the writer of the angle "demonstrates a distinct lack of adaptation, because this particular kind of connection is devoid of a sense of obligingness to the world, and opposes it by hardness and angularity. On the other hand, angular connections expresses that the writer makes no attempt to avoid or shirk difficulties, but prefers to overcome resistance and obstacles [in preference] to smooth adaptation" (121). Where arcade, garland, and thread writers adapt themselves to the world, the opposite is true for the angle writer—the world must adapt to him.

A person who writes with angles is sharp and uncompromising. Look for other features to offset this dictatorial aspect. Some writers have what are known as shark's teeth, which are extra sharp points that can be found atop m's, n's, r's, and h's. This is a sign of the potential for the expression of real venom. It is not wise to cross a person with this graphic pattern in his writing! The following chart is adapted from Mendel (1947) and Sonnemann (1950).

+		−	
decisive	logical, objective	domineering	cranky
purposeful	firm, reliable	rigid	obstinate
direct	determined	uncompromising	pitilessness
sharp	sincere	negative	argumentative
scientific	dutiful, moral	moralistic	aggressive
critical	unwavering	cold	hard
masculine	creative	hardened	rigid

VIII: Control

Control suggests "dominance of volitional forces in the organizing principle" (Anthony, 1967). The person is a take-charge type who may, on the other hand, have difficulty relaxing.

(37) Slant Consistency

If the slant is consistent, this shows control, dependability, and regularity. Mark the psychogram with a 6, 7, or 8. If there is a changing slant, this is a sign of division within the self, most likely caused by dissention between the parents during upbringing. It reflects conflict, competing emotions, fickleness, and on the positive side, flexibility and versatility.

(38) Space Between Words

Alfred Mendel describes spaces in his 1947 book, *Personality in Handwriting*:

There are wide and too wide spaces. As soon as they become too wide, we revise our favorable first impression and recognize the pedant or the person who keeps at a safe distance from us in better order to maintain a blasé attitude. Small spaces between lines, on the other hand, tell us of genuine spontaneity, perhaps also of a lack of reserve, and some muddle-headedness.

If we compare the idea of space between letters as compared to space between words, Klara Roman is suggesting by her placement of the variables in the psychogram that the former is more conscious than the latter. On the other hand, it is Mendel's contention that the space between words is nonconscious and non-deliberate. "Wide spaces may 'contain' more and deeper thoughts and emotions. But too wide spaces (in comparison, for instance, with the spaces between letters) must strikes us rather as emptiness" (Mendel, 1947). Drawing an analogy to speech, Mendel says wide spaces are analogous to a person who pauses between words. It therefore suggests someone who "ponders and considers" before he acts. If the spacing is very wide, this could be a sign of someone who is simply blasé, or it may suggest a sense of emptiness and loneliness, "afraid of establishing contacts on account of neurotic timidity and repression" (Jacoby, 1939). The following list is inspired by Mendel, (1947).

- ○ **Even spacing**: self confident, reasonable, orderly, disciplined.
- ○ **Large spaces**: artistically minded, deep feelings, rooted convictions, introverted. Such a writer enjoys time spent alone, for this a time for growth. If very wide, this could be a sign of the egotist with little care for others.
- ○ **Large uneven spaces** (with low form level): empty-headed, confused, tricky, conflicted, overcritical.

- **Very wide even spaces**: hiding instability behind a façade of order. In a mediocre Form Level writing, this extravagance suggests conceit with not much to back it up.

- **Small spaces:** dependency on others, unwilling to be alone, talkative out of fear of facing the self. There are no pauses between words. "As far as the surrounding world is concerned [such a writer] is much more strongly impelled by a direct impulse than guided by consideration or reasoning" (Jacoby, 1939).

- **Small uneven spaces**: lack of harmony, chatty, gullible.

- **Rivers**: Look at the entire page of writing. Rivers occur when you see paths of space meandering vertically down the page. Rivers area sign of existential loneliness.

Score a 7, 8, or 9 if there are wide spaces between words.

(39) Alignment Control

In general, we are looking here at the **baseline** and the relationship of one line to another down the page. If the writing follows a straight baseline, this shows a person who is ruled by an even keel. Where **space between lines** is associated with the writer's organizational skills and his "distance or proximity" between the writer and his environment (Karohs on Klages, 1980), the **space between letters** refers to the writer's inner feelings of social connection or isolation to others. In the case of **space between words,** this too symbolizes the writer's link to others, but symbolically, it is not as personal a connection. If the alignment control is good, mark the psychogram with a 6, 7, or 8.

Baseline alignment is also influenced by temporary moods. Some possibilities are as follows:

- **Descends**: depression, as in the case of Ernest Hemingway's handwriting.

- **Ascends**: optimism.

- **Wavy:** suggests emotion's rule. Mark the psychogram with a 4 or 3.

- **Arched:** the person starts off with enthusiasm, but then the energy wanes.

If the lines are crowded together, this shows lack of planning, thus the writer may lack foresight and may be prone to rely on the given rules. Yet they may also be highly imaginative, or, as Jacoby (1939) suggests, such a writing may be the result of "unchecked impulsiveness." On the other hand, if the alignment control is excellent, this shows order, planning, and discipline— mark the psychogram with a 7 or 8—but this may be at the expense of spontaneity (136). Poor alignment control, mark the psychogram with a 3 or 4. The following list is inspired by Mendel (1947):

○ **Wide spaces**: reasonable, analytical, ability to comprehend complex facts, sober, logical, concrete. On the negative, may lack spontaneity and be compulsive.

○ **Too wide spacing:** overly extravagant, blasé, fear of making mistakes, lonely.

○ **Small spaces:** impulsive, confused thinking, lack's introspective proclivities.

○ **Crowded:** lost in own world of fantasy, unrealistic, confused, regressive.

○ **Tangled:**

> ➤ **Lower loops invading line below:** uninhibited, sexually bold, domination of id.

> ➤ **Upper loops invading line above**: unrealistic aspirations, erotic fantasies.

(40) Regularity

What we are looking at here are those variables that can be controlled with deliberate effort by the writer, "specifically, size, pressure, tendency, form, movement and arrangement" (Anthony, 1967). Regularity is measured by heights and widths of the middle zone letters—they should be somewhat even—and the parallelism or lack thereof of the downstrokes (Klages, 1927). A regular handwriting should have a consistency in "dimension, slant, spacing, form and pressure." In general, Nezos (1992) states that regular handwritings reflect a "strong libido, stability and regularity in action" (120–121), predominance of reason over emotion, a person with self-control and a strong will, someone who tends to control situations. This type of person could therefore be, on the positive side, a leader; on the negative side, unyielding. See also #20, Fluctuation to Irregularity.

Regular

+		−	
discipline	moral	inflexible	mediocre
orderly	vital	routine	indifferent
strong	logical	obdurate	boring
sense of duty	persevering	antisocial	slow
evenness of emotions		insincere	

Determining Form Level and Functional Productivity Scores

After working with thousands of handwritings mainly for personnel selection, Dan Anthony (1967) has compiled a mathematical scoring system to differentiate between **Form Level** scores, which encompass the writer's "indicators of expressing, thinking and being," and also his or her cultural and intellectual level as compared to the **functional productivity** score that reflects the writers' "coping, adaptive and goal-seeking variables... the strength of one's thrust and drive towards success" (31). Where form level scores would be more linked to people skills and aesthetic sensibilities, the functional productivity will reflect how well that person will do in the workplace.

As stated earlier, the previous description of Roman's 40 indicators from the psychogram were compiled with almost no reference to Anthony's *The Graphological Psychogram: Psychological & Symbolic Interpretation of its Graphic Indicators*. The reason for this was to maintain the integrity of the Anthony text as a separate and distinct reference work on the same topic. However, I have taken his scoring system, which is based pretty much on a 100-point scale with an excellent score, with A = 85–100; B = 75–85; C = 55–75; and D or F, below 55. His scoring is as follows (32):

Form Level Score

A) Add the following 13 variables:

1–8 Organization, simplification, originality, expressiveness, rhythm, tri-zonal dynamics

11–15 Legibility, naturalness, garlands, speed, horizontal expansion

B) Compile the average of these four variables (by adding them up and dividing by 4):

23–26 Meagerness/fullness, lower zone strength, lower zone elaboration, pressure

C) Compile the average of these three variables (by adding them up and dividing by 3):

33, 36, 39 Arcades, angles, control

D) Add the totals of A + B + C to get the Form Level score.

Functional Productivity

Simply add up the following 14 variables to get Functional Productivity score:

1, 2, 5, 9, 10, 11, 12, 14, 15, 24, 26, 33, 36, and 39.

Organization, simplification, originality, "I" emphasis, middle zone height, legibility, naturalness, speed, horizontal expansion, lower zone strength, pressure, arcades, angles, alignment control.

A person might get a Form Level score of 70, but a functional productivity score of 85, which would suggest his social skills might not be the best, but he would have the drive to succeed. Do some Psychogram scores for both FL and FP for individual handwritings and see what you come up with. That is the best way to test out this scoring system.

Keep in mind these are just two scoring systems. For scientific studies, there are numerous additional possibilities that could be calculated for any number of different groups. For example: (a) psychoanalytically, such as for depressed, schizophrenic, or obsessive-compulsive individuals; (b) in the workplace, such as CEOs, car salesmen, politicians, policemen; (c) medically, such as stroke victims, epileptics, heart attack patients, colon cancer patients, asthmatics, and so on.

As you can see, the psychogram is a very powerful tool, because it transforms the abstract and very complex act of handwriting into a series of numbers.

Figure 4.23. The handwriting of best-selling author Nelson DeMille. The right trend, combined with a large, bold, tense, yet legible print script reveals a complex individual who is both independent and self-confident, yet in need of others, which could be seen as contradictory. Supremely self-confident, DeMille's generosity of spirit and his willingness to help other authors is revealed in the garlands, extreme slant, and largeness of the middle zone. He adheres to the rules (stays within the lines), but rebels by varying and rising above the baseline, and piercing through the left margin when necessary.

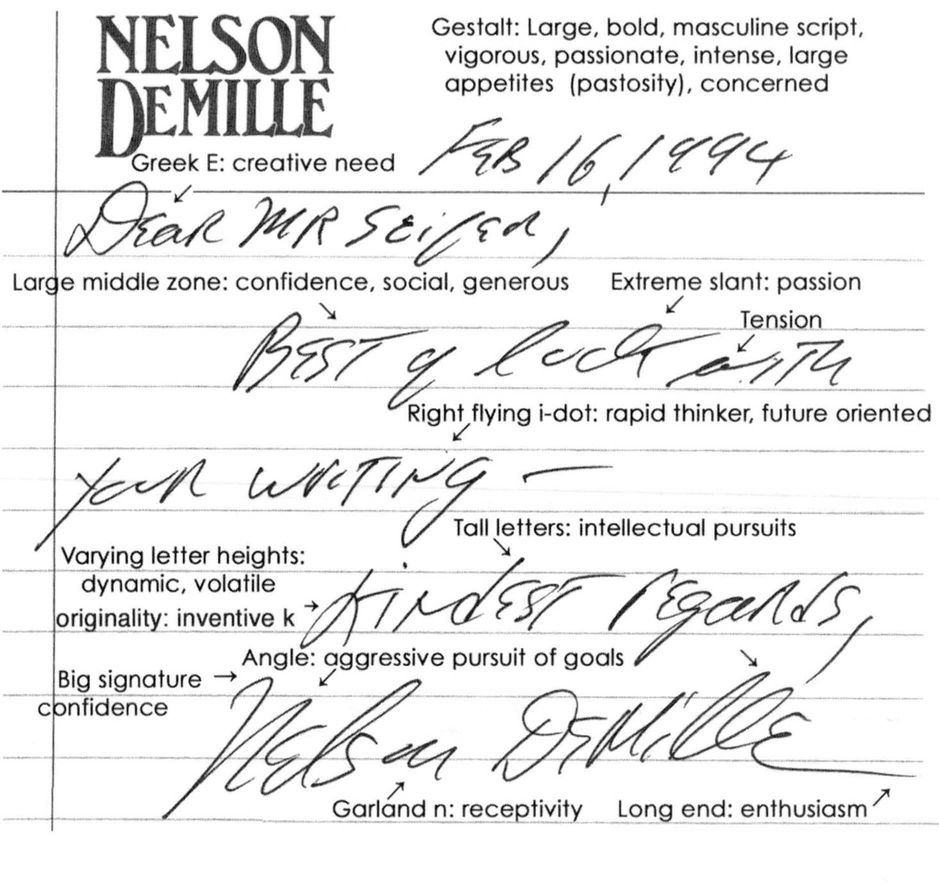

Gestalt: Large, bold, masculine script, vigorous, passionate, intense, large appetites (pastosity), concerned

Greek E: creative need

Large middle zone: confidence, social, generous   Extreme slant: passion

Tension

Right flying i-dot: rapid thinker, future oriented

Tall letters: intellectual pursuits

Varying letter heights: dynamic, volatile
originality: inventive k

Big signature →
confidence

Angle: aggressive pursuit of goals

Garland n: receptivity   Long end: enthusiasm

GRAPHOLOGICAL PSYCHOGRAM

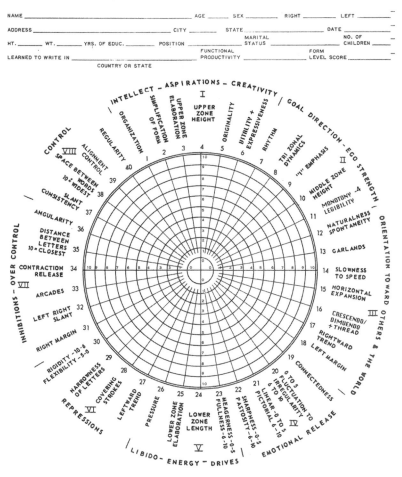

Roman-Staempfli Psychogram
1955 - Revised by Dan Anthony 1964
Revised by Marc J. Seifer © Copyright 2007

Figure 4.24. To construct the mandala-like psychogram for the handwriting being studied, rate each variable on a 1-10 scale.

The following is a list of traits to help refine your analysis.

abrupt
absent-mindedness
abusive
accommodating
accomplished
acerbity
acquiescent
acquisitive
adamant
adaptability
adept
addictive
adroit
adventurous
aesthetic interests
affable
affectation
affectionate
aggressive
agitated
agitation
agreeable
aimless
alcoholic
aloofness
altruism

ambiguous
ambitious
ambivalence
amenable
amiability
amorality
analytical
angry
animated
antagonistic
antisocial
anxious
apathetic
apprehensive
ardor
argumentative
arrogance
arrogant
aspirations
assertive
assured
astute
athletic
attention, desire for
audacity
authoritative

avaricious
balanced
bellicosity
beneficent
benevolent
bluffer
boastful
boldness
bossy
broad-minded
brutality
bully
busybody
calculating
callous
calm
candid
careful
careless
cautious
ceremonious
changeable
chattiness
cheater
cheerful
clannish

clear-minded
clever
cocky
cold-hearted
combative
color appreciation
commiserating
common sense
communicative
compassionate
competitive
complacent
compliant
composed
compulsive
concealment
conceited
concentration
conciliatory
conformity
confused
conscientious
conservative
considerate
constancy
contemplative

contrary
controlled
conventional
conviction
cool-headed
coquettish
courageous
cowardice
creative
criminality
critical-minded
crude
cruel
cultured
cunning
curious
cynical
deceitful
deceptive
decisive
deductive thinker
defensive
defiant
deliberate
demonstrative
denial
dependable
dependent
depressed
desirous
despondent
despotism

detached
detail-oriented
determined
devoted
dictatorial
dignified
diligent
diplomatic
direct
discouraged
discrete
discriminating
disdainful
dishonest
disillusioned
disorderly
disorganized
distracted
distrustful
docile
dogmatic
dominating
domineering
dreamer
driven
dynamic
eager
earnest
easy-going
eccentric
eccentric
economical
efficient

effusive
egocentric
ego strength
emotional
empathetic
emphatic
energetic
enterprising
enthusiastic
envious
equanimity
escapism
ethical
evasive
excessive
exacting
excitable
executive ability
exhibitionist
expansive
expedient
expert
expressive
extravagance
extroverted
facetious
fanatical
fanciful
farsighted
fastidious
fatalistic
fatigued
fearful
feeble-minded

fickle
firm
flexible
fluent
forceful
frank
friendly
frugal
gaiety
garrulous
generous
genial
gentle
goal-minded
good-natured
good-hearted
grandeur, delusions of
greedy
guilty
gullibility
harmonious
hasty
haughty
headstrong
helpful
hesitant
homosexual
honest
hopeful
hospitable
hostile
humanitarian
humorous

hypocrite
hysterical
idealistic
ill-tempered
imaginative
imbecile
immature
impartial
impassive
impatient
imperturbable
impetuous
impressionable
impudent
impulsive
inactive
inconsiderate
indecisive
independent
indifferent
individualism
indolent
indulgent
industrious
inferiority
inflexible
ingenious
inhibited
initiative
insecure
insincere
instable
instinctual
integrity

intelligent
intense
intolerant
introverted
intuitive
inventive
irrational
irresponsible
irritable
jealous
judgmental
judicious
jingoistic
jolly
kind
keen
lazy
leader
level-headed
literary
literal-minded
logical
loner
loyal
luxuriate
lyrical
lunatic
magnanimous
manipulative
materialistic
mature
meek
melancholy
mendacious

meticulous
modest
moody
motivated
modern
masculine
naïve
narcissistic
narrow-minded
negative
negligent
nervous
neurotic
non-conformist
nymphomaniac
obedient
objective
observant
obsessive
obstinate
offensive
open
opinionated
opportunistic
optimistic
orderliness
organizational
 ability
original
ostentatious
paranoid
passionate
passive-
 aggressive

passive
 dependent
pathological liar
patient
pedantic
perceptive
perfectionist
persecution
 complex
perseverance
persistent
persuasiveness
pessimistic
petty
physical-minded
poised
pompous
possessive
practical
precise
prejudiced
presumptuous
pretentious
prideful
procrastinator
progressive
promiscuous
pugnacious
realistic
reasonable
rebellious
reckless
recognition
refined

regressive
rejected
relatedness
repressed
resentful
reserved
resigned
resilient
resolute
resourceful
respectful
responsible
responsive
restless
reticent
ridicule,
 fear of
rigid
sadistic
secretive
sedate
seducer
self-abasement
self-aware
self-castigation
self-confident
self-conscious
self-controlled
self-deceit
self-esteem

self-pity
self-protective
self-reliant
selfish
senile
sensitive
sensual
sensuous
sentimental
serious
shrewd
shy
sincere
skeptical
social
spiritual
spontaneous
stabile
stamina
steadfast
stingy
stubborn
submissive
suicidal
superficial
suppressed
suspicious
sympathetic
taciturn
tactful

tactless
talkative
temper
temperament
tenacious
tender
tense
thorough
thoughtful
thoughtless
thrifty
timid
tolerant
trustful
trustworthy
truthful
tyrannical
unassuming
uncommunicative
unconcerned
uncooperative
undisciplined
unimpeachable
uninhibited
unpredictable
unreliable
unruly
unstable
unworldly
unyielding

urges
usurious
vacillating
vane
variety, desire
verbal facility
versatile
vindictive
violent
virile
visionary
vital
vitality
vivacious
vixen
volcanic
vulgar
wallflower
wanton
warmhearted
weak
welcoming
willful
willing
withdrawn
yes man
yielding
xenophobic
zany
zealous

How does one develop a personality? How much weight should be given to genetic or environmental factors? What are the instincts and how do they influence behavior? What are the causes of schizophrenia? How does one develop a normal personality? How can graphology be used to gain insights into these questions?

Sigmund Freud (1938) noticed that children developed in distinct stages. Personality factors, in turn, were greatly influenced and modified by biological processes and their interaction with the social world symbolized by the family unit. The child began as one ruled mostly by the primitive id. Through time, the center of personality, the ego, or self developed, as did the conscience or superego.

Brenner (1957) writes that two fundamental hypotheses lie at the basis of psychoanalysis: determinism, for every effect there is a cause, and the primacy of the unconscious, which is the state of being conscious is a rare event. What appears as conscious motivation may really be an unconscious attempt to placate instinctual urges. Biological drives can therefore be seen as a two-fold process involving both a motor and psychological response. "In a broad way," they are modified by individual experience and pressures from the environment (18). Somatic in origin, drives create a mental representation. From a graphological point of view, the basic inborn temperament most readily shows up in pressure, speed, slant, and prevailing type of connective stroke.

Drives "impel individuals to activity," which can either increase tension or lead to cessation of excitation through gratification of the drive (18). To a great extent, the effect can be seen as the ego's attempts to modify the demands of the id. The way the ego "handles" the instincts changes as the child develops, and the site of excitation (or the source of the drive) shifts.

Freud's theory of psychosexual stages of development presupposes that the libido, or life force, is most closely attached to the id, and further, that it is always active. As the child progresses from one stage to the next, in a biological sense, a new part of the body is developing, and therefore becomes more erogenous. From a psychoanalytic standpoint, in each case, an interaction takes place between the part of the body in questions, the mental state of the child, and the social consequences of the corresponding action. He says,

"Thus libido, which first cathected the breast [and mouth], or to be more precise, the psychic representation of the breast, later cathects feces [and anus], and still later, the really strong libidinal cathexis is never completely abandoned…but remains bound to the original [source]." Fixations can occur for either an object (for example, the mother) or stage of development; further, the fixation can be unconscious "either wholly or in part" (28).

Psychosexual Stages of Development

As handwriting analysts, we can pair various graphological indicators with their corresponding psychosexual stages. Frank Victor (1964) suggested that the **oral** stage was linked to roundedness and releasing movements, the **anal** stage with angularity and tension, and the **genital** stage with elasticity, energy, and pressure. This idea has been greatly expanded (Seifer, 1982; 1985). Please refer to the chart on page 132.

Naturally, with any topology, this schemata is to some extent artificial. Further, some graphic patterns appear to belong to different groups simultaneously;, for example, right and left slant would relate to the **trust vs. mistrust** sector, whereas changing slants appear to be more linked to the **phallic** part or **initiative vs. guilt** sector. Pressure relates to the **anal, latent,** and **phallic** periods; and simplification could be linked to the **latent** and **genital** stages or later, the **generativity vs. stagnation** sector. As a working hypothesis, I hope that this chart will be a valuable tool for delineating various personality factors, and for gaining insights into probable events (type of upbringing) occurring in early childhood.

Note that Freud's stages emphasize the biological component, whereas Erickson's delineations emphasize psychosocial elements. Where Freud had five stages ending at the culmination of adolescence, Erickson created eight stages spanning the whole of life.

Trust vs. Mistrust (Oral) Stage: Ages 0–1.5

Bruno Bettelheim (1967), regarded in his day for his success with autistic children, noted that breast-feeding was "the best paradigm of how combined action leads to a sense of trust in oneself and other persons" (19). If, for instance, the infant is kept from the breast against its own wishes, this can be destructive and can lead to "impotent rage…[the child becoming] a victim of inner tensions" (19). When the child's wishes are ignored, and affection is not genuine, this can lead to childhood schizophrenia. One way or another, if the mother is cold to the child during the early months of development, this will cause a trauma in the child, and, according to Bettelheim, some children will develop autism. Such a child not only loses interest in the world, but his ego turns inward and virtually disappears. Self-destructive actions such as hand banging may ensue, and social and linguistic development is arrested.

Graphology and the Psychosexual Stages of Development Marc J. Seifer © 1982/2007		
STAGE/AGE *Freud*	TRAITS *Erikson*	GRAPHIC PATTERNS
ORAL 0-1 1/2	TRUST VS. MISTRUST Dependence, love, intuition, transcendence, talkative, loyalty, affection, sensitivity, culture, brotherhood, warmth, contentment, laziness, inertia, attitude towards food and drink	Roundedness, connectedness, pastosity, loops, right slant, left trends, garlands, increasing margins, space between words
ANAL 1 1/2-3	AUTONOMY VS. SHAME AND DOUBT Control or no control, stubbornness, independence, punishment, aggression, fear, hostility, obsessions, compulsions, cleanliness, sloppiness, orderly or disorderly, responsibility, development of the censor and defenses, relationship to money, miser or spender, repetition compulsion, language development, secretiveness	Regularity, rhythm, pressure, arcades, retraced strokes, muddiness, fragmented and foreshortened letters, displaced pressure, organization, form level and aesthetic appearance, angles in middle zone, decreasing left margin, automatisms, upright slant, repetition compulsions
PHALLIC 3-5	INITIATIVE VS. GUILT Sexuality, libidinal, Oedipal and Electra complexes, incestuous thoughts, desires, pornography, the shadow and animal nature, curiosity, disobedience, awe, in touch with Nature's secrets, suppression, repression, evil, defense mechanisms, sense of morality, sexual identity, relationship to God and Garden of Eden	Length, angularity, quirks, curlicues, and other emphasis of the lower zone, primary width (within letters), and secondary width (between letters), vertical axis, changing slants
LATENT 5-11	INDUSTRY VS. INFERIORITY Industry, exploratory and ego-related behavior, enterprising, athletic, goal-oriented, curiosity, friendship, pride, socialization	Pressure, speed, simplification, rightward trend, horizontal axis, mid-zone height, upper zone elaboration, print script, foreshortened endings and downstrokes
GENITAL 12–18	IDENTITY VS. ROLE DIFFUSION Puberty, conformity, vanity, narcissism, reawakening of sexuality, emotionality, sense of identity, peer group pressures, originality	Middle zone, baseline, signature, capitals, personal pronoun I, simplification, left slant, lower zone elaboration, originality, legibility, secondary elaboration, e.g. circle I-dots

Figure 6.1.

Conversely, love, affection, careful attention to desires, and support for the infant's need for self-expression promotes ego growth.

Autism is a complex disease, with many variations and separate potential causes, such as genetic or neurological malfunctions, an undeveloped cerebellum, possible allergic reactions to inoculations while in infancy, and pollutants in the air. Bettelheim has a psychoanalytic theory on the cause of autism. Many researchers have dismissed his theories out of hand, because of the discovery of the other causes previously mentioned. This is an error in logic. If, for instance, the cause of autism in 40 children whose parents grew up near a Foster Grant plastics factory was air pollution, this does not rule out the possibility that another child going in for a shot could not also become autistic. One cause does not rule out the other cause, and yet that is what many researchers have done to Bettelheim's theories, which do, in fact, hold true in some cases.

Figure 6.2. Woody Allen's signature displays positive characteristics from the oral stage. Warm and rounded forms predominate, suggesting a positive relationship with the mother during the first few months of life. The hook at the top of the W and intertwined letters show selfishness and dependency needs. The drop of the n in the last name could be linked to his nihilist leanings. This tendency is offset by the right slant and bold clarity of the various letterforms. He also cares about others.

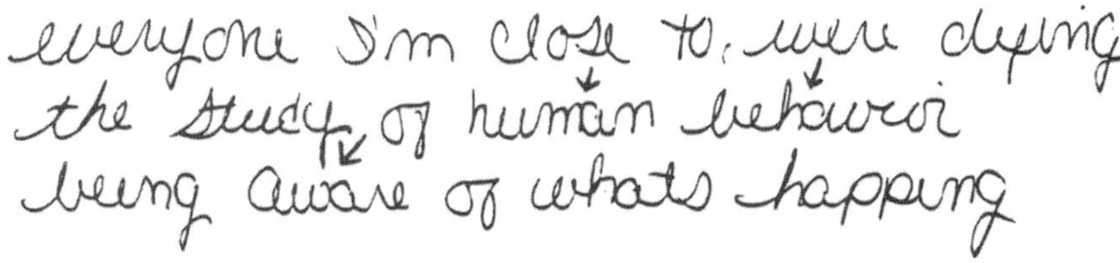

Figure 6.3. Note the predominance of rounded forms, lack of maturity, and tendency for letters to touch one another. This 19-year old female student was over-dependent. She following her best friend from class to class and even chose the same major and electives. Similar qualities of dependency can also be seen in Figure 6.2.

Harry Harlow's well-known studies with infant monkeys raised with surrogate dummy mothers made out of terrycloth or wire mesh supports Bettelheim's findings. Harlow found that monkeys raised with the terrycloth mothers tend to develop somewhat normally, whereas monkeys raised in the harsh cold environment of the wire mesh surrogate mothers tend to develop schizophrenia. Further, these latter monkeys are usually unable to get pregnant, and, if they do give birth, they tend to reject the newborn. Simply stated, Harry Harlow established that he could create schizophrenic monkeys by treating them harshly when they were in their infancy. This, of course, does not rule out other causes of schizophrenia, such as a defective gene. What his and Bettelheim's findings suggest is that, if a child is treated in an uncaring or abusive manner, the child's psychophysiology will be impacted in a negative way.

Figure 6.4. (written on lined paper). The highly disconnected nature of this script suggests schizoid tendencies. The writer was a female in her late 40s who was taking a course in abnormal psychology. She was poorly dressed, appeared extremely odd and did not make eye contact with the teacher. She attended most classes and received a high grade. She had probably been institutionalized at some point in her life and may have been on medication.

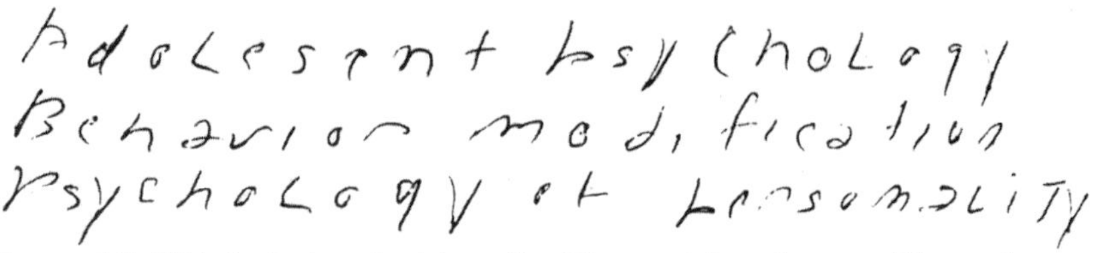

Figure 6.5. This is the handwriting of a 20-year-old student recalling a dream, the contents of which contain one element of truth: The student was adopted. If the adoption occurs before the child has had a chance to bond with the mother, the handwriting will usually reveal a disconnected aspect. In this case, the disconnections are coupled with an arrhythmia and changing slants, all which suggest discord between the adopted parents and some sense of isolation for the writer. One way or another, a disruption in bonding in the first few weeks and months of infancy will tend to show up as abrupt or arrhythmic disconnections in the writing trail.

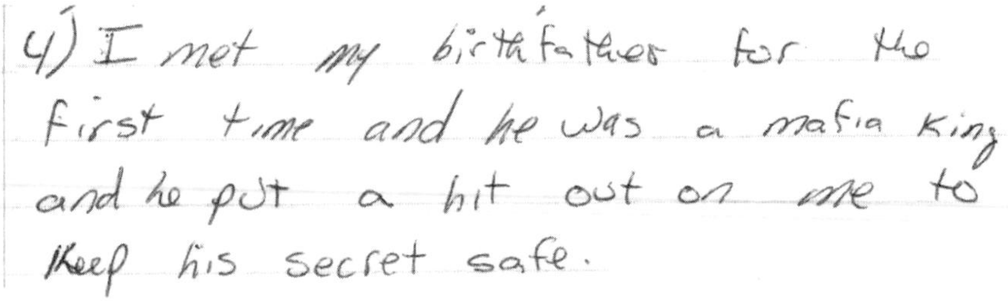

Autonomy vs. Shame and Doubt (Anal) Stage: Ages 1.5–3

This period is characterized by toilet training, but also walking, and the development of language. Erik Erikson (1968) notes that the anal stage is one of "conflicting patterns...[e.g.,] that of holding on or letting go." At this time the child is "subject to unequal wills, his [or her] own and in relationship to the parents" (107). Even the child's own will is subject to different forces, those which he or she can and can't control. It is a time of contradiction, a battle or a compromise to self-esteem; on the negative side, it is connected to hording and stinginess. Loss of self-control on the positive side leads to recognition of the biological imperative and psychoanalytically to generosity; on the negative side, it is linked to lack of discipline, doubt, and shame. Erikson notes that letting go can be destructive (letting loose) or a sign of relaxation (to let pass); holding can be cruel (withholding) or caring (to have and to hold) (109). And just as the child is learning to go on his own, he or she is also developing verbal communication skills. The autonomy stage is thereby linked to the terrible twos where defiance and self-definition are mastered with the powerful two-letter word: NO!

Because of all the various inherent contradictions in the anal stage (for example, cleanliness vs. dirtiness and biological necessity vs. social etiquette) this is also the stage where obsessions (unwanted thoughts) and compulsions (ritualistic actions) develop. In handwriting these can be seen as repetitive automatisms, which Freud tells us display through their action derivatives of former id impulses in conjunction with defensive measures against these impulses.

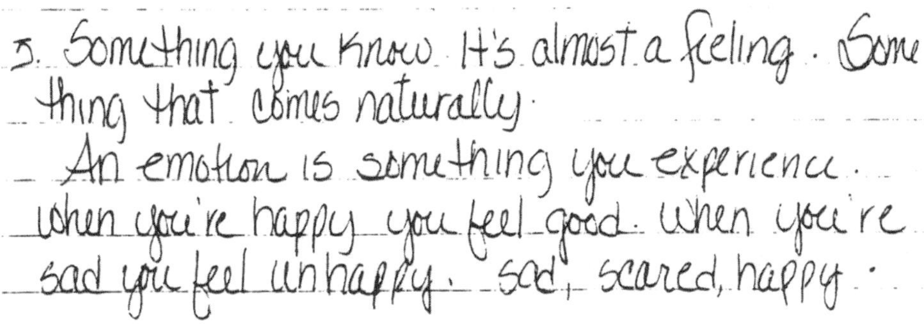

Figure 6.6. This person's handwriting is contradictory in a number of ways. The writer is a somewhat obese female freshman college student who does not appear to be meticulous. Generally, she wears blue jeans and a sweatshirt or sweater. One can see in this writing the superimposition of the oral stage (rounded graphics) with the rigid compulsive patterns of the anal stage (extreme regularity). The artificiality of the writing could be said to derive from the genital stage where self-identity or lack thereof (that is, conformity) would cause the defense mechanism of denial to play a key role. Although the writing appears to be over-controlled, at the same time there are changing slants (upright with a left-slanting f, some y's, and one of the g's). This all suggests great conflict and control vs. no control.

Figure 6.7. This is the handwriting of an extremely overweight female college student. Lack of discipline is evident in this slack graphic pattern (somewhat obscured during copying process). The pressure is very light, the sample bunched together and written with little dynamic energy. Similar to Figure 6.6, she dresses casually and is a compulsive eater, but, in contrast to the rigid sample, she is less guarded, although she does appear to be ashamed of her physical condition.

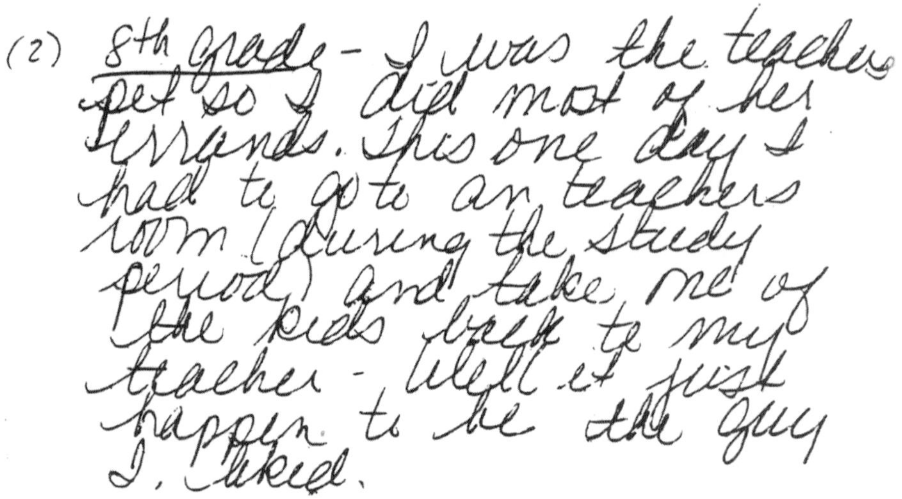

(2) 8th grade - I was the teacher pet so I did most of her errands. This one day I had to go to an teachers room (during the study period) and take one of the kids back to my teacher - well it just happen to be the guy I liked.

Figure 6.8.

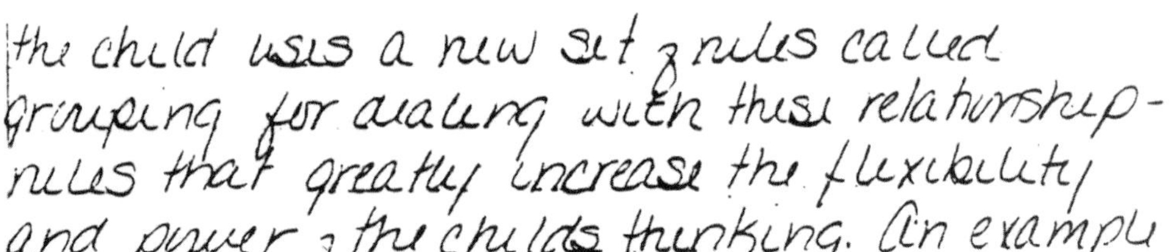

the child uses a new set 3 rules called grouping for dealing with these relationship-rules that greatly increase the flexibility and power 3 the childs thinking. An example

Figure 6.9.

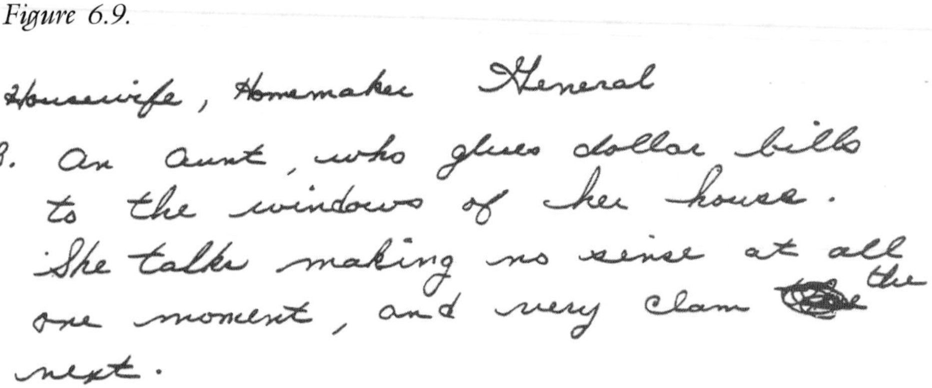

~~Housewife~~, ~~Homemaker~~ ~~General~~
3. An aunt, who glues dollar bills to the windows of her house. She talks making no sense at all one moment, and very calm the next.

Figures 6.8 and 6.9 are the handwritings of two anorexic females who have at one time been hospitalized for malnutrition. The refusal to eat is generally associated with a defiance stemming from the anal stage. Contradictions in this dysfunctional behavior are numerous. For instance, on the one hand an over-concern for appearance is evident (for example, they don't want to be "fat"), and yet, on the other hand, self-destructive tendencies and loss of feminine attributes (for example, breast size, menstrual cycle) ensue.

Figure 6.8 was a small and feisty 95-pound college student who seemed to be proud of her eating disorder. She was an only child whose mother was obese. In reaction to a caveat by the mother that the daughter would follow in her footsteps, this girl stopped eating. She said that she was overprotected and not in charge of her life. Not eating was one decision that she could make herself. Monitored by a doctor at the time of writing, she still ate very little (for example, a small bowl of cornflakes for a day's meal), and stated that in no way would she allow her weight to go above 100 pounds. A dancer, she smoked cigarettes, dominated her boyfriend, and appeared to be a selfish and spoiled child in general.

In many ways her persona handwriting resembles graphic characteristics of the overweight individual in Figure 6.6 even though their eating habits are opposite to one another. The anorexic writing, however, appears more schizoid (disconnected) controlled, and has retraced strokes and displays a lower form level.

Figure 6.8's bold writing also contradicts the meek graphic pattern of Figure 6.9, a lady in her late 20s or early 30s who dropped out of two psychology courses. Although feelings of inferiority lie at the basis of any self-destructive behavior, Figure 6.8 was also bold and overtly stubborn and defiant, whereas Figure 6.9 was shy and withdrawn, and displayed little, if any, fighting spirit. This sample can be linked to Erikson's shame and doubt category. Graphic variables include small, tight configurations and angle arcades, all indicating repression and concealment. Overcompensation and a tendency to gain an identity can be seen in the capitals and beginning strokes.

These four samples, figures 6.6–6.9, portray in vivid terms the complexity of human motivation, as similar over-eating disorders have been prompted by quite varying drives. One also notices that attitudes toward food can be influenced by the oral or the anal period.

Initiative vs. Guilt (Phallic) Stage: Ages 3.5–6

As the child grows, the libido shifts its biological focus from the mouth to the anus and then to the genitals. The phallic period is also associated with increased verbal and locomotive skills. The normal child is awakening his or her curiosity, but, at the same time, primordial sexual urges are also developing. Just as with the anal stage, contradictions abound. The processes of initiative, curiosity, and intrusion for the child can also be linked with the frightening thought of the phallus entering the female body (Erikson, 1968). The male and female child has mixed emotions about penis size.

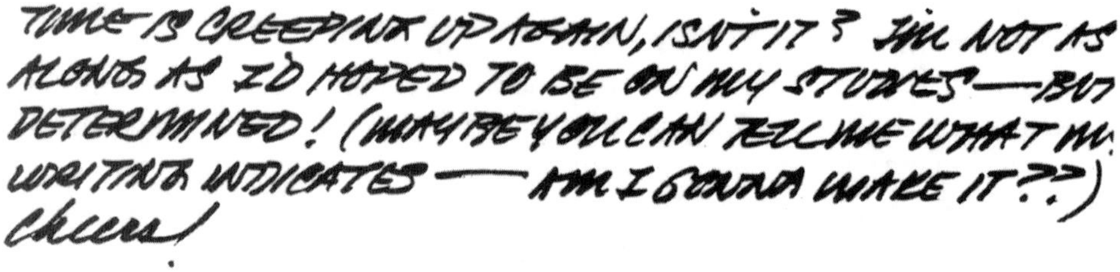

Figure 6.10. This is the handwriting of a creative female psychology doctoral candidate in her late 40s. Self-assured and individualistic, this woman made no secret of her homosexuality and interracial love relationship. From a graphological point of view, her handwriting appears to be fixated at the anal stage. Unsuccessful in facing the phallic period she did not resolve the electra complex. She over-identified with the male archetype and denied her own femininity. Although the writing appears over-controlled, the writer is obsessed with breaking rigid moral codes and to that extent is out of control; the id has been allowed free reign over the superego. Obsessive compulsions are seen in her tendency to fill in or muddy circular strokes.

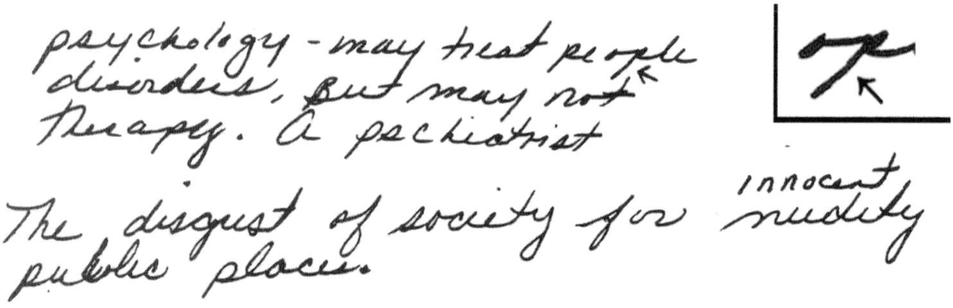

Figure 6.11. This signature belongs to a 37-year-old dental hygiene student who often used sexual innuendoes in class. Note the great changes in the length of lower zone forms and in broken downstrokes (see first line). This individual had had an emotional collapse earlier in life and appeared to be torn between reconciling her instinctual desires and giving in to societal restraints. She studied very hard and received high marks in class, yet her handwriting shows signs of great lack of honesty, at least with the self (tight letters, neglected or broken forms, and retracing particularly in the letter g, for example, disgust).

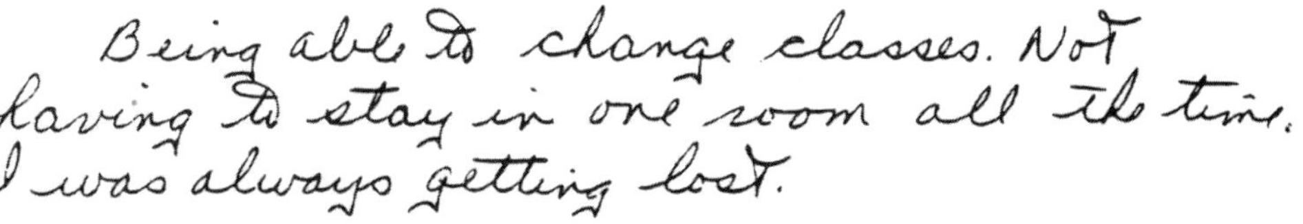

1. Being able to change classes. Not having to stay in one room all the time. I was always getting lost.

Figure 6.12. Also in her late 30s, this woman had been divorced and remarried, and had a daughter by each husband.

At the same time, each sex is in the midst of the oedipal and electra complexes. The young boy feels sexual desire for the mother and other females in his vicinity, and jealousy for the father and male siblings. The young girl feels the opposite. Erikson notes that, in conjunction with the rise of secret fantasies, a sense of guilt is awakened, and so the conscience or superego develops. It is felt as an inner voice of self-observation, self-guidance, and also self-punishment (119). Parents, who themselves may be fixated at the phallic stage, may also feel jealousy or sexual feelings toward their respective children. Fathers, for instance, often distance themselves from their daughters rather than face primal urges; mothers often make their sons their favorite children and alienate themselves from their daughters or husbands. Later in life, sons and fathers fight for dominance, while mothers and daughters oftentimes disagree.

Problems during the phallic stage can lead to over-compensation in the psycho-sexual sphere, homosexuality, promiscuity, hysterical denial, or self-restriction. Solutions for the oedipal and electra complexes involve successful repression or suppression of taboo urges, sublimation, and identification with the parent of the same sex. For just as the little boy competes for the affections of the mother, at the same time he wants to grow up to be just like dad.

In matter-of-fact fashion, the writer of Figure 6.12 informed me that she was unable to handle her eldest daughter, who was 15, and was sending the girl away to reform school. Fixated at the phallic stage, the writer was really unable to reconcile feelings of guilt and jealousy stemming for her own electra complex. Rather than show love and concern for a child whose real father had been replaced by the father of a half-sister, this woman rejected and punished the child. The compulsive use of broken lower-zone forms suggests that, in actuality, she was denying and punishing herself as well as the daughter. Note graphologically how the u-like t-bars (for example, "not," and "lost") echo the left-tending arcaded lateral lower-zone forms. The capital I also shows lack of completeness in both the upper loop and the angle on the left side, which stops before moving to the right. Coupled with hidden disconnections (between the letter *h* and the letter *a* of "having," and the letter *g* and the letter *e* of "getting,") all of this suggests a real breakdown of communication with both parents when she herself was a child.

Figure 6.13 is a sample of a recently divorced 30-year-old lady whose son was continually being molested by the estranged husband. The double loops on the lower zone of the letter *f*, invade the line below it, and the changing slants indicate excessive sexual fantasies and libidinal conflicts especially with the father. Whether the charges about the husband were real or imagined, this writer became enmeshed in perverse sexual activity.

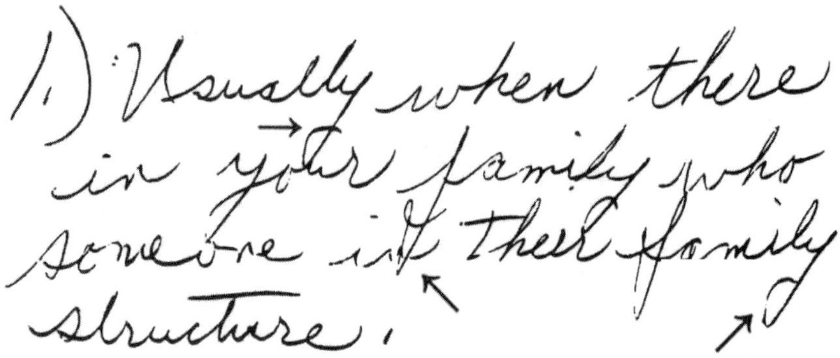

Figure 6.13. Signs of sexual dysfunction.

Figure 6.14 (opposite page) contains two samples of Ernest Hemmingway's handwriting. The bottom sample to F. Scott Fitzgerald was probably written while drunk. Note the dropping lines and club-like downstrokes, which indicate a depressive and violent temperament.

When writing to the grandson, the male, phallic-like club-strokes were transformed into female triangular forms. One would guess that part of Hemmingway's suicidal nature was linked to sadistic repression of homosexual or bisexual tendencies. He tried to foster the macho image, but to some extent it was a ruse against strong identification with a feminine archetype. The club-like downstrokes are classic signs of brutality. One would guess that he took some delight in his big game hunting, able to kill and thus cathect dark energies in a way that was socially accepted. The signature, C, was taken from another document. Hemingway routinely wrote his H-bar in such a way as to slash into the first name, Ernest. This symbol foreshadowed the great writer's decision to ultimately commit suicide by shooting himself with a shotgun.

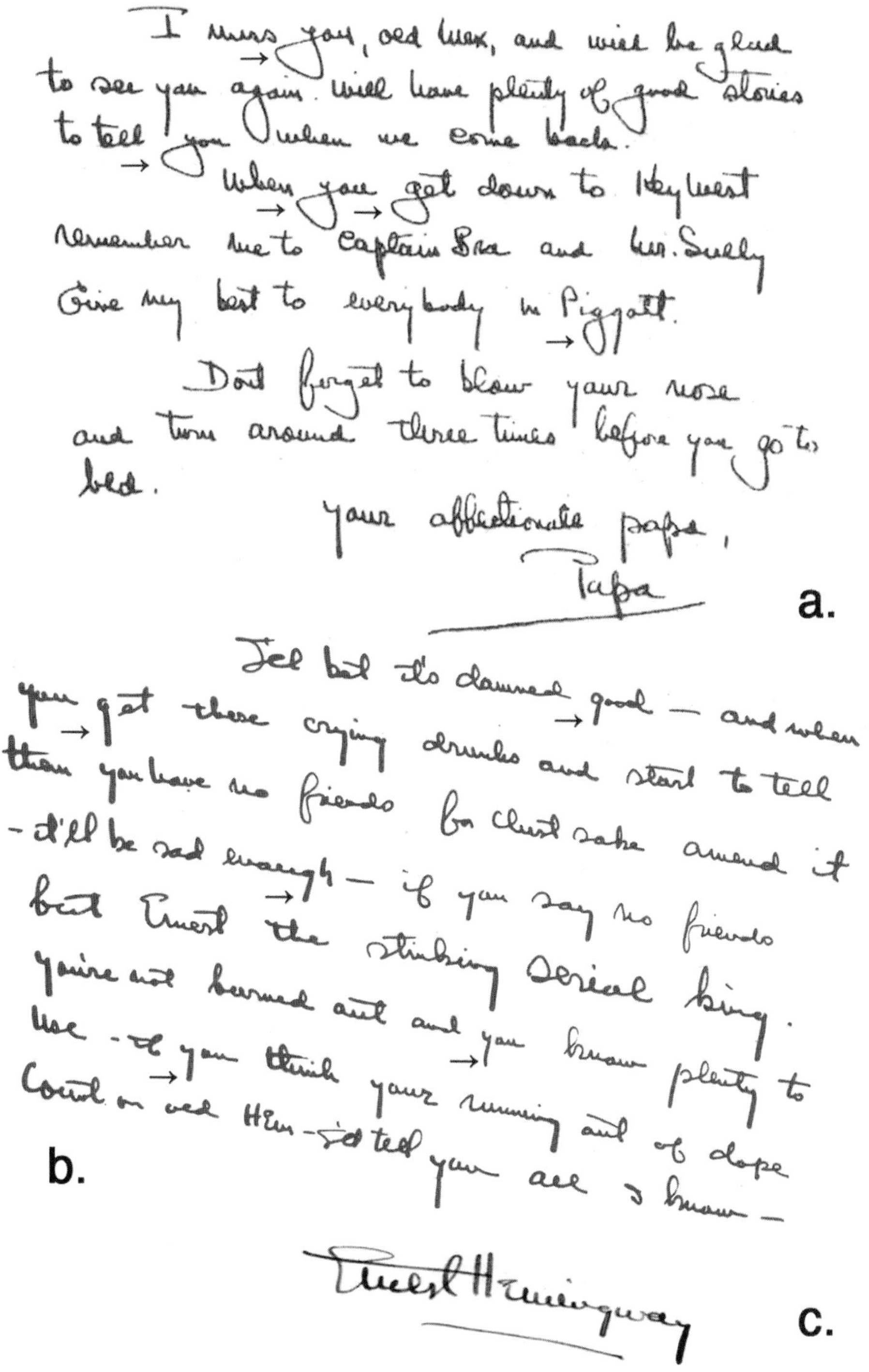

I miss you, old man, and will be glad to see you again. Will have plenty of good stories to tell you when we come back.

When you get down to Key West remember me to Captain Bra and Mr. Sully. Give my best to everybody in Piggott.

Don't forget to blow your nose and turn around three times before you go to bed.

Your affectionate papa,
Papa

a.

Tell but it's damned good — and when you get these crying drunks and start to tell them you have no friends for Christ sake amend it — it'll be sad enough — if you say no friends but Ernest the stinking serial king. You're not burned out and you know plenty to use — if you think your running out of dope Count on old Hem — I'd tell you all I know —

b.

Ernest Hemingway

c.

Figure 6.14. Two different styles from Ernest Hemingway. The first writing to his grandson in 1933, and the second to F. Scott Fitzgerald in 1929. The date of the signature is unknown.

Industry vs. Inferiority (Latent) Stage: Ages 7–11

Figure 6.15.
Political satirist,
sardonic gonzo
journalist Hunter
Thompson
committed suicide
by shooting himself
in the head.
Similar to the
symbolism in
Hemingway's
signature,
Thompson slashes
his H-bar through

his first name (the C-like capital H). This essential cross-out of the first name
suggests that Thompson harbored ill thoughts of self for many years. This would be
a sign of feelings of inferiority.

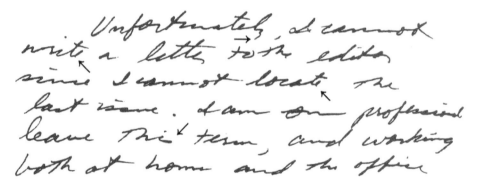

Figure 6.16. The handwriting of a person fixated in the latent stage, whereby
sexual feelings are thwarted, and more emphasis is placed on pushing forward
into the future and plowing his energies into work. See arrows for signs of sexual
inhibition and repression. The small capital I further supports the case for a
repressed self-image. This is the writing of a successful scientist interested in
metaphysics.

During the latent stage, the libido becomes diffused throughout the body and the sexual sphere is no longer energized. Children become more active in school, in socializing with members of the same sex, and in playing sports or working on hobbies. Erikson says that on the negative side, if solutions from preceding conflicts are insufficient, estrangement from the self can occur, along with feelings of inferiority.

Signs of fixation in the latent stage, such as denial of biological urges and over-emphasis on work can be seen in Figure 6.16. The individual is a male college professor and science writer in his mid-30s. Note the linear style, small capital I, fore-shortened word endings, and truncated lower zone. Over-compensation at the office at the expense of romantic or social interaction is indicated. This individual is involved with abstract ideas. He is very active in his field and has edited a number of books.

Ego Identity vs. Role Confusion (Genital) Stage: Ages 12–15

Erik Erikson writes that identity formation is "an evolving configuration of successive ego syntheses." This process culminates during the period of early adolescence just as the physical body matures. How does the ego integrate these new changes? "Great suffering may occur for the adolescent in gaining his identity…. [The person] may be defenseless against latent disturbances…[or there may be] playful and daring experimentation." One way or another, there is likely to be a "pre-occupation with the self-image" (163).

Figures 6.17 and 6.18 are the handwritings of two Caucasian ladies who have decided to follow different Indian gurus. At the same time, both have elected to adopt Eastern names. The writer of Figure 6.17 dresses in orange robes. She is around 33 years of age and wears a ring through her nose. This masseuse presents a smiling and happy disposition. She confided in me that she had left her 8-year-old daughter to travel to India on several occasions to be with Bagwan Shree Rajneesh, and this resulted in a strained relationship with the daughter. This is a conforming handwriting displaying little, if any, individuality. Alienated from her real self (see small personal pronoun I), she has adopted an artificial name (possibly suggested

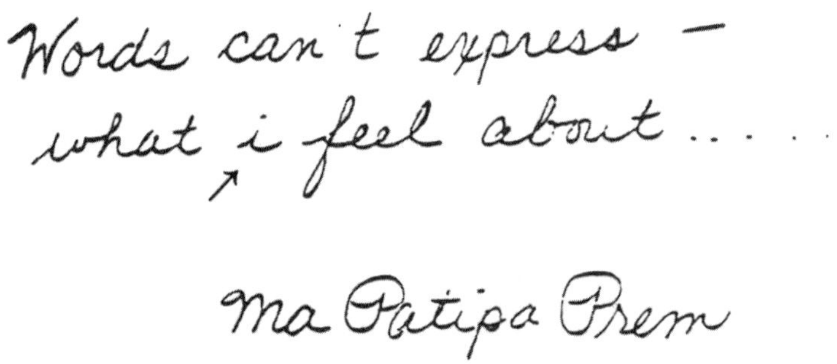

*Words can't express —
what i feel about .. . .*

ma Patipa Prem

Figure 6.17.

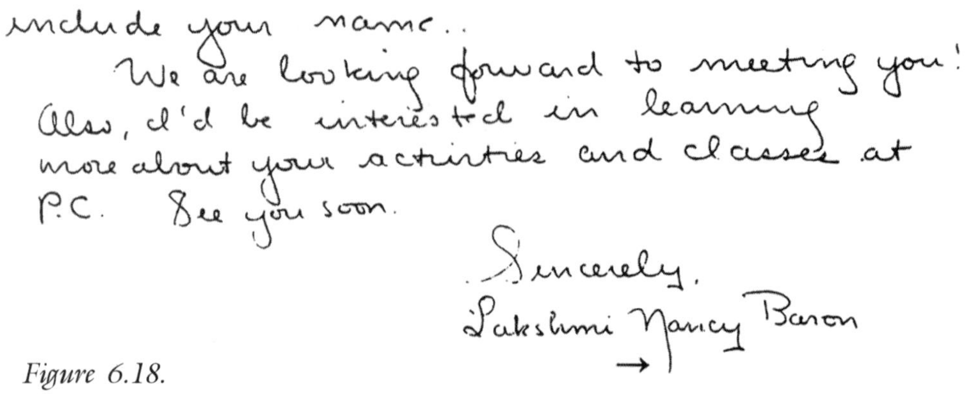

include your name..
We are looking forward to meeting you!
Also, I'd be interested in learning
more about your activities and classes at
P.C. See you soon.

Sincerely,
Lakshmi Nancy Baron
→

Figure 6.18.

to her) and a corresponding persona that satisfies the feelings of non-self that she seeks.

The young lady in Figure 6.18, whom I have not met, has a much higher Form Level than Figure 6.17. Lakshmi follows the Sufi leader Pir Vilayet Kahn (1916–2004), who in my opinion, was a wise and learned individual. Unlike Rajneesh (1931–1990), the "sex guru" who owned something like 20 Rolls Royces and was obviously too interested in material gain, Pir Vilayet Kahn, son of the esteemed spiritual leader Hazrat Kahn, was very involved in creating symposia that tried to combine such diverse fields as quantum physics and consciousness. Nevertheless, the Pir Vilayet seeker suffers from an identity problem as well. Note the double arch in the word *learning* and an abundance of artificial forms in the lower zone, especially in the signature. Sonnemann (1950) associates the double arch with lack of purpose and over-adaptability in the social sphere, for example, a follower (87). Intellectually, she is drawn to an abstract and high-level philosophy; however, in terms of self-knowledge, because this is a persona writing, she remains alienated from the true self, and ultimately, she does not know who she is.

Erikson's Last Three Stages

Graphology has its limits. One of the points of this chapter is to show that one could look at a handwriting, even of a person who is 40 or 50 years old, and gain some insight into that person's childhood rearing. This is not a small accomplishment.

Freud had five stages, ending with the genital stage at about age 15. Erikson proposed three more stages that we are about to discuss: (1) early adulthood, when most people get married, (2) mid-life, the 30s, 40s and early 50s, which would be associated with the person's career; and (3) advanced years, which Erikson started at age 55. In terms of graphology, and the maturation of the handwriting trail, at a certain point in the maturity of

Figure 6.19.

the writer, there may not be too much that changes for many years. However, handwriting will also reflect daily moods and other situations. For instance, it would be interesting to log Arnold Schwartzenegger's handwriting in his adult years, from his start as a body builder to a movie star to governor of California.

Figure 6.19 is the writing and signature of the dancer Ginger Rogers while she was still relatively unknown as compared to the quantum leap her career took when she teamed up with Fred Astaire. Not only did she take direction from the brilliant dancer and choreographer, she also emulated his signature.

During a cursory exam of comparing the handwritings of high school friends of mine at age 18 and then 40 years later, certainly one can see maturation in their writing. In general, the middle zone got larger in most cases and the writing became more refined, more rapidly written and simplified, and in some cases more legible (see Figure 6.22). Sometimes, a writer will abandon the Palmer script and change to printing because the writing is more legible. This is usually done by a male.

Figure 6.20.

Figure 6.20 is another example of a well-known individual, Mickey Mantle, whose signature changed as he became more famous. Note in the first instance, that the rookie year signature is big and confident, but somewhat conservative. Nevertheless, we can see in the salutation that the Yankee slugger does have a sense of style. After his fame grew, these additions made their way into his handwriting. The top signature is very rare, the bottom one more reflective of the thousands of signatures that the Mick handed out.

At the age of 18, the handwriting is usually still immature, and the graphics will ripen as the individual goes through his or her 20s, 30s, and so on. Except for the health of the writer or some significant change in life, the handwriting will generally stabilize for the next 30, 40, or even 50 years, but there are great variations, and it is very hard to generalize. In general, writing, and particularly the signature, may be executed more rapidly and get more and more simplified with each decade. In old age, of course, the writing begins to weaken and get shakier. There will be more missteps, patching, and quivers at this stage.

There is also a distinct difference between someone in their 50s, 60s, 70s, 80s, and 90s, in part because so many people die in their 70s. Anybody older than the age of 70 is certainly much more aware of their mortality because of this. A few years ago we attended an exhibit of Claude Monet's water lilies, and one could see that as he made it into his 80s the pictures became more and more simplified, as the artist kept refining his work to get to the essence of the archetypal water lily image that was his leitmotif.

With that in mind, we can say that as a person ages, his writing probably becomes more fluid and simplified, but there are many exceptions to this rule (that is, that some people's writings barely change through the decades). Let us continue with the discussion of Erikson's three stages.

Intimacy vs. Isolation Stage: Ages 16–29

This is the time when marriages and deep adult friendships are formed. In a sense, it can be seen as a rebirth of the oral phase, just as the last two Eriksonian stages can be seen as rebirths of the latent and genital phases.

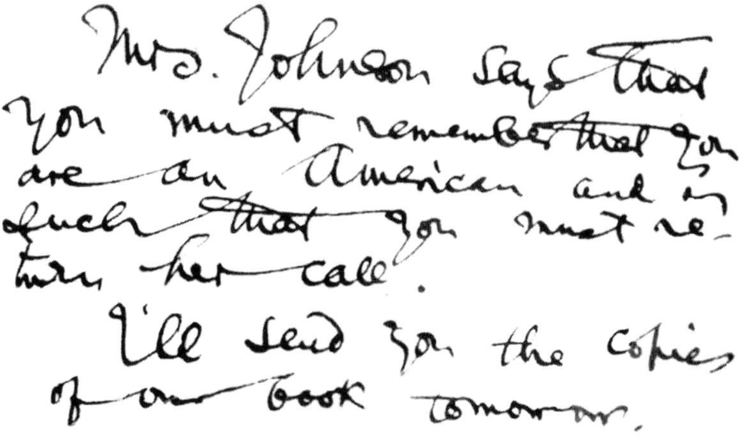
Mrs. Johnson says that
you must remember that you
are an American and as
such that you must re-
turn her call.
I'll send you the copies
of our book tomorrow.

Figure 6.21. Robert Underwood Johnson, editor of The Century, *circa 1898.*

Figure 6.21 is a sample of the writing of Robert Underwood Johnson, a man who has achieved much intimacy in his life. Johnson was editor of *The Century*, a literary magazine from the turn of the century. A poet and eventual ambassador to Italy, Johnson deeply cherished his long-standing friendships with such individuals as Rudyard Kipling, Mark Twain, Nikola Tesla, and Theodore Roosevelt. He was also a family man, devoted to his children and deeply in love with his wife. Although the connecting of separated words was a style of the day, it also symbolized Johnson's wish to integrate all aspects of his experience. Note the artistic and pastose nature of the script. His home became a haven for many luminaries of his day, and his dynamic style of writing stayed very much the same for decades.

Figure 6.22 (page 148) shows the handwritings of a female and male spanning 40 years, from age 18 to 58. Both writings got larger and bolder, and both have maintained a consistency of the pattern throughout the four decades. In the female's case, she increased secondary elaboration by creating overly large loops for her p's, but her threading and tensing up of some letters, such as the *a*, has stayed the same. In the male's case, his large spacing between words has stayed the same, but the middle zone has enlarged, suggesting a positive growth of the ego. Both are high-functioning individuals,

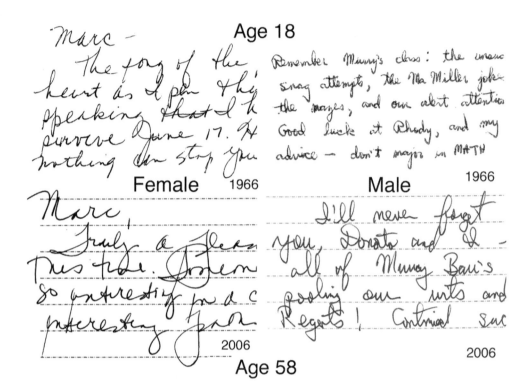

Figure 6.22.

so it remains a curious aspect that the female felt the need to overcompensate in her style, when, in fact, she is an accomplished success in her field.

Generativity vs. Stagnation: Ages 30–55

At this stage, the time of mid-life crisis, the individual reflects on the worth of his or her life. Is the person growing and advancing in the career, or is he or she simply marking time? Clearly Robert Underwood Johnson has an exciting dynamic writing that reflects "generativity." See also Figure 6.19, the signatures of Ginger Rogers, Gene Kelly, and, most notably, Fred Astaire. His, in particular, is rhythmic, dynamic, and aesthetically pleasing. An all around individual, one way or another, this is the signature of not only a highly productive individual, but also one considered to be a genius in his field. It's lyrical quality was so infectious that Ginger Rogers adapted it as her own, and wrote with a larger hand as a way to mask her benign pilfering.

Ego Integrity vs. Despair: Ages 55–105

Erikson is suggesting that the individual is always evolving, always seeking new horizons, and always facing various identity crises. In the later years, the individual must reconcile the whole of his or her life. Does the person face this period with bitterness and longing for the past, or courage and attention to the present and future?

Figure 6.23 is that of a happily married lady who is in her early 90s. Yes, we can see some frailness to the trail, but also there is rightward trend, a lyrical aspect, and still the energy to display full lower zone elaboration. Curiously, the capital J in the signature appears foreshortened and the middle zone is flattened. Overly humble, this is a generous lady who, even at this great age, is preparing food for an elderly friend. The writing has zest, tenacity of spirit, and an exclamation point, which reflects the generally optimistic spirit of a lady who has lived nearly a century and is still looking forward to the next day!

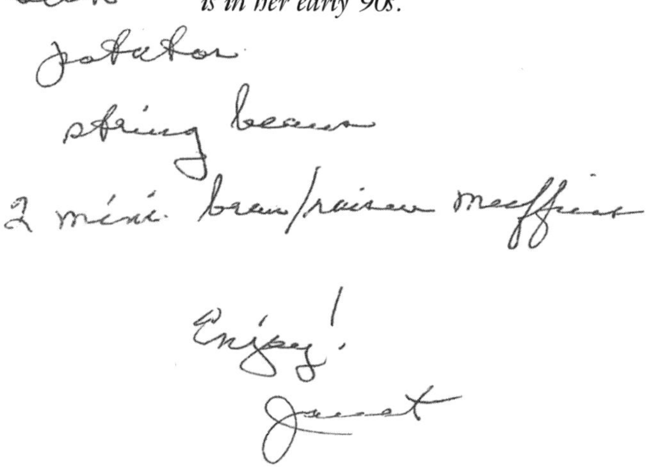

Figure 6.23. Janet, still happily married, is in her early 90s.

Identity formation is an ever-changing process. Fixation at one stage hampers development at the next. In handwriting, this generally shows up as arrhythmic disconnectedness, slant inconsistencies, repetition compulsions, and peculiar lower-zone forms. However, if the individual is successful in passing from one stage to the next, his or her writing tends to show dynamic forms, spontaneity, rightward trend, aesthetic balance, and high Form Level. Different characteristics from different stages can be superimposed on the same graphic form, and also distinct stages can be discerned. If used correctly, this typology could help pinpoint blocked areas of personality, and perhaps even lead the person to new insights and ways to change outmoded patterns of behavior.

Chapter adapted from: Seifer, Marc. (1982–1985) "Graphology and the Psychosexual Stages of Development," *National Society for Graphology Newsletter*, 13 (1985): 1–5. Seifer, Marc (1987), Handwriting and the Psychosexual Stages of Development. N. Bradley (Ed.) *Oxford, 1987: The First British Symposium on Graphological Research*. Derbyshire, Great Britain: British Institute of Graphology, pp. 128–145.

Psychoanalysis through the mechanism of graphology is a powerful tool. Not only can one analyze the personality of an individual long dead, but also insights can be gleaned in a new way, and sometimes things can be uncovered that could never be known by any other means.

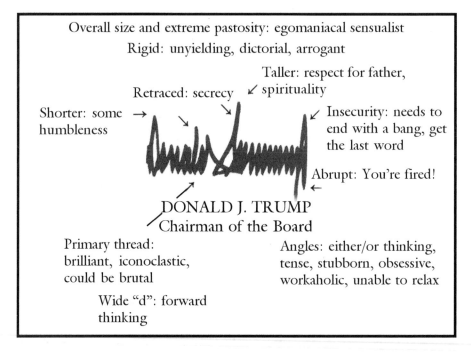

Overall size and extreme pastosity: egomaniacal sensualist

Rigid: unyielding, dictorial, arrogant

Taller: respect for father, spirituality

Retraced: secrecy

Shorter: some humbleness

Insecurity: needs to end with a bang, get the last word

Abrupt: You're fired!

DONALD J. TRUMP
Chairman of the Board

Primary thread: brilliant, iconoclastic, could be brutal

Angles: either/or thinking, tense, stubborn, obsessive, workaholic, unable to relax

Wide "d": forward thinking

Figure 7.1. Real estate entrepreneur, capitalist, casino owner, builder of luxury apartment buildings, and TV personality Donald Trump. Although extremely arrogant, he has the ability to make fun of himself, and can be generous. Essentially, however, this is the handwriting of a dictator, unwilling to yield.

Working with biographers, handwriting analysts can bring to the fore a new understanding of well-known historical characters and also secondary individuals, who, for one reason or another, may have been overlooked or misunderstood.

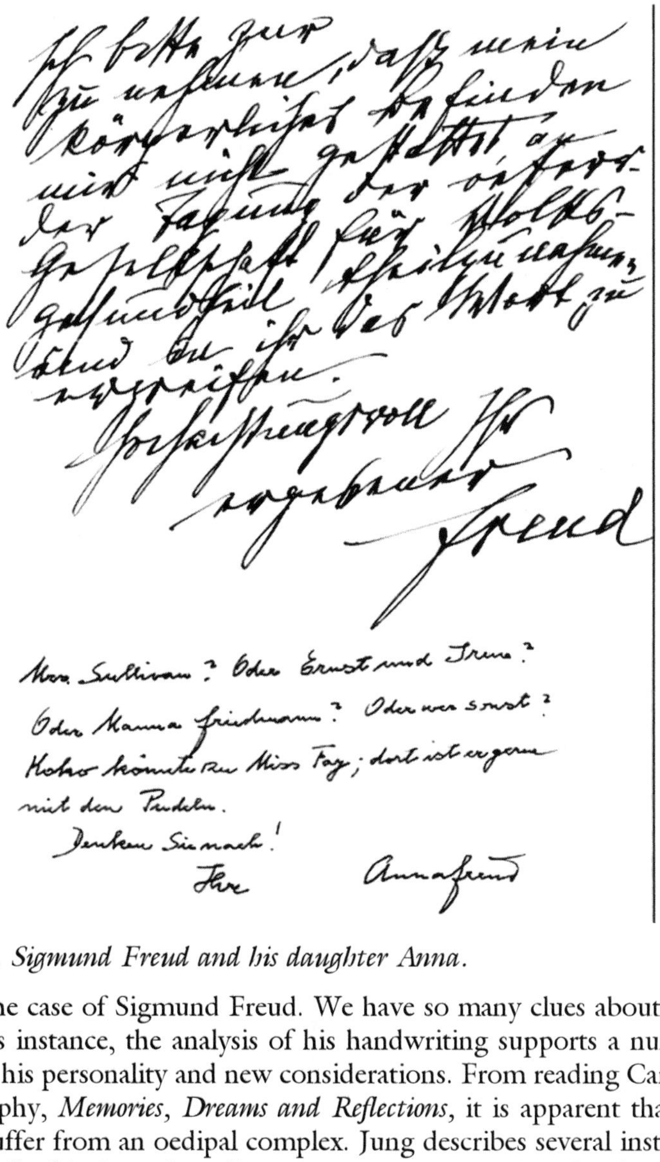

Figure 7.2. Sigmund Freud and his daughter Anna.

Take the case of Sigmund Freud. We have so many clues about his life, and, in this instance, the analysis of his handwriting supports a number of oddities to his personality and new considerations. From reading Carl Jung's autobiography, *Memories, Dreams and Reflections*, it is apparent that Freud truly did suffer from an oedipal complex. Jung describes several instances of Freud actually fainting when discussions arose concerning the theme of father and murder. In one spectacular instance, Jung, the younger man by 20 years, picked Freud up into his arms and carried the unconscious master into another room, Freud eerily awakening as Jung lowered him onto a couch.

Figure 7.2 is a wonderful example of the handwriting of Sigmund Freud at the prime of his life. One can see the vigor and enthusiasm seen in the rising baseline and long endings to words, offset by the falling off of one of the lines. The margins are also telling. His wide left margin supports the hypothesis of a forward thinker, but his planning is poor, and the signature actually runs off the page. It is a handwriting of opposites. The most curious feature is the rather long capital F in his name, displaying an expansive ego and overpowering sense of self, but this is offset by the fact that the letter is written in the lowercase form. He is optimistic and pessimistic, full of himself and plagued by a sense of inferiority. Here, in the lowercase "capital" F we see the symbol of Freud's oedipal dilemma. On the one hand, he is proud of who he is, even haughty, but he can't get over the negative feelings he had toward a father he secretly wished were out of the way, so that he could break the taboo and take his mother. Freud's great interest in the unconscious is indicated by the long lower zone letters, which truly plunge into the depths. The sharpness of the writing reflects his perspicacious nature.

When we turn our attention to his daughter Anna who became a foremost psychoanalyst in her own right, we see, similar to her father, the very tall, deep plunging f's, which stand for Freud. But also like her dad, she too uses the lowercase style. The question is why. It seems obvious that Anna was stuck. She dare not use a capital F if her great father used a lowercase one. So, her use of the understated, yet quite large first letter for the last name is for a very different reason than Freud's. In his case, it refers symbolically to a sense of inferiority he had in relationship to his father, a relatively poor Jewish man unable to stand up in the dangerous anti-Semitic climate in which they lived. It also refers symbolically to his wish to overtake the father, to gain the affection of the mother. Yet in Anna's case, her reason for using the small f is almost the opposite. She is emulating her father, and at the same time living in his shadow, probably afraid to capitalize the letter for fear that she would lose the love her father had for her because if she used a real capital F, she would be trying to outshine him. So her small capital F appears because of her identification with her father, and probably out of a fear of him, whereas Freud's taking on of the lowercase F was done symbolically in opposition to his father, Anna's grandfather.

Nikola Tesla

Born the same year as Freud, in 1856, the electrical inventor Nikola Tesla was a very different sort of man, one who claimed no interest in the unconscious. In fact it was Tesla's contention that every thought he ever had derived from an outside source. In that sense, Tesla and Freud were opposites, because Freud hypothesized that many of man's thoughts stemmed from primitive instincts.

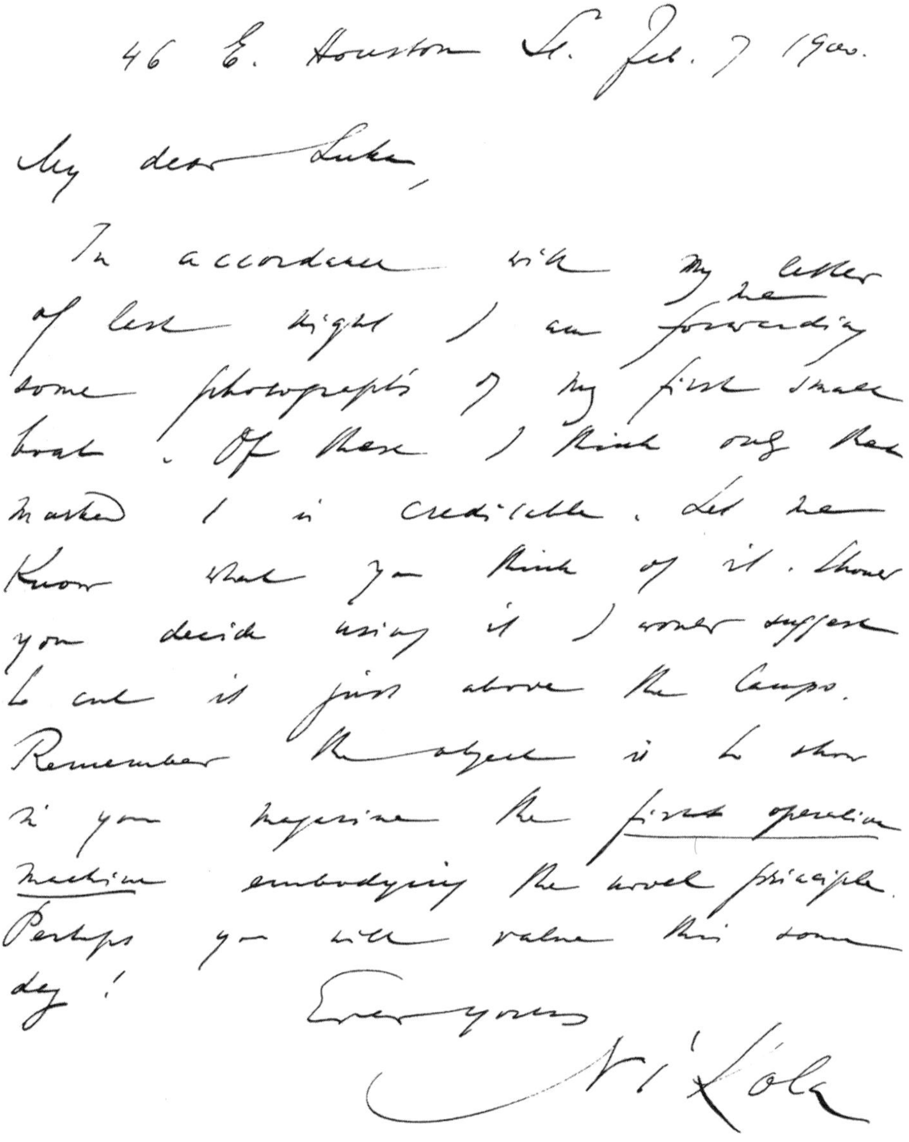

Figure 7.3. The handwriting and signature of a genius, Nikola Tesla, circa 1900. The written out text follows.

46 E. Houston Street (Tesla's lab)   February 7, 1900
My Dear Luka,

In accordance with my letter of last night, I am forwarding some photographs of my first small boat. Of them, I think only those marked 1 is credible. Let me know what you think of it. Should you decide using it, I would suggest to cut it just above the lamps.

Remember the object is to show in your magazine the first operative machine embodying the novel principle. Perhaps you will value this some day!

Ever Yours, Nikola

Tesla is writing to his friend Robert Johnson, who he called affectionately "Luka," at the very pinnacle of his career. Inventor of the AC electrical power transmission system, which had just been put in at Niagara Falls and which still runs the world today, Tesla is referring here to another great invention, his "teleautomaton." This complicated creation, which he displayed at Madison Square in New York City in November 1898, had within its design the foundation for wireless communication, remote control, artificial intelligence, cell phone technology, radio guidance systems, and even encryption devices. Writing this letter to *Century Magazine* editor R.U. Johnson, concerning a major article they are planning, Tesla is well aware that his incredible boat is the work of genius. This remote controlled robotic device, in Tesla's own words, was the first prototype of "a new type of species on the planet, one not made out of flesh and bones, but rather, wires and steel."

Tesla is envisioning at this moment R2D2, CP30, and I-Robot all wrapped up into one device. He also constructed it in such a way that it responded to a combination of transmitted frequencies, so that perfect privacy was obtained and the means were devised for creating a virtually unlimited number of wireless channels. Note the superior spacing, the simplicity, and the combination of speed, sharpness, control, and legibility. This letter is written at this culminating moment, and

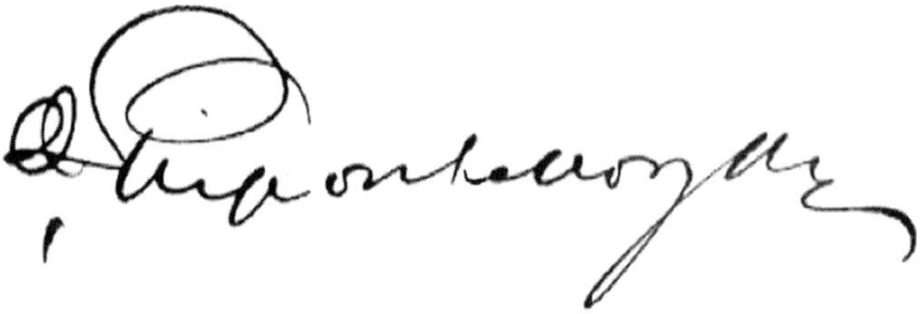

Figure 7.4. The imperial signature of J. Pierpont Morgan.

so his signature, as counterbalance to relatively short upper zone, expands dramatically to reflect the great feelings of self-confidence he had at this time.

In the signature, note the spectacular three-dimensional capital P and the insignificant capital M. It would seem that Morgan held his paternal grandfather, Pierpont, in more esteem than his father, whose financial thumb he lived under for much of his early adult life. The incredible power that Morgan wielded can be seen in the vigor, pastosity, and general boldness of the writing coupled with the heavy-pressured endstroke. A sensualist who had his concubines and indulged to the tune of tens of millions of dollars in purchasing rare coins, ancient artifacts, original manuscripts, and rare paintings, Morgan, in control of the railroads, banking, shipping, mining, electrical, steel, and other endeavors, was also a philanthropist, heavily providing funds for museums, universities, and churches. His maternal grandfather, John Pierpont, was a highly regarded poet, minister, and abolitionist, whose son, James Lord Pierpont, wrote the Christmas song *Jingle Bells*.

Due to the success at Niagara Falls in providing clean electrical power for nearly half a continent, Tesla formed a partnership with J. Pierpont Morgan, then the most powerful financier on the planet. Cartoons of the day depicted Morgan as an atlas holding up the world, a giant able to hold Wall Street in the palm of his hand, and as emperor, greater than such minions as the king of England, kaiser of Germany, and William McKinley, president of the United States.

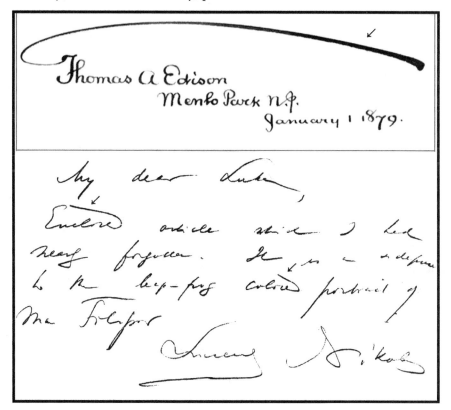

Figure 7.5. The famous signature of Tom Edison along with a frivolous letter and signature by Nikola Tesla to his friend Robert Johnson written at the peak of his career, circa 1900.

Tesla's competitor was Thomas Edison, whose signature became his trademark, placed on his many inventions, particularly the ubiquitous phonograph. Edison's moniker is a persona, a mask, quite unlike his natural spontaneous script. Because Edison's bold overstroke was known, Tesla produced one like it, but did it to the left, as a lighthearted counter to the cornucopic symbol in Edison's.

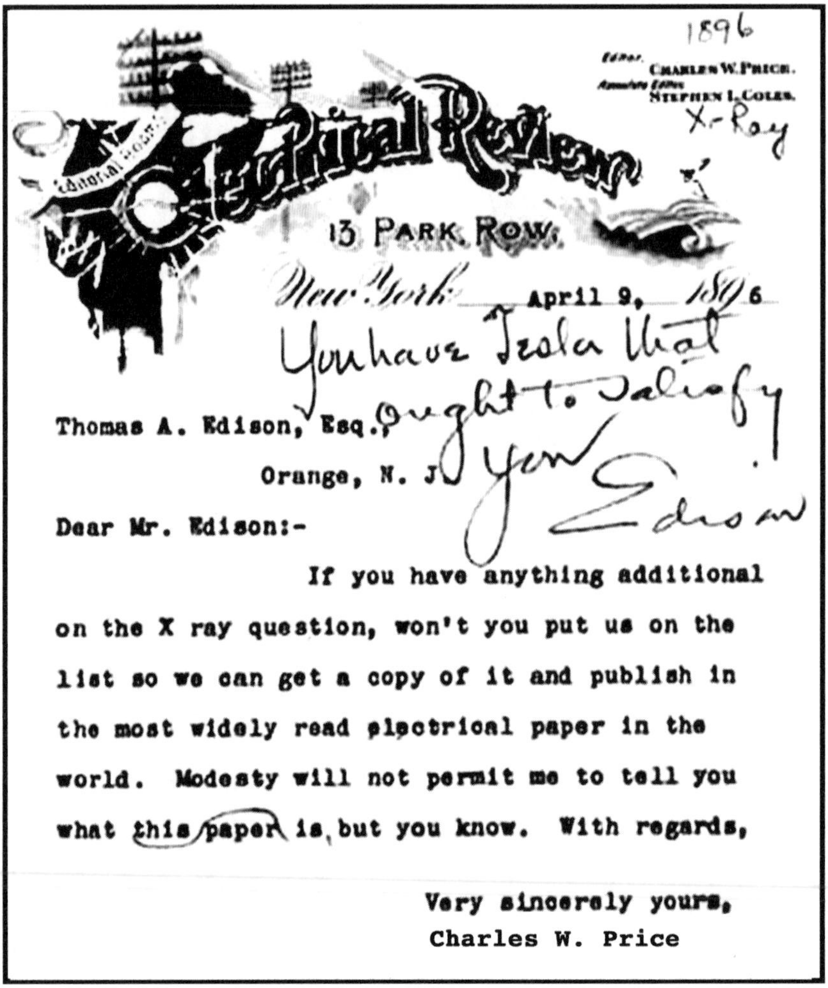

1896

Editor. Charles W. Price.
Associate Editor Stephen L. Coles.

X-Ray

Electrical Review

13 Park Row,

New York, April 9, 1896

You have Tesla that ought to satisfy you

Edison

Thomas A. Edison, Esq.,

Orange, N. J.

Dear Mr. Edison:-

If you have anything additional on the X ray question, won't you put us on the list so we can get a copy of it and publish in the most widely read electrical paper in the world. Modesty will not permit me to tell you what this paper is, but you know. With regards,

Very sincerely yours,
Charles W. Price

Figure 7.6. A wonderful and rare example of Edison's "true" signature and writing. Note the combination of printscript and persona writing as seen in the first line with the Greek ∊'s, and then the dropping of pretense with a stunning burst of spontaneity as his t-bar in "to" becomes the s in "satisfy." This unguarded spirit continues enthusiastically with the vigorous ending upstroke in the word you *and the bold natural signature with the large capital E and high-flying i-dot.*

Figure 7.7. A political cartoon of J. Pierpont Morgan in 1901 as emperor above Kaiser Wilhelm of Germany, King George of England, and President McKinley. At right is Tesla's Wardenclyffe wireless tower, and below, the inventor, holding a wireless fluorescent lightbulb, which he displayed before the public in the 1890s.

Figure 7.8. Tesla's handwriting in 1906. Here we see a total breakdown of the writing trail as Tesla writes a rough draft to Morgan, asking once again to not pull the plug on Wardenclyffe. Envisioning an enterprise that would combine the advantages of AT&T, GE, and what would come to be radio, wireless fax machines, and cell phone technology. Tesla cannot believe that Morgan will not give in, and so his handwriting crumbles to reflect a corresponding mental state.

In 1901, Tesla began his quest to construct a high-tech industrial center starting with a world wireless telegraphy plant on 1,800 acres out on Long Island, 60 miles from New York City. The architect for the project was the brilliant Stanford White of McKim, Mead & White, and the backer was J. Pierpont Morgan. With $150,000 provided by the Wall Street giant, Tesla

Figure 7.9. A time line of Tesla's signatures spanning 10 years, from the height of his fame and success in the 1890s to the depths of his despair as seen in 1906.

initiated construction of a laboratory and a 180-foot-tall transmitter, but for various reasons, including Tesla's unilateral decision to construct a more expensive tower in order to bury the competition, (Marconi), and a stock market crash (caused by none other than Morgan himself) Tesla ran out of funds. After raising another $50,000 on his own, Tesla still required another $75,000 to $100,000 to complete the plant, but Morgan refused to supply these additional funds, and even blocked Tesla from obtaining the money from any other financier.

As time goes on, and Tesla continues to be thwarted by Morgan, the inventor's signature begins to show continuing signs of anger, seen in Figure 7.9, in the whipping down endstroke in the 12/2/03 signature. Tesla's last chance to turn Morgan around occurs at about this time when he is successful in negotiating with such millionaires as Jacob Schiff, Henry Clay Frick, and Thomas Fortune Ryan, who actually gave Tesla $10,000 at this time. It takes Tesla nearly three more years to arrange a meeting between these financiers and Morgan, but the deal falls through and Morgan instead sets Ryan up as head of a large insurance company. That is the last straw, and in 1906 Tesla crumbles, and something qualitatively changes in his writing and in his nature.

"May gravity repel instead of attract, may right become wrong. All reason must founder on the rock of your brutal resolve," Tesla writes in yet another plea to the obdurate financier. "I tell you I shall advance the world a century."

"Every night my pillow is bathed in tears, but you must not think me a weak man for that.... I harnessed Niagara Falls, Mr. Morgan. This is not a boast, only my credentials.... I am like a man swimming against a tide that carries me down." Year after year, from 1902 until 1906, Tesla writes letters, appeals, and meets with the "Wall Street Monster," but all to no avail. Finally, in 1906, his nerves gave out, and Tesla suffered a mental breakdown.

Note the loss of verve to the letters in the 1907 aftermath signature, whereby the capital N leans over and loses all of its finesse. One can also see in this time line the varying self-images Tesla had. For instance, he is confident and bold in the first and last signature in the left column. The curved capital N's written on 8/21/1899 and 10/14/99 are aesthetically pleasing gracious gestures written to Katharine and Robert Johnson, his closest friends, when again, he had a positive view of himself. The tiny N, written on 12/12/1899, is associated with an impulse the wizard received on his wireless equipment at his Colorado Springs Experimental Laboratory in 1899, which Tesla attributed to extraterrestrial intelligence. Considering the possibility that martians had initiated contact with humans, Tesla's capital N shrinks to reflect the sense of smallness he felt in trying to comprehend the vastness of the cosmos and the possibility that humans were not alone. Simultaneously, his capital T, in this instance, resembles an antenna.

As can be seen in these examples, a person's handwriting and self-image can change daily, even momentarily. And thus, by this means, a heretofore unrecognized nervous collapse of this great inventor is uncovered and reported by the author in my doctoral dissertation, several published articles, and in the biography *Wizard: The Life & Times of Nikola Tesla: Biography of a Genius*.

Note that, through graphology, one can come to understand the interplay of other players in the story as well, in a way very difficult to achieve by other means. I will end this chapter with a great letter Johnson sends Tesla in 1916, after it is wrongly reported in the *New York Times* that Tesla was to share the Nobel Prize in physics with Edison. Tesla owed Johnson money. Unfortunately, neither Tesla nor Edison received this prize, although both individuals certainly deserved the accolade. Interestingly, there is some evidence that Tesla actually declined the nomination because he did not want to share such an honor with Tom Edison, who in Tesla's words was a mere

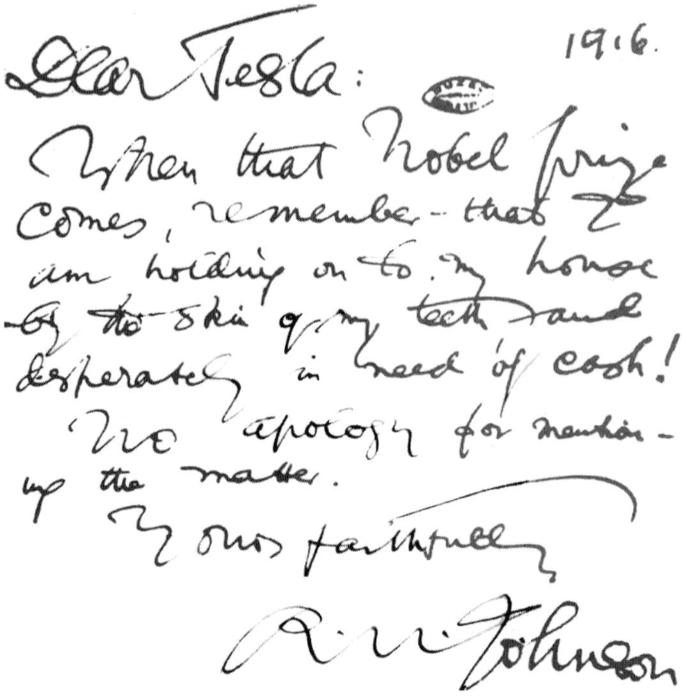

1916.

Dear Tesla:

When that Nobel Prize comes, remember—that I am holding on to my house by the skin of my teeth and desperately in need of cash! No apology for mentioning the matter.

Yours faithfully

R. U. Johnson

Figure 7.10. Robert Underwood Johnson (1853–1937).

inventor. Tesla, on the other hand, saw himself as a discoverer of new principles, and thus he felt he was in a different league.

In Figure 7.10 Johnson attempted to recoup some monies he had invested with Tesla out of the inventor's supposed winnings from the Nobel Prize. Unfortunately, Tesla never received the award, but Tesla actually did repay Johnson out of other funds several years later. Johnson's personality seems to just leap off the page, with his large gracious opening "Dear Tesla," and his aesthetically pleasing pastose/pictorial script. One way or another, Johnson was an artist at heart. A poet, editor, and latter-day ambassador to Italy, Johnson, along with his wife, Katharine, were Tesla's closest friends. Other close associates who often came to dinner included Mark Twain, Rudyard Kipling, Marguerite Merrington, and two gentlemen with whom Johnson started the Sierra Club, naturalist and poet John Muir and Teddy Roosevelt. (Part of Johnson's full signature was added to the text.)

1916

Dear Tesla,

When that Nobel Prize comes, remember that I am holding on to my house by the skin of my teeth and desperately in need of cash! No apology for mentioning the matter.

Yours faithfully,

R.U. Johnson

The Criminal Mind and Handwriting

Specific graphic trait clusters that graphologists have traditionally associated with integrity problems reflect, in varying degrees, tendencies referred to as covering up, evasiveness, inhibition, defensiveness, lack of clarity, self-consciousness, deliberate calculation, impulsiveness, deceit, dependency, vanity, and ostentation. In addition, graphic characteristics take on alternate meanings when combined with other traits such as speed [and slowness] or pressure.

—Patricia Siegel

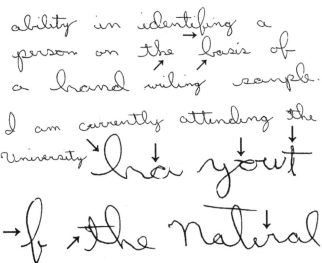

Figure 8.1. The handwriting of a fraternity brother who turned into a thief. Arrows point out various signs of weakness in character: the foreshortened lower zone in the f, left-tending arcade on the h, sway-back or broken back verticals such as on the b, h, and f, double loop on the a, patching between the y and o to make it look connected, twisted loop on the t, unusual circle under the t-bar, and neglect, such as, missing parts of letters. See the ur in "natural" as an example.

Anita Muhl, MD, lectured on graphology at the University of Melbourne in Australia in 1939. She is known for her studies in analyzing hundreds of delinquent and criminal handwritings. Following in the footsteps of Saudek (1928) and Pulver, Muhl (1949) lists eight signs most often found in dishonest writers: left tending half ovals, small tight loops, covering strokes,

Dishonesty Saudek	Insincerity Pulver	Unreliability Muhl
*1. Slow writing (sentence impulse reduced to better impulse).	A. *In slow handwriting:*	*1. Leftward tending half oval.
2. Unnatural impression—stylistic, leftward tending slant, lifeless, frequent arcades.	1. Phony, artificial, calligraphic.	*2. Small tight loops.
3. Instability and liability: loose without pressure, thread and waving lines.	2. Covering strokes.	*3. Covering strokes.
	3. Partial covering, supported forms, sharks teeth.	*4. Abrupt stops above the line.
4. Touch-ups without improving legibility.	4. Arcade—internal and left tending final.	5. Breaks and mends.
5. Letter written like other letters with cover strokes, replacement, neglect of size ratios.	5. Elaborate circular forms, cross cuts and tie ups.	6. Smeariness.
	6. Puntuation, dots where they shouldn't be.	7. Slowness.
6. Interrupted writing: punctuated or blobbed, resting points, fitful speed.	7. Broken letters and broken off lower loops.	8. Combined form: leftward tending half oval to covering stroke to angle to rightward tending half oval.
7. Frequent lifts from paper.	8. Omitting of letters.	9. Looped arcade.
8. Important parts of letters omitted (decisive only in slow, mature writing).	9. Stumbling and repeated starts.	10. Resting points.
9. Marked initial emphasis.	10. Retouching, corrections.	11. Letters mistaken for each other in slow writing.
10. Letters o, a, d, g, and q open at base, and written clockwise in two strokes, leftward tending half oval.	11. Counter strokes, open forms at bottom, increased left trend in capitals or end strokes.	12. Neglected letters in slow writing.
		13. Letters open at the bottom of the middle zone.
Iris Holmes Hatfield	B. *Graphics not determined by speed:*	14. Breaks in large loops of upper zone.
1. Spoon e formations.	12. Thread.	15. Double curves.
2. Twisted loops.	13. Smooth unclear connector strokes, neglect and illegible forms.	16. Acute angle of 30 degrees in a right-slanted school model.
3. Double loops.	14. Substitution of letters, smooth errors.	17. Too great difference in lengths of strokes.
4. Ambiguous numbers.	15. Mixed writing systems.	18. Aggression strokes.
5. Missing letters.	16. Difference between handwriting and siganture.	19. Clubbed end strokes.
6. Displaced pressure.	17. Exaggerations and inconsistent strong pressure.	20. Double t crossings.
7. Extreme slant (R or L).	*To determine insincerity requires a number of the graphics and experience in evaluating handwritings.	21. Signs of exaggerated fantasy.
8. Muddy writing		22. Too great secondary width.
9. Unstable baseline.		23. Marked oscillations of the writing angle.
10. Left bend vinal arcade.		*To determine unreliability requires the first four starred graphics or any five recurring repeatedly.

Figure 8.2.

abrupt stops above the line, breaks and mends, smeariness, slowness, and looped arcades. Extremes in tension, for example, either very tense or very slack writings, are also associated with the antisocial personality (Schuler, 1982).

The chart (Figure 8.2) lists more than 50 variables associated with unreliability, insincerity, and dishonesty. One must be very careful in using such a chart. In general, it is the combination of four or more that would lead the analyst to suspect deceitfulness. The bulk of the chart was taken with permission from "Integrity & Handwriting" by Siegel, *ASPG*, 1991, pg. 58. The section by Hatfield was taken with permission from *A Question of Honesty*, 1988, 52.

Mendel (1947) would add the counterstroke, which is a contrary movement that goes in the wrong direction. This can be seen in an opening when continuity is expected, an arcade where there should be a garland, a downstroke when an upstroke is called for, and a movement to the left when a rightward movement is expected. Depending on other features such as form level, the counterstroke would be found in "braggarts, corruptors, seducers, forgers, felons, embezzlers and potential murderers" (206–7).

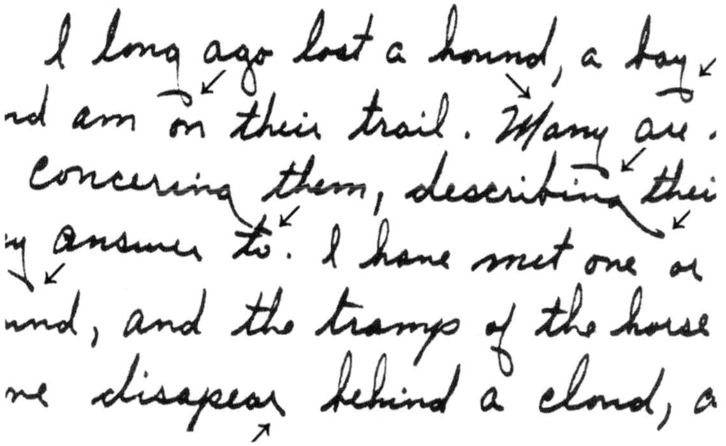

Figure 8.3. A drug dealer who murdered one of his suppliers for money. Note the recurrent counterstrokes on the lower loops, the overall narrowness, suggesting a sense of secrecy, the saw-tooth capital M, double-crossed t in to and the clubbed ending to the r of "disappear [sic]." The combination of these signs supports the case for someone with a anti-social personality and violent streak. From Hatfield (1988).

In more recent days, Iris Holmes Hatfield (1988), who did her research in the prison system in Kentucky, and Paul de St. Colombe (1967) have listed additional signs of dishonesty including unnatural openings, broken and distorted letters, initial and terminal strokes turned up (showing avarice), smeary writing, retouched letters, spoon "e" formations, double looped ovals, twisted upper loops, and numbers that are purposely written in an ambiguous fashion.

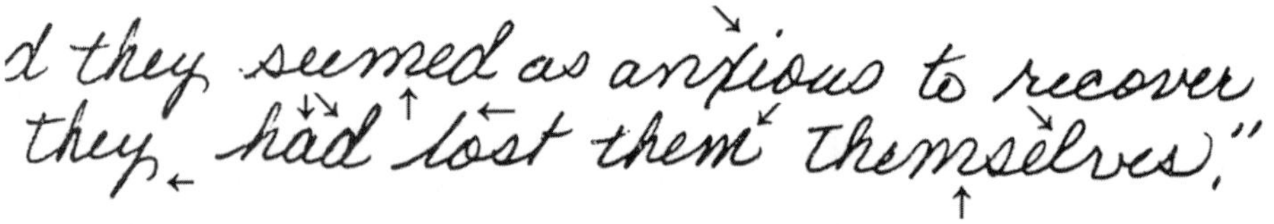

Figure 8.4. Handwriting of a 27-year-old man in prison for armed robbery and rape. From Hatfield (1988).

Note the pulsating quality of the size of the writing as it gets smaller and larger as seen in the words *seemed as anxious*. The x-bar is large and ends with pressure (lack of impulse control). We also see left-tending ends to arcaded letters such as the m, upper loops that almost twist seen in the d's (a counterstroke), peculiar curved-down strokes on the ends of y's, and sharp endings to the m's as in the word *them* (aggression).

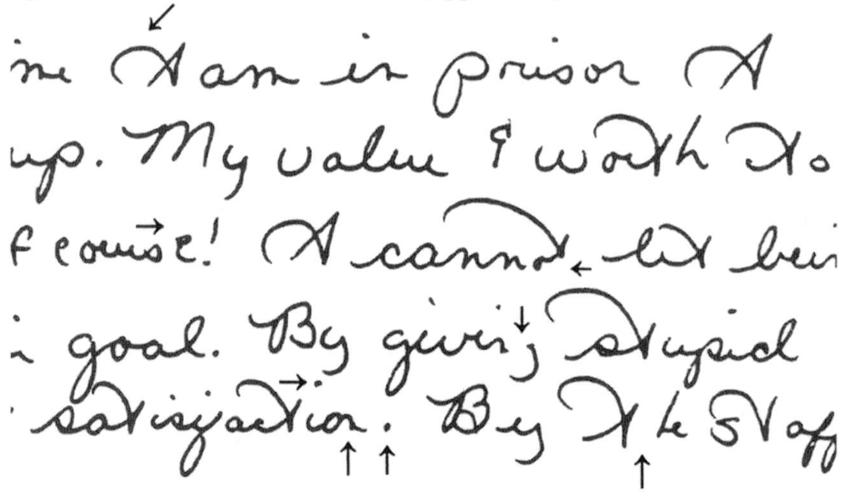

Figure 8.5. A 28-year-old mother in prison for armed robbery (from Hatfield 1988).

Note the repetition compulsion in Figures 8.5 and 8.6. Figure 8.5 has many signs of dishonesty, aggression, and anti-social behavior. The capital I is really the letter A. This implies deception in the self-image. Some letters or parts of letters are written small or missing altogether, as in the *ot* in "cannot," *ng* in "giving," and ending *n* in "satisfaction" (relating to a Machiavellian tendency). Note also the great emphasis on diacritics, such as the i-dots in "satisfaction" and period at the end of the word. A schism in herself, and thus in her relations with others, is evident in the great split in the word *the* in the sentence at the end that reads, "But the staff." The back-slashing *t*'s, because of their prominence, suggest a need to emphasize the self but in a violent way. These are bold counterstrokes symbolic of the charge she gets from robbing people at gunpoint, or perhaps with a knife. This is the writing of someone with an negative identity.

One of the most famous serial killers is Ted Bundy. His handwriting appears below. Bundy was a fairly good looking snake charmer, who murdered unsuspecting college girls by luring them into his car in a variety of ways. One method involved the use of crutches and a false cast. He would ask his victim if she would help him open his car, and that was that. Among other things, this is the writing of a psychopath and a liar. The use of the word *Peace* as a salutation in this instance is a cruel joke—the personification of a twisted mind.

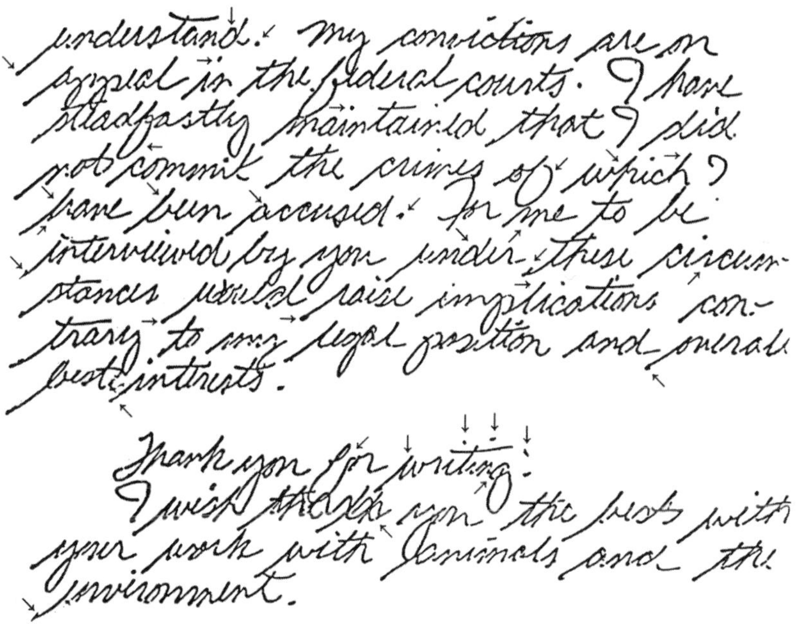

Figure 8.6. Ted Bundy, serial killer.

Note the repetition compulsion of the beginning strokes. This need to "touch the base every time," suggests that Bundy was superstitious. His obsessive compulsive nature lurked in a very dark place. Many of these exceedingly long, dark phallic upstrokes have a sharp initial hook. Much like a fisherman, he reeled in his catch. The swollen lower zone f-loops reflect his sadistic sexual appetites, when combined with the combination of long, dark covering strokes in both upper zone loops and in curved letters, such as the tops of *a*'s and *d*'s. Look at the word *for*, first line, second paragraph. Here we see a counterdominant. The *f*-loop is ballooned out and awkward. It invades the letters below it, yet the very next letter is essentially missing. So he expands the first letter and neglects the second (the *o*). It's a bizarre contradiction and peculiar arrhythmia. Note also the overall pastosity (obsessive need for pleasure), sickle-like capital *I*'s (angel of death?), bludgeoning *i*-dots, left-tending understrokes which many times are angles that cut back (*h* in *have* and *m* in *me* line 5; *i* in *with* and *n* in *and*, second to last line), and broken forms (*h* in *which*, line 4; *g* in *writing*, line 9). These last two features are associated with his psychotic/schizophrenic nature. He cuts off relationships, viciously severing ties. Ironically, the right slant, coupled with the general curved nature of much of the writing, is related to his dependency needs. Note the well-formed circular stroke for the p in *peace*. This horrible individual can be charming. One way or another, the handwriting reflects the writing of a cold-hearted, self-indulgent, repressed, secretive, and mean-spirited liar.

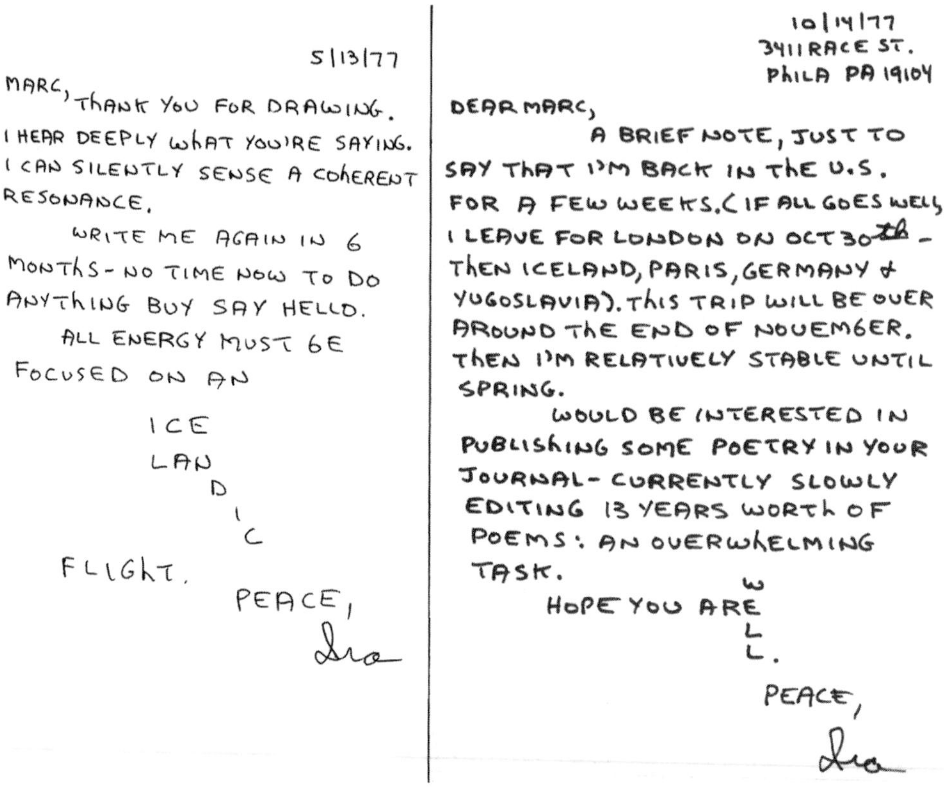

Figure 8.7. The handwriting of New Age guru Ira Einhorn. The first sample, at age 37, was written a week after he chaired a noteworthy conference on consciousness and quantum physics at Harvard University. The second sample, five months later, was written 35 days after he murdered his girlfriend, Holly Maddux.

Einhorn was a leader of both the ecological and anti-war movements of the late 1960s and early 1970s. A charismatic figure, stocky, with a ponytail and full beard, Einhorn was able to bridge the gap between various left-wing groups and corporate America. At one time, he was a candidate for mayor of Philadelphia. In 1972, he met Holly Maddux, a blonde cheerleader from

Texas and graduate from Bryn Mawr College. Einhorn introduced Holly into a psychedelic world that included many luminaries of the day, from renegades such as Abbe Hoffman; to Andrija Puharich, MD, author of *Beyond Telepathy*; Arthur Bell, inventor of the Bell helicopter; and Arlen Spector, who became Einhorn's lawyer before he became a United States senator.

When I received the letter on the left, frankly, I was stunned, because it struck me as so childlike. It certainly was different, with a scrabble-like originality, but it was slowly written, and the signature was particularly immature. By the time of the writing of the second letter, everyone knew that Holly was missing. Einhorn speculated that a right-wing paramilitary group, perhaps associated with the CIA, had taken her. This was a time of conspiracies: the assassinations of JFK, RFK, and Martin Luther King; the fiasco in Vietnam; Nixon's Watergate break-in; the Black Panthers kidnapping of Patty Hearst; and the disappearance of Abbe Hoffman after being arrested for drug trafficking. Anything seemed possible, and Einhorn continued to live his high-profile social activist lifestyle for two more years, until Holly's body was found drained of all its blood, locked in a trunk at Einhorn's Philadelphia flat on Race Street. With $4,000 bail paid by Barbara Bronfman, who was part of the family that owned Seagrams, Einhorn skipped town and lived underground in Europe for the next two decades. He even got married.

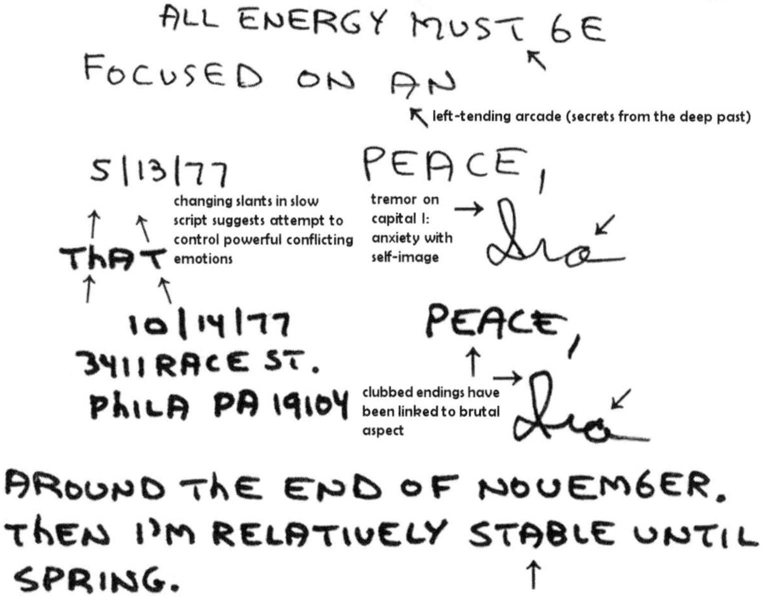

Figure 8.8. Note left-tending arcades at the ends of his a's, change of size and slant for a slow and controlled writing, clubbed ending to the e of Peace (brutality), increased tremor in signature on the capital I, after the murder, (anxiety with the self), and double loop on the a of the signature, which is associated with locked in secrets.

Arrested in France, it took the authorities about a year to extradite Einhorn, because he had been tried in absentia and this went against French ordinances.

Einhorn's handwriting before and after the murder is primitive, child-like, and slowly written. Its great pastosity is related to his sensual nature. He had a habit, for instance, of taking long baths and spending much of his time in his apartment in the nude. One has the sense that this is the writing of a person haunted by oedipal memories from early childhood, perhaps associated with a taboo relationship with the mother early on, probably also during the toilet-training stage. The roundedness reflects the warmth or bonding that he experienced with the mother early on, but this is off-set by the segmented nature of the script, a sign of isolation and distance from the primary caregiver. This all suggests schizophrenegenic tendencies in the mother. She's not crazy, but she drives her son crazy by giving him mixed signals, some-times too intimate, other times cold. Einhorn had repressed rage to-ward the mother. He almost strangled a girl to death while in col-lege, years before he met Holly. The great slowness of the writing trail is most likely also associated with the influence of a powerful psychedelic that impeded the speed and connectedness. Thus he may have been tripping when he penned both letters. In that sense, he could escape to a different state of consciousness, and distance himself from a corpse that he kept as an odd trophy in a back closet in his apartment.

Figure 8.9. Ira Einhorn and Holly Maddux.

Many people in the building complained of the smell. The simple fact that Einhorn never took it upon himself to remove the body could be interpreted in a variety of ways. Similar to any other classic Freudian re-pression, he simply buried the ugly memory and tried never to deal with it. Ironically, had he gritted his teeth and gotten rid of the body, he probably would never have been charged with the murder. Freud would say that Einhorn wanted to be captured. He was a man of opposites, idealistic, aware of moral obligations, interested in a new world of expanded con-sciousness and peace, but at the same time a slave to his primal instincts and repressed anger concerning some deep secret from early childhood that continually sparked his creativity but also plagued him, and caused him to occasionally erupt in horrible ways.

Osama bin Mohammed bin Laden

On October 15, 2002, the Associated Press called me from New York to analyze a new bin Laden letter and signature that had just arrived in their London office from Al-Jazeera, the Arabic TV news organization. Within 24 hours, they had a full camera crew at my doorstep, and by dinnertime the next day, the story went out to 300 television stations worldwide.

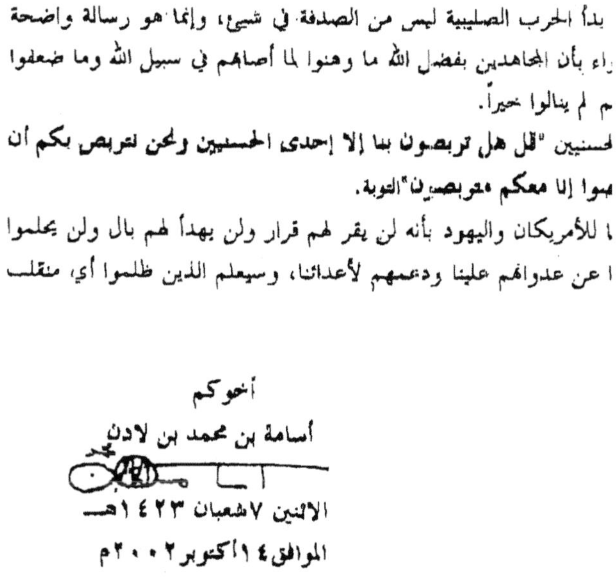

بدأ الحرب الصليبية ليس من الصدفة في شيء، وإنما هو رسالة واضحة رآء بأن المجاهدين بفضل الله ما وهنوا لما أصابهم في سبيل الله وما ضعفوا م لم ينالوا خيراً.

لحسنيين "قل هل تربصون بنا إلا إحدى الحسنيين ونحن نتربص بكم أن بوا إلا معكم متربصين"التوبة.

ا للأمريكان واليهود بأنه لن يقر لهم قرار ولن يهدأ لهم بال ولن يحلموا ا عن عدوانهم علينا ودعمهم لأعدائنا، وسيعلم الذين ظلموا أي، منقلب

The AP was interested to know if the signature was genuine. I thought that it probably was, but requested color copies of the original along with one or more exemplars to make the comparison. Soon after, it became apparent that bin Laden was most

أخوكم
أسامة بن محمد بن لادن
الإثنين ٧ شعبان ٤٢٣ ١هـ
الموافق ٤ ١أكتوبر ٢ ٠ ٠ ٢ م

Figure 8.10. A letter to the West signed by Osama bin Laden, October 15, 2002. Courtesy of the Associated Press.

likely alive and so the questioned document aspect of the case became moot. The following discussion concerns a personality assessment.

One notices immediately that the signature is not really in Arabic, but rather it is a symbolic ideogram that bin Laden designed himself. Resembling an assault rifle as a whole (Dresbold, 2006, 80), the right part, which looks like the letters "L" and "T," is geometric and a little too pat. If we look at the pair of circles on the left, to the right of the right circle there is a long lateral line that connects to a very small sphere. This lateral line is extremely shaky. I was unable to determine if this was caused by the fax or if it was written that way. Assuming that this lateral line is a fair representation of the original, and that it was written by bin Laden himself, he may have been ill at the time of writing. He is known to have a kidney disease.

Anna Koren, working for the Israeli government, had written a very astute analysis that can be seen on her Website. I had this to refer to, but based most of my analysis on a Jungian interpretation. Because I had worked with Anna in Haifa and New York in the past, I e-mailed her to see if she had translated any of the symbols; I was delighted to hear from her associate, Dafna Yalon, who I knew from one of the British conferences. Dafna had worked with Dalia Agmor, an Israeli graphologist born in Iraq who is an expert in Arab handwriting. Dalia compared the signature to the name written in standard Arabic.

Figure 8.11. Dafna Yalon and Dalia Agmor's illustration and notes. Arabic goes from right to left. The words Osama bin Mohammed bin Laden, Osama,

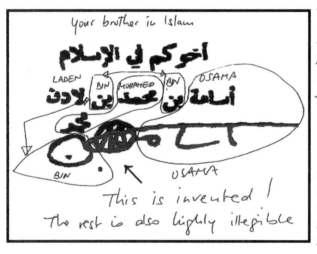

son of Mohammed, son of Laden, do bear a striking similarity to parts of the signature that they identify. The first section on the right, the part that resembles the letters "L" and "T" match the Arabic word Osama, *and the Arabic word* Mohammed *can be seen above the left-most circle, which Dalia attributes to a morphed sign for the word* bin.

The dark second circle (arrow), according to Yalon and Agmor, is purely invented and bears no relationship to Arabic.

Figure 8.12. The Anarchy symbol resembles one of the circles in bin Laden's signature.

The large original signature reveals a narcissistic personality. Much duality can be seen within its structure. There are lean geometric forms on the right side and circles on the left. This could be seen as the split in his nature between his Eastern philosophy, symbolized by the circles, and his engineering background and interest in high technology seen by the architectural forms on the right. His father was a builder who became a billionaire and advisor to the Saudi King. If we look at the two large circles, the leftmost one would symbolize bin Laden's anima or feminine side and the dark circle would symbolize his animus or masculine bellicose side. As one of my students pointed out, this dark section bears a striking resemblance to the symbol for anarchy. Mohammed, or God, sits above the feminine archetype as a lightning-like thunderbolt.

Taking a Gestalt perspective, every aspect of the signature would be linked to various parts of bin Laden himself. The dot in the center of the left circle would be him as a single man surrounded by the world with God protecting from above. Osama lives under God's law, but we also see a small dot outside the circle. This could symbolize that he also lives outside the law. He creates his own laws. The dark circle corresponds to his terrorist activities and also the father. Growing up as one of more than 50 children, the small circle attached by the umbilical cord to the right of the dark circle could correspond to bin Laden as a child living in the household of a very powerful man.

Figure 8.13. The pen, mightier than the sword. Peace Agreement between Yitzhak Rabin of Israel and Yasser Arafat representing the Palestinians, 1993 (JASPG, 1995/96, 4, p. 6).

Most of this signature stays under the umbrella of the long, dark overstroke. One of bin Laden's accomplishments was to bring together under one roof many competing terrorist organizations. And in that sense, this overstroke could symbolize his ability to coordinate many disparate groups. The umbrella stroke also appears to be born from the anarchic darker circle. This is a man with megalomaniacal designs. One of his trademarks is to coordinate two terrorist acts at one time. They bomb a bank in Turkey and, when people think it is all over, another bomb is detonated, killing more. Duality can be seen in the numerous signs of pairing in his signature: two circles, a left circular side and a right architectural side. He is a complex man who has identified with his vision of a multifaceted light and dark god.

Since the time of this analysis, additional entreaties and bin Laden's voice have been sent to Al-Jazeera, and there are still conflicting conclusions, but most people assume that as of October 12, 2008, bin Laden is still alive.

Based on: Seifer, Marc (December 2002). The Bin Laden Affair. *The Vanguard*, pp. 1–2.

Japanese Handwriting

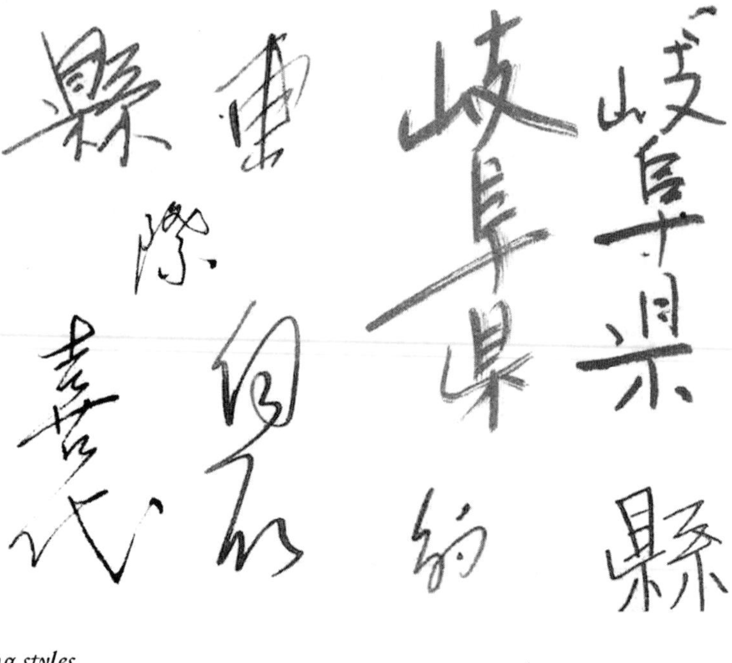

Figure 8.14. The magnificent graphics of the Japanese script. These words were taken from the addresses on a number of envelopes. Note the same long graphics in two different scripts at the top right and the similarity of the ideograms catty-corner, top left with bottom right. Clearly graphological principles are cross-cultural, as we see here a mix of pastose, sharp, more carefully drawn and more free-wheeling styles.

Part

II

Handwriting and Brain Organization

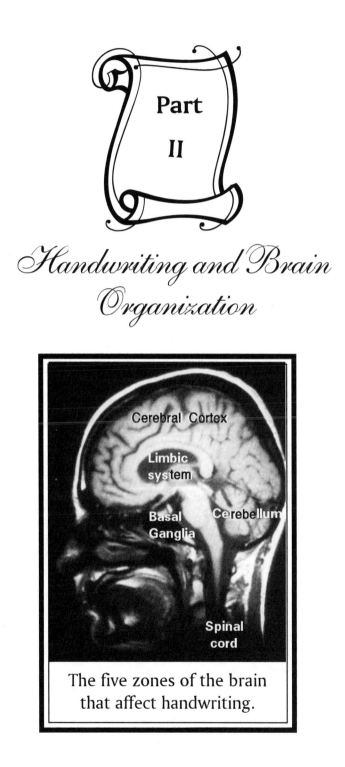

The five zones of the brain that affect handwriting.

Chapter 9
Historical Considerations

Oh, what a curious combination of corporeal structure, mental character and training must handwriting depend!

—Charles Darwin

From an evolutionary perspective, it becomes apparent that the process of handwriting is linked neurologically to the process of speech, and in a certain sense is a further development of human language production. Writing is about the most advanced process that a human brain can achieve.

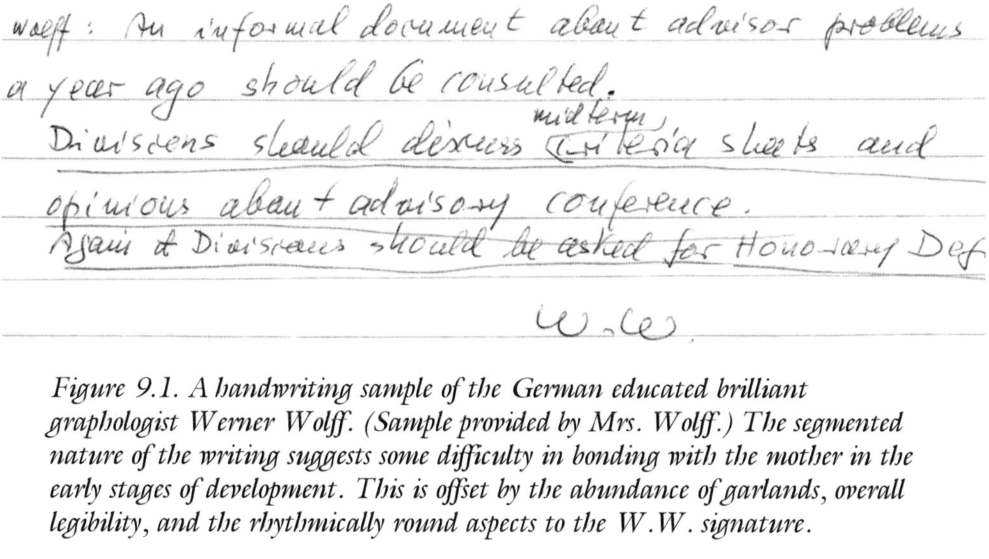
Wolff: An informal document about advisor problems
a year ago should be consulted.
Divisions should discuss mid term criteria sheets and
opinions about advisory conference.
Again the Divisions should be asked for Honorary Def
W.W.

Figure 9.1. A handwriting sample of the German educated brilliant graphologist Werner Wolff. (Sample provided by Mrs. Wolff.) The segmented nature of the writing suggests some difficulty in bonding with the mother in the early stages of development. This is offset by the abundance of garlands, overall legibility, and the rhythmically round aspects to the W.W. signature.

Werner Wolff

Born in 1904, Werner Wolff was only 53 years old when he died. A tireless researcher and prolific writer who taught psychology at the University of Barcelona and at Bard College, Wolff's articles and books cover a wide range of topics, including unconscious expressions of behavior, dream interpretation, the child's expression of self, and a study of the culture of Easter Island. Frankly, I was shocked when CIA consultant and long-standing matriarch of the field, Thea Stein Lewinson, dismissed Wolf's contributions. In my humble opinion, Wolff's masterwork, *Diagrams of the Unconscious* is one of the most important graphology textbooks published in the English language. It is an indispensable and highly original reference work that covers such topics as psychoanalysis, symbolism, and depth psychology as it relates to handwriting. His idea of the principle of configuration, an unconscious organizing factor to the writing, stemmed from some of the more philosophical aspects of Klages's theories and that of Gestalt psychology. Each part of handwriting, including so-called individual signs, for example, the lower loops, the way a "t" is crossed, and so on, must be linked to the whole.

Wolff was able to discern principles of configuration such as symmetry, periodicity, and consistency manifesting in precise ways in the unconscious aspects of writing. By working with a compass and ruler, Wolff noted that many signatures had an exact midpoint, either the ending stroke of the first name, the beginning stroke of the last name, or the dot in the middle initial. Wolff also noticed that certain favorite psychomotor movements, such as a t-bar or ending stroke, would be a particular length that would bear a precise geometric relationship to the size ratios of the signature. These relationships persisted throughout the life of the writer.

Wolff's findings were expanded by Daniel Anthony (1967), who noticed "geometrical forms, interlocking units and touch points" in creative writings. These ideas were further expanded by Seifer (1976), who applied Jung's concept of synchronicity to the study of a full page of writing. Oftentimes, particular letters, i-dots, symbolic features, or the same word would line up to the millimeter down a page. Thus, Wolff's exacting "diagrams of the unconscious" have been expanded beyond signatures and words to include the entire writing field.

Alexander Luria

Russian neurophysiologist Alexander Luria (1902–1977) describes a relationship between the organization of handwriting, language, and the coordinated workings of the various lobes of the brain:

> Writing starts out as a chain of isolated motor movements,
> but with practice the process is radically altered and writing
> is converted into a "kinetic melody" no longer requiring
> the memorizing of the visual forms of each isolated letter
> of individual motor impulse for making every stroke.

> —Alexander Luria

Born in Kazan, a university town east of Moscow, Luria entered the university at the age of 16. Shortly after the World War I, while still an undergraduate, he established the Kazan Psychoanalytic Society, exchanging letters with Sigmund Freud. With the onset of a new all-embracing Soviet philosophy, Luria had to temper his interest in psychoanalysis and shifted his studies to neurological organization and cognition.

In 1924, Luria met Lev Vygotsky (1896–1934), whose ideas on language development influenced him greatly. Vygotsky was a brilliant professor, whose lectures were so riveting that when his class was filled, the overflow of students would stand alongside nearby open windows to take notes. Essentially, what Vygotsky had realized was that children do not develop in isolation, but rather they interact with adults when they learn such things as language and social rules and regulations. Vygotsky thus suggested that human brains were, in a sense, open systems. Once language was acquired, cerebral complexity would increase, and thinking

Figure 9.2. Alexander Luria (right) with child psychologists Jean Piaget and Natalia Morozova.

would now be augmented by inner speech. Handwriting can thus be seen as frozen expression of this complex development in the evolution of man.

By studying and testing humans who had various forms of brain damage, Luria would rise to become, perhaps, the most important neuroscientist of the 20th century. His theories on the neurological organization of handwriting and how it develops are seminal accomplishments in the history of the field.

Rudolf Pophal

Neurophysiological investigations have been conducted by Rudolf Pophal (1893–1966), a medical doctor who taught graphology at the University of Hamburg from 1946 to 1958. His work has been translated into English along with the studies of other researchers by Marie Bernard and Erika Karohs. Pophal hypothesized that four different personality types were linked to four different areas of the brain:

1. Intellectual/Cerebral cortex.

2. Instinctual/Brainstem.

3. Impulsive/Globus pallidus.

4. Inhibited/Corpus striatum.

These types could be determined through analysis of the handwriting. Pophal also suggested that each motor center in the brain was also reflected in the quality of the stroke. His student Heinrich Pfanne continued this line of investigation, but his works, similar to most of the German authors, have never been translated into English.

Integrating the ideas of Luria, Vygotsky, and others, this author (Seifer, 1985) expanded Pophal's work to suggest that the three-zoned vertical cerebral division: cerebral cortex, mid-brain, and brainstem, which MacLean associated phylogenetically with human/intellect, mammal/emotion, and reptile/instinct, should also be reflected in handwriting. For instance, Albert Einstein would have a handwriting that would reflect the cerebral cortex type by displaying high Form Level and excellent organization; James Belushi would be the emotional mid-brain type, with tendencies toward curves, changing slant, and wavy baseline; and the fierce Napoleon would display in his handwriting aspects stemming from brainstem activity such as rapidity of writing and erratic explosions of motoric impulses.

In brain-damaged writers, Luria (1980) discovered that, if a person had damage to the left parietal/occipital lobe (visual cortex), when the person copied a drawing, the right side of the drawing would be missing. Studying the MRIs and handwritings of multiple sclerosis patients, coma patients, and stroke victims before and after the onset of trauma, I worked with medical doctors from Brown University to point out alterations, tremors, and breaks in the writings and correlate them to the damage seen in the brain scans. Different kinds of brain damage caused different aspects of the handwriting trail to be affected.

Hemispheric Dominance

Current president of the American Society of Professional Graphologists, Patricia Siegel, has studied the neurophysiological organization of left-handed writers. As a lefty herself, Siegel has noted that there is a sense of alienation peculiar to lefties as they live in a right-handed world. Her categories of lefties take into account the hold of the pen (for example, inverted or non-inverted hold) and link between left-handedness and hemispheric dominance. Siegel suggests that different kinds of lefties may have "different neural subsystems" (1985).

This work is related to Klara Roman's research on the handwriting of twins. Having studied nearly 300 pairs of identical twins for the Medical School of Budapest in 1942, Roman discovered that "the dissimilarity in the handwritings of identical twins is due to a difference in lateral dominance, since in most cases, one twin was right-handed and the other left-handed" (Roman, 1962). The brain is organized contralaterally—that is, the opposite hemisphere rules. Most people are right-handed because the language center of the brain is almost always located in the left temporal lobe. In general, right-handers tend to be left brain dominant, and left-handers tend to be right-brain dominant, but there are many exceptions to the rule. Some lefties slant to the right or upright and some slant to the left. It is generally more comfortable for a lefty to slant to the left, even though he or she was taught to slant to the right. Thus, a left slant in lefties has a different connation than a left slant in a righty. Simplistically, a left slant for a lefty is more natural and suggests right-brain dominance, whereas a right slant for a lefty suggests left brain influence. A left slant in a righty could reflect right-brain dominance, or it may be linked to a psychoanalytic tendency not to conform. Graphology is very complex. In the study of left slant in lefties and righties, other tests for brain dominance (for example, projective measures, MRI, or eye dominance tests) would help in the investigation.

The link between hemispheric dominance and handwriting has also been investigated by Jeanette Farmer (1995). Based on the work of Ned Hermann, who extrapolated from Carl Jung's four types, Hermann identified four thinking styles with four quadrants of the brain: Thinking and Sensing for the left hemisphere, and Intuitive and Emotional for the right. By plugging in graphic indicators that are graded for each type, a mandala-shaped chart can be constructed for each different person mapping out, in derivative form the type of brain dominance he or she has (Farmer, 1995).

As a student of Anthony's, I undertook a study of muscle tension in the handwritings of schizophrenics as compared to normals at Billings Hospital, University of Chicago, under the direction of two medical doctors, Herbert Meltzer and David Goode. I isolated 10 of the 40 indicators from the Roman Psychogram that related to muscle tension. These included pressure, narrowness, speed, and rhythm. In a blind study of 20 individuals, each handwriting was graded for each variable, with a 1 corresponding to a non-tense handwriting, and 10 corresponding to an extremely tense script. This procedure proved statistically significant in separating schizophrenics who were more tense from normal people (Seifer and Goode, 1974). German graphologist Bernard Wittlich studied tension in psycho-motor movements and has discovered "a method of determining through handwriting whether under stress a given personality would lean towards compulsion, depression, hysteria, or schizophrenia" (Schuler, 1982). Seifer's study uncovered a link between arrhythmic disconnections within words and schizophrenia as compared to the handwriting of normals. The implication is that interruptions in the bonding process between mother and child at an early stage of development will translate into abnormal breaks in the continuity of the writing.

In a blind study utilizing the entire Psychogram, Seifer and Siegel were each independently able to differentiate eight epileptic split-brain writers from eight normal matched pairs ($p \leq .05$). The study found fragmented and foreshortened letters, tremors, and misspellings in the writings of many of these epileptic patients who have had their corpus callosum's surgically severed (TenHouten, Seifer, and Siegel, 1988).

Alfred Kanfer

Burdened with a tremulous hand from his earliest years, Kanfer became interested in psychological disorders and detecting them through study under high magnification of handwriting. A Viennese handwriting expert for the Department of Justice and a survivor of the Dachau concentration camp, Kanfer came to New York City in 1940 to work as a diagnostician for the Hospital for Joint Diseases. There he worked with the director of the laboratory, Henry Jaffee, MD, After decades of research and examining thousands of handwriting samples of cancer patients, Kanfer, later at the Strang Clinic, enlarged handwritings 500 to 1,000 times. By this procedure he was able to detect minute neuromuscular spasms indicative of cancer in the connecting strokes of the writing, which occur when muscle groups involved in contracting movements change to releasing strokes.

Figure 9.3. This 70-year-old lady survived stomach cancer and an operation to remove the tumor two years earlier. Kanfer states that cancer will create a

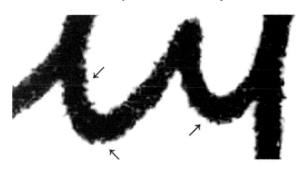

segmented pattern in the writing trail under high magnification (see arrows). Part of the trauma in the writing could be caused by chemotherapy, which cured the patient, but almost at the cost of her life.

Similar to Saudek, Alfred Kanfer (1902–1974) made use of a microscope in his graphological investigations. Although an accomplished handwriting psychologist who analyzed Howard Hughes's writing for *Life Magazine* in the early 1970s (the sample that Clifford Irving used for his famous forgery), Kanfer's major contribution to graphology was in cancer detection.

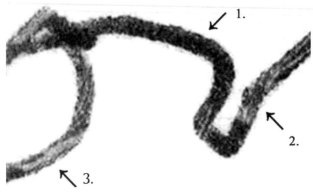

Figure 9.4. The handwriting of an 81-year-old rather agile male who survived throat cancer three years earlier and eats through a feeding tube. In relatively good health, we can see two types of trauma in the writing: (1) an ataxia or slight tremor not

as pronounced as the segmented effect seen in Figure 9.3; and (2) a kink in the writing trail more likely the result of the advanced age of the writer.

Figure 9.5. High magnification of the writing trail of a 71-year-old male who survived colon cancer 15 years earlier. The writing is vigorous with no signs of tremor reflective of his being cured of the disease. As with Figure 9.3, this gentleman endured debilitating chemotherapy shortly after the operation to remove the tumor.

Due to my own interest in this topic, I met with and interviewed Kanfer briefly at his downstairs laboratory at the Strang Clinic in 1971. He had many file cabinets filled with studies and also a projection system used to magnify his samples when flashed on a screen. He preferred to study handwritings filled out in fountain pens rather than ballpoints, as the fountain pens more aptly displayed the telltale tremors that differed depending upon the kind of cancers being studied. As fountain pens are now so rarely used, felt-tipped pens would be a better indicator of minute tremors than ballpoints. In a study for the American Cancer Society with coauthor Daniel Casten, MD (1950), involving 935 handwriting specimens, 88 with cancer, Kanfer was 85 percent correct in detecting cancer cases and 79 percent accurate in distinguishing non-cancer writings (Hartford, 1973).

Figure 9.6. The wife of senator and perennial presidential candidate John Edwards,

Elizabeth Edwards

Elizabeth Edwards was diagnosed with breast cancer in 2004 at the age of 55. This sample was taken three years later.

Figure 9.7 is an enlargement of the original inked signature. Note two separate types of tremors in the writing: the large tremor in the z-loop at 8 o'clock and numerous more subtle tremors throughout the writing (see enlarged area at right). Here we see clearly the segmented pattern identified by Kanfer as an indication of cancer. Certainly a question remains as to whether or not this kind of segmented fine motor tremor can exist in the handwriting of people who are simply under stress, or that it might be caused by some other illness. However, in this instance, we know for sure that Ms. Edwards has cancer and she also has this tell-tale tremor.

What does it mean? If we consider that the brain is an antenna of sorts, monitoring the health of the organism, then it makes perfect sense that the brain would register the onset of any illness. Handwriting as a measure of neurological organization and fine motor control can thereby be seen as serving the same function that the canary does in the mineshafts. But Kanfer goes a step further. He states that different types of cancers will generate different types of tremors. Because the substantial nigra in the midbrain modulates fine motor control by supplying dopamine, one would guess that the tremor we see here in Elizabeth Edwards's handwriting may indeed be associated with some type of insult to that area of the brain. This would suggest the dopamine receptors might also be involved with the immune response. This theory is supported by L. Bryndon, et al., Department of Epidemiology, University of London, who conducted MRI studies of immune responses to vaccinations and their impact on this area of the brain.

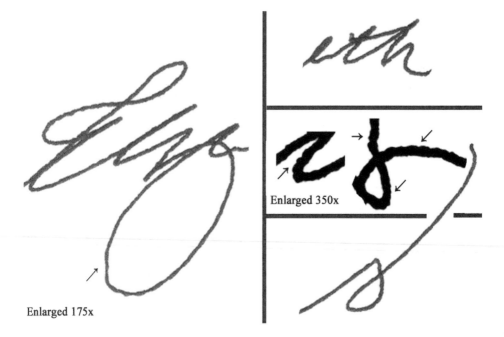

Enlarged 350x

Enlarged 175x

Figure 9.7. The handwriting of Elizabeth Edwards enlarged 175 and 350 times. Note two types of tremors: a larger tremor as seen on the bottom left side of the z-loop and a fine motor tremor throughout the entire script.

Handwriting, as a reflection of brain organization and neurophysiological processes, is certainly influenced by emotions, brain trauma and disease. In the case of cancer, Kanfer is stating that the study of handwriting can reveal its onset as much as five years before the disease is apparent in other ways. He also claims to classify "typical aberrations of stroke quality" for different cancers (Fluckiger, 1961). In an interview with Patricia Siegel, Israeli handwriting expert Arie Naftali, MD, suggested that the tremors Kanfer detected may be an indication of a breakdown in the immune system, rather than an indication of the cancer itself. One way or another, if we look at the brain as a kind of antenna, or sensing device, it would make perfect sense for it to know ahead of time that the organism is being attacked, and this trauma could affect fine motor control, and thus handwriting. Here is fertile ground for young researchers to study the link between cancer, the immune system, and the neurological apparatus involved in fine motor operations, for example, the substantia nigra, sensori-motor cortex, cerebellum, and parietal lobe (angular gyrus). In a rare interview, Kanfer stated:

> No matter what they call my test: cancer test, neuromuscular test, etc...it is still a handwriting test.... I cannot, and I do not want to deny that my work is closely related to graphology. I consider graphology my spiritual parent.
>
> —Alfred Kanfer

Difficulty in Testing

> Now and then, in the United States, come sporadic investigations of one or more claims made by graphologists, but regardless whether findings tended to support or to refute such claims, American psychologists in the main remain highly skeptical and largely indifferent to graphology as a testing device.
>
> —Rose Wolfson

Allport and Vernon (1933/1966) note that psychologists in America seldom take the findings of graphologists seriously. Rather, they tend to "regard handwriting as unrelated to the deep lying factors of personality, and as a product of essentially peripheral manual movement" (186). Written nearly 80 years ago, this statement is probably true today. For instance, Emery (1985) reported that findings of E. Karnes, chairman of the psychology department at Metropolitan State College, Los Angeles, who studied the so-called "Barnum effect" (names after the famous circus manager) whereby "people will rate as 'very accurate' any personality profile that is general and flattering, as long as they are led to believe it was written specifically for them" (1).

Karnes commissioned a Graphoanalyst to analyze the handwritings of nine individuals from a local business. Each person was then asked to choose his or her analysis. They were unable to do so beyond chance expectations. Karnes concluded that the use of Graphoanalysis (or graphology) could be "harmful" to corporations who may employ this diagnostic tool for personnel evaluations (2). Starting from a similar premise, Jansen (1973), a psychologist from the Netherlands, had 79 scripts analyzed for characteristics of "energetic versus weak." Using 10 graphologists, 10 psychologists, and 10 psychologists briefly trained in graphology, Jansen found "a positive, but very slight agreement between graphological judgments and business personnel ratings" (126). These, to Jansen, were "disappointing results... show[ing] precariously low reliability" (126).

An often-quoted study cited as disproving graphology (which lies as the basis for Karnes work) was by Hull and Montgomery (1919) whereby they had 17 fraternity brothers compare graphological analyses based on a copied paragraph to their own psychological assessment of such traits as ambition, bashfulness, and perseverance. Correlations (of –.016) were not significant. Allport and Vernon (1933/66) concluded that "the deficiencies of this method are so patent that one is neither surprised nor convinced of the negative result" (193). Yet, the poor status of graphology in America prevailed.

Part of the problem is associated with such variables as the intricacy and subtlety of personality investigations in general, the impreciseness of language, semantic differences in comprehending the meaning of the analysis, and also the caliber of the analyst. Wolfson (1951) wrote "clinical validation...[of handwriting analysis] does not yield satisfactorily [to] statistical treatment" (425). Many experimental studies performed by academically trained psychologists, however, have had positive findings. Harvey (1934), for instance, testing 50 college females with handwriting analysis, and measuring 26 variables, with the Thurstone Personality Schedule, obtained significant correlations. Binet (1907) and Eysenck (1942) found positive correlations between handwriting analysis and certain personality variables including intelligence and emotional stability. Lewinson and Zubin (1944) successfully differentiated between the handwritings of delinquent and non-delinquent students for such graphic traits as balance and extreme tendencies (for example, in size, slant, and pressure).

Wolfson (1951) recognized that there is a difficult problem in finding the meaning to variables that have been objectively delineated. Harvey (1934) questioned the reliability of relating a graphic trait to a personality variable, as the meaning of the graphic trait remains somewhat subjective and would vary based upon (a) the school of thinking that the analysis reflected; (b) the graphologist's psychological training; and (c) the insight of the graphologist. Graphology is a highly complex method of personality investigation.

Wolfson writes that handwriting analysis is "fundamentally a study of relationships. Absolute measures do not exist (442).... The central
problem...relates to evaluation and interpretation" (453).

Upstrokes and Downstrokes

Upstrokes and downstrokes, Sonnemann states, are executed as the hand
moves across the page in time. Contraction involves movement toward the
body and thus ego emphasis, volitional processes, control over emotions,
and cognitive functions. Releasing movements away from the body involves
spontaneity, object emphasis, impulsivity, and fantasy life. The structure of
individual letters, the person's backbone and expression of volitional control
are linked to the downstroke. The upstroke is mainly just a way to get to the
next downstroke. Thus, downstrokes are more linked to conscious procedures, whereas upstrokes are move unconscious procedures. In Sonnemann's
book, he clearly points out that, if all the upstrokes of writing are eliminated,
much of the writing is still legible; whereas, if all the downstrokes were
eliminated, the writing becomes illegible.

It is at this point that a leap to a discussion of brain organization can
occur. Downstrokes are apparently more linked to left brain activity, and
upstrokes more linked to right brain activity. This hypothesis is supported by
Jeanette Farmer, who suggests that contracted writers tend to be more left-
brain dominant, whereas released writers tend to be more right brained.

Taking it a step further, we know that language is centered in the left hemisphere, and pictures are more centered in the right. However, there is some
evidence from Luria (1980), that consonants are more left brain centered, and
vwls r mr rght bn cntred. Note that the last phrase is possible to read even
without the vowels. This is analogous to the fact that one can read handwriting
if all the downstrokes are present, but cannot do so if only upstrokes are present.

Abstracting from this work and discussions by Klages and Sonnemann
on rhythm, Seifer (2004, 2005) hypothesized that upstrokes would be a
more right brained process whereas downstrokes, which, akin to consonants,
really define the word, would be more linked to left brained processes. The
suggestion is that the up-down movement of handwriting and corresponding
changes in muscle groups would also be linked to language, inner speech,
automatization, and the dynamic interplay between left and right hemispheres.

What all of this suggests is the possibility that the process of language
and the creation of written speech—that is, handwriting—apparently involves
a close interplay of interhemispheric communication. The language center is
not just located in the left hemisphere, but involves both. An example of this
was pointed out by an associate of mine who suffered a temporary but debilitating stroke to the left temporal lobe, Broca's area, which is the language

center for speech production of his brain. He could "think" the alphabet, but he could not "say" the alphabet for a full 12 hours. Rhythm, which Klages tells us is the balance between contraction and release, therefore also suggests a balanced relationship between left and right hemispheres of the brain as well.

Taking this a step further, we can thus see that the concept of Connectedness is directly associated to the link between to conscious and unconscious processes, and perhaps, also, to the left and right hemispheres of the brain.

High Form Level scores would display natural connections, excellent organization, and rhythm of spatial arrangement. Neurophysiologically speaking, this would translate into well-coordinated inter-hemispheric communication, that is, easy access between left and right brains, conscious and unconscious processes, and well-developed areas of the different lobes of the brain such as the following four areas of the cerebral cortex:

1. Cerebral Cortex:
The most "human" part of the brain.

- Frontal lobes: where goals, higher cognitive processes, and abstract thinking is formed, and where motor output begins.

- Motor cortex: where muscle coordination is controlled.

- Temporal lobe: where sounds, words (left hemisphere), and music (right hemisphere) are processed.

- Occipital lobe or visual cortex: where words and letters, symbols, and images are formed.

- Parietal lobe: where coordination of these lobes will take place.

On two sides of the left temporal lobe are Broca's area, where speech is produced and Wernicke's area, where speech is comprehended. In brain-damaged individuals and those who suffer from dyslexia, there may not be easy access between the visual cortex and the temporal lobe and Wernicke's area. These types of people have difficulty reading words as they have trouble getting from the visual cortex to the region of the brain that can interpret what they have seen. Reading aloud helps offset this problem.

High Form Level involves an integrated use of emotional factors, and thus easy access to deeper brain centers such as found in the midbrain and brainstem.

2. Limbic Area:
Where emotions are tied in.

- Thalamus: the main switchboard of the brain that transfers information from the lower centers to the higher centers. It is also believed that one's self-image is tied to the thalamus.

‣ **Hypothalamus** (in the midbrain): controls sexual and aggressive drives, emotions, and link to the endocrine system, hormone production, and the pituitary gland.

3. Basal Ganglia:
Where important mechanical and instinctual aspects are organized.

‣ **Corpus Striatum** (in the brainstem): which is an inhibitor of instinctual drives.

‣ **Globus Pallidus** (in the brainstem): which is an expresser of instinctual drives.

‣ **Substantia nigra:** which produces dopamine sent to the rest of the basal ganglia for augmenting fine motor control.

4. Cerebellum:
Handwriting is initially organized in the cerebral cortex and is then transferred to the cerebellum via the thalamus as an automatized subroutine. Because this process is mostly a preconscious activity, symbolic correlates will be transferred as well.

A fifth area would include physical factors outside the brain such as, in the negative sense, any injury to the shoulder, arm, or hand.

High Form Level suggests that the writer would have a well-coordinated, integrated, and highly developed brain.

Figure 9.8. Prehistoric petroglyphs, writing and images created by removing rock by carving and engraving the stone.

Chapter 10
Handwriting and the Structure of the Brain ———

Language evolved as a social necessity, beginning with hand signals and facial expressions in conjunction with primitive vocalizations. If we tie language to tool-making, its onset would be at least a quarter of a million years old. From a neurological point of view, language always had a motor aspect through its active link to gesturing, speaking, and interacting with other brains. Handwriting is thus a natural outcropping from this already highly complex ingrained human procedure. The Russian neurologist A.R. Luria (1980) points out that the development of language allowed humans to create symbolic representations of events and physical objects. Through the process of "inner speech," unlike any other animal, man was freed from the confines of the present, to reflect upon the past, learn from others, and plan for the future. Luria goes so far as to say that the very acts of consciousness and voluntary behavior evolved because of the development of language, and, further, that using this process of thinking in words to organize the world, dramatically increased cerebral complexity. Quoting Pavlov, Luria concludes that "speech is the highest regulator of human behavior" (32). Handwriting can be seen as a further advance of this development.

The modern alphabet can trace its roots back 35,000 years, from awe-inspiring prehistoric cave drawings and more simplistic petroglyphs, to about 9,000 years ago with the advent of pictograms and hieroglyphics. As early as 6,000 years ago, merchants marked their property with Cuneiform signs on soft clay. Papyrus scrolls go back 5,000 years. Phoenician (which evolved into Hebrew) and Chinese writing trace their roots back about 4,000 years, Mayan writings appeared several thousand years later. About 1000 BC, the lean Greek and Latin alphabets came into being. This was a full millennium before the time of Christ. Along with the creation of the alphabet came handwriting. Where the Western culture creates their words with 26 letters, the Chinese have thousands of abstract symbols. Nevertheless, both groups have their predominant language center situated in the left hemisphere, although signatures and other graphic pictograms generally get transferred to, and/or are processed by the right hemisphere. Interhemispheric communication is a necessity because the essential picture of the event, or point being made, located in the right hemisphere, must be translated into the language center, located in the left.

Brain Writing

As a neuropsychological procedure, handwriting is an evolutionary culmination, and, as such, a tangible window to the complex interplay between mind and brain. If the brain is injured through accident or disease, it will affect the handwriting in specific ways, and conversely, in some instances, it may be possible to locate the site of the brain trauma from studying the handwriting. Higher mental processes are the given form in the act of handwriting.

Anatomically, the process of scrawling out a message is a complex voluntary procedure, engendering the cooperative efforts of all the lobes of the cerebral cortex with other parts of the brain. Seen as a five-stage procedure, this would involve (1) the cerebral cortex; (2) the thalamus, hypothalamus, and limbic system; (3) the basal ganglia and brainstem; (4) the cerebellum; and (5) the spinal cord, which sends the impulses out to the hands and fingers. An injury to any one of these parts will affect fine motor control, and show up as some type of break in rhythm or ataxia in the handwriting.

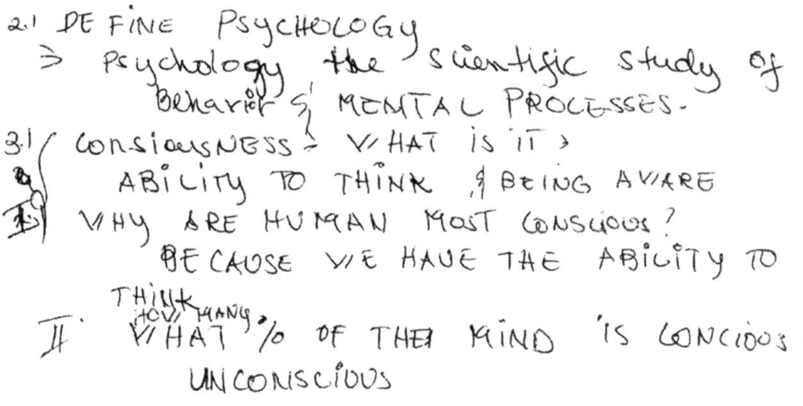

Figure 10.1. The handwriting of a 19-year-old recent émigré from the Philippines. What looks like some type of brain dysfunction is really caused by the confusion she is experiencing in her frontal, temporal, and parietal lobes, as she changes her culture, language, and handwriting from Filipino to English. The end result is a style that combines both. Most likely, through time, if the writer stays in the West, her handwriting will begin to lose some of the design features associated with the Filipino written language.

The sequence begins at the central control center in the frontal lobes in association with the limbic system for initiating the intent and emotional coloring of the communiqué, and for controlling the onset of the motor sequence. Figure 10.2 shows a flow chart of the different brain centers, reduced from the five stages above into the following three: (1) cerebral cortex; (2) mid-brain/limbic system; and (3) brainstem. All subcortical impulses go through the thalamus to get to the cerebral cortex.

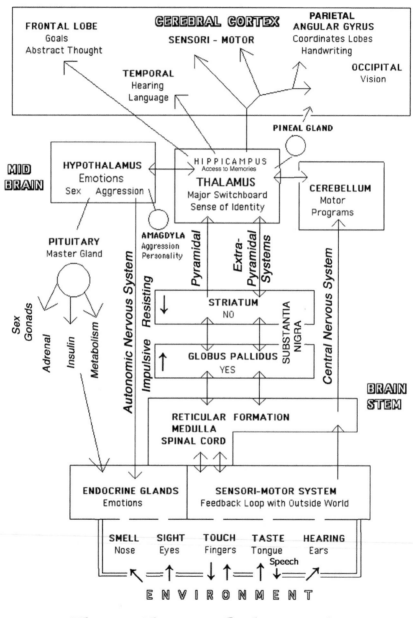

Flow Chart of the Brain

© 2008 Marc J. Seifer

Figure 10.2.

A person's mood, for example, uplifted or dejected, will affect motor output. This control center is closely tied to Broca's and Wernicke's areas of the temporal lobe for speech production and comprehension, the occipital lobe for seeing the page and for picturing associated ideas, and the parietal lobe writing center, which includes the left angular gyrus, for converting visual perception of letters into the comprehension of words. The parietal lobe is also involved in the global coordination of all these lobes with the motor cortex, which has specific areas for arm, hand, and finger movements.

The downward track of the extrapyramidal and pyramidal nervous systems, which monitor gross and fine motor control, will pass through a second level that comprises a multifaceted interplay of limbic system regions that include the amygdala for regulating aggression, temperament, and other aspects of personality; the thalamus, which is the main switching center for the brain, and also an area now believed to be associated with one's self-image; and a very complex system tied to the hypothalamus and pituitary gland. This area involves the endocrine system and the sympathetic and parasympathetic nervous systems, which, as a unit, controls neurotransmitter and hormone production for regulating mood, behavior, metabolism, and movement.

Below the thalamus are the basal ganglia structures that include the caudate nucleus, putamen and globus pallidus, and the sub-thalamic substantia nigra, which supplies dopamine to the neurotransmitter on this third tier for the modification of fine motor control. There are also proprio-kinesthetic feedback mechanisms linked to the cerebellum, the reticular formation for modifying consciousness, and the continuing downward path of the extrapyramidal and pyramidal track, which passes through contralateral connections in the medulla en route to the spinal cord, arm, hand, and fingers.

Add to this the corpus callosum for connecting pictorial/holistic right brain procedures with sequential/linguistic left brain counterparts, along with the hippocampus for memory retrieval, parts of the brainstem for expression of primitive impulses and unconscious desires—the pons, for instance, has a motor aspect, but also controls dreaming with a feedback loop to the pineal gland for serotonin and melatonin production—and the thalamus for augmenting the transfer of this hierarchical functional complex to the fourth tier, the cerebellum, where the entire process is reprogrammed as a habit or subroutine. Note that the cerebellum, by necessity, not only contains the physical aspects of this repetitive psychomotor pattern, that is, the automatic procedure of handwriting, but also the intrinsically linked psycho-social aspect. Handwriting or "written language" is not an isolated muscular function, but rather, a dynamic representation of a complex process of thought that is as Vygotsky (in Luria) suggests, "social in origin." Just like speech, handwriting is taught through interaction with other people. It is thus influenced by social and environmental variables as well as by the person's own neurological architecture.

"Handwriting starts out as a chain of isolated motor movements, but it is radically altered with practice, and converted into a 'kinetic melody' no longer requiring the memorizing of the visual form of each [separate] letter or motor impulse for making every stroke" (Luria, 1973). Thus, its cerebral organization changes by becoming more deeply ingrained, yet at the same time it requires less energy to execute. The process of handwriting, according to Nielsen (1962), is located on the border between the occipital and parietal lobes. It is a multi-layered dynamic kinesthetic memory involving the picturing of how the letters are formed (supramarginal gyrus), how it looks (occipital lobe), and how it feels (motor cortex/parietal lobe) to move the pen across the page (29).

As one writes, inner speech plays a crucial role. Figure 10.3 is the writing of a 20-year-old warm-hearted female community college student with a severe

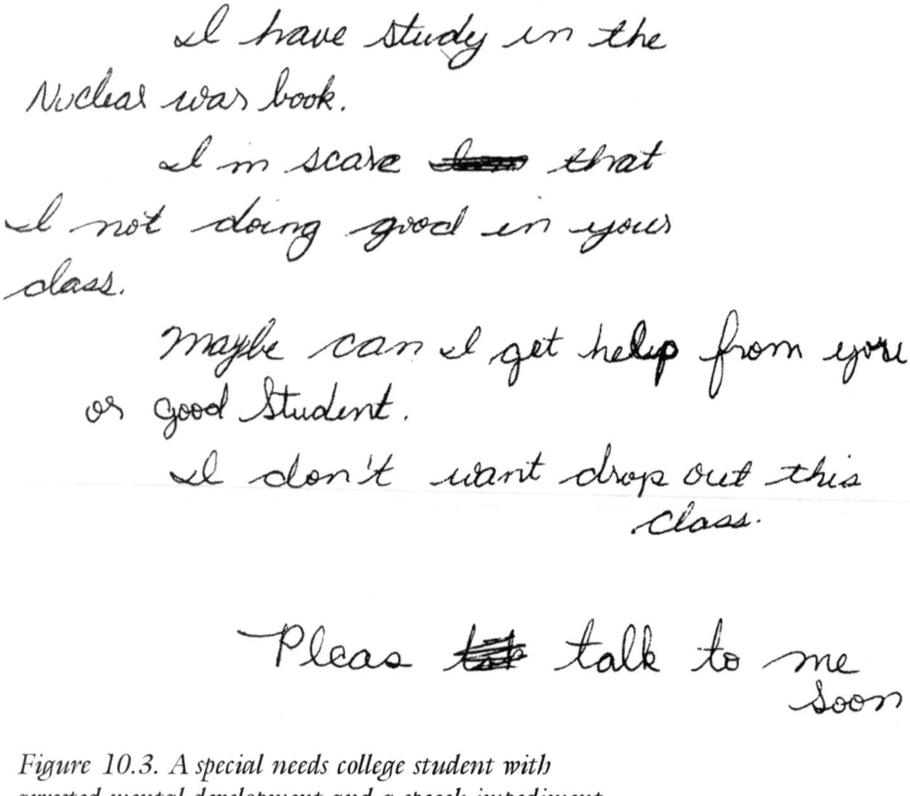
I have study in the Nuclear war book.
I m scare that I not doing good in your class.
maybe can I get help from you or good Student.
I don't want drop out this class.
Pleas talk to me soon

Figure 10.3. A special needs college student with arrested mental development and a speech impediment.

learning disability. She also has a speech impediment, is dyslexic, and, most likely, has auditory aphasia. She can take up to two hours to partially complete a 45-minute exam. When she speaks, the subject leaves off the ends of many words. This tendency is reflected in the handwriting where she writes the word *scare*. Because she doesn't say "scared," when she speaks, she doesn't hear the *d*, and so does not write it. Her dyslexia is seen in the next sentence where the word *I* is placed in the wrong part of the sentence. One would guess that she has a dysfunction in her frontal lobes and in Wernicke's area (speech comprehension), which, in turn, has caused a problem in Broca's area (speech production) and also, no doubt, the left angular gyrus whose task it is to combine speech with the visual perception of words and their kinesthetic output.

The first attempts to explore the relationship between handwriting and neurological organization were performed by William Preyer. Preyer was an Englishman by birth and German university professor, who, in 1895, established that handwriting was really brain writing. Preyer proved this by demonstrating that the basic pattern of one's script stays the same if the person writes with the hand, the foot, or mouth. Figure 10.4 was written at the age of 32 by Joni Earekson, author of *Joni: The Unforgettable Story of a*

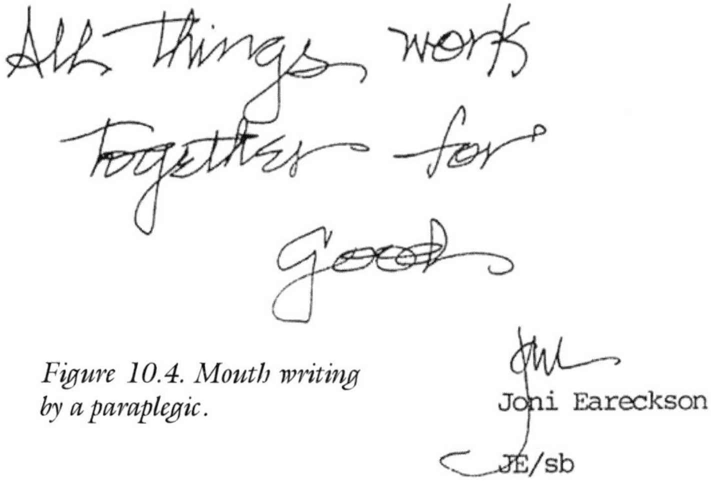

Figure 10.4. Mouth writing by a paraplegic.

Young Woman's Struggle Against Quadriplegia and Depression, who held the pen adeptly between her teeth to produce this message.

This extraordinary example of mouth writing was written 15 years after she was injured in a diving accident. An artist and horseback rider before the tragedy, it is known that the pleasing aesthetic aspect stemmed from a similar style, which she had developed with her hand in the normal way before her injury. The automatized aspects of her handwriting, augmented by some mobility of her shoulders, was simply shifted from the pyramidal fibers that control the hand to the ones that control the neck and mouth.

The Preconscious in Handwriting

The preconscious is a complex theoretical structure located between the Freudian conscious and the unconscious. It is a realm that encompasses latent memories, the censor, the defense structure, symbolic behavior, and the automatism. Graphologically, preconscious automatisms can be seen as habitual psychomotor movements and/or as written symbols. These, in turn, have neurological and psychological counterparts. Handwriting crosses that border between thoughts and physical expression. This chapter explores the nature of that crossover.

Since William Preyer's times, it has been found that the organization of each of our psychophysiological functions is localized in different areas of the brain. Handwriting, although a unified procedure, is also made up of component parts. As a psychomotor procedure, it utilizes each of the following lobes of the cerebral cortex for different purposes.

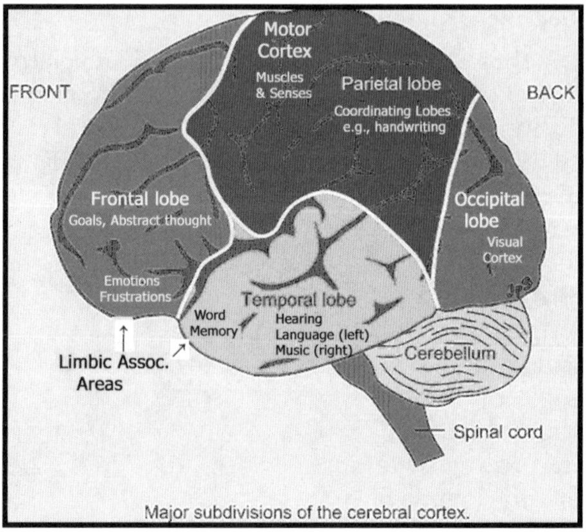

Frontal lobes situated in the forehead are involved with all higher thought processes including goals, reasoning, and abstract ability. It initiates volitional action and me-

Figure 10.5. The five major lobes of the cerebral cortex.

diates intentional and/or other conscious activities, and therefore analyzes information from all other areas of the cerebral cortex. Note in particular the limbic association area. This has two divisions: emotions stemming from the hypothalamus (sex and aggression), insula, and amygdala (temperament and anger).

Motor and sensory areas are located atop the head, midway between the frontal cortex and the occipital lobe. Made up of giant pyramidal cells that are involved with movement, the motor areas contain motor neurons that direct the movement from the brain to the muscles of the hand and body. The sensory pathway takes the information from the hand and brings it back to the brain. This area has an input (sensory)/output (motor) system.

The **occipital lobe** is also called the visual cortex. Located in the back of the brain, the occipital lobe contains the projection area for all visual data. Dreaming produces EEG activity on the occipital lobe as well. The process of mentally or physically visualizing letters is carried by this area of the brain.

The **temporal lobes** situated on the sides of the head above the ears, analyze acoustical data as well as verbally related procedures involved in language comprehension and thinking. The left temporal lobe contains the speech center whereas the corresponding right temporal lobe contains the music center. Two important subdivisions:

1. **Broca's area** involved in speech production, located between the left temporal and frontal lobes.

2. **Wernicke's area** associated with speech comprehension, located between the temporal lobe and visual cortex.

The Parietal lobe is involved with eye/hand coordination, spatial organization, and simultaneous synthesis. During the act of handwriting, this area, also called the **left angular gyrus**, coordinates input from the occipital and temporal lobes, thereby aiding integration of the seeing and mentally "saying" of words and letters as one writes. Simply stated, reading and handwriting are predominantly coordinated in the left angular gyrus.

Psychophysiology of Handwriting

The well-known Soviet neurophysiologist Alexander Luria tells us that for a movement to take place, there must be constant corrections and, thus, a feedback loop between sensory and motor areas. Every **movement** has the character of a **complex functional system**. This "system" is dynamic and flexible. Its holistic structure accounts for Preyer's discovery of the similarity of hand, foot, and mouth writing. "The same results can be achieved by different methods" (Luria, 1973). Therefore, the concept of localization of a function, such as handwriting, does not have only one focus, but incorporates the entire cortex.

The thought of writing originates in the frontal lobes where goals and intentions can be found. It is visually and mentally seen in the occipital lobe, makes use of language located in the temporal lobe, is manually executed by the motor cortex, and is coordinated as a single action of the parietal lobe. Certainly, handwriting is brain writing. It utilizes individual areas as well as the total brain in its production. This displays the holistic ability of the brain to create a complex act by dynamically integrating each specialized area of the cerebral cortex with all other areas.

> During ontogeny, writing initially consists of complete expanded series of manipulative movements which gradually become condensed and have acquired the character of mental inner actions. As a rule they are based on external aids such as language [and other forms of social interaction].... They are mediated by them and cannot, in general, be conceived without their participation.
>
> —Lev Vygotsky in Luria, 1973

Luria (1970) tells us why **mental functional systems** "cannot be localized in narrow zones of the cortex or isolated cell groups." Instead, he says, complex functional systems such as bike riding, thought, and inner speech "must be organized in systems of **concertedly working zones**, each of which performs its role in complex functional systems and which may be located in completely different and often distant areas of the brain" (30). In the case of the process of handwriting, it is not located in the left angular gyrus, but rather coordinated there. Stated differently, Werner Wolff (1948/63) tells us that "an individual's movements are the result of specific muscle groups.... There is a reflection of inner relationships" (21). Handwriting reveals intracerebral coordination, but handwriting is even more than brain writing.

Mind Writing

Handwriting as a psychophysiological mechanism reflects the organization of the physical brain as well as the psychology of the mind. On the **biological side**, it expresses various neurological mechanisms of the various lobes of the cerebral cortex, hemispheric dominance, influence of the mid-brain, brainstem, endocrine system, and so forth; on the **psychological side**, it displays conscious, preconscious, and unconscious aspects of the psyche. Handwriting lies on that magical border between mental reality and physical actuality. The will, which is related to the intentional aspects of the instincts and ego, also lies on this border. In a derivative or Jungian sense, handwriting as a symbolic expression also reveals the personality of the species. Just as mind interacts with matter through the brain, thoughts are transcribed into physical reality through handwriting.

Psychology and Neurophysiology of the Preconscious

The preconscious is a theoretical construct originally postulated by Freud. It is a complex domain with many components to it. The PCS (preconscious) mediates between the CS (conscious), which has access to the outer world, and the UCS (unconscious), which taps the mental world. Therefore, the preconscious lies between inner and outer reality. It houses all latent memories (that is, ones that can be brought to the surface) and contains the censor or mediator between the CS and UCS. The censor contains the defense structure that decides which information should or should not reach consciousness (self-awareness). Because the PCS houses the censor, it can also be thought to contain the superego.

A highly repressed person will have a strong defense against his unconscious and therefore a rigid preconscious. Palmer scripts, abundance of covering strokes, and monotony would be indications of an inflexible PCS.

Looking at Figure 10.6, note the slow, arcaded writing. There is an overabundance of covering strokes as well as extreme slant to the right. This is the writing of a repressed young man who is afraid to be alone or think independently. His censor is symbolized by the stop sign and the dead end sign. His

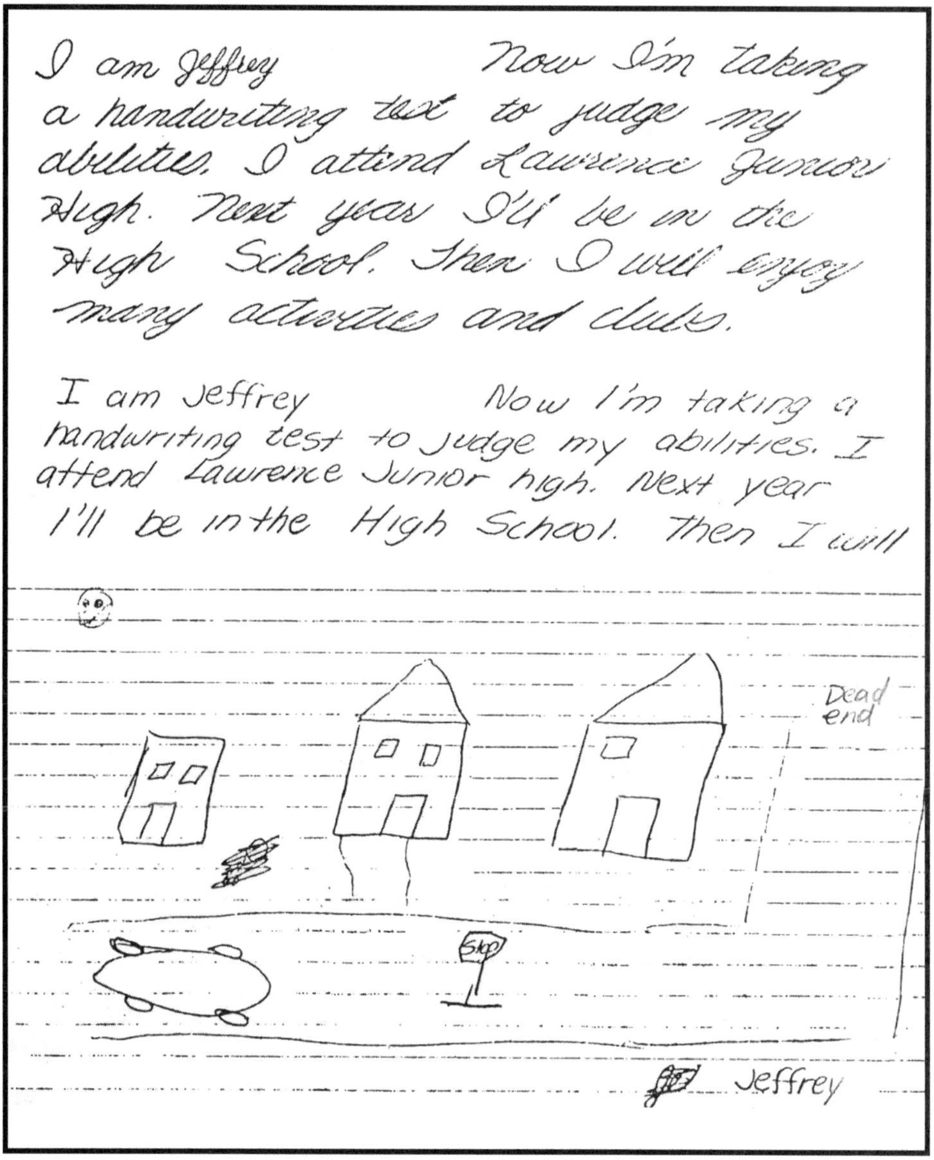

Figure 10.6. The handwriting, printscript, and drawing of a 12-year-old boy.

creative unconscious is being guarded too strictly by a strong defense structure. Although, the drawing lacks imagination, and the writing appears monotonous, the printing shows some flexibility and independence of thought noted by the simplified capital *I*'s and by the rebellious disregard for the i-dots. This boy is in a transitionary stage and that his censor, although strict, does enjoy some flexibility. There is a clear battle here between pressures to conform (top cursive handwriting) and a tendency toward individual expression (bottom printscript).

Conscious

The conscious (CS) has two functions. It is an organ of awareness, and it is also an apparatus that gives the UCS (unconscious) access to motility (that is, to the physical body). Consciousness as a process is actually, for Freud, a function of the UCS. Thus, in an ironic sense, Freud's UCS is linked to intentionality and self-awareness through its CS apparatus. Note that it is possible to use the CS apparatus and not be conscious, for example, sleep-walking, hypnosis, or driving past one's exit on the highway. One can be conscious of inner or outer states as well. The more CS, the more one is aware of and makes use of the UCS, but also, the more purposefully one's fate is directed. The layout of the page of writing, and the general direction of the total movement is a conscious procedure. Slow scripts are more self-conscious than faster ones.

Preconscious

By definition all memories we can remember are in the preconscious (PCS). The PCS also houses the censor and thus the defense structure. The PCS is the repository of the automatism and corresponding prelogical be-havior patterns. To continue one of the previous examples, if one drives past one's exit on a highway, that person, caught up in some reverie (for example, talking on a cell phone), is driving preconsciously. These ideas are explained in more depth in the following paragraphs.

Unconscious

The UCS houses all memories we cannot remember because they are forgotten or because they are repressed. At the same time, Freud tells us that the UCS is the true psychic reality. Our real self (our soul) is hidden in the unconscious. Consciousness can be thought of as one of many functions of the all-inclusive unconscious. In the same sense, the PCS is actually also part of the UCS. The UCS is *everything*, but it has PCS and CS aspects to it. The UCS continues to think during the day while consciousness naively consid-ers the UCS to lie dormant. We as graphologists and psychologists know that the UCS contains a great percentage of one's motivating impetus.

Freud compared the iceberg, which is 90 percent below the surface, to the UCS. In a sense, the UCS is an iceberg with part of itself above the surface. This corresponds to the CS, which is really part of the UCS. We are essentially unconscious beings.

All that is repressed is in the UCS. It is through the (PCS) or the censor that UCS thoughts must pass in order to reach either self-realization or self-expression. In Freudian terms, this *release* of unconscious energy is called a **hypercathexis**. It is the function of the censor and defense structure to **countercathect** or *oppose* the release of this energy. Although the censor is asleep at night, these repressed thoughts tend to surface, although they are still distorted by the weakened censor; but because consciousness tends also to be asleep, most dreams, although released through the CS apparatus (that is, hypercathected), are barely and rarely consciously perceived. We tend to remember a small percentage of our dreams.

CS and PCS movements are learned, but the overall pattern of movement is neither CS or PCS.

> We cannot bring to consciousness why we incline a certain letter, why we put the dot over the i in a certain place, why we emphasize a curve.... While the direction of the total movement is CS and single steps are PCS, its form and quality are UCS.
>
> —Werner Wolff

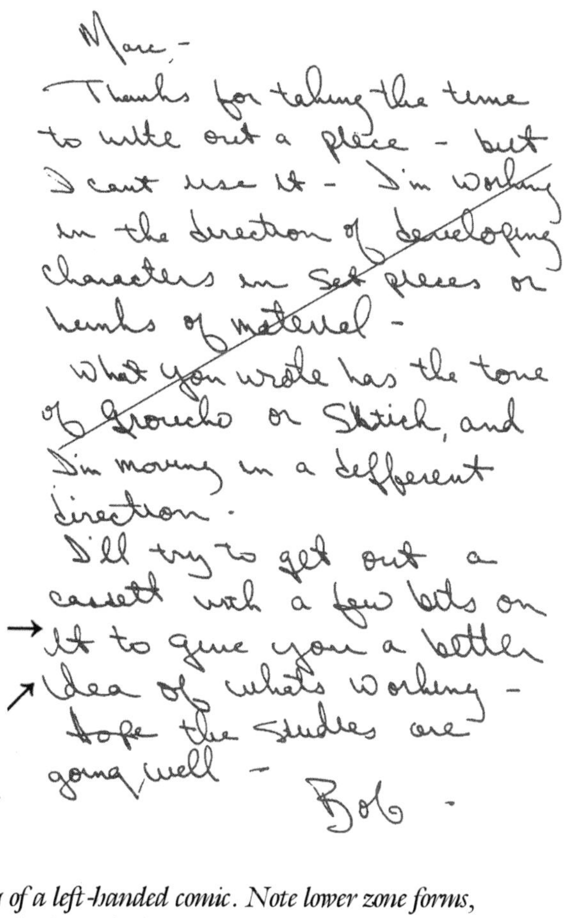
Marc -
Thanks for taking the time
to write out a piece - but
I cant use it - I'm working
in the direction of developing
characters in set pieces or
hunks of material -
What you wrote has the tone
of Groucho or Shtick, and
I'm moving in a different
direction.
I'll try to get out a
cassett with a few bits on
it to give you a better
idea of whats working -
hope the studies are
going well -
Bob -

Figure 11.1. The handwriting of a left-handed comic. Note lower zone forms, rhythmical integration, and emphasis on the lowercase i *as in "it" and "idea" on the left side of the last paragraph. The word* of *lines up diagonally down the page in spectacular synchronistic fashion, and this same automation can be found in his signature.*

In order to fool the censor, the UCS may use defense mechanisms, such as displaced aggression, denial, rationalization, reaction formation, and intellectualization. During the day, this tendency to circumvent the censor and release tension may result in prelogical or symbolic behavior patterns, for example, quirks. At night, when the censor is weakened by sleep, the repressed material may be disguised, and thereby released, by various primary process maneuvers during dreaming, for example, substitution, compression, or representation by the opposite. Similar kinds of hypercathexis of repressed material can take place through the symbolic act of handwriting.

Figure 11.1 is that of a left-handed, 26-year-old successful comedian and comedy sitcom/screenplay writer. It is replete with symbolic psychomotor expressions stemming from the preconscious. At the time of this writing, two years before he actually established himself, there may have been some displaced aggression or feelings of competition toward the addressee. This is evident in the heavy pressured downstroke of the M of Marc. Bob was just starting out in the entertainment business at the time and wanted to control his ego drives. His hidden or disguised need for recognition is evident in many of the lowercase *i*'s, which force themselves into the upper zone, that is, they become disguised capital *I*'s. Bob wants to be humble, so the displaced ego drives, evident in the handwriting, are also evident in his controlled discussions concerning his rise in the entertainment profession. The angular lower loops seen especially in the letters *g* and *y* near bottom of page, relate to his rebellion from the ways of the parents as well as to his aggressive

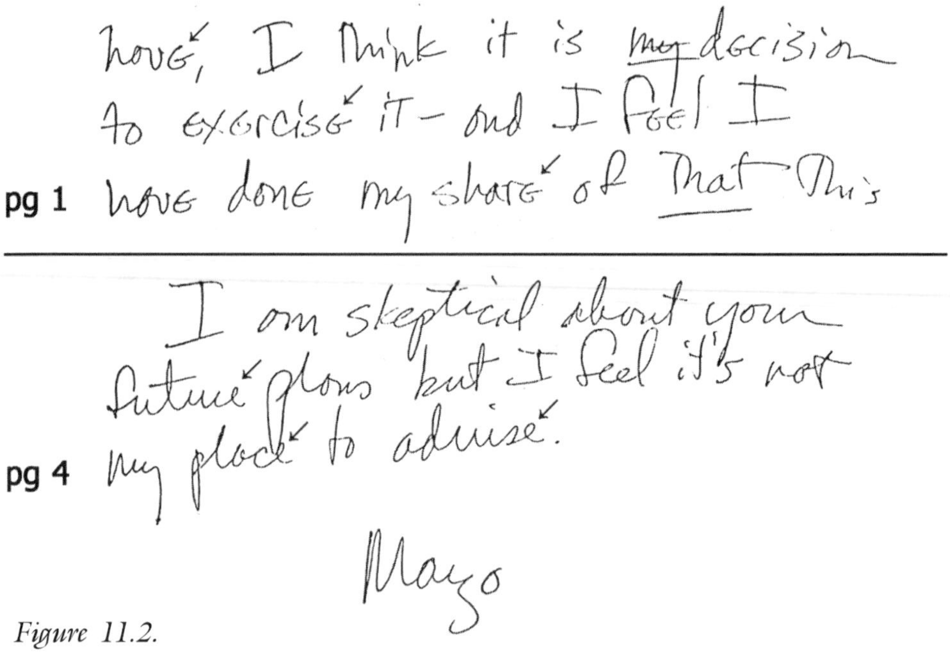

Figure 11.2.

sexual humor. The rhythmical integration and emphasized rightward trend reflects his conscious motivation to succeed in a difficult field, keen interest in music, and in the timing that a comic must have to get his laugh. The aesthetically pleasing pattern is reflective of a dynamically creative unconscious.

Figure 11.2 contains an analogous type of prelogical or symbolic psychomotor movement in that the writer tries to emphasize the ego without doing it overtly. Both sections of this sample are part of the same four-page letter. The top part is from page one. Note curious G-like *e*'s throughout this sample, and their total absence in the last, more spontaneously written page. Her signature has a prominent *G* in it. And so the G-like *e*, although chosen consciously for aesthetic reasons, was actually intrinsically motivated by unconscious ego drives.

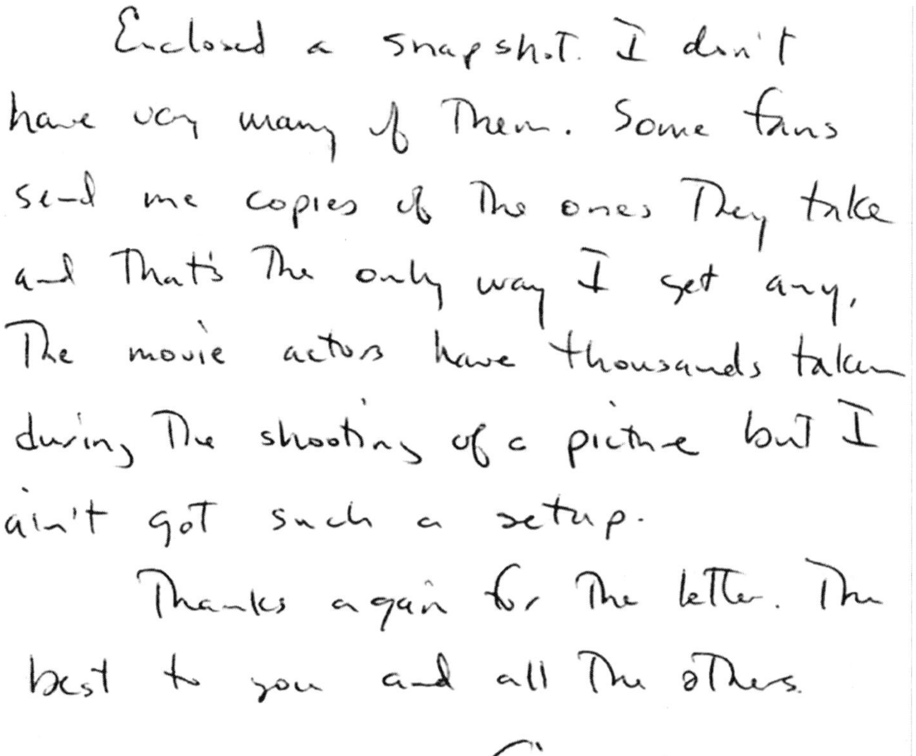
Enclosed a snapshot. I don't have very many of them. Some fans send me copies of the ones they take and that's the only way I get any. The movie actors have thousands taken during the shooting of a picture but I ain't got such a setup.

Thanks again for the letter. The best to you and all the others.

Sincerely
Paul Newman

Figure 11.3. The fluid handwriting of 30-year-old TV actor Paul Newman from May 1955. He had completed just one motion picture at that time.

It is an inventive letter, but also it is a disguised pat on the back. Due to the multidimensional nature of symbols, this letter also displays a creative unconscious, which serves to express her individuality, while also circumventing preconscious defenses involving feelings of inferiority. Note also the overly large capital I's. This young lady is an identical twin and clearly needs to assert her uniqueness. In attempting to adapt this G-like *e* into her writing, Margo is trying to produce an original and spontaneous graphic pattern. But it is a fad, and the artifice will be unsuccessful because of its contrived nature. The proof is her inability to maintain false airs throughout the duration of the text.

The Automatism

Besides housing the censor and latent memories, the preconscious, in physiological terms, also contains the automatisms that are learned responses that develop after practice. These habits or gestures contain our idiosyncrasies, and also our individuality. They display how the person mediates between conscious, spontaneous, and inhibited psychomotor movement patterns.

In Figure 11.3, note the rapidity of the writing, its simplification and abundance of such automatisms as the *th* combination, the thready *m*'s and *n*'s, and the simple downstrokes to replace the loops on the lower zone letters. To continue the analysis, we see several dichotomies. For instance, the writing is small and linear, suggesting a technical nature, but this is offset by a broad pastose stroke, which is the choice stroke of the artist. The capital *I*'s are small, yet the signature is quite large. At just age 30, and by this time a successful TV actor, Newman already has a high opinion of himself and his abilities. The handwriting drops off a little at the ends of the lines, but the signature is on an upslant. He is ambitious and enthusiastic, but beneath there is a sober side and some sense of isolation (separated letters). Another contradiction is the large capital P as compared to a smaller *N*. Paul is asserting himself over his father who ran a successful sporting goods store of which Paul wanted no part. This suggests some alienation from the father, which is echoed by the wide spacing between words, again supporting the contention of some sense of isolation. In this instance, the content of the letter is key. He has simply decided to send an everyday snapshot of himself to a fan. He's a good soul, with a fine sense of humor, and this is seen by the overall fluid, curved writing and its spontaneity. In touch with his inner self, Newman likes people and respects the average man.

A certain "trust" of unconscious processes and instinctual mechanisms are required in the development of PCS automatisms. They are learned responses, which are developed with practice over time.

> Just as we are unaware of single steps made by our moving
> feet, and just as we do not plan the movement of our typing
> of piano playing hand, so we are unaware of single writing

movements…. They are automatized and function almost without direction of the details…. Our impulse is: get this object, walk to that goal, play this music…. How the general command which we give ourselves is fulfilled usually lies beyond our attentions… but these single movements can be brought into consciousness—what is PCS can be made CS.

—Werner Wolff

Werner Wolff says that we are preconscious of each step of the writing, but that CS and PCS movements are learned. The PCS develops through time; because it houses the censor (which is guided by the superego), the PCS is under the direct influence of the demands of the environment. For example, if the society suggests that "one should not be egocentric," the UCS id forces could influence the PCS to emphasize egocentricity through a disguised fashion. Graphically this is seen as large lowercase *i*'s in Figure 11.1 and the G-like *e*'s in Figure 11.2.

Automatisms are mental as well as physical expressions. They are adapted for efficient operation of our bio-psychological machine. Heinz Hartmann describes them this way: "Physiological automatisms facilitate the transformation and the saving of energy. The success of many complicated achievements in central mental regions depends on automatization. Purposeful achievements depend on some functions taking a flexible form, others an automatized form, and still others combining these two forms in various proportions."

Habitual forms of behavior, says Hartmann, are "relatively stable" ways for the individual to adapt to the environment, which to a great extent modifies and even controls the automatism. Located in the preconscious, the automatism is

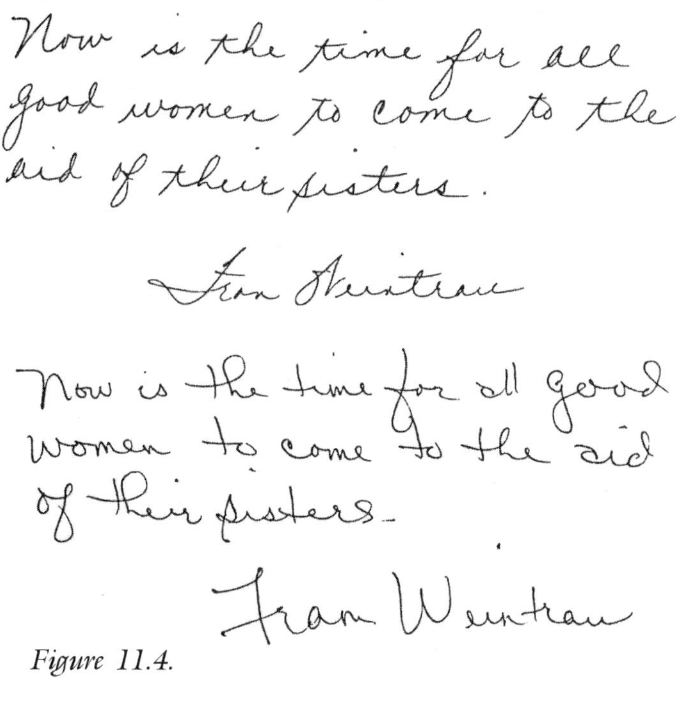

Figure 11.4.

under the sway of the censor, whose job it is to protect the ego of the individual by somehow reconciling powerful id impulses with the dictates of society. In that sense, automatisms "function as a stimulus barrier in the mental apparatus" holding these instinctual urges in check (91). The problem is, the more powerful the censor and the more coalesced the automatism, the more likely that creative forces will be held at bay as well. This would be seen in a more controlled or regulated handwriting as compared to one that is dynamic and rapidly written.

Figure 10.7, young Jeffrey's handwriting, shows its arcadedness and adherence to the Palmer method. These automatisms are certainly stimulus barriers preventing individualized expressions, whereas the egocentric automatisms in Figure 11.1, Bob (his *i*'s) and Figure 11.2, Margo (her G-like *e*'s), are actually displaying an underlying non-conformist streak expressed to satiate the demands of the UCS ego drives.

Figure 11.4 displays the ability of the PCS to mediate between the demands of inner needs versus outer reality. The upper writing is the one this 19-year-old girl usually uses. Note the Palmer script, beginning strokes, and arcadedness. This script obviously shows conformity to the demands of the environment.

The writer stated that the top sample was her "normal" handwriting. The lower writing is just something she "fools around with"! Note the numerous positive changes in the lower script. The middle zone is larger and more full, the writing stands up taller, the capitals are original and simplified, and unusual letter forms appear that enhance the writing, such as the elegantly simplified highly original "a" in "aid," line 2. As soon as the demands of the inner (true) self emerge, the entire structure of the writing, and also the cerebral organization, changes and new automatisms appear. Beginning strokes are abandoned, angles replace arcades, loops are dropped, and original forms appear. This young lady's PCS defense structure is one of suppression rather than repression. The upper handwriting now can be seen to display a coping mechanism rather than unconscious defense mechanism. Her automatization displays an adaptable ego, which has not yet decided to truly align itself with the individualized personality that is seeking unfoldment, but rather she hides her originality because of her perception of the repressing demands of a conforming society. Her PCS adapts both to the demands of society and that of the self, and has not allowed one to rule out the other. Graphologically we can see that with a disciplined yet flexible mind, the demands of the self yield a more creative expression, the lower handwriting displaying more advanced automatization.

Automatisms are highly important in understanding the economical structure of the psyche, for they allow one to think and write at the same time.

Their central organization must therefore lie in the parietal lobe (left angular gyrus), which, we remember, deals with simultaneous synthesis. Once learned, such automatisms as walking, biking, step climbing, handwriting, typing, piano playing, and probably some aspects of talking and social forays, are also reprogrammed in the cerebellum, a lower brain center.

> As the child develops any type of complex conscious activity, at first it is expanded in character and requires a number of external aids for its performance [such as mouthing the letters and words to the self as one writes].... Not until later does it gradually become condensed and converted into an automatic motor skill.

> —Alexander Luria

Concerning handwriting and the process of automatization in the initial stages (ages 4 to 7) "every sound or speech...is associated with a definite visual image or a letter" or word (Luria, 1973, 79). From hearing the letter or word, a mental picture is created and transformed into a kinesthetic response, and, at the same time, all lobes of the cerebral cortex participate in the activity. The frontal lobes deal with the goal of writing, the motor cortex controls the muscles, the occipital lobe allows the child to see what he is doing, the temporal lobe locates the specific letter or word being acted upon, and the parietal lobe coordinates the entire activity.

Each lobe has three layers to it:

1. **The primary projection area,** which receives impulses and first impressions, and transmits impulses to other locations.
2. **The secondary association layer** where incoming information is processed, prepared, and catalogued.
3. **A tertiary association layer** that is less localized, is deeper in the cortex, and is in greater connection to surrounding lobes.

So, for instance, when the child writes the letter a: a a a a a a a, his whole brain and a good part of his body, such as his hand, arm, shoulders, and maybe even his head is actively involved in drawing a perfect circle, adding a downstroke, and saying the letter "a," and then performing the activity again and again sounding "a," "a," "a" as he practices. Eventually, the process sinks into the secondary and then the tertiary layers of the brain, and the process becomes more and more condensed and automatic thereby freeing the primary projection area so that the person can think and/or perceive his environment even as he writes: *aaaa.* Writing starts out as a chain of isolated motor movements, but with practice the process is radically altered and writing is converted into a "kinetic melody" no longer requiring the memorizing of the visual form of each isolated letter or individual motor impulses for making every stroke. Similar changes take place also during the development of the higher psychological processes, which changes its cerebral organization.

Alexander Luria said, "The participation of the auditory and visual areas of the cortex, essential to the early states of formation of [this] activity is no longer necessary in its later staged and the activity starts to depend on different systems of concertedly working zones. During ontogeny [i.e., during the growth of the child] it is not only the structure of higher mental processes, which changes, but also their relationship with each other, i.e., their interfunctional organization."

Luria is stating that a beginning writer such as a young child organizes his writing in different areas of the brain than mature, practiced writers. Automatisms reflect a special interfunctional organization and integration of the cerebral cortex, so that in order to adapt a new letter into a script, as Margo tries to do, there is actually a cerebral restructuring and regression back to a former model of operation until the letter becomes fully automatized and thus is produced subconsciously.

The use of automatisms displays the hierarchical nature of the cerebral cortex. As the formation of a letter becomes a preconscious procedure, the conscious is freed once more so that more intricate forms of thinking can take place. While writing, for example, one can think about the content of the page rather than how each letter or word is formed. The variations and inventiveness of the automatisms can also display a dynamically flexible cerebral cortex, one that is able to shift gears and learn to deal with its deeper strata.

The paradox is that, although automatisms are consciously learned, they reflect UCS processes because the CS is trying to learn how to produce the same movement unconsciously. Once automatisms are achieved, less energy is used in their creation (as in cursive writing, driving, playing the piano, and so on) and so consciousness can begin to operate on other levels while the PCS takes care of the rest.

Kinetic Melodies

Luria states that signatures are automatic "kinetic melodies." They take an ideographic form and are so impressed into the psyche that they are no longer simply perceived by the language-centered left hemisphere, but are actually transferred over to the more abstract, symbolically oriented right hemisphere.

Words, abbreviations, and logos such as STOP, USA, GULF, NBC, and ETC are also ideograms, which are perceived holistically and therefore penetrate into deeper layers of the psyche. Because of their symbolic stature, they

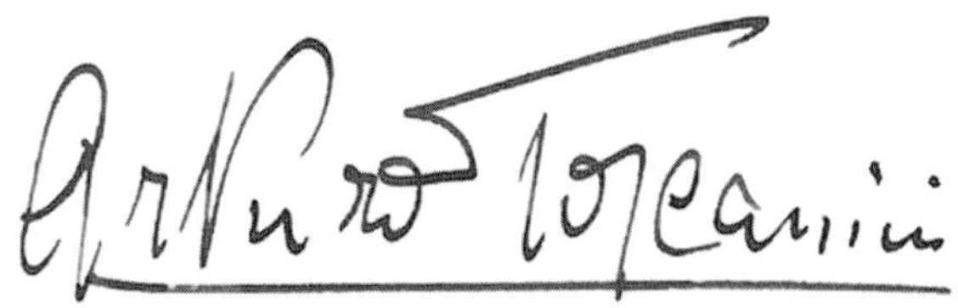

Figure 11.5. The signature of Italian cellist and conductor Arturo Tuscanini. Note the rich originality, pictorial quality, creative letter forms (for example, the t in the first name), the highly rhythmical nature of the script, and the symbol of the conductor and his baton as the o in the first name becomes the T-bar in the last name. This is just a wonderful example of an energetic, dynamic, and artistically advanced autograph.

too are shifted to the right non-verbal hemisphere and are perceived as ideas or pictures rather than mere words. From this we can deduce that the automatism involves more abstract and deeper layers of the psyche, and, correspondingly, use of the non-verbal right hemisphere (and also use of the left hemisphere's parietal lobe/angular gyrus, which is involved with simultaneous synthesis).

Automatization reflects psychophysiological restructuring and thus different use of the brain as a whole and also as the sum of its parts. Automatization develops through practice, but can act as a stimulus barrier if the demands of the environment prevent flexible use of the PCS. Automatisms also become ideograms, or symbols reflecting deeper layers of the psyche, for example, the limbic association area in the lower part of the frontal lobes where emotions are catalogued. Pictorially, through the PCS, automatisms portray CS and UCS (repressed) desires and needs. This is because the PCS is influenced by the CS as well as the UCS. All handwriting is automatized; it is the degree of automatization—its rigidity or flexibility and inventiveness—that reflects the dynamic interchange between the demands of the self (in the UCS) and the demands of the environment (perceived by the CS). The meeting ground is the preconscious. If we define the self as the ego it is the PCS aspects of the ego that we are talking about.

Symbolism

Written language, as an advanced form of human communication, developed out of the ancient cave drawings, which were attempts by our ancestors to portray objects and important events from their lives. These, in turn, evolved into the pictorial hieroglyphics of the Egyptians, the less concrete forms as found in the Chinese and Hebrew alphabets, and the more abstract characters as seen in the Latin alphabet. Wolff (1948/65) notes that letters live beyond the individual, and thus transcend time and space. "In ancient times, letters had a magic value and were considered symbols of conjuration from the innermost depths of existence." Writing displays not only intentional information, but hidden massages as well.

This relationship between the magical structure of the formation of the letters and the symbolic structure of man is explained by Klara Roman (1970):

> We tend to perceive letters as having volume: three dimensional configurations standing upright like a man standing on the ground. This ground is symbolized by the implied baseline. For we speak of upright letters, in spite of the fact the they actually lie flat on the plane of the paper. This attests to something that projection theory has long recognized—man's tendency to project the self onto the object that meets the eye, and to invest this object with the tensions and emotional impulses actually operating in himself. In writing, this leads to an identification with the letter form, upon which the writer projects his psychic activity in the guise of images and symbolic gesture.

Symbols are expressions of intense emotional cathexes. "Through repeated occurrences...an entire train [of thought] may ultimately be concentrated into a single unit. This is a fact of compression or compensation" (Freud, 1938) whereby, through a single gesture, a constellation of suppressed or repressed material can be hypercathected (released) and thereby be expressed.

All language and writing is symbolic, as individuals tend to choose and create certain idiosyncratic psychomotor configurations in order to satisfy the wants or desires of the CS, PCS, and UCS. Symbols can reflect a unifying factor in the organization of personality. If conceived as "kinetic melodies" they display the physiological integrative function of the multidimensional cerebral cortex; if conceived of as psychological projections, they display the symbolic "nodal points" of whole trains of thought that Freud talks about. They are prelogical and/or preverbal compromises that are allowed by the censor to be expressed.

Figure 11.6 is the signature of the famous astrologer Noel Tyl, who has written a series of textbooks on the topic. Its excessive height and roundedness emphasizes the highly sensitive nature of this 6'6" opera singer/newspaper editor/professional astrologer. He is egocentric, outspoken, caring, and oftentimes brilliant. But as noted in the knot-tied script, he is caught up in an inflated self-image. He is

Figure 11.6. The spiraling handwriting of famous astrologer, Noel Tyl.

future-oriented, optimistic, and highly ambitious, but held back emotionally by the unresolved problems from the past. Although the writer may have difficulty communicating his true self to himself (as well as to others), he is empathetic (roundedness) and a knowledgeable guide in therapy. The abstract signature pairs well with the astrologer. The circular movements look almost similar to spiraling progression of the earth as it goes around the sun, as the solar system progresses through the galaxy. The figure 8 supports the hypothesis of an ambiguous self-image. He really does lead a cork-screw life.

Another giant figure 8 is evident in the signature in Figure 11.7. Both of these men's accomplishments reflect the idea of an infinite potential, but the composite nature of the symbol tells the graphologist that the figure 8 also points toward a certain ambivalence or difficulty in releasing the past, always tying it in, as the writer progresses into

Figure 11.7. The signature of creative artist, Robert Adsit.

the future. This signature is that of an artist who was adopted at 4 1/2 years of age. With this information, the figure 8 now seems to point to the mystery of his birth and a continuing concern regarding the womb from which he sprang.

If we compare both signatures we find that both are illegible, use rounded forms, are rather large and abstract, and both are highly creative, warm-hearted, self-contained, and interested in metaphysics; however, it is also clear that the same or similar automatized habitual psychomotor patterns (that is, symbols) will reflect different psychological trains of thought dependent in part on the experience of the writer and in part on some inner symbolic psycho-biological need.

Signatures Can Portray One's Profession

Many writers generate symbols in their signatures that portray their profession. Sometimes these symbols are done on purpose and sometimes they are done either preconsciously or unconsciously. The level of self-knowledge in these kinds of signatures varies greatly. One way or another, what we see here is the very identity of the individual becoming associated with the abstract symbolic process of signing one's name. You will note, however, in some instances, important symbols show up elsewhere in the handwriting as well. The following sections on signatures and profession, and signatures and body parts or body image, contain obvious examples of this phenomenon. Most of the time, this is *not* the case. Symbols can become more and more abstract. The more the handwriting analyst knows about the writer's life, the more chance he or she has of uncovering the meaning of such symbols.

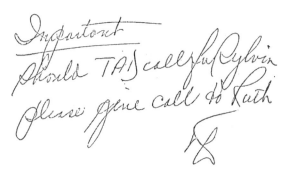

Figure 11.8. The writer plays the violin. The signature is a personalized initial for the name Doris. The heart-shaped lower loop relates to her warm personality and the flashy releasing upswing visually pairs well with the fact that she is a violin teacher. The ideogram itself looks abstractly like a musician moving her bow over the stringed instrument.

Figure 11.9. The signature of the famous medical doctor Karl Menninger, founder of the Menninger Clinic. Note the sign of the caduceus used for the letter g.

In Figure 11.10, Alfred Hitchcock draws his famous profile that he used to open up his TV show. Peter Benchly is the author of *Jaws*. Liberace had a great sense of humor and appreciation for camp. The famous pianist draws a piano with his ever-present candelabra with his signature. Harold Takata, who played Odd Job in the James Bond movie *Goldfinger*, was famous in the film for throwing a boomerang hat that could take people's heads off! The inventor of the steamboat, Robert Fulton, writing 200 years ago, clearly places a boat-like design in his signature.

Figure 11.10. All of these writers have knowingly created signatures or cartoons associated with their signatures that are obviously linked to their profession.

Figure 11.11. The signatures of Neil Armstrong and Buzz Aldrin, the first two humans to step on the moon. Where Aldrin's signature looks like a plane taking off, Armstrong's has a number of symbols that resemble a rocket ship flying and its booster.

Figure 11.12. Fred Astaire and Ginger Rogers. Note how both signatures resemble each other and look like a couple dancing.

Figure 11.13. (Below) Here we see two great athletes, the Olympic champion sprint runner, Jesse Owen, who won a gold medal for the United Sates in 1936. On the right is Pelé, considered by many to be the world's greatest soccer player. Note how Owen's handwriting with the long J-loop and rumbling O resembles a sprinter taking off, and Pelé's signature clearly corresponds to his spectacular acrobatic abilities.

Figure 11.14. contains the signature of guitarist and rock star Bruce Springsteen on the left and golf champion Jack Nicklaus on the right. Springsteen's signature clearly resembles his classic pose with guitar in hand. Nicklaus has placed the sign of his golf clubs in the salutation and the golf swing in his capital N.

Figure 11.15. contains two signatures of Count von Zeppelin, the inventor and designer of the airship. Note that his signature looks very much like a blimp, and the p's in his last name look more like the letter Z. Thus we see the Count placing symbols of his name and profession in his signature in a variety of ways.

Figure 11.16. Walt Disney's very famous signature became the logo for his company. Here is a more spontaneous example. This is clearly the handwriting of a right brained thinker, whose signature seems to be imbued with the very cartoons that Disney brought to the world. The signature on the right is that of Sidney Toler, a Caucasian actor who became famous playing the Chinese sleuth Charlie Chan. Clearly, the writing simulates Chinese-like graphics.

Parts of the Body Showing Up in the Signature

Just as some writers portray their profession in the signatures, other writers place symbolic features associated with parts of their body. Again, sometimes this is done consciously, but it is also done preconsciously (that is, with some subconscious knowledge) or unconsciously.

Figure 11.17. Signatures from Jimmy Durante and Hedy Lamarr.

eyebrows

Figure 11.18.

Figure 11.17 on page 214 contains the photographs and signatures of two Hollywood stars from the 1940s at two ends of the spectrum: the comedian Jimmy Durante, known for his large proboscis and the lovely Austrian actress Hedy Lamarr. Note how a symbol for Durante's nose apparently finds itself in the capital *P* of Pleasure. One could make the case that the large *J* might also symbolize this feature of his body even though it doesn't resemble a nose at all. Symbols are abstract representations. In Hedy Lamarr's case, she tends to make a double loop on her *e* and on the *y*. In both cases (see arrows), they appear to resemble her lips. Graphologically, this double loop in the lower zone also relates to an exotic fantasy or sex life. The styles of the letters reflect her European upbringing.

Figure 11.19. Jayne Mansfield's image was closely tied to revealing her full bosom. Note the double J in her first name (the second J created with the y-loop), the prevocative heart-like i-dots and the colossal sensual curves that resemble full breasts in her signature. Sofia Loren forgot to look at the camera for this photo.

In figure 11.18 on page 215, note Theta Bara's eyes appearing in her handwriting, Dali's double moustache with a doubled D, playwright Noel Coward's unusual pose, and union leader John L. Lewis's famous heavy eyebrows all showing up in their signatures.

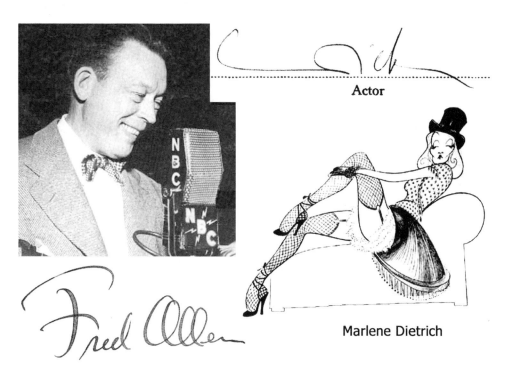

Actor

Marlene Dietrich

Figure 11.20. The famous radio star Fred Allen. When I obtained this signature, it occurred to me that the capital F resembled Allen's profile. Marlene Dietrich's highly simplified signature, with its sensual curves resembles, perhaps, a lady in repose.

The image on page 218 is that of Lloyd Boucher, the captain of the military intelligence ship the *USS Pueblo*, which was captured by the North Koreans in 1968. Notice how Boucher not only draws the ship surrounding his name, but also has a series of waves going in two different directions! The top signature is that of World War I flyer/industrialist Anthony Fokker, inventor of a machine gun that could fire its rounds through the propeller of a plane. This astonishing accomplishment, which seemed like magic at the time, was achieved by the elegant decision to have the propeller itself fire the rounds. Thus the release of the bullets through the openings was perfectly timed. When Mr. Whitehead requested a signature, Fokker wrote his right on top of Whitehead's. This is a highly unusual decision and corresponds to the goal of his weapon, which was to obliterate the other guy!

Figure 11.21. On the top, Anthony Fokker. On the bottom, Lloyd Boucher.

Touchpoints and Synchronicity in Handwriting

The discovery of touchpoints among the letters and words in the signature and on the page helps give the analyst a greater understanding of the formative pattern of thinking of the writer. According to Dan Anthony, who explored this line of investigation that began with Werner Wolff, when playing with a compass and ruler in analyzing the writing, the more touchpoints in a spontaneously written script, the more creative the writer. Neurologically, when touchpoints occur, this is most likely to reflect hemispheric communication.

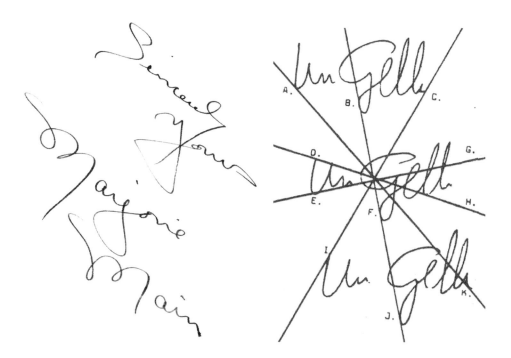

Figure 11.22. On the left is the signature and salutation of 1940s Ma and Pa Kettle actress Marjorie Main. The second writing is the signature of Uri Geller.

Note how Marjorie sets up her own touchpoint by bisecting the *y* of yours in precise fashion with the downstroke of the ending *y* of sincerely. The second writing is the signature written three times of Israeli psychic and spoon bender Uri Geller. When connecting *A* with *K* and *C* with *I*, the giant *X* meets in the center of the middle *G*. The *G* loops also line up precisely in touchpoint fashion, all cross lines meeting in the same *G*. Both of these handwritings display in spectacular fashion the "diagrams of the unconscious" that Werner Wolff talks about. The writing and scribbling that we do on a page is not random. There is a hidden order, and, the more precise the relationships are, the more in tune the writer is with his or her own unconscious. These cases are unusual because these two writers are very gifted individuals, one as a performing artist and the other as a creative individual endowed with extraordinary mental powers. (Note: The break between the e and l in the last signature of Geller's was caused by the reproduction. The original is connected.)

Figure 11.23. Here are two examples of the Diagrams of the Unconscious *taken from Werner Wolff's book by the same title. Note that, as Mussolini got older and more powerful, the entire length of his signature was still contained in the same space. In the case of author and poet Christopher Morley, Wolff uncovered two interesting measures. In the top signature, the length of the t-bar was the same length as the entire last name from beginning stroke to end stroke. In the bottom signature, the lengths of the first and last name are the same if measured from the beginning to end stroke of each name.*

Dan Anthony's technique for finding touchpoints include the following:

- If it is a page of writing, draw a big X on the page, starting with the beginning point of the first line to the end point on the last line as the first diagonal. The second diagonal is created by finding the endpoint of the first line and drawing that line down to the beginning stroke of the last line (see Figures 11.22 and 11.24).

- Do the same thing for a signature. You create an X by drawing a line from the top of the beginning letter to the bottom of the end letter and another line from the top of the last letter to the bottom of the first letter.

- Use a ruler and draw a line when any three points or more line up. Often you will see i-dots, t-bars, and tops of upper and lowercase letters line up. Sometimes you will see the tops of the first name line up in a diagonal, which becomes the baseline of part of the last name.

- Thelma Seifer suggests using colored pencils to fill in different kinds of symbols with different colors, for example, assign different colors for upper and lower loops, t-bars, favorite letters, unusual symbols, repetitive patterns, and so on.

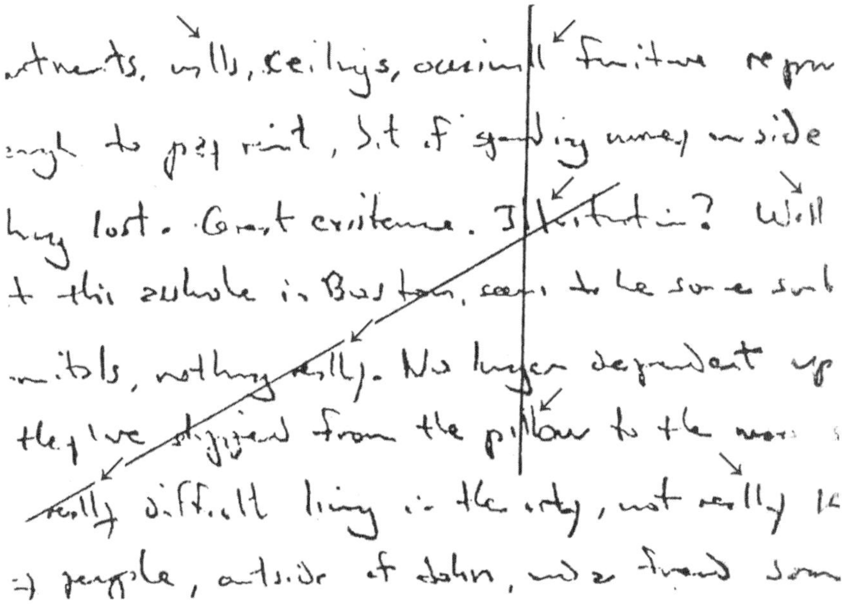

Figure 11.24. This writer has used words with double l's in them eight times in this paragraph. Note that some of them line up as well. The last name of this writer has a double l in it.

▶ You can also draw on Werner Wolff's idea of using a compass to find either the length of the first name or a significant length such as a t-bar or *y* downstroke, and make that the measure to see if the entire length of the signature is a multiple of this figure.

In general, this is the kind of technique with which you need to experiment. Your tools are a pen, colored pencils, compass, and ruler. By playing this way with the signatures or a page of handwriting, different patterns begin to emerge, and the analyst will find that this procedure helps discover aspects of the writing that would be overlooked otherwise. What Werner Wolff is saying is that there is a consistency to the pattern of the writing, an internal organizing principle that stems from a very deep realm.

From my studies, I have come across many people who have favorite letters or diacritics or other symbolic forms, and because of them, whole written pages are preconsciously constructed to maximize their use. Oftentimes, they cluster or line up synchronistically down a page, or, as Dan Anthony has noted, they create touchpoints with other rhythmically executed strokes. Werner Wolff's (1948/65) text *Diagrams of the Unconscious* attempts to explore the tendency towards wholeness expressed in writing by

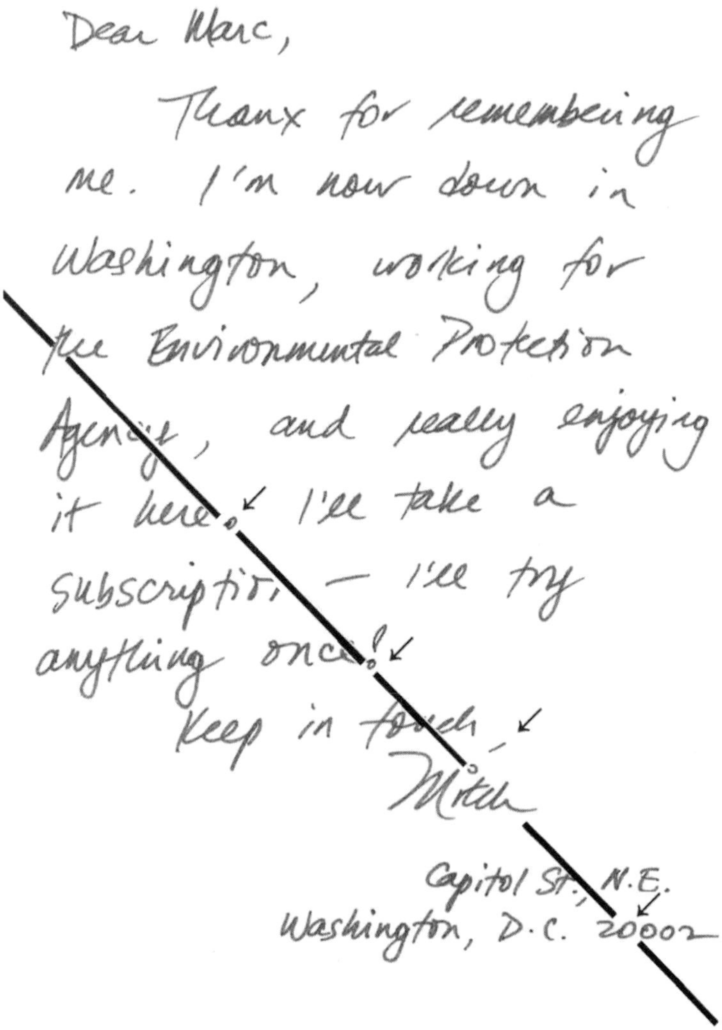

Dear Marc,

Thanx for remembering me. I'm now down in Washington, working for the Environmental Protection Agency, and really enjoying it here. I'll take a subscription — I'll try anything once!

Keep in touch,

Mitch

Capitol St., N.E.
Washington, D.C. 20002

Figure 11.25. Note how the circle i-dot lines up diagonally down the page and even goes through the zipcode, which also has three circles inside it.

measuring the **symmetry, consistency, rhythm,** and **periodicity** of, in particular, the **signature**. Wolff coins the term *configuration* to stand for the unconscious harmonious arrangement of these various aspects of the writing. This configuring principle is unlearned. "Whatever the personality trends are which determine expressive movement, they seem to become configurated just as spread iron filings are configurated by a magnet" (96).

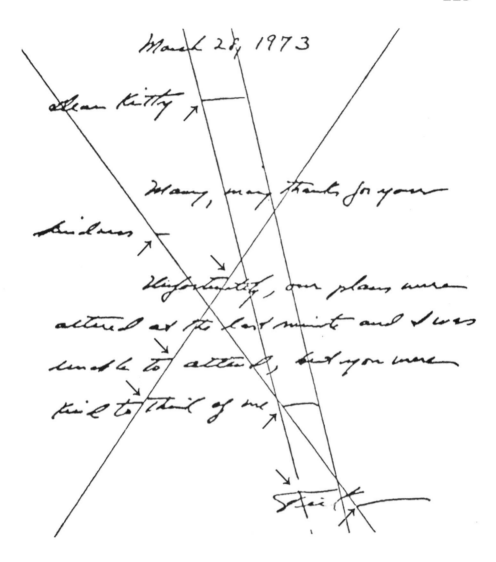

Figure 11.26. Note how the lateral strokes (dashes and t-bars) line up in spectacular synchronistic fashion in Rick's script.

Figure 11.25 is the handwriting of the top student from my high school class who got an 800 on his SAT's. There is the possibility that the unusual zipcode tuned Mitch into writing circle i-dots. One way or another, one can see that the dots line up exactly down the page.

Jung's hypothesis of the archetype as a "formative pattern or tendency towards a particular style of life" is a concept linked to these ideas, as is his idea of synchronicity, or meaningful coincidence. In the case of the comedian's handwriting discussed earlier, Figure 11.1, note how the word *of* lines up precisely, diagonally down the page. The automatized pattern of this word is identical to the last two letters of Bob's signature. The capital *I* is another configuration, which often lines up in touchpoint fashion down a page (not shown). This synchronistic configurating expression of the centralizing ego is also evident in Rick's signature, Figure 11.26, whereby the kinetic melody of the dash predominates with 15 t-bars and five dashes in this short page of writing. Note how the dash replaces both the curved part of the top of the capital *R* in Rick and the period at the ends of sentences. This lateral stroke also lines up precisely down the page along with other similar graphics, in this instance, in five lines with five t-bars. Extreme precision of this tendency toward patterning is evident. This neurophysiological holistic propensity stems from very deep layers of the unconscious.

In his 1959 book, Ira Progoff states that: "These archetypes, motifs or themes underlie the patterns of symbolism that belong to the process of growth in the psyche... the essence towards depth then is a growth towards wholeness."

Certainly a self-actualizing and unifying tendency was evident in a variety of ways in the previous signatures whereby the depth and scope of the person's existence is expressed as a stylized insignia.

The preconscious is a vast area of the psyche. It is not only a meeting ground of the conscious and unconscious, but also a repository for the symbols, automatisms, defense mechanisms, and structure of the censor. As the first layer of the unconscious, the preconscious is a gateway to the deeper strata of the mind.

Chapter 12
Handwriting and Brain Trauma

Any illness that disrupts the basal ganglia will adversely affect fine motor control, because signals being sent to the frontal lobes, motor cortex, and parietal lobe via the thalamus will become tainted. These illnesses include Parkinson's disease, which involves a diminishment of dopamine production in the substantia nigra; Fredrich's ataxia, which causes the loss of cells in the posterior root of the ganglia; and Huntington's disease, which affects the caudate nucleus. According to Dr. Robert Iacono of the Neuroscience Clinic at Loma Linda University, basal ganglia diseases will cause "negative symptoms [including]…akinesia and loss of postural reflexes …[and] positive symptoms [such as…] tremors, rigidity, and involuntary movements." Parkinson's disease has been known to cause tremors and reduction in the size of letters and words. Other diseases that affect the higher centers, particularly the major lobes of the cerebral cortex, will also adversely influence fine motor control. These include heart attacks and strokes, which can restrict blood flow to specific areas of the brain; cerebral palsy, which involves the atrophy of cortical cells; dyslexia, which affects the left angular gyrus; and multiple sclerosis, which can create cerebral lesions. Other diseases in this category include epilepsy, schizophrenia, brain tumors, head trauma, and coma.

Luria informs us that writing can be affected by disorders occurring in widely separated areas of the cerebral cortex. Hearing problems especially created difficulties for kinesthetic analysis and synthesis.

If the motor cortex is damaged, the writing is jerky. Ability to end movements can also be impaired. Local lesions of one area of the brain causes symptoms and compensations in other areas. Thus the diagnostician must identify the primary defect as well as secondary consequences. These related problems can be widely separated from one another. Three such problems are:

- **Agnosia:** a motor defect disturbing perception of the nature of sensation while still being able to experience sensation.
- **Apraxia:** a sensory defect or disorder of skilled action with elementary motor functioning remaining in tact.
- **Aphasia:** a speech disorder.

All three are disorders associated with symbolic activities. They are not, however, independent, isolated disturbances, for the simple reason that, when one link in the chain is weak, the entire integrity of the system is affected.

Speech, for instance, is a highly complex function, because a wide range of disorders can disturb it. As previously stated, speech and language are generally programmed in the left hemisphere (even in many lefties). Nevertheless, the right hemisphere is intimately involved with the abstract nonverbal understanding of what the word means.

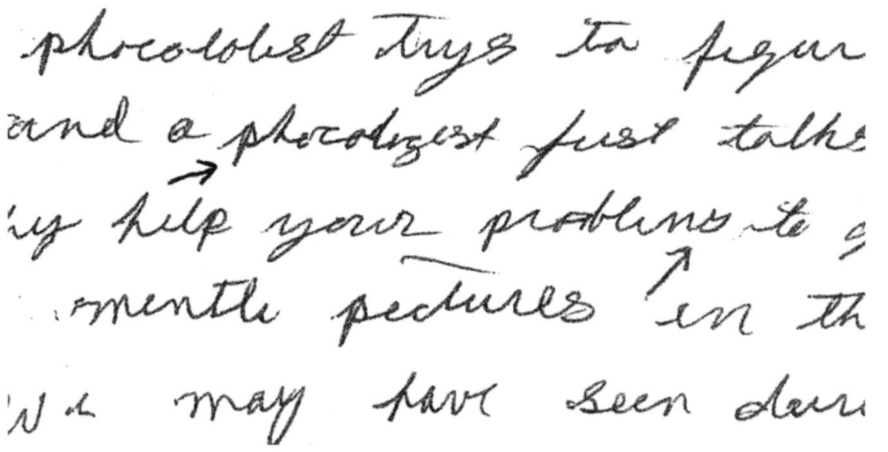

Figure 12.1. The handwriting of a 19-year-old male with a consequential speech impediment shows a number of motor disturbances, spelling mistakes ("phocololist" for "psychologist"), and patching (see o and s in the word problems). The writer may have had a hearing impairment, but, if so, it was not noticeable. The problem could be linked to aphasia in Broca's area or another area of the temporal/motor lobes associated with speech.

In the case of auditory problems, the process of phonemic hearing is impaired. If words are not heard correctly, they cannot be spoken correctly; therefore, spelling and handwriting are also affected. There could be a problem in the motor aspect of speech, the systematizing of language, or the understanding of individual words. Writing from dictation becomes extremely difficult and "the patient makes mistakes with words requiring special sound analysis" (123). Writing while holding the tongue between the teeth also becomes difficult.

Frontal lesions have been linked to depression, lack of interest, indifference, and impaired intellectual synthesis. These people may also be impulsive. A lesion of the prefrontal region can also affect the motor ability.

Figure 12.2 contains two samples of the handwriting of former press secretary James Brady. The bottom signature was written shortly after he began his recovery from the gunshot wound to the head, which he sustained during

Figure 12.2.

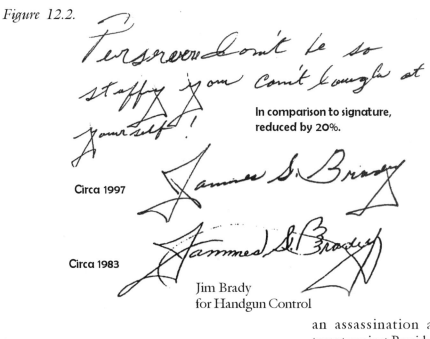

In comparison to signature,
reduced by 20%.

Circa 1997

Circa 1983

Jim Brady
for Handgun Control

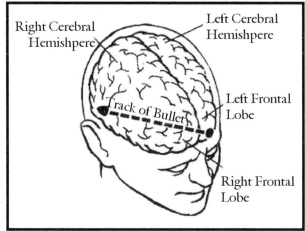

Figure 12.3. The track that the bullet took when it entered Brady's brain.

an assassination attempt against President Reagan in 1981. The top sample was created about 15 years later for Lorne Adrain's book *The Most Important Thing I Know*.

According to Brady's surgeon Richard Cytowic, who described "the long ordeal of James Brady," in the magazine section of the *New York Times* on September 27, 1981, "the more frontal the injury, the more severe the spasticity." Mr. Brady survived the gunshot wound because the bullet did not hit the deeper centers of his brain. Clearly, his abstract thinking has been impacted, but his well-known wit miraculously survived. Through physical therapy and alternative techniques, such as printing the B instead of writing it in cursive, one can see that Mr. Brady's signature became more fluent over time.

Figure 12.4. Loss of the left half of the field of vision in a patient with optic impairment from a tumor of the contralateral right parieto-occipital region. Because he doesn't see the left part of the picture, he doesn't draw it (simulated, based on Luria, 1980).

Specimen   Specimen

Performance   Performance

"Truck"   "Don't know"

Figure 12.5. Disturbance of the perception of crossed-out figures in a patient with optic agnosia. This patient has an extracerebral tumor of the occipital region. He can see the truck on the left side, but he cannot see the truck on the right side (simulated, based on Luria, 1980).

Note the inability to shut off a motor program once it is initiated. This is seen particularly in the earlier sample in the letters *m* and *B*, but also in the *n*'s in "don't" and "can't" and the *m* in "James" of the second sample as well. The inhibiting feedback loop has been disrupted. Figure 12.3 shows the path the bullet took, shattering the forehead, and tearing through the tip of the left frontal lobe, through the right frontal lobe, cutting off part of the corpus callosum, and lodging itself near his right ear. Paralyzed on the left side and confined

6/4/1994 6 days before a major seizure	
6/5/1994 5 days before a major seizure	
6/15/1994 5 days after a major seizure	
7/29/1994 1 month after surgery	
10/10/1994 4 months after surgery	

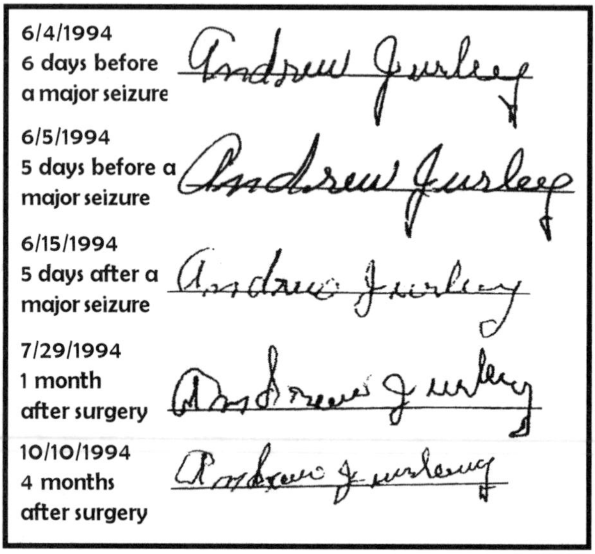

Figure 12.6. The handwriting of a man with a parietal lobe tumor before and after surgery.

to a wheelchair, Mr. Brady's movements became awkward and jerky. Although he did not sustain a direct injury to the motor cortex, his motor functions were severely disabled, because the prefrontal lobes control motor functions.

Figure 12.6 is that of a man in his early 70s who had a brain tumor on the front part of the right parietal lobe near the post-central gyrus that left him dizzy and caused him to have seizures (middle initial replaces capital letter of last name). The top writings were performed five and six days before a major seizure. One can see great differences in the fluidity of the 6/5/94 sample as compared to the day before. Clearly, this subject had suffered a debilitating neurological event on the 4th of June, and he recovered the following day. Nevertheless, even in the better sample, one can see arrhythmic disconnections. Note the lack of ability to connect the *d* with the *r* in the name "Andrew." This kind of arrhythmia is indicative of some type of disruption in interhemispheric communication caused either by the seizures, or the tumor in the parietal lobe. Five days later this subject suffered a major seizure that caused him to collapse to the floor, and then walk in an awkward manner. The third signature was taken five days later. Note the evidence of akinesia—the handwriting appears flaccid and has weak pressure. Two weeks after this sample, A.J. underwent brain surgery to remove the grade 4 glioblastoma. The fourth sample was given one month after surgery. One can see that the ability to integrate simple curved movements has been severely disrupted. The subject also has trouble in the directionality of the writing trail and the baseline undulates. The increased ataxia suggests an additional problem in the central nervous system. The last sample, given four months after surgery, shows that the writer was still severely disabled and continuing to degrade. At this time, he was paralyzed on the left side and restricted to lying in bed. This writing sample reflects not only the grave disruption of the activity of the right parietal lobe, and brain damage caused by seizures, but also problems from deeper areas of the brain, perhaps the basal ganglia.

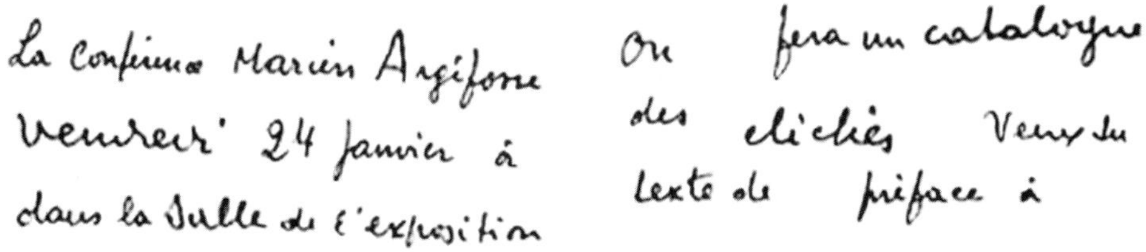

Writing from dictation with tongue in the free position.

Writing from dictation with tongue gripped between the patient's teeth.

Figure 12.7. Changes in the writing of a patient with a tumor of the left post-central division of the motor cortex (near the language center). Once Luria prevented the patient from mouthing the words (right column), the patient was unable to write the sentences smoothly. Note uneven spacing on right column (simulated, based on Luria 1980). Here we see the important role that internal speech has in organizing our thoughts and coordinating (via the parietal lobe) the motor cortex with the occipital and temporal lobes.

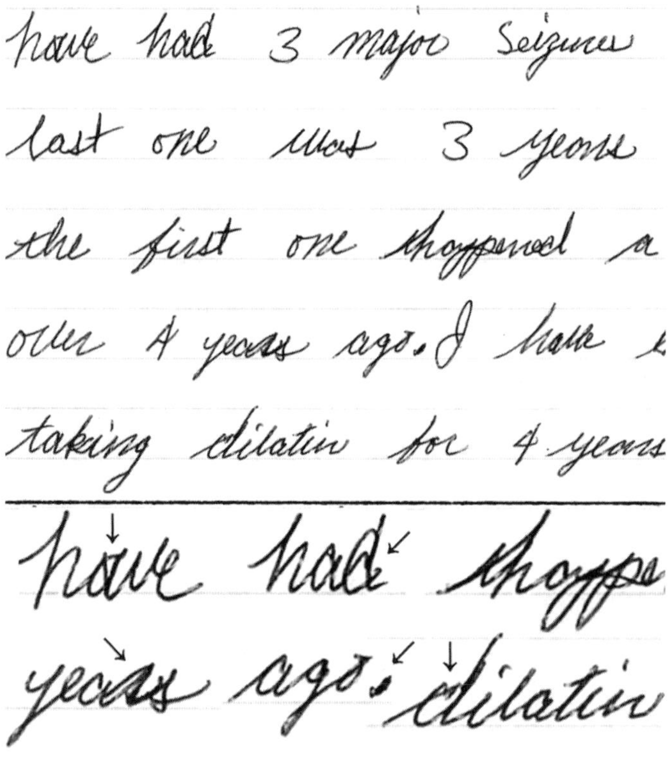

Figure 12.8. Handwriting of a male who has grand mal epilepsy.

Figure 12.8 is the handwriting of a 24-year-old male who suffers from grand mal epilepsy. Note the hard, slow pace, the brittle nature of the connecting strokes, such as in the *l* of "last," the false starts, and the numerous corrections, as seen in the *d* of "had," the extra beginning stroke in the word *happened*, and the *k* of *taking*. Clearly, the psychomotor pattern associated with the creation of letters has been affected. To compensate, the writer digs into the paper with extreme pressure, in part to relieve the tension, and in part to slow the writing down, so less mistakes will be made.

The Epileptic Split-Brain Writer

In the 1950s Roger Sperry performed the first surgery to separate the two cerebral hemispheres of individuals suffering from severe epilepsy. What Sperry did was to cut the corpus collosum or connecting link. This broke the electrical circuit and greatly alleviated the epilepsy. At the same time, it created individuals who had, essentially within themselves, two separate brains: a **left** brain where language was housed, and a **right** brain where music and pictures were catalogued. Further study revealed that the left brain tends to think sequentially and sees the parts, whereby the right brain thinks intuitively and sees the whole. In a general sense, because we tend to think in words, the left brain can be considered the dominant/conscious side, and the

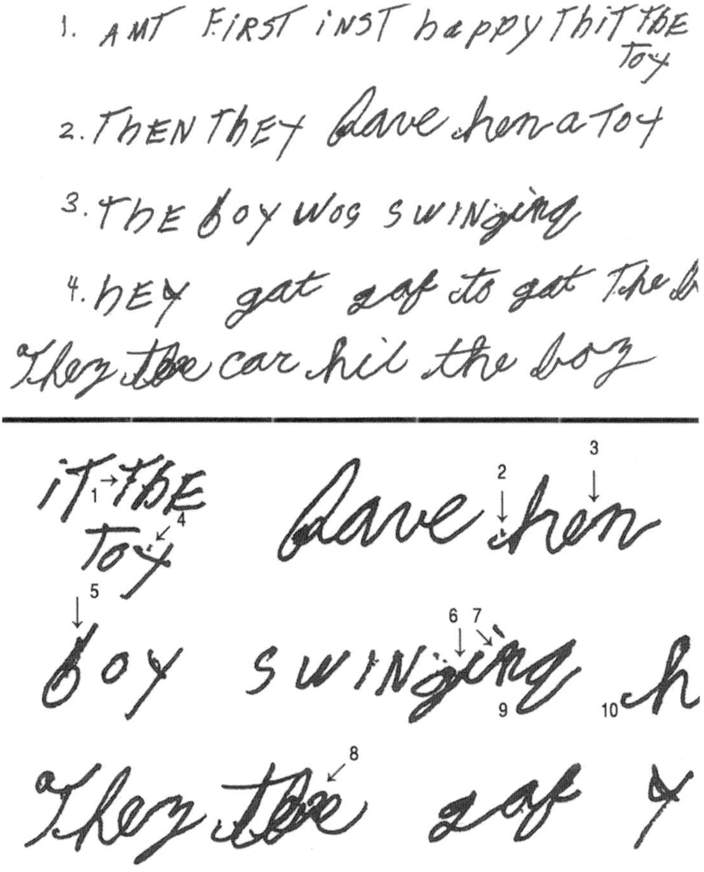

Figure 12.9. Low functioning split brain patient.

right brain, the subordinate/unconscious side. Nevertheless, if a person has a stroke in the left temporal lobe, although he cannot speak, he knows what he wants to say. The same injury in the right temporal lobe would create an individual who could talk with no problem, but substance will be lacking. Clearly, one needs both hemispheres to speak and think correctly.

One of the greatest dangers during an epileptic seizure is that the electrical storm in one hemisphere can cross over, via the corpus callosum, and cause corresponding mirror-image damage in the same lobe of the opposite hemisphere. Roger Sperry was the first to realize that if the corpus callosum was cut above the optic nerve in severe cases of epilepsy, the electrical storms would subside and no more damage would be done to the opposite hemisphere.

Figures 12.9 and 12.10 are two epileptics who have had their corpus callosums surgically severed. The first is an example of a low-functioning

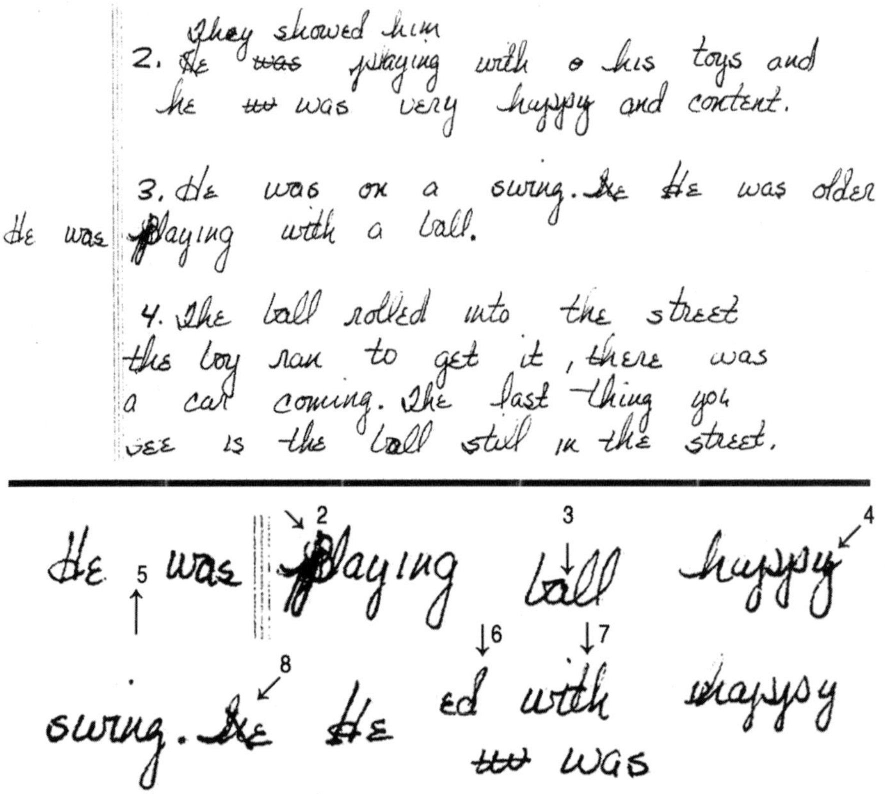

2. They showed him
   He was playing with o his toys and
   he was very happy and content.

3. He was on a swing. He He was older
   He was playing with a ball.

4. The ball rolled into the street
   this boy ran to get it, there was
   a car coming. The last thing you
   see is the ball still in the street.

He ₅ was ↓2 playing ball happy ↗4
   ↑   ↓6   ↓7
swing. He He ed with happy
   ↙8   was

Figure 12.10. High-functioning split brain patient. Note simplified cross outs and overall maturity and coherence of the handwriting, but also evidence of operation as seen in the split y, arrow 4.

split-brain writer, and the second, an example of a high-functioning split-brain writer. In the first case, Figure 12.9, it is clear that a great amount of brain damage had been done prior to the operation. This writer was never able to truly automatize his handwriting due to the great trauma that occurred to his brain as he was growing up. The writing shifts between printing and cursive, the spacing and spelling are poor, the style is childlike, and there are signs of dyslexia; letters have been substituted for other letters, and many words are unintelligible. The second line probably reads, "Then they gave him a toy." If this is the case, we see the substitution of an *h* with a *g* and an *m* with an *n*.

Without seeing a pre-surgery sample of this person's handwriting, there is no way to know for sure how the operation affected the output. However, in general, those who have had this operation tend to have arrhythmic "splits," or unnatural stops and starts, between and within letters. Note the extra dots in the last two words *the toy* on line one, and the clear break in the connecting stroke between the *e* and the *n* in the word *hen* on line two. One would suspect damage not only to all or most of the lobes of the cerebral cortex, but also the deeper centers including the basal ganglia and cerebellum.

The second case, Figure 12.10, is that of a writer who is educated. The handwriting is clear and well formed. Because of the deep-rooted automatized aspects of the writing, the subject is able to mask the disruption in interhemispheric communication, but careful analysis reveals evidence of the operation. To the writer's credit, mistakes are crossed out simply. This suggests that the writer is not too hard on herself. The wide spacing between words reflects some sense of distance from others, or feeling of isolation. Note the unnatural breaks between letters, such as between the *a* and *s* in *was*, line one (bottom), and the false starts, as seen in the *h* in *happy* on line 2. There is also patching and misalignment of some letters, such as *t* of *with* line 2, where she tacks on an extra vertical loop, and in the *y* in *happy*, arrow 4, which is actually made with two separate movements. Misalignments such as this are found frequently in the handwritings of split-brain writers.

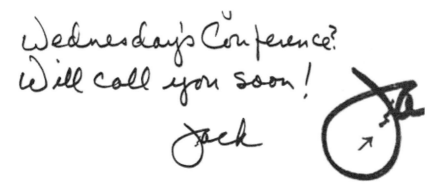

Figure 12.11. False starts and misalignments occur in this sample of a 65-year-old engineer who has suffered 12 minor strokes that have left him temporarily confused, but generally all right.

At first look, the handwriting appears to be unimpaired. In fact, this is an excellent example of a high Form Level writing. It is well organized, spontaneous, balanced, rhythmic, clear, and aesthetically pleasing. The only hint that there has been neurological damage can be seen in a false starting stroke (not depicted) and in the involuntary zig-zag extra stroke seen inside the signature. This is a subtle uncontrolled tremor, which in some way is disconnected from the rest of the automatized aspect of this first-rate graphic pattern. The unimpeded handwriting supports the case that these strokes have indeed been mild. However, after 10 more years, they would eventually be the cause of his death.

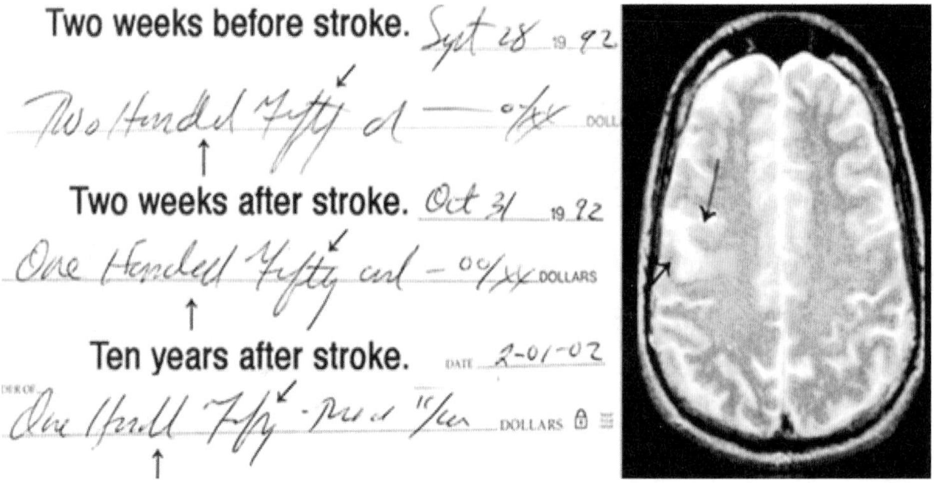

Two weeks before stroke.

Two weeks after stroke.

Ten years after stroke.

Figure 12.12.

Figure 12.12 is the handwriting of a 41-year-old male stroke victim. For the victim, this was a powerful single event, which left the subject hospitalized and incapable of talking for 12 hours. As he struggled out unintelligible moans, being a psychology teacher, he monitored himself by realizing that he could not even say the alphabet. However, he watched the show *Jeopardy*, and knew many of the answers at this time. Throughout the next few days and weeks, his speech came back, but he noticed he had difficulty spelling. Yet, 45 days later, except for occasional blockages, he was talking fluently and so delivered a lecture before the public that had been scheduled months earlier. Ten years later, the effects of the stroke can still be gleaned, as he occasionally stumbles for words when he speaks. This stroke caused a permanent lesion to Broca's area, seen in his MRI. The top check was written two weeks before the stroke, the middle check was written two weeks after, and the bottom check was written 10 years later.

A fluent speaker and dynamic high school psychology teacher, the subject is easily able to mask any remnants of the stroke to those who had no knowledge of its occurrence. At first look, the handwriting seems unaffected. In all cases the writing is a rapidly written, slightly chaotic script that makes great use of primary thread, a technical term in graphology used to describe the simplification of the writing trail, which is achieved by the elimination of lateral strokes. Primary thread can be seen in the words *Hundred* and *Fifty*. Notice how easily one can read the words, yet in the top and bottom examples, the *u* and the *n*, the *dred* and the *ty* have all been combined to create this abbreviated writing. This type of simplification is indicative of superior intelligence. From a neurological viewpoint, although a bit awkward, the primary maneuver has created a neat kinetic melody, which shows proficient use of the lobes of his brain. By using such a shortcut, less energy is invested in the creation of the letters and words, so that the frontal lobes are freed up to think on other levels. The key for this writing is that the simplification has not hampered legibility. Note that after the stroke, the well-designed automatism has suffered. The *e* has been put back into the word *hundred* and the *t* has been put back in the word *Fifty*. Here is clear evidence that the stroke caused a regression to a slightly less effective, and, most likely, earlier rendition of the automatic aspect of his writing trail. Ten years later, the automatism has progressed even further with the writer having almost eliminated entirely the second *d* and t-bar and *t*.

The MRI of the patient below reveals lesions in the frontal lobes, the left pons, central and right medulla, and corpus callosum. The writer has also suffered three heart attacks during the last 15 years.

The writing in figures 12.13 and 12.14 is bold, clear, and rhythmic, even though there is brain damage. Clearly, the frontal lobe lesions have not made much impact on the graphic pattern. The writer speaks well, drives, and has a part-time job. Evidence of the disease can be seen in occasional hesitations within and between letters, for example, the *2* in the date, the *g* of "*writing*," and the *a* of "*taking*." Involuntary movements

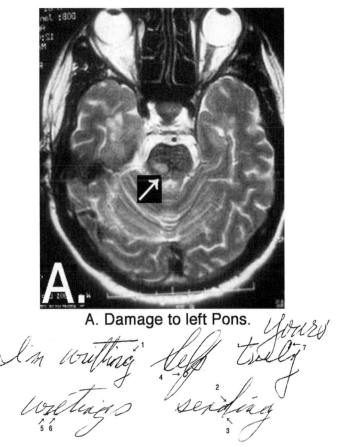

A. Damage to left Pons.

Figure 12.13. The MRI and handwriting of a 61-year-old male with MS and multiple brain lesions. Arrow points to brain damage of pons, which probably results in various tremors in writing trail.

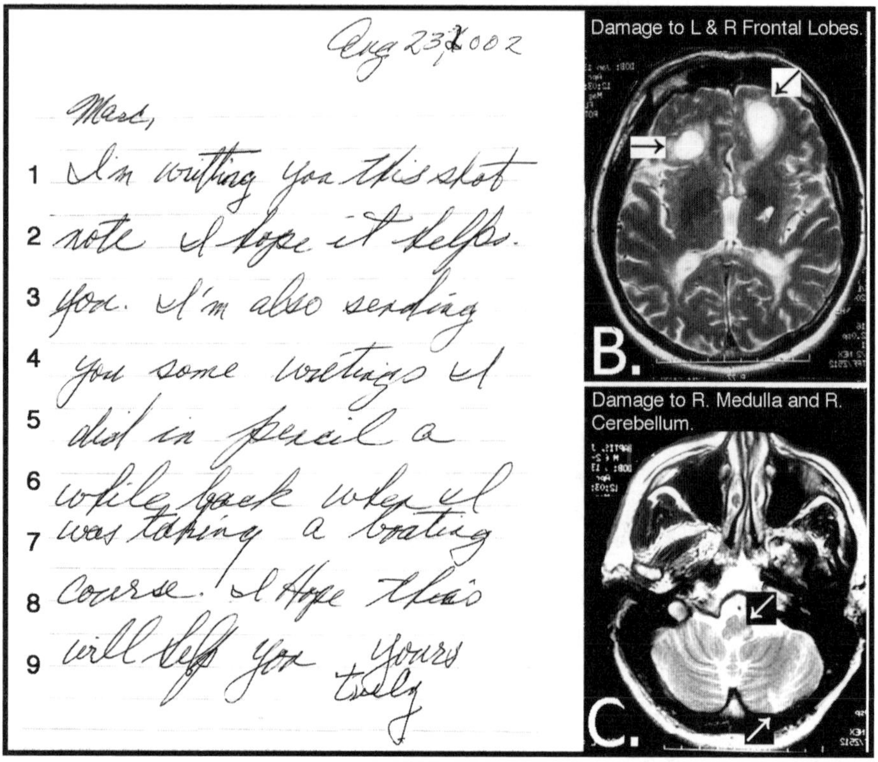

Figure 12.14. This is the handwriting of a 61-year-old male suffering from multiple sclerosis, a disease that attacks the nervous system and causes a breakdown in the myelin sheath of neurons in the brain.

suggestive of deep brain lesions in the corpus callosum and medulla can be seen in the *i* of *this*, and the *s* for an *h* and *l* of *help*, and *l* of *truly*.

The large blank areas in the MRI on the frontal lobes are *not* a true measure of damage. It is more likely that fluids in the frontal lobes have magnified the white areas so that the damage to the frontal lobes looks a lot worse than the real situation. In reviewing this patient's MRI upon my request, Harvard neurologist and MS specialist Ferenc Jolecz stated, "Brain swelling is very well seen on MRI, but cannot be easily distinguished from dead brain tissue." Here is an instance where the handwriting is a better measure of neurological integrity than the MRI.

Sometimes illnesses can create symbolic representations in the writing trail. The fragmentation, ataxia, size distortions, and bizarre elaborations in the handwriting of the schizophrenic patient in Figure 12.15 can be correlated psychologically to her emotional outbursts, tension, and strange ideas, and neurophysiologically, to the disturbances in the cortical/subcortical/cerebellar motor circuit and to imbalances of such neurotransmitters as serotonin, dopamine, and noradrenaline.

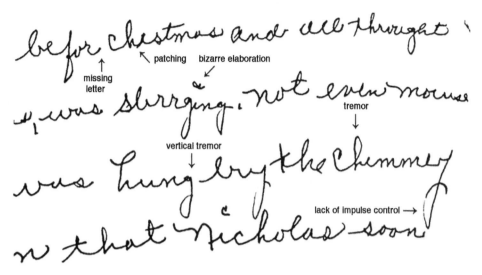

Figure 12.15. The handwriting of a schizophrenic patient (Billings Hospital, University of Chicago, Seifer and Goode, MD, 1974).

The writing sample of the 75-year-old poet was written three years before her death of a heart attack is well organized and aesthetically pleasing. It is hard to analyze the flow of the writing, because it is really a print script. Nevertheless, there is little, if any indication of neurological impairment. However, two curious signs can be seen (right box): a trailing stroke leading into the top of the number *3*, and an extra loop above the *W* in the word *West*. These miscues may indicate some type of neurological interference or symbolic representation of her natural concern about the tumor.

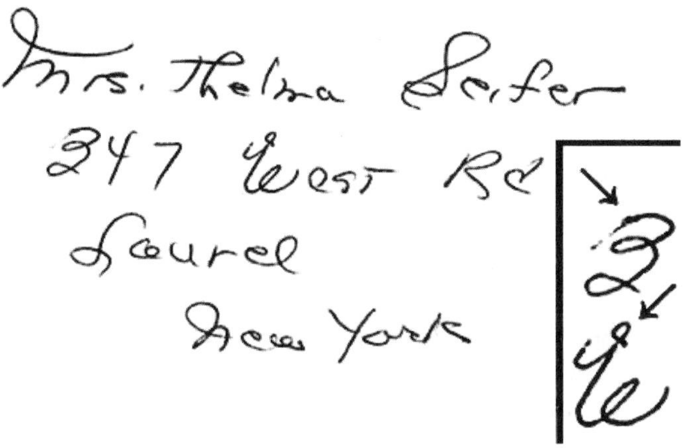

Figure 12.16. The writing of a 75-year-old female poet who had a brain tumor removed 20 years before this sample was written, only to find out 20 years later that the tumor had returned.

In Figure 12.17, the lack of clear spacing between words is due to a variety of factors including the neurological trauma suffered, and the fact that it was physically hard for him to progress his non-dominant hand across the page because of his infirmity. Although the writer makes some *y*'s of a normal length, other *y*'s are truncated, as in the words *anxiety* and *inability*. This cutting off of the bottom of the vertical stroke appears to be a subconscious symbolic recognition of the unfortunate status he is in as having his legs paralyzed.

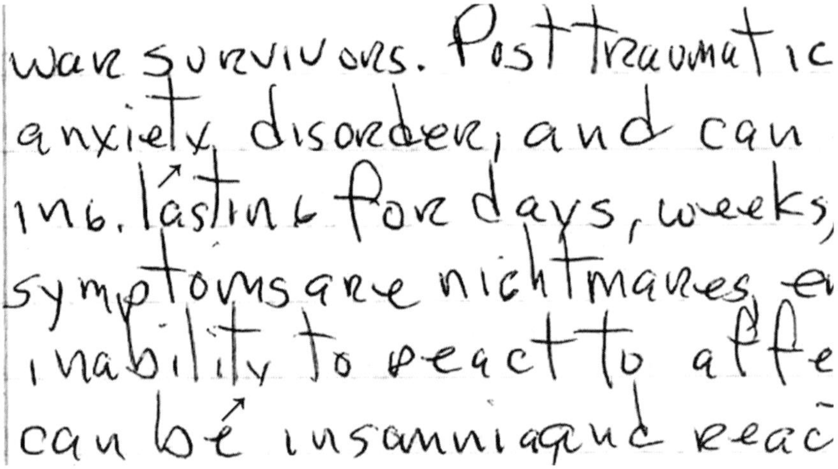

Figure 12.17. This is the handwriting of a 23-year-old male who lost the use of the dominant hand, and both legs in a car accident.

In Figure 12.18, on page 239, the victim's car was totaled and it flipped over. The subject broke both pubic bones and left shoulder, and there was significant brain injury, which included an edema on the right temporal lobe that was removed shortly after admittance to the hospital. After two months, the patient was transferred to Braintree Hospital in Massachusetts, which specializes in treating brain trauma victims. This subject was fed with a tube directly to her stomach for weeks after she recovered from the coma because her swallowing reflex had been impaired. Unable to walk, and only able to communicate by nodding yes or motioning to a "no" card, upon admittance, she undertook three months of physical and speech therapy before leaving the hospital after a total stay in both places of 152 days. At that time she could walk with a walker, and she still uses one 14 years later.

The top sample was written on a postcard at the age of 46, two years before the accident when the subject was in excellent health. The writing is a combination of cursive and print script. Incidental minute tremors can be seen in the

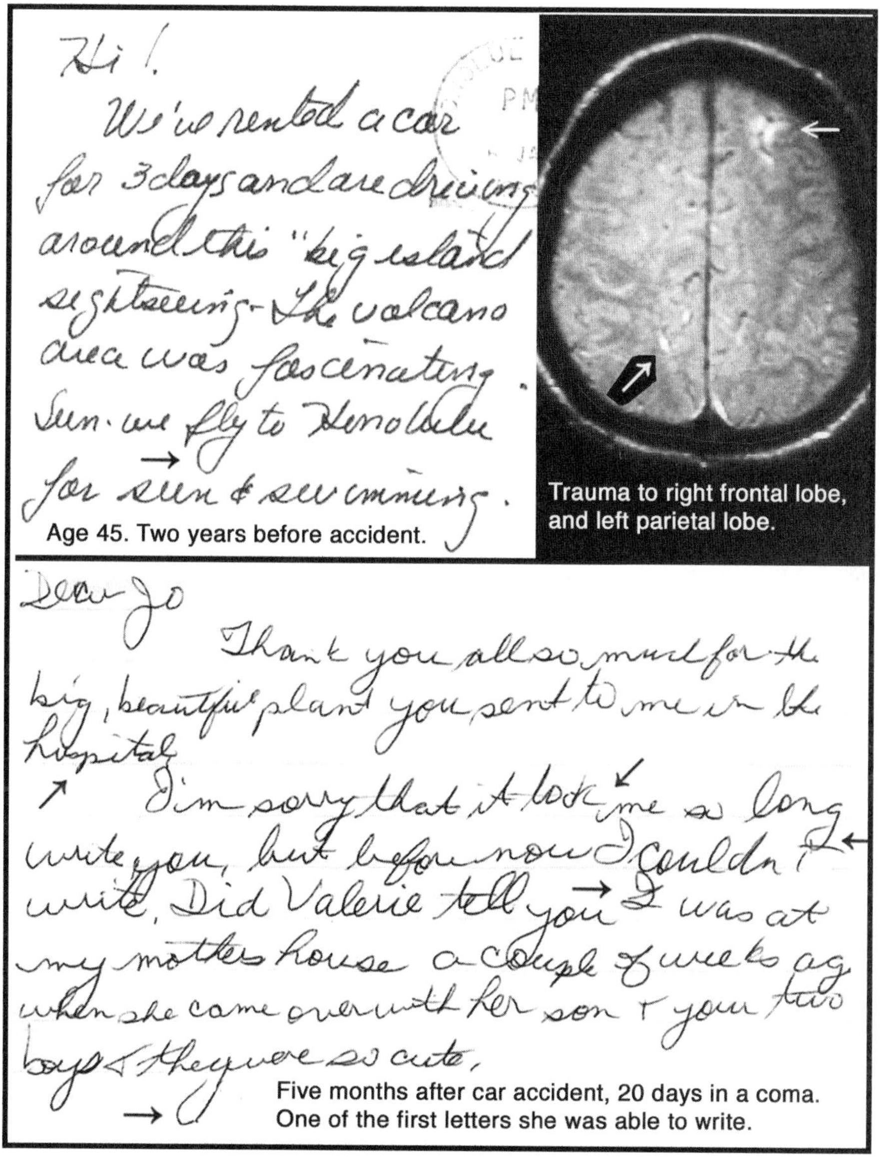

Trauma to right frontal lobe, and left parietal lobe.

Age 45. Two years before accident.

Five months after car accident, 20 days in a coma. One of the first letters she was able to write.

Figure 12.18. Two samples of the handwriting of a female in her mid-40s who was in a coma for 21 days and became severely debilitated as a result of a car accident, which smacked her violently on the left side.

a of *area* and the *n* of *fascinating*, which could be attributed to slight nervousness or impatience. In general, the writing is clear, mature, legible, and stylistic, with flowing fanciful *f*'s, *g*'s, and *y*'s.

The bottom sample of Figure 12.18 was written five months after the trauma, and represents one of the first letters the subject was able to write. At the time, she was still severely incapacitated, mentally confused, simplistic in her responses, and emotionally still very upset. The writing is slow, unsteady, but deliberate. Note changes in pressure, the rising up of words off the baseline, for example, *took*, line 5, *now*, line 6, and the great variation in size of letters, such as, the *l*'s in *beautiful*, and *plant*, line 3. Each word is written separately with no continuity between words. See the lack of connection between *you sent*, line 3. A dyslexic movement associated with the partial memory of an automatism neurologically linked to the parietal lobe and cerebellum can be seen in the misplacement of the apostrophe in the word *couldn't*, line 6. In voluntary movements can be see in the *a* of *Dear*, line 1 and the word *I*, line 7. Both of these movements would be linked to the premotor area of the frontal lobes; the first is a hesitation associated with the beginning of the entire motor sequence of the creation of the letter, and the second, on the word for *I* is associated with some inhibition or trauma attached to the self-image. Fourteen years later, the writer has been left with permanent physical and mental injury. She walks precariously with extreme motor ataxia of the lower extremities, uses a cane or walker, has difficulty completely focusing her eyes, and the voice apparatus is permanently impaired. She thinks slowly and can get confused. Nevertheless, her memory is intact, and, she has depth, empathy, compassion, a sense of humor, and great fortitude, most of which is seen in the content of this letter. She runs a small business, and for the next 15 years, was able to drive a car in a confined local neighborhood.

Concerning the MRI of Figure 12.18, the frontal lobes will influence the overall style and grace of the writing. From the subject's MRI, we note damage to the right frontal lobe. This injury is probably responsible for regression of the writing to a more primitive form. Although the subject is now a slower thinker and unable to concentrate enough to read a book, as stated previously, she has retained her depth, her sense of humor, most of her memory, and her tremendous fortitude. The writing, however, does accurately reflect the severe damage that was done to this subject mentally as well as physically. If we were to put her functioning ability on a 100-point scale, she now operates at about 65 percent of what she had been before the accident.

Figure 12.19 has the handwriting of a lady who was in excellent health at the age of 97. She walked without difficulty and was mentally sharp. Note the youthful friendly nature of the writing offset by sharp angles. This was one tough senior citizen—vigorous, disciplined, congenial, and well organized. A few months after providing this sample, she suffered a mild stroke while on a staircase, lost her balance, and died from the fall. The enlargement of the top of the D and the double-crossed *h* indicates that she may have had a series of mild undetected strokes at least a year before her unfortunate demise.

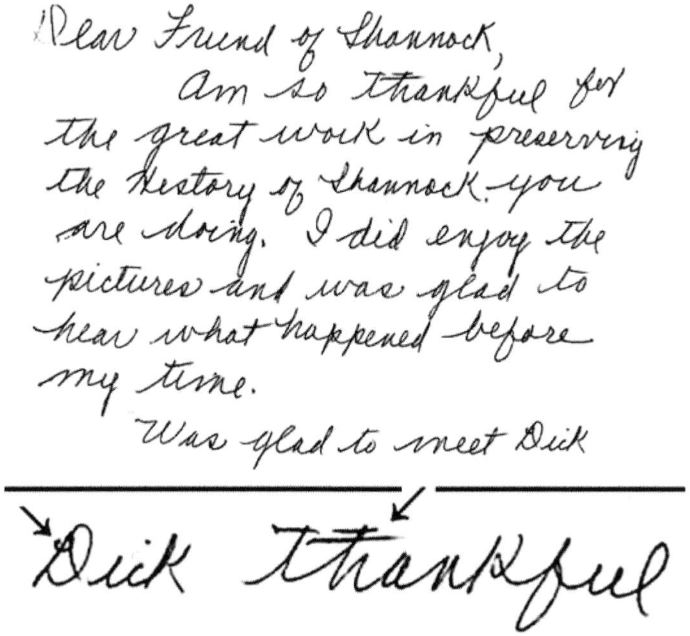

Figure 12.19. The youthful handwriting of a 97-year-old lady.

Handwriting as an outward manifestation of inner speech reflects how the brain uses words, pictures, thoughts, and emotions to express itself. A complex neurological process, handwriting, as an example of fine motor control, is organized essentially, in four separate zones of the central nervous system, in the lobes in the cerebral cortex, in the thalamus and basal ganglia, in the cerebellum, and exterior to the brain in the arm, hand, and fingers. Different diseases and brain traumas attack different parts of the process. In general, unnatural breaks between letters reflects cerebral cortex and interhemispheric communication difficulties, whereas tremors, breaks within letters, broken forms, and a regressive style reflect subcortical problems stemming from the basal ganglia, brainstem, or cerebellum. By working with the MRI and cataloging the progression of each disease, and by obtaining handwriting samples through time, new insights may be revealed concerning how disease affects the brain, and how voluntary behavior and cognitive functions are organized.

This chapter on handwriting and brain trauma was adapted from "The Telltale Hand: How Writing Reveals the Damaged Brain" by Marc J. Seifer, PhD, *Cerebrum*, 2002: (27–420). For their guidance, MRIs, and handwriting samples, I would like to thank the following handwriting experts: Kathie Koppenhaver, Thelma Imber Seifer, Pat Siegel, and Sheila Lowe; also Barry Horowitz, MD, National Institute of Mental Health; Ferenc Jolec, MD, Harvard Medical School; Herbert Meltzer, MD, and David Goode, MD, Billings Hospital, University of Chicago; Lorcan O'Tuama, MD, and Syed Risvi, MD, Department of Neurology, Brown University; Warren Tenhouten, PhD and Joseph Bogen, MD, UCLA.

Chapter 13
Handwriting and Brain Organization

> *Klages himself stresses the fact that every expressive movement is being unconsciously molded by expectations of a pleasing aesthetic effect, in other word by the control of the eye and neurology speaks of a "design for movement" which determines the resulting vital movement of a person.... The process of forming precedes the writing movement, and censure and control by the eye occurs later.*

—Wilhelm Muller and Alice Enskat

The human brain can really be looked at as three brains: brainstem and spinal cord, midbrain and limbic system, and cerebral cortex, "which operate like three interconnected biological computers, each with its own special intelligence, its own subjectivity, its own sense of time and space and its own memory" (MacLean, 2006). By combining the ides of Luria (localization of brain functioning), MacLean (threefold structure from an evolutionary perspective), and Pophal (pallidium and striatum), this chapter attempts to discuss not only how handwriting is organized neurologically, but also how different types of writers will reflect the dominance of different brain centers. For instance, verbal/analytical intellectuals, such as an Einstein or Arthur Conan Doyle, have handwritings that tend to be dominated by the cerebral cortex, whereas a Michael Jackson or Marilyn Monroe type reflect more the limbic system. Also discussed are writers who have had brain damage.

In order to understand the relationship of brain functioning to the psychophysiological process of handwriting, it is helpful to discuss not only the overall structure of the brain, but also the multidimensionality of the writing trail.

The process of writing is intimately related to the processes of speech, reading, thinking, drawing, and social interaction. In the case of brain-damaged people, lesions of the temporal lobe that impair the process of hearing also tend to influence the structure of writing, because the writer is unable to "sound" the words mentally as they are written. In fact, the close cooperation of all major centers of the cerebral cortex are intimately involved with the act of placing one's thoughts on paper, for goals are processed in the front of the brain (frontal lobe), language is processed on the side (temporal lobe), eyesight is processed in the rear (occipital lobe), muscles are directed from the top (motor complex) and coordination of all lobes is taken care of by the area between the motor, temporal, and occipital lobe (parietal lobe/angular gyrus). To complicate matters, this discussion has only taken into account the cerebral cortex, or topmost layer of the brain. This chapter will also discuss the role played by the midbrain, cerebellum, brainstem, and also the basal ganglia, this last area having been of particular interest to the German graphologist Rudolf Pophal (Bernard, 1981).

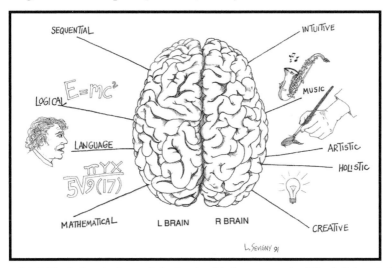

Figure 13.1 Each hemisphere of the brain thinks separately. The left hemisphere programs language, whereas the right programs pictures. In a general sense, the left is the more "conscious" hemisphere because we think in words; to complicate matters, the left sees the parts and the right sees the whole.

Dyslexia

Visual dyslexics have trouble reading, and they reverse letters and numbers when they write. An article from *Scientific American* (Vellintino, 1987) attributes this to a "problem in storing and retrieving information." Dyslexics tend to confuse similar words and letters, they can lose their place when reading, and they can have difficulty interpreting words and sentences, because they may be seeing letters and words backward, or upside-down.

Many years ago at a community college, I had a severely dyslexic student whose high school teachers thought he was retarded. Working with a handicapped association for the blind, this student (male, 28 years old) had all of his textbooks placed onto books on tape, and, once he did that, his grades improved dramatically. In fact, he got a B in the class. There are many different levels of dyslexia, and this student had a profound visual dyslexic problem, but there was nothing at all wrong with his ability to acoustically transcribe words into meaning. Therefore, when he *heard* the words, the information was already in the temporal lobe, so he had no trouble correlating the symbolic information (for example, the word *house*) with its visual association. His difficulty was in bringing the visual information into the language center of the temporal lobe, not in bringing acoustical information into the language center.

Figure 13.2 is that of an 18-year-old female student with a much more mild form of dyslexia. Note the dramatic change in slant in the word *individualized* and the reversal of the *s*'s into what looks like *z*'s.

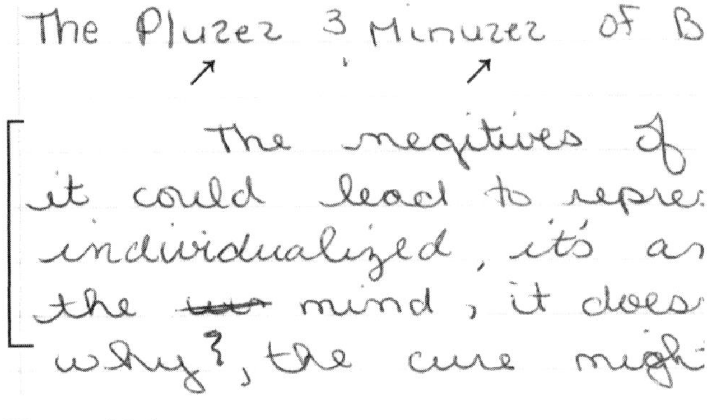

Figure 13.2.

Let's consider what has to happen when one reads. Take the following word: *tree.*

The reader must (1) see the symbolic design in the occipital lobe at the back of the brain; (2) transfer the image to the temporal lobe, where words are stored; (3) find the meaning of the word; and (4) go back to the occipital lobe to create a pictorial image of a tree.

The left angular gyrus in the parietal lobe coordinates this transfer. Visual dyslexia is caused by some kind of problem or disconnect from getting from the occipital lobe to the temporal lobe and getting back to the occipital lobe. Another potential cause of dyslexia is when both the left and right hemispheres of the brain compete for dominance. This happens all the time in children (Toys Я Us).

For most people, one hemisphere dominates. Either the person is a left-brain or right-brain type, or these people tend also to be left-eyed or right-eyed as well; the ipsilateral (same side) eye that's dominant reflects the hemisphere that is dominant. However, some people are "counter-dominant," meaning that both hemispheres vie for power. Most counter-dominant people are also ambidextrous, and their handwriting tends to have an upright/mixed slant. The hypothesis here is that if a dyslexic had a pronounced mixed slant, then their dyslexia is more likely to be caused by counter dominance rather than by some type of minimal brain dysfunction in the left angular gyrus.

Higher Cortical Functions in Man
(Title after A. Luria's classic treatise, 1980)

Localization of Brain Functions

In 1861, Broca discovered the language center in the left temporal lobe of the human brain. This discovery was the first major step in the realization that psychoneurological processes were localized in special areas of the brain. Fritsch and Hitzig continued the search for the specialization of brain functions in 1870 when they discovered that certain muscles of a dog moved when particular neurons were stimulated. This discovery process began to get rather complex by 1881, when Munk discovered "after extirpation of the occipital portion of the brain [i.e., the visual cortex], a dog could still see but lost the power of visual recognition of objects" (Luria, 1980).

It became clear by the turn of the century that "highly complex mental functions [were] located in circumscribed areas of the cerebral cortex" (12). However, a question remained as to how more abstract psychological functions could fit into this neat compartmentalized materialistic view of the brain.

The Anti-localization of Brain Functions

The first major jolt to the localization of brain function theorists came from Karl Lashley, who in 1929 "extirpated different areas of a rat's brain who was going through a maze." Because the rat could still go through the maze even after losing a good portion of his brain, Lashley concluded that a particular type of behavioral disturbance cannot be ascribed to a defect of a particular area of the brain" (14).

The Functional Complex

Pavlov correctly realized that Lashley was not studying specific physical functions, but rather integrated relationships within the brain. By revising the definition of a function (for example, maze meandering), various Russian neurologists came to see that a function is a complex activity comprising (21):

- Analyzing and integrating stimuli.
- Uniting excited and inhibited areas.
- Forming a system of temporary connections.
- Creating an equilibrium of organism with environment.

With regard to movement and thus to handwriting, in 1935 Bernstein noted that "continuous feedback" was necessary between muscles and brain, and that the process involved goal-directed activity from subcortical as well as cortical structures. Motor tasks involved systems that incorporated interconnected areas. Therefore a function, such as **handwriting**, harnessed a "plastic system utilizing differentiated and interchangeable elements." Due to this plasticity, **brain-damaged individuals** would often be able to recover most of their abilities because the process was not directed by one specific lobe, but rather by a coordinated effort of the entire brain. The function in this instance became cortically reorganized.

The Mediate Structure

> When a person ties a knot in his handkerchief or makes a note in order to remember something, he carries out an operation apparently quite unrelated to the task at hand. In this way, however, the person masters his faculty of memory; by changing the structure of the memorizing process and giving it a mediate character, he thereby broadens its natural capacity.

—Alexander Luria

Luria is discussing here the mnemonic device, which, he states, is *characteristic of all higher mental processes*. As an example of the power of this mechanism, I recently was apologizing to my class for not remembering the names of all the students. As I have around 85 of them, perhaps this is understandable, but it can be embarrassing. I was discussing Luria's ideas on memory, and said to one of the girls that because her name was Julie and she wore jewelry, I could remember her name by remembering this characteristic of her appearance. A few weeks later I forgot her name but remembered the example and recovered the lost jewel!

Luria states that **speech** is one of the most important mediate structures involved in all higher mental activity. "As a result of language, man can evoke a particular object and use it in absence of the original.... The reorganization of mental activity by means of speech...and their incorporation into larger processes [separates men from animals and allows them]...to acquire consciousness and volition" (31–32).

The previous paragraph is worth rereading and considering. It is perhaps Luria's most profound insight, for he places speech in the same category as the mnemonic device.

Self-direction, by this definition, operates in conjunction with the internalization of the social activity of speech. Once the child has learned language, he now begins to *think in words* and thereby order his world, both inner and outer, with **inner speech**. If we stay with this idea of how we think, we have to also realize that we also think in non-verbal and pre-verbal ways, for example, through emotions, feelings, sense impressions, and so on. Walking along a Caribbean shoreline, making love, listening to the *White Album*, watching a great old movie, seeing your favorite quarterback throw the perfect game-winning touchdown pass, strolling through an art gallery—these are all areas where thought will probably not be processed in words.

Handwriting, when seen from this perspective, crosses some boundaries, not only reflecting left brain activity of inner speech, but also right brain activity linked to symbolization, emotional expression, and pictorial imagery.

Central Nervous System

Where the **pyramidal nervous system** controls fine motor control, such as carefully dotting *i*'s, eating with a fork, and playing a musical instrument, the **extrapyramidal nervous system** controls gross motor movements such as standing and walking. In a general sense, we can thus see that the voluntary nervous system has two divisions: Pyramidal is more conscious, and extrapyramidal is more unconscious.

Aside from processing acoustical data, the left **temporal lobe** processes language, whereas the right temporal lobe processes more abstract stimuli such as music.

Based on 40 years of research, Luria (1980) concludes that consonants, which make up the important parts of the words "r prgrmmd n th lft hmsphr," whereas vowels form the background of the words and are programmed in the right hemisphere. Also, because different languages stress different processes (for example, Chinese pictograms vs. abstract English), the cortical organization of the brains of people from different cultures will be different.

Well-known words, the signature, ideograms (for example, **STOP, USA, EXXON, ETC**), and automatisms also tend to be programmed more in the right brain, whereas access to the larynx tends to be located in the left hemisphere.

Concerning the **parietal lobe**, as mentioned earlier, the left angular gyrus is involved in processing reading and handwriting, whereas the entire parietal lobe is involved in what Luria calls "simultaneous synthesis." In other words, its function is to coordinate all the lobes. In this sense, the parietal lobe operates very much like the **cerebellum**, which contains, among other things, automatisms or psychomotor programs learned over time, such as bike riding. As a child learns to become more proficient in riding a bike his ability to coordinate all the lobes involved (muscles, eye-hand coordination, knowing where one is going) is coordinated by the parietal lobe, and, once it becomes a habit, the program is *transferred* to the cerebellum.

It is known that the **cerebellum** is less developed in people who have autism, which can be defined as a form of childhood schizophrenia. It is quite possible that social programs (*Hello, how are doing? Fine, how are you doing?*) are also facilitated by this brain center in the same way. As the child learns to communicate, the parietal lobe probably shifts the various routines to the cerebellum. Because autistic children have difficulty communicating, one way or another the ability to coordinate the various lobes to partake of these everyday social programs malfunctions.

The Split Brain

LEFT HEMISPHERE	CORPUS CALLOSUM	RIGHT HEMISPHERE
CONSCIOUS	PRECONSCIOUS	UNCONSCIOUS

The CS/PCS/UCS relationship can exist *within* the cerebral cortex, between the two hemispheres and also with regards to subcortical organization. Of course there is the problem of trying to apply these Freudian psychoanalytic concepts to the physical brain, and so we are only looking at this chart loosely. Nevertheless, there are some truths herein. There *are* CS, PCS, and UCS aspects to the cerebral cortex within and between each hemisphere, and there are also these same threefold relationships to the midbrain/limbic and brainstem areas. For instance, if it is sunny out and we have an emotional high because of this, the limbic area has been activated, and, the more we are aware of its activation, the more conscious of it we become. In the same sense, if a jerk cuts you off on the highway and you experience road rage, elements of the survival mode brainstem have kicked into gear. Some people are more "road rage"/brainstem types, some more emotional, some more cerebral, and these differences will be evident in the handwriting.

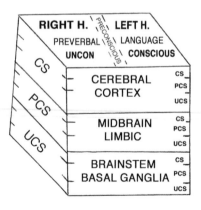

A word about the corpus callosum: It takes approximately eight years for it to develop in the growing child. One way or another, the corpus callosum facilitates interhemispheric communication, and thus would be associated with the censor, which lies between the CS and UCS and also automatisms, habitual psychomotor patterns, in this case, the seemingly automatic way a person cross-talks between hemispheres. Certainly Freud's preconscious correlates in some ways with the corpus callosum.

Figure 13.3. Applying psychodynamic theory to the Triune brain.

There is the implication here, based on Luria's findings, that consonants are in the left hemisphere and vowels in the right, that (1) there must be a subordinate language center in the right hemisphere, and (2) during the process of reading and writing, there will be constant cross-talk between the hemispheres because the **left** must access the **right** in order to retrieve vowels, and to obtain the deeper meaning of words and sentences. Following this line of thinking, **downstrokes** are associated with movements *toward* the body, they are an expression of self, and thus are more conscious, more left brained. **Upstrokes**, on the other hand, are mostly just a way to get to the next downstroke, and thus are less conscious. It may in fact be the case that just as vowels are located in the right hemisphere, upstrokes may be as well. In the left will be the words, and in the right will be pictorial aspects to the writing, such as symbols and ideograms (for example, highly practiced writing sequences, such as one's signature).

Rudolf Pophal

Rudolf Pophal, a German doctor from the University of Hamburg from the 1930s through the 1950s, undertook an extensive study of the specific neural pathways that handwriting takes. It was Pophal's theory that the center in the brain that governed in the writing would also govern the personality. Pophal created four types of writers, those ruled predominantly by the (1) cerebral cortex, such as intellectual types; (2) those ruled by the repressive corpus striatum, such as strict and inhibited individuals; (3) those ruled by the globus pallidus, such as impulsive and violent types; and (4) a fourth category that he called brainstem writers, which were instinctual/emotional types. The components of the basal ganglia that surround the thalamus, the corpus striatum, and globus pallidus, although located in the center of the brain in the midst of the limbic system, are still brainstem (reptile) organs. Before discussing Pophal's ideas, it is best to briefly define the various subcortical components.

Thalamus

This is the major switchboard (kind of like the Grand Central Station) relaying all sensory information to the rest of the brain. It elaborates and integrates sequences. It is in close communication with the cerebellum, hypothalamus, and basal ganglia (below it), and hippocampus and cerebral cortex above it. One's sense of identity has also been located in the thalamus.

Medulla

This is an extension of the spinal cord housing the reticular formation. This area is involved with vital functions such as muscle tone, heartbeat, breathing, and states of consciousness.

Brainstem

The brainstem has the pyramidal and extrapyramidal nervous system (voluntary nervous system) running through it. The medulla and brainstem can be considered one and the same.

Reticular Formation

Reticular formation controls the brainwaves, muscle tone, and the energy level to allow consciousness to operate. This is a complex area linked to the **pons**, which controls dreaming, and the **REM cycle**. The **RF** is modulated by the **pineal gland**, which controls the wake/sleep cycle through the production of hormones serotonin and melatonin (which are structured very much like **LSD**). In terms of handwriting, it is well known that the production of **serotonin** is associated with an uplifted mood. If a person has signs of an elevated mood (for example, rising baselines), this would suggest the influence of serotonin or perhaps **adrenaline**. Conversely, **depression** is linked to reduced levels of serotonin. The hormone **gaba** inhibits serotonin production. Depression is complicated, but it could be associated with increased levels of **gaba** and **noradrenaline** and corresponding decreased levels of serotonin.

The Cerebellum

The cerebellum is the great coordinator conveying impulses from the senses, balance, body position, and brainstem processes. A cat has a highly developed cerebellum. It coordinates muscle activity and also sensory data. It is well connected to the thalamus, and also influences the cerebral cortex. Acting much like a mini-brain, it also houses automatisms, which are learned habitual behavior patterns that originate in the cerebral cortex. The cerebellum, in a sense, stores subroutines. After these automatisms are gained and transferred, the cerebral cortex is freed to learn additional information.

Hippocampus

Much like a reference librarian, the hippocampus accesses memories, and, in that sense, it can almost be seen as a specialized extension of the thalamus.

Hypothalamus

The hypothalamus is also a kind of mini-brain whose responsibilities include emotions, hunger, thirst, body temperature, aggression, sexual impulses, and metabolism. It has a direct line to the pituitary gland, which sits adjacent to it. Thus, the HT also modulates the autonomic nervous (involuntary) system.

Pituitary Gland

The pituitary gland is the Master Gland. It controls the other endocrine glands and their hormone production: thyroid (body metabolism), adrenal, pancreas (which produces insulin to control sugar metabolism), and the gonads (male and female sex hormone production). It also controls growth. Clearly, handwriting will be influenced by the production of different hormones. For instance, estrogen would soften a personality (graphologically it would be associated with connectedness, curves, garlands, and pastosity), whereas testosterone would make one more aggressive (pressure, angles, emphasis on upper and lower zone lengths). Adrenaline production would be seen in the pressure, speed, and expressiveness of the writing.

Amygdala

The amygdala is involved with survival processes, temperament, personality, and aggressive behavior. A disorder of this organ could cause autistic-like behavior in children or rage.

Automatonic Nervous System

The automatonic nervous system in the old days was called the involuntary nervous system, because it involved procedures that were not controlled by volitional activity (heartbeat, hormone production, dilation of pupil in the eye, and so on). The ANS has two divisions:

- Parasympathetic nervous system produces noradrenaline and generally slows down the system (for example, slows heart rate).
- Sympathetic nervous system produces adrenaline and generally speeds up the system.

The autonomic nervous system controls involuntary smooth muscles such as ones found in the esophagus and heart, blood pressure, and also various glands.

Basal Ganglia

The basal ganglia is a complex structure involved with voluntary movements and is somewhat independent of the cerebellum and cerebral cortex. "The basal ganglia and cerebellum are large collections of nuclei that modify movement on a minute-to-minute basis. Motor cortex sends information to both, and both structures send information right back to cortex via the thalamus. (Remember, to get to cortex you must go through thalamus.) The output of the cerebellum is excitatory, while the basal ganglia are inhibitory. The balance between these two systems allows for smooth, coordinated movement, and a disturbance in either system will show up as movement disorders" (*wustl.edu/course/cerebell*, 2007).

Globus Pallidus

The globus pallidus (pallidium) receives information from the cerebral cortex and is also connected to the hypothalamus on top of the brainstem. This organ is intimately associated with voluntary movements and the pyramidal and extrapyramidal nervous systems. Damage can cause wild, flying movements. It is probably the active or excitatory organ of the basal ganglia. (Note that this definition contradicts the implication of the definition from *wustl.edu*, which says only the cerebellum is excitatory. Either way, there is excitatory and inhibitory systems associated with the basal ganglia, which will correlate to the thrust of Pophal's argument.)

In their book, *Subcortical Correlates of Human Behavior*, Manuel Riklan and Eric Levitz talk about the basal ganglia.

> The multiplicity of connections of the basal ganglia would indicate that these structures are inextricably involved in the activities of the remainder of the brain. The flow of impulses through the basal ganglia is modulated by the thalamus and the cortex.... [The basal ganglia] also defines connections of major efferent paths to the motor nuclei of the brainstem and to the anterior horn cells of the spinal cord [i.e., from spinal cord to cortex].... The precise functions of the basal ganglia are still not clearly understood as they cannot be determined apart from other brain areas with which they are in functional relations.

Substantia Nigra

Located in the midbrain region, the substantia nigra, by supplying dopamine, modulates fine motor control and regulates mood. (Parkinson's disease results when this system breaks down.)

Striatum

The striatum receives information from the suppressor areas of the frontal cortex. It is involved with manual skill and tends to be an inhibitory factor.

Handwritings such as that of Beethoven and Napoleon are pallidium writers, raw and passionate, whereas the everyday conforming writings show influence of the inhibitory striatum.

The more automatized the script, the greater the integration between hemispheres; conversely, the less automatized, the less cerebrally organized, and the less "plastic" the cortical zones.

Pophal's Topology			
Pallidium		**Striatum**	
rising lines, illegibility, great pressure, speed and richness of movements		smallness, small endings, narrowness, meagerness weak pressure, falling lines, and monotony	
+	**−**	**+**	**−**
mobile	excited	slow	dry
spontaneous	irritable	disciplined	anxious
vivacious	uncontrolled	cautious	depressed
active	aggressive	regulated	inhibited
sexual	careless	patient	over regulated
humor	instable		

Figure 13.4. In the chart, you can see traits of basal ganglia writers (adapted from Bernard, 1980).

Figure 13.5. Note the spontaneous and bold graphic movements and the predominance of primary thread (as seen in the rapid up and down and v-like movements in the signature) of Napoleon's handwriting. This is an example of a high-functioning pallidium writing.

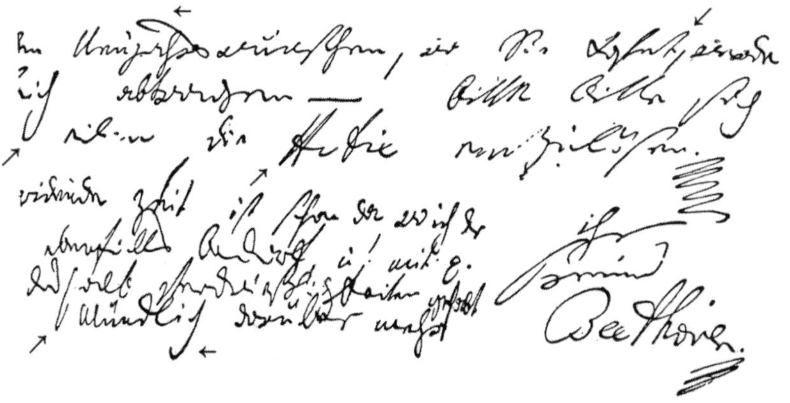

Figure 13.6. Another example of a high-functioning pallidium handwriting, that of Beethoven, early 1800s. Note great size and pressure changes, yet aesthetically pleasing vigor of the writing. The curves and shading of the stroke soften the so-called brainstem aspect. Arrows point to length differences in lower zone.

Figure 13.7. Jack Dempsy and Jake LaMotta, two boxers who have the influence of both the pallidium (large J's in both cases) and the restrictive striatum (tight, constrained middle zone). Dempsy even cuts off his lower zone, removing and converting any amorous feelings he may have had into the fight game.

Field Marshall Erwin Rommel, 1941.

Sincerely,

H. Norman Schwarzkopf
U.S. Army, Retired
1995

Figure 13.8. Two generals, Erwin Rommel and Norman Schwartzkopf. Both display the unbridled zigzag movement of the pallidium writer, although in Rommel's case, the bold impulse is more along the lateral axis, whereas Schwartzkopf's is classic up and down primary thread. In both cases, their primitive aggressive impulses are tempered by foresight and high intelligence, evident in Rommel's case in the clarity of the signature; in Schwartzkopf's case, for almost an opposite reason, the signature's abstract bold multidimensionality.

A third category Pophal has is for writers who have rhythmical, flowing, garlanded, looped scripts. Curiously, Pophal labels these **brainstem** writers, which appear to this author to be a misappropriation. Because the pallidium and striatum are part of the brainstem, it seems Pophal would have been better served to have named this category the **limbic** type.

A last category Pophal suggests is the cortex writer. These writers have simplification, regularity, discipline, and rhythm to their scripts. This group includes high form level scientific, professorial kinds of scripts, heavily modulated by the workings of the cerebral cortex. These are very high-level individuals who interact with their environments more through their minds than through the emotional sphere. Examples for the last two types will be discussed. The important point to keep in mind is that Pophal was the first major theoretician to categorize handwritings according to specific brain structures.

The Triune Brain

The brain can be divided into three major functional units (Luria, 1973):

1. **Brainstem** for cortical tone and waking.
2. **Midbrain** for receiving, analyzing, and storing information.
3. **Cerebral cortex** for programming, regulating, and verifying information.

Paul MacLean (1976), a neuroscientist from Bethesda, Maryland, who coined the term *triune brain* links these same three divisions to the evolutionary structure of the brain:

1. **Brainstem** (basal ganglia, reticular formation, spinal cord, medulla, pons, and cerebellum) comprise what he calls the **reptile brain—Instinct**.
2. **Limbic system** (thalamus, hypothalamus, hippocampus, and amygdala) comprise the **mammal brain—Emotion**.
3. **Cerebral cortex** (frontal, motor, temporal, parietal, and occipital lobes) make up the **human brain—Intellect**.

This is a hierarchical arrangement, whereby the evolutionary process seeks not to undo what has already been achieved, but to build upon the more primal brains.

He also states: "The three brains are radically different in structure and chemistry and in an evolutionary sense countless generations apart. We are obliged to look to ourselves and world through the eyes of three quite different mentalities. To complicate things, two of the mentalities appear to lack the power of speech."

	MacLean	Luria	Freud
Cerebral Cortex	Human brain Intellect	Programming Regulating Verifying	Conscious Awareness Ego
Midbrain Limbic system	Mammal Emotion	Receiving Analyzing Storing info	Presonscious Latent memories Defense structure Superego
Brainstem	Reptile Instinct	Cortieal tone Waking Reflexes	Unconscious Forgotten and repressed memories Id

Figure 13.9. This diagram explores the relationship between the threefold Freudian structures for thinking (that is, conscious, preconscious, and unconscious) and the three major hierarchical divisions of the brain, cerebral cortex, midbrain/limbic system, and brainstem.

One cannot help but see a clear parallel to Freud's threefold delineations of id, superego, and ego, and also unconscious, preconscious, and conscious. However, there are also great differences between the thinking styles of the left hemisphere as compared to the right hemisphere, so we now come up with four major divisions that can be correlated to Jung's four personality types and, also, loosely to Freud's four divisions:

LEFT HEMISPHERE	RIGHT HEMISPHERE
Thinking	Intuition
Ego	Ego Ideal

LIMBIC SYSTEM

Emotion
Superego
Erotic Id

BRAINSTEM

Sensing
Aggressive Id

Figure 13.10. In the chart, we can see that the human brain has two hemispheres and two major lower centers for four divisions.

In a general sense, the limbic system appears to be more correlated to right brain activity and the brainstem/sensing type, correlates more with the left brain. Ultimately, we begin to run into some difficulties when we try to fit such things as Freud's and Jung's psychological typologies to various physical brain structures and eventually to handwriting. Is there really a "brainstem" or "limbic brain" human type? Yes and no. Marilyn Monroe is certainly an emotional type and thus she should be more dominated by her limbic system than, say, Albert Einstein. To further complicate matters, Freud's id really has two main divisions, an instinct associated with sex/pleasure and one for aggression/survival. From a neurological point of view, it would make more sense to break the id up into these two divisions and place the more aggressive/reptilian part of the id with the brainstem and the more erotic side of the id with the limbic system. We thus come up with the following fourfold brain with two divisions for the cerebral cortex and two subcortical divisions, one under the domain of each hemisphere.

LEFT HEMISPHERE	RIGHT HEMISPHERE
Thinking /Ego **(Left Frontal Lobe)** Sees parts/Analytical high Form Level, organized, sharp, simplified, mixed connecting strokes, garlands, diacritics EINSTEIN, DARWIN, CONON DOYLE	**Intuitive/Ego Ideal** **(Right Frontal Lobe, Thalamus)** Sees whole/Pictures spontaneous, innovative, pastose, elaborated, pictorial, expressive, rhythmical, horizontal axis garlands, secondary thread WALT DISNEY, MARC CHAGALL, RU JOHNSON
BRAINSTEM	LIMBIC SYSTEM/MIDBRAIN
Sensing/Id **Globus Pallidus/Striatum** Aggression/Athletic heavy pressure, pastose, angles, vertical axis emphasized, conforming in low level, primary thread in high level MIKE TYSON, JACK DEMPSY, MARLON BRANDO, ROBERT DINERO, HEMINGWAY	**Emotion/Superego** **Hypothalamus—Endocrine system** Eroticism extreme right or left slant, also changing slants, curves, left trend, big lower loops, Palmer style, arcades, secondary elaboration MARILYN MONROE, TOM CRUISE, GLEN FORD, BILLIE HOLIDAY

Figure 13.11. In the chart, we can see Jung's four types: thinking, intuitive, sensing, and emotional, and Freud's ego/superego/id loosely correlated to four major divisions of the brain.

This typology is very similar to that of Jeanette Farmer's (1995), who based her work on Ned Hermann's Brain Dominance typology.

LEFT CEREBRAL	RIGHT CEREBRAL
A. Analytical	**D. Imaginative**
Thinking style: logical, factual, critical, technical, and quantitative	**Thinking style**: visual, holistic, intuitive, innovative, and conceptual
Preferred activities: collecting data, analysis, understanding how things work, fact-based, logical reasoning	**Preferred activities**: looks at big picture, taking initiative, iconoclastic, visual, metaphoric thinking, creative problem-solving, long-term thinking
LEFT LIMBIC	RIGHT LIMBIC
B. Sequential	**C. Interpersonal**
Thinking style: safekeeping, structured, organized, detailed, planned	**Thinking style**: kinesthetic, emotional, spiritual, sensory, feeling
Preferred activities: following directions, detail oriented work, step-by-step problem-solving, organization, and implementation	**Preferred activities**: listening to and expressing ideas, looking for personal ideas, looking for personal meaning, sensory input and group interaction

Figure 13.12. Farmer and Hermann's fourfold brain dominance chart and its link to handwriting. Farmer also linked these four types to Pophals's.

	LEFT CEREBRAL	LEFT SUBCORTEX	RIGHT CEREBRAL	RIGHT SUBCORTEX
Ancients:	Fire/Lion	Earth/Bear	Air/Eagle	Water/Man
Jung:	Thinking	Sensing	Intuitive	Emotional
Hermann:	Analytic	Sequential	Imaginative	Interpersonal
Freud:	Ego	Aggressive Id	Ego Ideal	Superego/Erotic Id
MacLean:	Human/Intellect	Reptile/Instinct	Human/Art	Mammal/Emotion
Luria:	Cerebral cortex	Brainstem	Cerebral cortex	Midbrain
Pophal:	Cortex writer	Striatum	Globus Pallidus	Brainstem
Seifer:	Left Brain type	Brainstem/Primal	Right Brain type	Limbic

Figure 13.13. A comparison of numerous theoreticians to the fourfold structure of the brain, whereby the top layer of the triune brain has two parts: right and left hemispheres.

Although we have a good amount of correlation, we see a discrepancy between Pophal and Luria. Part of the problem is that Luria would be defining the characteristics of the brainstem in a different way than Pophal, who appears more to define the brainstem as an emotional realm.

It seems that the limbic system is more tied to the right brain, and brainstem energies appear to be more under the domain of the left brain. This hypothesis would be a topic for research, to either refute or support. In any case, there are still four divisions: (1) left brain; (2) right brain; (3) limbic; and (4) brainstem; there would be subdivisions for each type. Pophal's model leads us to speculate that there is a restricted and unrestricted brainstem type, and there are also high Form Level/high functioning and low Form Level/low functioning types for each division.

The brain is very complicated. No person is a pure type, but clearly, from our discussion, it is certainly evident that there *are* different types whose handwritings are organized in different ways.

Endocrine Glands

The last category is writers who appear to be dominated by the **emotions** and thus the **endocrine glands**. The neurotransmitters produced by the pituitary and pineal gland and at the synaptic junctions of every neuron powerfully influence cerebral organization and behavior. These writers are perhaps being controlled more so by the workings of the hypothalamic-pituitary system. Three of the four examples in this category have low Form Levels, which suggests poor ego integrity and some type of arrested development. Thus, they may be even more subject to the whims of the emotions than higher functioning **limbic** types discussed in the next section.

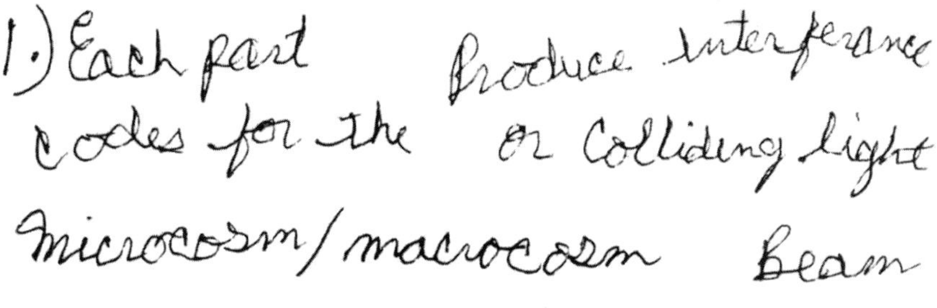

Figure 13.14. This young man has an alcoholic stepfather who probably abused him (and his mother) when he was a child. He is a bright student whose voice quivers. The roundedness displays dominance of the limbic region (symbolically, the maternal related instincts) and activity of the endocrine system. The shakiness reveals inner conflict and tension.

Figure 13.14 is a vocal and somewhat bright student who told me he wants to become a clinical psychologist! He has missed all three exams (stating that his grandfather died for the first one) and making up excuses for the others; however, he did make up the tests and pass them. His voice has a quiver to it, but, without seeing his handwriting, it would be highly unlikely to realize the gross motor disturbances that affect his psychophysiology. He says he is nervous. Quite frankly, his writing disturbs me as he seems "quite normal" in day-to-day contact. Although it is clear that he does have problems, he is friendly and extroverted. In any event, one would expect a borderline schizophrenic personality from the writing, and this is not the case.

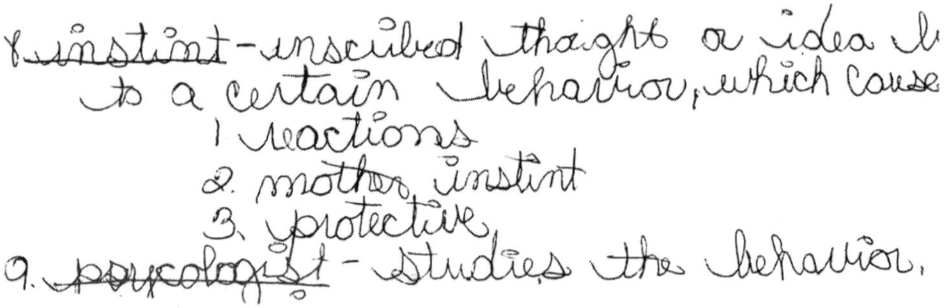

Figure 13.15. The handwriting looks similar to Figure 13.14. This a quiet female student who had a C-average. She appeared to be shy and unconcerned.

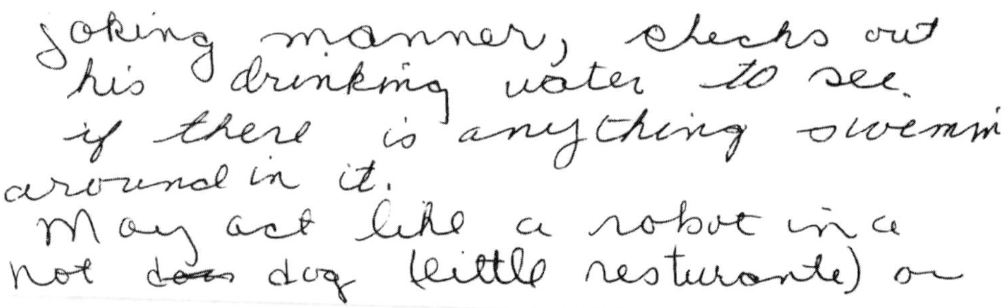

Figure 13.16. The handwriting of a 20-year-old female religious fanatic with a high scholastic average.

The next writing in this category, Figure 13.16, was that of an A+ student! She memorized everything for the exam and asked many questions. She did say that she almost suffered a nervous breakdown (having been brought up with eight other children—although that, in and of itself, means very little)...until she found Jesus. She inundated me with her beliefs and could not understand why I would not commit myself to her specific religious view.

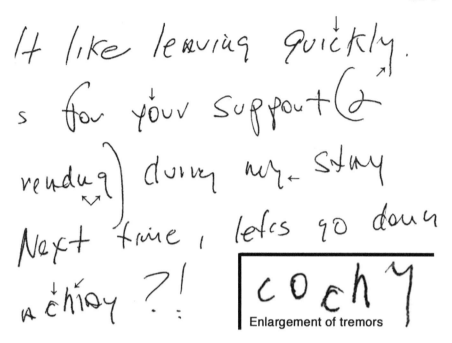

Figure 13.17. A doctoral student who has taken LSD possibly hundreds of times.

She saw parapsychology as evil and riled me so that I had powerful pallidium urge to clobber her! She was overbearing, egocentric, and a general pain. Nevertheless, she was intelligent, caring, and truly searching for a more meaningful existence. She could not see, however, that salvation comes from within. She sought an external source, which had the net effect of substituting an all-powerful god for a true willing self. She memorized everything but learned nothing.

The last writing is that of a highly intelligent PhD student in psychology who had edited a small journal on psychedelics and is considered an expert in that field. His friends included Timothy Leary. Note the fuzziness of the line strokes. This is probably caused by an imbalance of the pineal gland and a dopamine imbalance, which, in turn, affected the reticular formation that is intrinsic to fine motor control through the pyramidal nervous system and substantia nigra.

Limbic System Writers

The predominance of loops, left trend, and essentially modified Palmer writings separate the **limbic system** writers from higher Form Level **right brain** intuitive/holistic writers discussed. The top two writers, Billie Holiday and Jim Belushi, were both brilliant entertainers, but also both addicted to drugs. We see a predominance of left trend in the lowercase y's and an over-abundance of tall loops in Billie Holiday's ample signature. The writing suggests strong elements of hysteria and mania. In Belushi's case, we see a marked change in the slant in the *y*, and a lower zone loop that hangs in the depths. There also is a marked difference between Belushi's tight and somewhat over-controlled handwriting as compared to his rather freewheeling signature. His huge appetite for drugs can be seen symbolically in the large lower loops and psychologically in his wish to escape a rather mundane sense of self, seen in the surprisingly staid and essentially humble handwriting.

Michael Jackson was a rock star by the age of 5. For some peculiar reason, this striking African American was never satisfied with his appearance and kept going in for more and more nose jobs, face lifts, and skin whitening procedures. One can see how handsome he is in this photo, which was taken before his face changes really entered the realm of the truly bizarre. He was also arrested for allegedly molesting a young boy who he admitted to sleeping with, but he said it was platonic. Although he was not convicted, it was his second arrest for this kind of possible crime. One way or another, Michael is fixated on the success he had as a boy and surrounds himself with children, mostly young boys. His dancing and lyrics can be very masculine, for example, *Beat It!,* but when he talks he sounds meek and feminine. He is a man of opposites.

A question arises as to the limitations of handwriting analysis. Michael Jackson has been, perhaps, the most famous person in the Western world for more than 30 years (circa 1977–2007), and we all know his story. So, when we analyze his handwriting, in a way, we are working backward. That said, we see a number of key symbols in his writing that give us a key to just who he is. The signature is exceedingly tall; one way or another, MJ has a high opinion of himself, but the signature is artificial, and thus it suggests planning in its design, and, in that sense, it is a ruse, as it hides the real person. Nevertheless, we do see strong masculine signs and influence of the **pallidium** as seen in the overall height and very tall sharp second hump in the *M*, and feminine signs, the circle i-dot, and long tapered tails to many letters that trail into the lower zone. His last name has the *J* clearly bisected, symbolizing the duality of his self-image, black/white, and male/female. The name also ends with a counterstroke, the *l* that cuts back to the left when it should go right. It suggests deception, offset by another opposite, the very tall capital letters that relate to his sense of spirituality, thus the id/superego duality is also present. The large circles, curves, and pastosity of the stroke all relate to the influence of the limbic region.

Marilyn Monroe's signature shows a strong right slant, circles tumbling onto other circles, rhythmic shading to the letters, and an illegible middle zone. She also seems to have more trouble with the first name than the second, all suggesting a highly sensitive erotic disposition with feelings of self-doubt. John Belushi has the highest form level of the group. His legible middle zone and well-spaced letters suggests a clarity of thought, friendliness, and loyalty, and also an ability to keep a secret. The biggest problem in his writing is the changing slant. Belushi is being pulled in opposite directions. All of these figures led tragic lives and, in all cases, their egos (that is, sense of identity) were overpowered by emotional factors that led to their undoing.

Figure 13.18. The handwriting of four limbic systems emotional writers under the sway of neurologically, the pleasure center of the hypothalamus, and psychologically, the erotic side of the id.

Glenn Ford was one of the most successful actors of his day. Having acted in more than 100 movies, he is most remembered for *Blackboard Jungle*, *Tea House of the August Moon*, and *Pocket Full of Miracles*. The large curves, pastosity, and general conformity of the middle zone are the signs of the **limbic** writer. But we also see the influence of the **pallidium**, in the strong powerful upstrokes on the *F* and *G*. One can see his large sexual appetites evident in the strong masculinity of the writing, and the grasping lower loop of the *G*. Ford's conquests included Joan Crawford, Dinah Shore, Bridget Bardot, Connie Stevens, Debbie Reynolds, and Rita Hayworth. The vigor of the writing reflects his longevity as an actor.

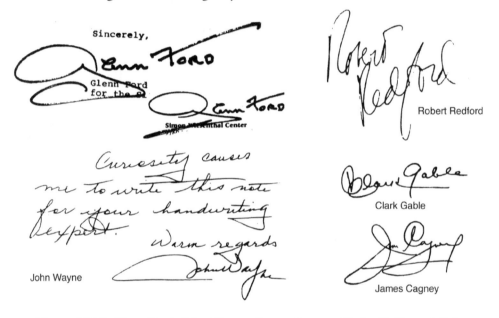

Figure 13.19. Glenn Ford, John Wayne, James Cagney, Clarke Gable, and Robert Redford, five high-functioning limbic system writers.

One can see in John Wayne's writing the powerful influence of what Pophal calls the **striatum**. Take away the big loops and the name on the signature and the writing looks like a non-descript conforming Palmer writing. The middle zone is straightforward, well organized, and disciplined. His originality shows up in the secondary elaboration, the big lower loops, which bespeaks his wish to be creative, but the writing is not intrinsically so. Wayne's aggression shows up in the sharp angles in the lower zone, the large capital *J*, and long t-bar. John Wayne was a big man, in some ways "larger than life," but on some level, he felt ordinary. Perhaps that is what endeared him to his many fans. From a psychoanalytic point of view, he did not truly connect to his big star persona. He was addicted to cigarettes and died of lung cancer because of it.

Clark Gable's writing is similar to John Wayne's in that it does not come across as particularly masculine. The capital *C* looks more like a heart than a *C*. It is awkward, and, similar to Wayne, Clark Gable cuts off his lower zone in the lateral stroke that goes through the lower loop of the *G*. The overall warmth of the writing through its unassuming curves corresponds to the charm that Gable had as one of the premier leading stars of his day.

James Cagney's writing with the very large lower zone letters shows the influence of the **pallidium**. He was an aggressive actor who understood what power was and how to use it. The **limbic** influence is seen in the curves. Both brain centers, the aggressive and emotional side of the id, are evident in this signature.

The highest form level of the group by far can be found in Robert Redford's writing. There is a lot of warmth evident as well as clarity of thought, and strong sense of self. Unlike the other writers, there is no sense of overcompensation in Redford's writing. You get what you see. He is sincere, warmhearted, self-confident, spontaneous, and bold. We see here the influence of both the **limbic** region as well as the marked influence of the **right cerebral cortex**. Glenn Ford would be more a combination of **limbic** and **left cerebral cortex**, seen in the almost mathematical aspect to his linear middle zone. Redford started his career as an artist. This tendency is evident in the graceful curved nature of the graphic trail.

Striatum Writers

A good way to learn how to analyze handwritings is to know the history of the writers; and compare similar types to see what is similar and what is different. The top writing in Figure 13.20 has a larger middle zone and better tri-zonal dynamics. The bottom writing has larger spaces between letters and is more tense. Try to list other similarities and differences between these two writings.

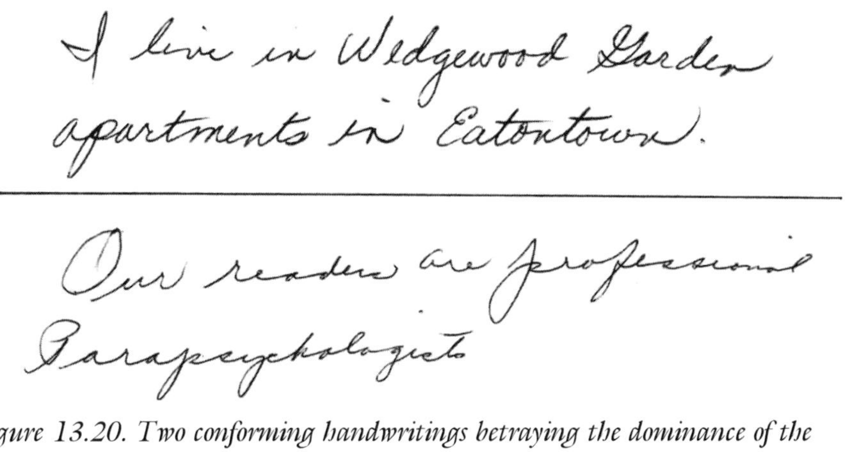

Figure 13.20. Two conforming handwritings betraying the dominance of the restrictive striatum, the part of the brain that keeps the pallidium at bay.

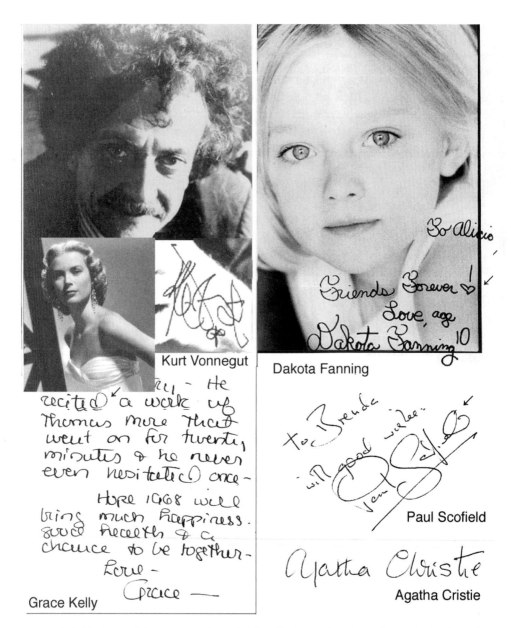

Figure 13.21. Kurt Vonnegut, Grace Kelly, Dakota Fanning, Paul Scofield, and Agatha Christie—all right-brain writers.

Cerebral Cortex Writers

There are essentially three types of cerebral cortex writers, right-brain and left brain types and positive mixed types that exhibit interhemispheric communication. In general, all three will display spontaneity, fluidity of movement, simplification, innovative connections, excellent organization, and high Form Level. Where the left brain types will tend to be sharp, linear, well-regulated and lean, right brain types will have pastosity of stroke, fullness, a pictorial quality, primary elaboration, and a strong sense of form.

Right Brain

The signature of the prolific satiric author Kurt Vonnegut appears in Figure 13.21 on the top left. It looks somewhat like a cartoon self-image. There is a tortured quality to the writing, and it is doubtful that a graphologist would necessarily know that the writer was high functioning if all he had to look at was this whacky scribble. Vonnegut ended up in a prisoner-of-war camp in Dresden during WWII. Many prisoners and guards died during the bombing of that beautiful city. Vonnegut survived by hiding in a slaughterhouse, thus the title of his most famous book, *Slaughterhouse Five*. Sixty years later, he was still writing. The pictorial quality of the signature places him as a right brain type.

Another handwriting that has a whacky aspect to it is that of the brilliant child star Dakota Fanning. For some offbeat, symbolic reason she has come up with a highly unusual capital *F*. It brings to mind a cartoon-like caricature of an extraterrestrial. Dakota also places the unusual design in the capital *T* as well. The writing is clear, round, and pastose. Her warm-hearted disposition is reflected in the heart she places in her exclamation point. It will be interesting to see how this unique yet peculiar and somewhat artificial capital *F* evolves as she gets older.

Heart-like symbols can also be seen in Kurt Vonnegut's signature at the far right, and in the ending *d*'s of Grace Kelly and Paul Scofield. Both Grace Kelly and Agatha Christie have large middle zones, whereas Scofield's is rather small. The two ladies are social bugs, but Scofield's handwriting suggests an introverted nature with some sense of isolation. This *Man For All Seasons* actor shows left brain influence in the regulated lean middle zone and strong right brain emphasis in the large, round pictorial signature. Grace Kelly's right-brain pictorial/symbolic style also shows much influence of the limbic system emotional sphere. This is tempered by the upright slant, which shows self-control associated with left-brain logical thinking. The foreshortened lower zone (influence of striatum—she married a king but at the expense of her career), and the general clarity of the middle-zone bumps this writing up from the subcortical limbic writer to the cortex right brain writer.

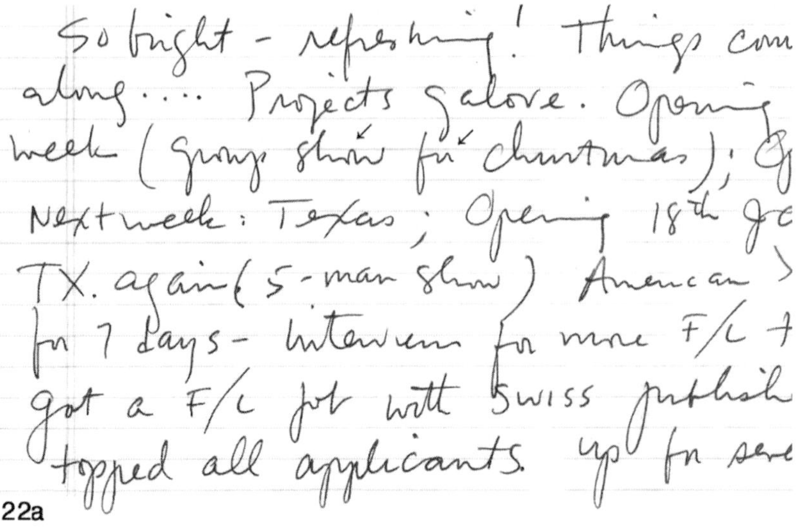

So bright - refreshing! Things com along.... Projects galore. Opening week (group show for christmas); Of Next week: Texas; Opening 18th of TX. again (5-man show) American for 7 days - Interviews for more F/L + got a F/L job with Swiss publish topped all applicants. up for seve

22a

I opened it. Oddly, I bought Dreams in, I think, 1975. Still brown now 80 and a little w in; into something, when I turne around 18. I don't know when o be back. Very fortunate to b you in 85-6 Though... I'm

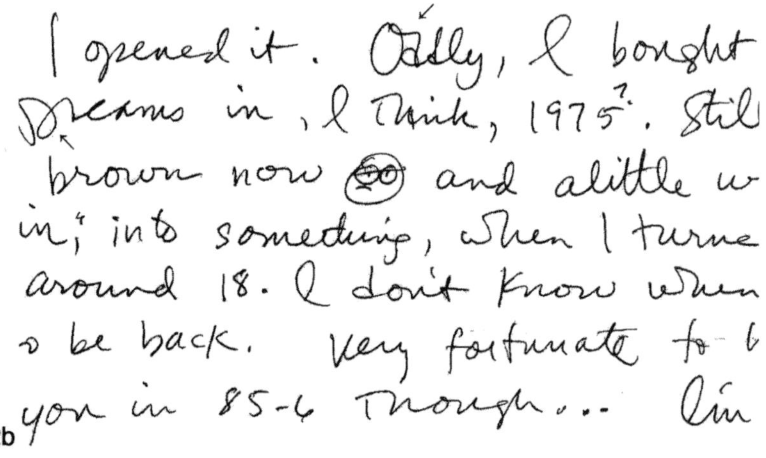

22b

Figure 13.22. The handwriting of two very talented artists with high Form Level.

The most integrated of the five is that of Agatha Christie. The sense of form, spacing, and roundedness in the writing displays the influence of the right brain. The upright slant and overall regulated nature shows the influence of the left brain and the missing top part of the *g* suggests some type of restriction linked to the striatum. See also Figures 13.23 to 13.33 for other examples of right brain writers.

Figure 13.22 shows two right-brain cerebral cortex writers who both earn their living as artists. The top example is the handwriting of painter and graphic designer Robert Adsit, whose figure 8 signature appears in Figure 11.7 in Chapter 11. (See also Figure 3.2 from the Form Level chapter.) A prodigy who was adopted at the age of 4, Robert worked in oils and watercolors; he also created etchings and collages, and even worked with finger paints. One of his etchings appears in Figure 13.23. Note the fluid nature of the writing trail, its sense of enthusiasm and imagery, ability to switch between writing and printing, use of diacritics (ellipses and exclamation points), bold decision to set his own parameters, ignoring the vertical and horizontal margins on the page, and speed. The ar-

Figure 13.23. Night Vision, an etching by Robert Adsit, circa 1976.

rows point to primary thread, (up and down movement), which suggests signs of genius supported by his ability to cover the vertical *and* horizontal axes with both primary (-or combination), and secondary thread (-ing endings), and at the same time create a letter that is completely legible.

Figure 13.22b is that of Lynn Sevigny, whose illustrations can be found in the frontispiece and in Figure 13.1 in this chapter, the technical drawing of the split brain. The arrows show original and spontaneous connecting strokes. Note also the use of a caricature in the center of the page, the arcades in the upper zone as in the word *when*, the dynamic quality of the writing as the size changes seem to pulsate, and the use of diacritics (question mark, commas, and ellipses). These all show the workings of the right brain. In both cases left brain influence can be seen in the excellent organization, simplification, and legibility, which shows a measure of control within the spontaneity. Both writers also have calligraphic print scripts that display their highly developed fine motor control (pyramidal nervous system and substantia nigra), which can also be seen in their drawings.

Left Brain

These three individuals (Figure 13.24) are some of the premier thinkers of their day. They all have well-organized connected writing with simplification and upper zone elaboration, particularly with t-bars. All three are left brain dominant, but also strong right brain influence seen in the high form level, variety of connections, use of garlands, and aesthetic pictorial sense.

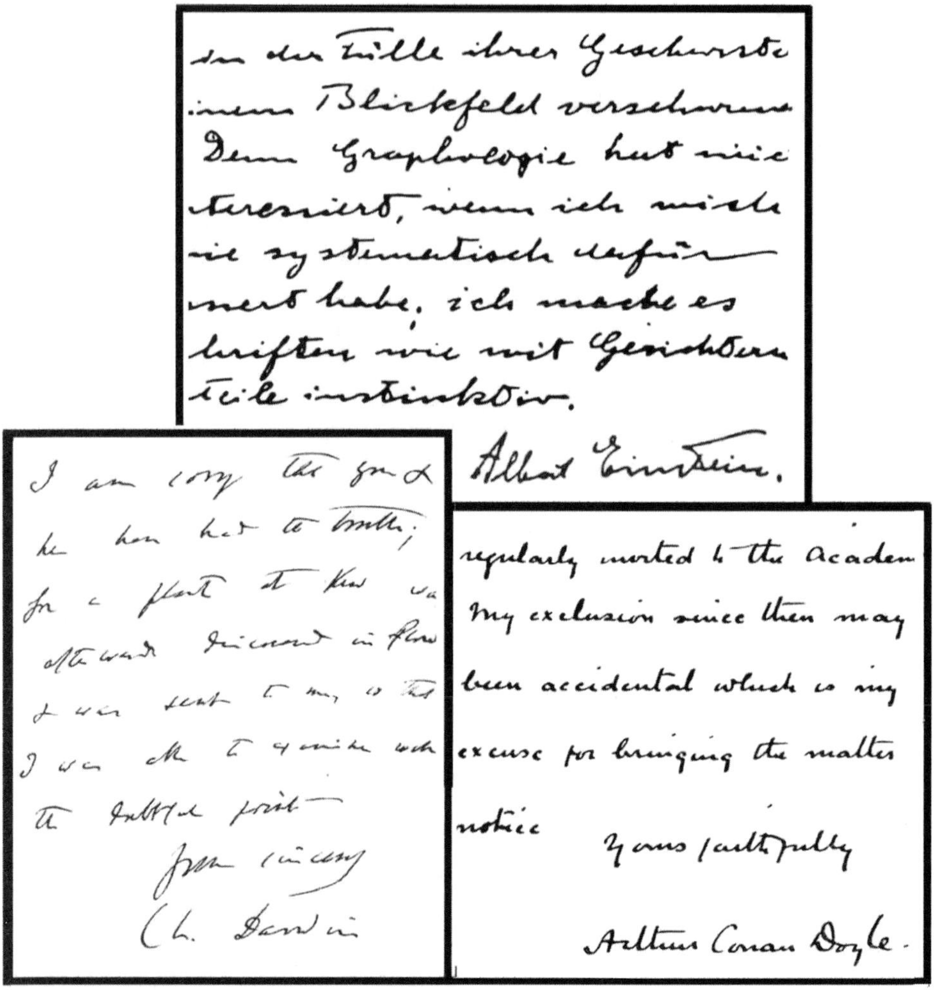
Denn Graphologie hat mich
interessiert, wenn ich mich
nie systematisch dafür
bemüht habe, ich mache es
Schriften wie mit Gesichtern
Teile instinktiv.
Albert Einstein.

Yours sincerely
Ch. Darwin

regularly invited to the Academ
My exclusion since then may
been accidental which is my
excuse for bringing the matter
notice
Yours faithfully
Arthur Conan Doyle.

Figure 13.24. These writers: Einstein, Darwin, and Doyle are extremely regular and display high form level to their writing. Neurologically, the dominance of the left brain cerebral cortex is evident, combining linear thinking from the left brain with symbolic activity from the right. The frontal and prefrontal lobes of abstract thought and the predominance of the left temporal lobe (neurolinguistics) is also evident. Darwin's writing is the most spontaneous.

Interhemispheric Communication

In particular, Figures 13.22 and 13.24 are examples of writers who display graphologically interhemispheric communication, some type of balanced

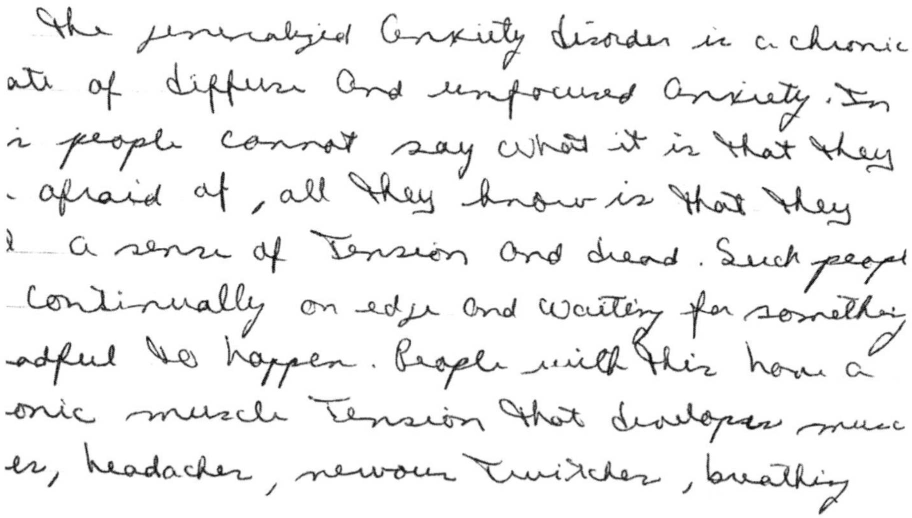

[handwritten sample]

Figure 13.25. Twenty-year-old male writer. Note radical changing slants indicating interhemispheric conflict and counterdominance.

activity of both left and right hemispheres, with the artists in Figure 13.22 being more right-brain dominant and Figure 13.24 more left brain dominant.

The term counter-dominance refers to a situation where, because neither hemisphere is in charge, they each vie for power.

The following handwritings are examples of interhemispheric communcation, namely instances where there is positive cross-talk between the two hemispheres. The first example is that of Lawrence Tenney Stevens (1896–1972), a sculptor whose work can be found in both the Brooklyn and Will Rogers Museum and the Arabian Stallion Museum of Scottsdale, Arizona. Winner of the Prix de Rome for three years running (1922–1925; the time of writing of the enclosed sample), Stevens was described as "a lean, sinewy man galloping through life in Western pants and cowboy boots, his goatee quivering with laughter or indignation, his longish hair never seeming to settle on his head." This description seems to aptly relate to his handwriting as well.

If we grade Stevens's handwriting from a neurological point of view, we note that there is a strong sense of form, shading, and pastosity, which is linked to right-brain procedures. Simultaneously, there is a linear quality and a somewhat rigid slant consistency, which suggests influence of the left brain. Stevens is a complex individual who, as an artist, is bold, creative, sensual, even unbridled, but also he has the discipline to be the complete craftsman. His handwriting shows high-level interhemispheric communication.

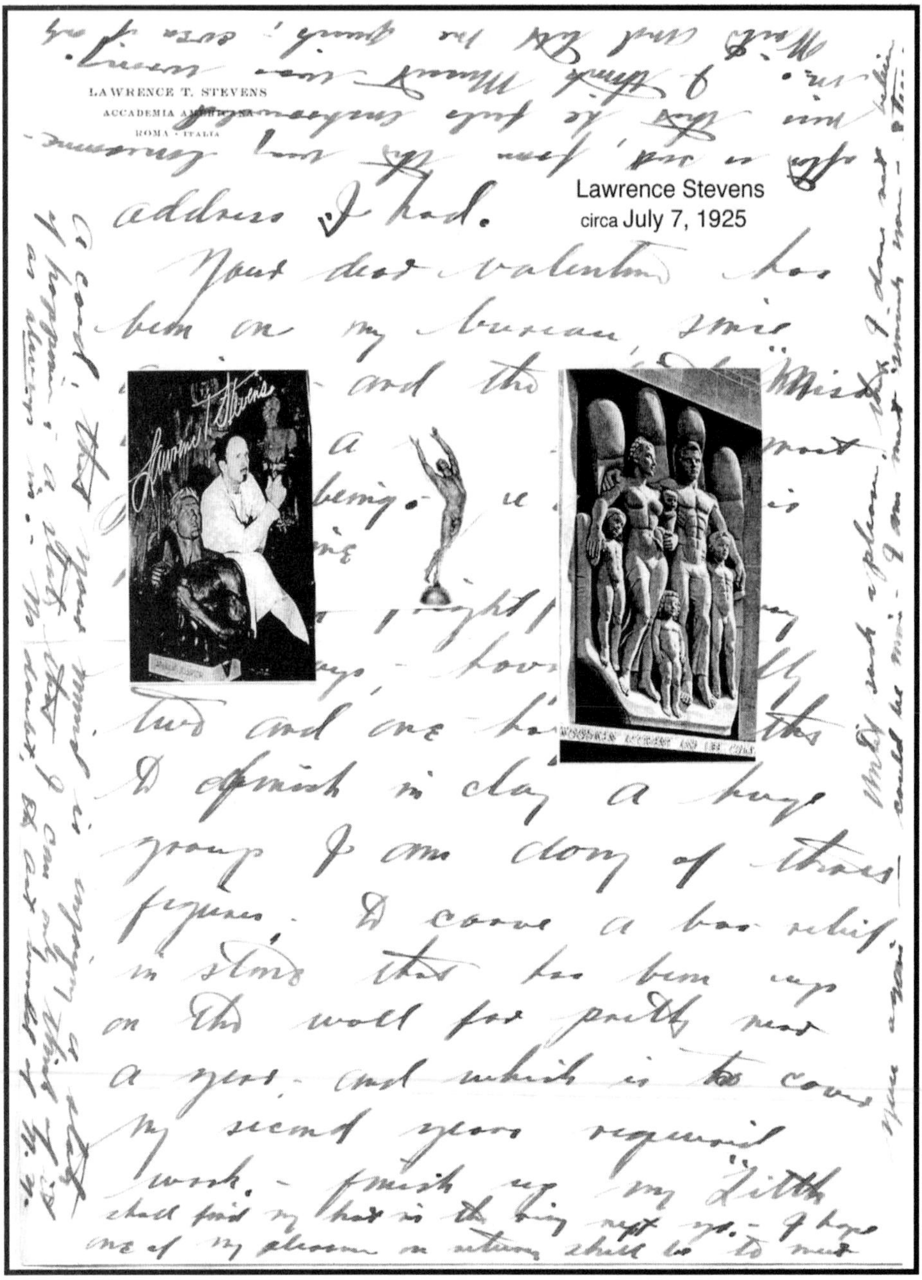

Figure 13.26. The handwriting of sculptor Lawrence Stevens, writing from Rome. The pictures of the sculptor and his works have been superimposed over the writing.

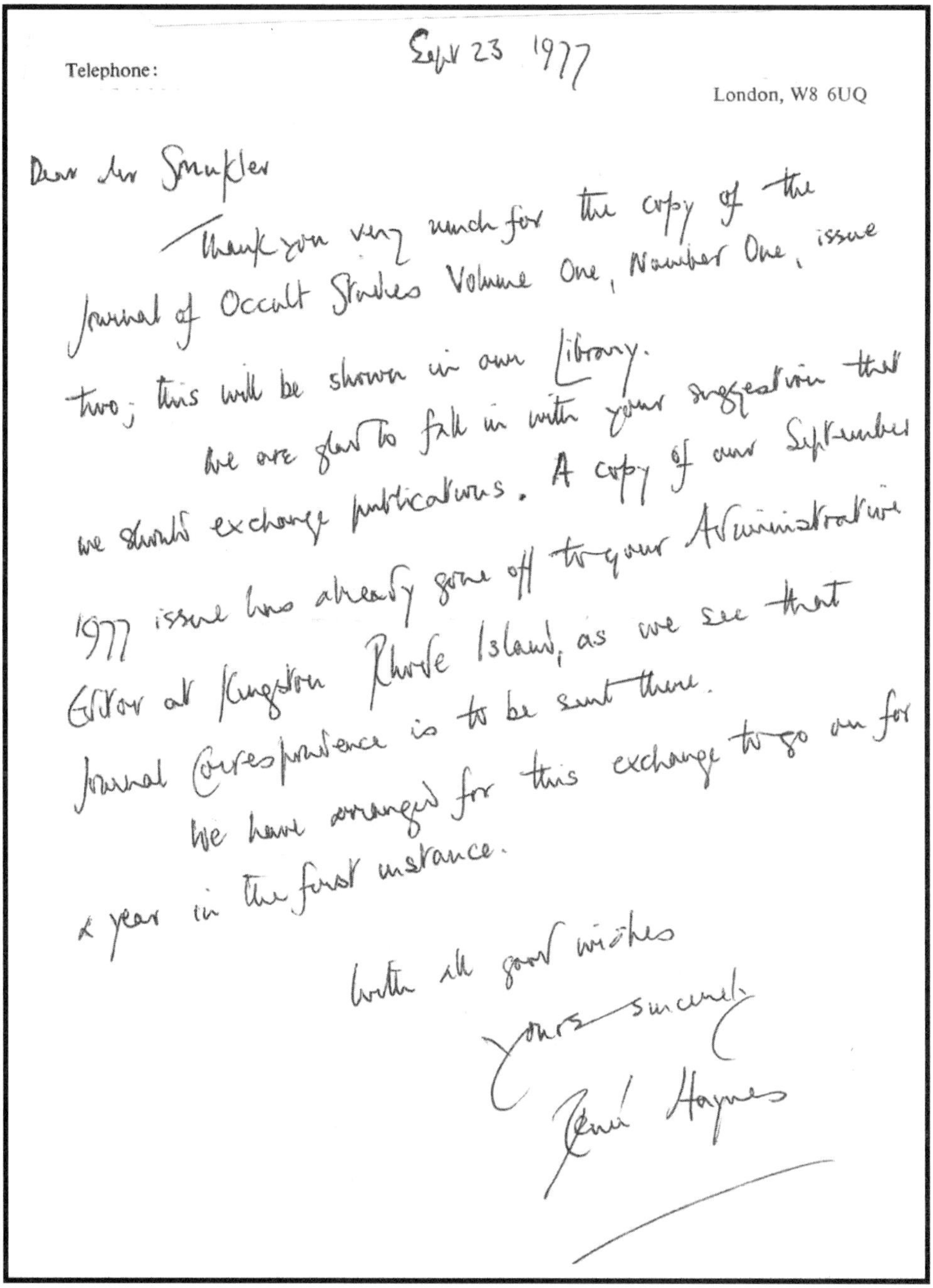

Telephone:

Sept 23 1977

London, W8 6UQ

Dear Mr Smukler

Thank you very much for the copy of the Journal of Occult Studies Volume One, Number One, issue two; this will be shown in our Library. We are glad to fall in with your suggestion that we should exchange publications. A copy of our September 1977 issue has already gone off to your Administrative Editor at Kingston Rhode Island, as we see that Journal Correspondence is to be sent there. We have arranged for this exchange to go on for a year in the first instance.

With all good wishes

yours sincerely

René Haynes

Figure 13.27. The handwriting of Reneé Haynes, editor of a British science journal.

The last handwriting in this group is a superb example of interhemispheric communication, as one can easily see the influence of both the left brain through the well-executed lean, linear, and simplified middle zone as compared to numerous flourishes, unusual connections, sense of form, and aesthetically pleasing pictorial elaborations such as the interesting capital *L* in "Library" and *C* in "Correspondence." Note in particular the stunning way Haynes's d in the word *glad*, 4th line down, becomes the t-bar to the word *to*. This writing is a simply wonderful example of a well-integrated cerebral cortex writer.

Conclusion

Handwriting analysis is a powerful tool with many rich areas for new exploration. This chapter has been an introductory attempt to explore the relationship between major brain structures and the graphic trail. In general, such a study would be augmented by continuing to use the MRI in correlating specific brain injuries to different graphic patterns. Such a course of action would help refine this first step in mapping out the specific relationship between the graphics of the handwriting trail and cerebral organization. The avenue of investigation may prove fruitful in diagnosing disorders, and, perhaps, in guiding people toward a greater understanding of the mind/brain connection.

Figure 13.28. The lyrical, inventive, and visually stunning signature of Basil Rathbone, the versatile actor who could play a villain as easily as Sherlock Holmes.

Part

III

Questioned Documents

Sherlock Holmes

"The old gentleman wrote, but nobody couldn't read it. The lawyer looked powerful astonished, and says:

'Well, it beats me'—and snaked a lot of old letters out of his pocket, and then examined the old man's writing and then them again and then says, 'These old letters is from Harvey Wilks…. And here's this old gentleman's handwriting, and anybody can tell, easy enough, he didn't write them."

—*The Adventures of Huckleberry Finn*

The science of the study of questioned documents can be traced back several thousand years to the time of the Greek and Roman empires. European graphology began in earnest in the 1600s in Italy, and the practice spread to France, where they instituted the legality of the study of questioned documents into law in 1737 (Hayes, 2006). Yet up through the mid-1800s, throughout Europe and Great Britain, the assessment of whether or not a signature was genuine was based solely on the testimony of witnesses *seeing* with their own eyes the person in question putting down his signature. Exemplars were not admitted unless they were already involved in the evidence based on other factors in the case, and handwriting experts were not allowed to give an opinion, because they had not witnessed the actual act of signing.

"In 1854 the English Parliament enacted the Common Law Procedure Act for the admission and comparison of handwriting in civil cases only. This allowed the expert or trier of fact to use exemplars…for the purposes of comparison," and 21 years later, in 1865, "the law was extended to apply to criminal cases as well" (104). But in America, the QD expert was still prevented by the old system.

An early weighty American treatise is *A Manual of the Study of Documents; To Establish the Individual Character of Handwriting and To Detect Fraud and Forgery* by Persifor Frazer, J.B Lippincott Company, 1894. Frazer, a geologist and professor of chemistry and natural philosophy at the University of Pennsylvania, identified three postulates:

1. "Everything capable of being observed is capable of being measured."

2. "The method employed must be capable of that which is essential from that which is accidental."

3. "Handwriting is the result of the action of a motor (the will) on a machine (the bony structure of the arm with the particular muscles and nerves attached to it) attempting to reproduce a pattern which habit has gradually rendered permanent in the mind" (109).

Frazer explains the absurd situation that the questioned document examiner faced during the turn of the 20th century, because the courts in America still prevented the expert to compare in court exemplars (known samples of the writer) with the document or documents that were in dispute! In no uncertain terms, Frazer states that this is "bad law." "If one who is an expert be forbidden to juxtapose and make comparisons before a jury of the handwriting admitted to be genuine with the one in doubt, it is consonance with the spirit of such a law that he should be forbidden from using such comparison in forming an opinion" (200–201). Logic would dictate, however, if the expert was able to make such comparisons in his lab in order to come to certain conclusions, he should also be able to replicate this work in court. Therefore, the law must change.

The courts during the late 19th and early 20th centuries were highly suspect of supposed expert witnesses, because many of them were hired advocates rather than objective scientists, a problem that still exists today. Oftentimes, defense attorneys would hire expert forgers to simulate the writing of a signature in question, and then ask a witness if he or she recognized that signature. Invariably, these witnesses, not knowing they were being duped, would simply state that said signature was genuine. The clever defense attorney would then admit to the ruse, and the case against his client would dissolve (203).

One of the most famous of these expert witness forgers was a Mr. Reilly, who, throughout a 50-year period, testified in nearly 400 cases. Here is a bit of testimony of Mr. Reilly from a case from the 1930's:

Q. Have you ever prepared any spurious writings whereby you have successfully misled Mr. John F. Tyrrell?

A. I don't know whether he was on the Patrick Rice case. I may have.

Q. What did you do on the Patrick Rice case?

A. I wrote nine signatures of W.R. Rice.

Q. For the purpose of deceiving the people who would testify on the other side?

A. [No, for the purpose of] testing their ability.

(Testimony from the Haupmann trial, *Law.umkc.edu*)

These duped witnesses were often not handwriting experts, but simply individuals familiar with the defendant's signature. Unprepared for this kind of tactic, naïve witnesses continued to walk into the same trap and, by this method, case after case would be thrown out. Today, witnesses are much better prepared, and it would be a rare day that an expert witness on the stand would form an opinion on a new signature that he or she had not seen before.

Progress for allowing a handwriting expert to present evidence in a clear manner was painfully slow. Clark Sellers (1947), president of the American Society of Questioned Document Examiners in the 1940s, informs us that as late as 1914, handwriting experts were still not able "to give effective testimony in most courts, due to restrictions and suspicions which surrounded all expert testimony. In a trial involving questioned documents in many states, no standards for comparison could be introduced in evidence unless they were admissible for other purposes; enlarged photographs were either excluded or looked upon with grave suspicion; it was not permissible to give reasons for an opinion on direct examination; and even the use of a magnifying glass or a microscope was strenuously objected to or excluded altogether" (75–78).

Albert Osborn

The individual most responsible for changing the status of the questioned document examiner in America was Sellers's mentor, Albert S. Osborn (1858–1947), without doubt, the most important handwriting expert of the 20th century. Predated by Rexford's (1902) work on anonymous letters, forgeries, and disguised writing, Osborn's magnum opus, *Questioned Documents*, became the standard bearer, a superlative 1,000-page reference work that could be brought to court to help change the way lawyers and judges looked at the field. Osborn states in his second edition, written in 1929, that "these restrictive conditions are now nearly all changed" (xi). And the reason was, in great measure, this book. Even today, nearly 100 years later, Osborn's work remains the standard bearer that all questioned documents books must be compared with.

With a detailed bibliography, index, and 36 chapters, Osborn covers a vast range of problems that the QD expert could encounter. Chapter topics include standards of comparison, the microscope and special instruments, pen position, pressure, shading, page arrangement, size, proportions, spacing, slant, use of different writing instruments, simulated, traced, and copied forgeries, guided and assisted signatures, anonymous letters, disguised writing, printing, typing, types of inks and papers, and the law and legal procedures in disputed document cases.

Osborn achieved international fame in 1932 when he testified about the ransom note in the Lindbergh kidnapping case. The venerated handwriting expert captured the imagination of the media and the world when he proclaimed that the note was a disguised writing penned by a left-handed individual.

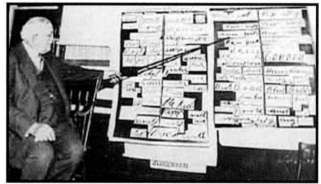

Figure 14.1. Alfred S. Osborn at Hauptmann trial.

Wilson Harrison

It would be another 30 years before a work of comparable stature was written—*Suspect Documents* by Wilson R. Harrison in 1958. Born in Wales in 1903, and educated at Cardiff University with a doctorate in physical chemistry, Harrison came to head the university's forensic science laboratory from 1938 until 1963. There, he studied more than 7,000 handwritings. Waiting nearly 20 years to write his masterpiece, Harrison's work advanced the field by providing many more samples to study. He also explained in greater detail a number of key topics first introduced by Osborn.

"I believe what cannot be demonstrated is not evidence," Harrison wrote. "In criminal cases, in particular, there should never be any appeal to conclusions based on flair or on the 'eye of the expert'. Consequently," this chemist/handwriting expert wrote, "I have endeavored to treat the subject as a branch of physical science with a broad basis of demonstrable fact for every opinion I have expressed."

Harrison's exposé on disguise in writing is exhaustive and groundbreaking. His understanding of nuance and discussion of details of fundamental structure of writing, and his ability to explain how an expert makes a final determination on authenticity is first rate. "The rule is simple—whatever features two handwritings may have in common, they cannot be considered to be of common authorship if they display but a single consistent dissimilarity in any feature which is fundamental to the structure of the handwriting, and whose presence is not capable of reasonable explanation" (342).

> The writer who is methodical, definite, matter of fact and practical does not produce with his hand that which is slovenly and uncertain; neither do the bungler and the sloven produce a page of writing that is graceful, balanced, artistic and finished without excess. Certainly to that extent here specified, graphology points in the right direction, although most of the deductions are based on foundations too slender for scientific accuracy.
>
> —Albert Osborn

The QD Examiner's Views on Handwriting Analysis

> The art of attempting to interpret the character or personality of an individual from his handwriting... is beyond the realm of the document examiner's work.
>
> —Ordway Hilton

Although ruled a forgery in court, the Howard Hughes Mormon Will was considered genuine by some of the foremost QD experts from Europe that Harold Rhoden hired. Referring to Figures 14.2 and 14.3, note the extreme similarity of Hughes's known signature with the signature from both the will and the envelope that contained the will. The top signature, which is from page 3 of the will, was damaged by water. See *High Stakes* by Harold Rhoden, 1983.

Where many QD examiners dismiss out of hand the field of graphology, or handwriting analysis, both Osborn and Harrison state unequivocally, "There can be no doubt that handwriting does, to some extent, at least, reflect the personality of the writer" (Harrison, 1958). With this clear-cut premise, the issues that follow are then twofold: to what extent, and whether or not handwriting analysis can ever be raised to the level of an experimental science. Both Osborn and Harrison suggest that graphology cannot attain the status of being called a "science."

Osborn notes that writing as a "mental act" may reflect the "mental or even spiritual stature of a man" (1929). Writing may also reveal a person's occupation, nation of origin, handedness, and, sometimes, the sex. "The scientific student [of questioned documents examination] is of course bound to study the subject and test its claims and enlist its aid if it will assist in any way in discovering and showing the facts in a disputed document case" (436). Graphology, however, for Osborn, remains a "pseudo-science" because there are too many uncertainties and "unknown and outside influences…in this method of human character or personality evaluation" and this, for Osborn, is its "fundamental defect" (438–9). In other words, the study of the human personality is too complex to be reduced to a discipline that could attain the level of a true science. This view, Osborn notes, "is made with full appreciation of the empirical skill acquired by certain experienced exponents of the subject of graphology" (439).

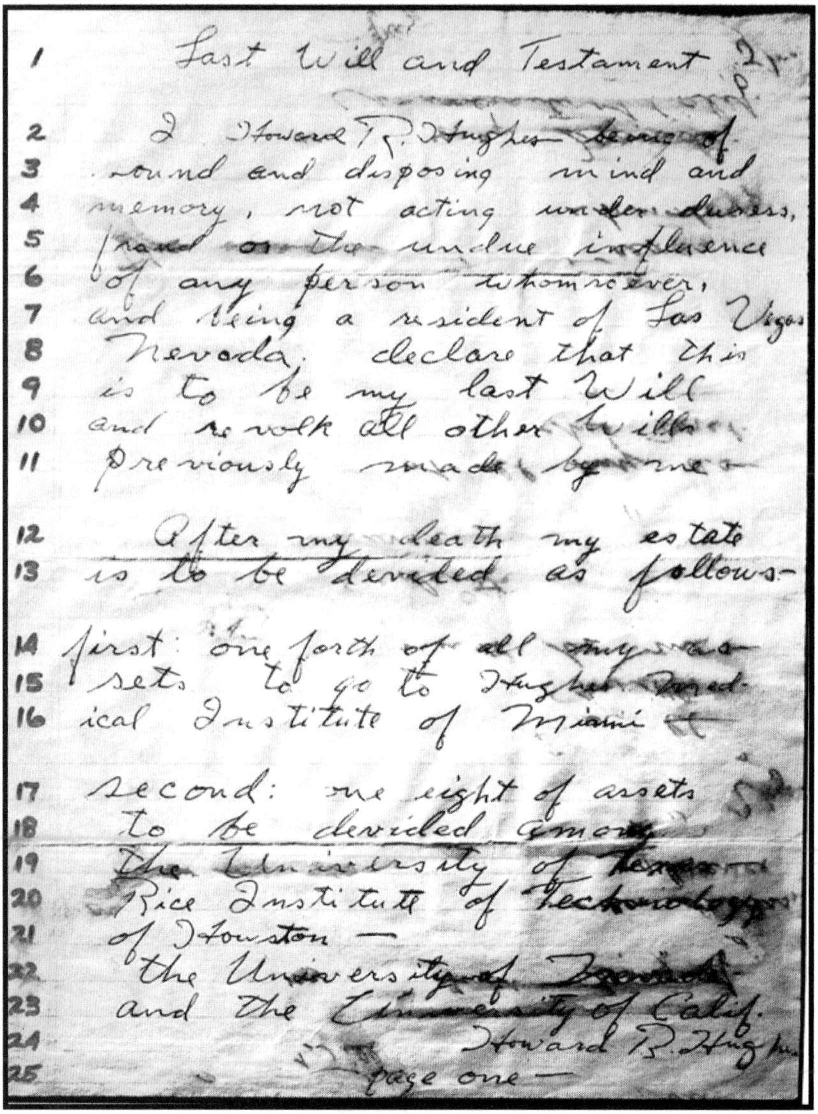
Last Will and Testament

I Howard R. Hughes being of sound and disposing mind and memory, not acting under duress, fraud or the undue influence of any person whomsoever, and being a resident of Las Vegas Nevada, declare that this is to be my last Will and revolk all other wills previously made by me —

After my death my estate is to be devided as follows —

first: one forth of all my assets to go to Hughes Medical Institute of Miami —

second: one eight of assets to be devided among the University of Texas Rice Institute of Technology of Houston — the University of Nevada and the University of Calif.

Howard R. Hughes

page one —

Figure 14.2. Mormon Will of Howard Hughes. This questioned document has water damage. Photo of the original, courtesy of Harold Rhoden (1983), author of High Stakes.

Osborn clearly has his eyes open. He has studied the precepts of graphology, sees its merit and its flaws, and recognizes that attempts have been made by serious experimental graphologists to catalog and statistically analyze their findings. However, when compared to questioned documents examination, the graphologist can never attain an equivalent level of demonstrable proof. My argument with Osborn has to do with the definition of science and perhaps even with the definition of graphology.

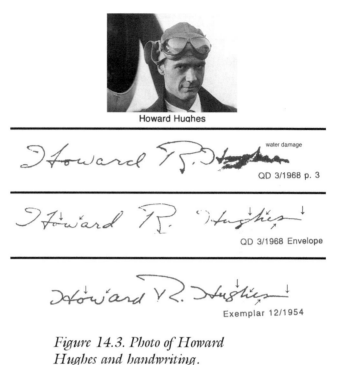

Howard Hughes

water damage

QD 3/1968 p. 3

QD 3/1968 Envelope

Exemplar 12/1954

Figure 14.3. Photo of Howard Hughes and handwriting.

> The American attitude is hard to account for, and it is all the more strange when one considers that forensic uses of handwriting expertise in cases of forgery long have been perfectly acceptable, which means the law admits that handwriting is unique and individually identifiable.
>
> —Paul de St. Colombe

By breaking it into three branches—handwriting analysis or behavioral profiling, neurophysiology, and questioned documents—one begins to see that the cataloging of handwritings for corresponding neurological criteria can be studied in a scientific manner. For myself, in two separate studies with medical doctors, a professor of psychology, and another graphologist, we were able to distinguish between schizophrenic and normal writers, and epileptic split-brain patients and normal writers to a statistical degree of certainty (Seifer and Goode, 1972; Tenhouten, Seifer, and Siegel, 1989). There also have been other studies done to measure writings for personality differences, but I would agree with Osborn that such studies encounter large stumbling blocks, because, as Osborn notes, the study of personality involves so many variables, including ones that cannot be known.

Famous Questioned Document Cases

Captain Arthur Quirke once said:

To us, graphology must be an applied science. Such data [are...] of little but academic interest to us, except insofar as we can apply the information gleaned to the all-important task of determining identity or non-identity of authorship from comparisons of documents.

This is very far from asserting that a working knowledge of the principles underlying the psychological analysis of handwriting is of no value in the realms of legal handwriting experts.... The handwriting [expert] who brings to bear upon his work the barest minimum of specialized knowledge, absorbed blindly and unquestioningly from textbooks... can never achieve anything, unless to be discredit for himself and unavailing regrets on the part of those rash enough to rely on him.

This deficit in the training of one group of QD experts that otherwise have excellent resumes has led to some grievous errors. The most famous case, no doubt, involved the handwriting of Howard Hughes. In 1972, McGraw Hill announced a publishing coup when they signed Clifford Irving to write the authorized Hughes autobiography. Although still alive, the recluse billionaire had not been seen in more than a decade. But McGraw Hill had a series of letters written by Hughes giving Irving permission to cowrite his memoirs. These letters were sent to Russell and Paul Osborn, sons of the late Albert Osborn, venerated author of *Questioned Documents* cited above and prestigious New York City QD experts in their own right. After comparing these letters to Howard Hughes exemplars, the Osborns informed McGraw Hill that the letters were genuine, and Clifford Irving was given an advance of several hundred thousand dollars.

Clifford Irving's signature.

QD from McGraw Hill letter forged by Clifford Irving.

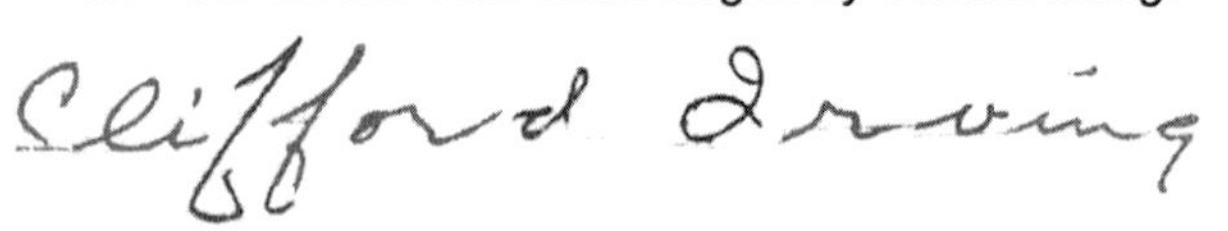

Howard Hughes' handwriting piecing Irving's name together.

Figure 14.4. The swing of the top of the I of Irving is similar between Irving's known signature and his attempt to write his name in Hughes' handwriting style. The f's and ing do not match Hughes's known handwriting.

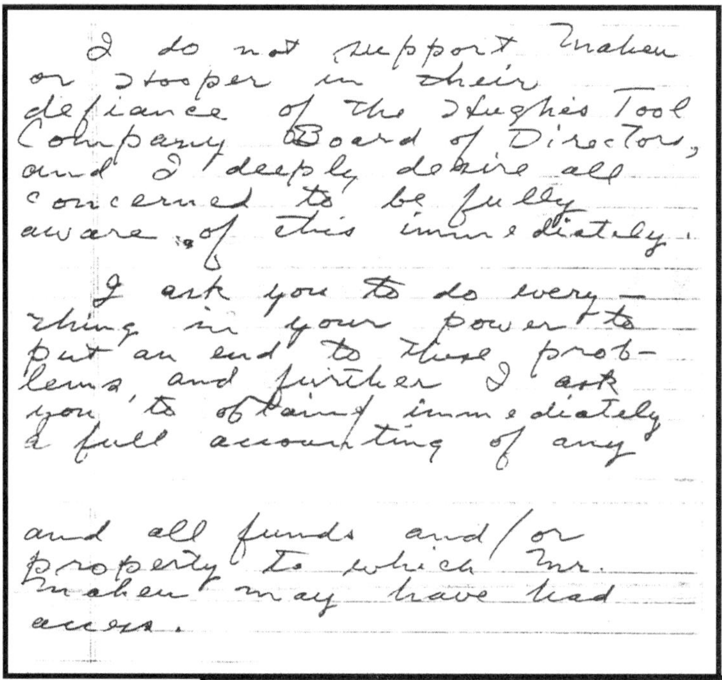
I do not support Maheu or Stooper in their defiance of the Hughes Tool Company Board of Directors, and I deeply desire all concerned to be fully aware of this immediately.

I ask you to do everything in your power to put an end to these problems, and further I ask you to obtain immediately a full accounting of any

and all funds and/or property to which Mr. Maheu may have had access.

Figure 14.5. The handwriting of Howard Hughes published in Life Magazine, *January 1971. The writing was analyzed for personality characteristics by Alfred Kanfer.*

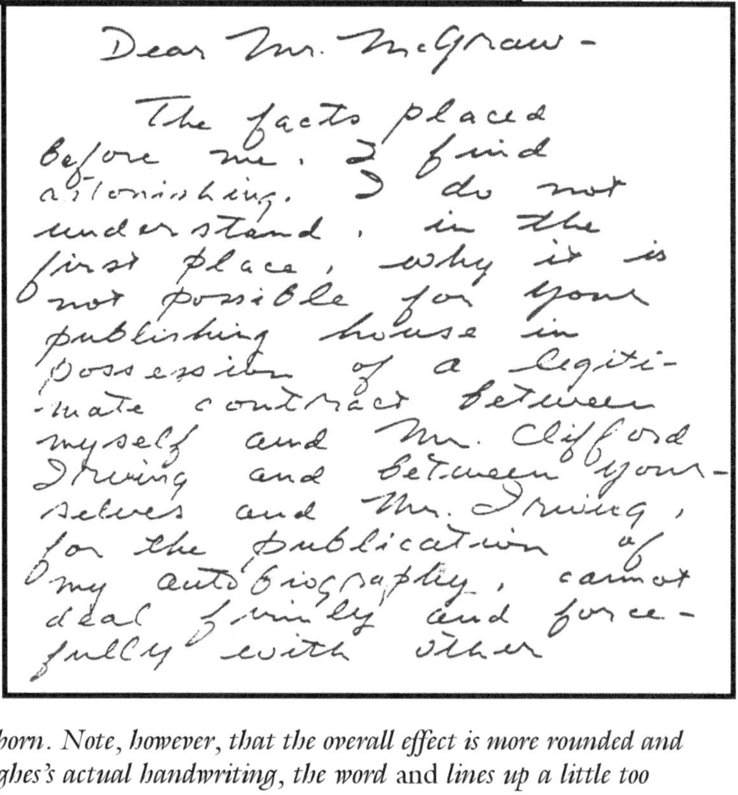
Dear Mr. McGraw -

The facts placed before me, I find astonishing. I do not understand, in the first place, why it is not possible for your publishing house in possession of a legitimate contract between myself and Mr. Clifford Irving and between yourselves and Mr. Irving, for the publication of my autobiography, cannot deal firmly and forcefully with other

Figure 14.6. The famous Clifford Irving forgery of Howard Hughes's handwriting telling the publisher, Mr. McGraw of McGraw Hill that he had assigned Irving to write his autobiography. At first glance, this is a superb forgery, and it fooled the Osborns, the sons of Alfred Osborn. Note, however, that the overall effect is more rounded and pastose than Hughes's actual handwriting, the word and *lines up a little too mechanically, and key fundamental details are different.*

For example, one would agree that it would take a certain level of aggression for a person to become president of the United States. Therefore, Jimmy Carter, Ronald Reagan, Bill Clinton, George Bush, and George W. Bush are all aggressive individuals. But clearly, each are aggressive in different ways. In the case of Al Gore, he won more popular votes than George W. Bush, but he had less electoral votes so he lost the election. Is he less aggressive than George W. Bush?

Personality is very complex, but it can be studied in a scientific manner. Handwriting analysis cannot be measured as a science with the same ruling stick that governs the hard sciences or even questioned documents examination. But even in the case of physics there are theories, for example, black holes and string theory, that are accepted as factual aspects of reality, but really are speculations. The important point to reiterate is that two giants in the field of document examination, Osborn and Harrison, are both in agreement that handwriting does indeed reflect personality, and that, to be a top handwriting expert, one should be versed in this branch as well, even if it is controversial. And another handwriting expert, Captain Arthur Quirke, handwriting analyst to the department of justice, attorney general, and police headquarters of the Irish Free State in the 1930s, goes even farther by devoting a full chapter on the psychology of handwriting in his text *Forged, Anonymous & Suspect Documents*. In support of the view that questioned documents examiners should also have training in handwriting analysis, Quirke quotes Dr. Hans Gross (1924), professor of criminology, in his "classic work," *Criminal Investigations*, who writes the following with a caveat against untrained or unscientific graphologists: "The most important thing which an Investigating Officer can extract from a writing is the character of an individual."

This view contradicts many other QD experts who reject whole-heartedly handwriting analysis, know none of its precepts, and disdain handwriting experts who are versed in that branch of the field.

Shortly thereafter, Howard Hughes himself called McGraw Hill to inform the publisher that he did not know Clifford Irving and he did not write those letters. Two full pages of Hughes's handwriting had been published in *Life Magazine* one year earlier. Irving had simply used those exemplars as models to create the elaborate forgery. Having studied the Irving forgeries and the Hughes's exemplars, it is clear that, if one looks at the entire writing as a total pattern, it is not a good comparison to the exemplars. The problem with the Osborns was their reliance on only measuring individual letters and not taking into account the dynamic pattern of the whole, something stressed in the field of graphology, but not stressed in QD examination.

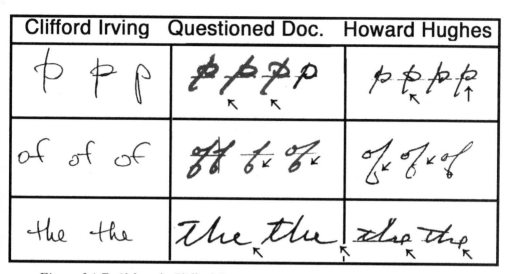

Clifford Irving	Questioned Doc.	Howard Hughes

Figure 14.7. Although Clifford Irving got the overall shape of the letters and odd spacing correct in his McGraw Hill forgery of Howard Hughes's writing, he erred on the word endings. For instance, Irving's f's end to the left and Hughes's ends to the right. Irving's e's end to the right and Hughes' e's end to the left. This consistent difference of a fundamental detail is the key in determining separate authorship. The person who wrote the Hughes's exemplars (Howard Hughes) is not the person who wrote the McGraw Hill letter.

A decade later, QD experts from Europe made a similar faux pas when they authenticated Adolf Hitler's personal diaries only to find out soon after that these also were frauds. In this instance, one of the errors that these experts made was in using fake exemplars to make their comparisons. In both cases, the QD experts were fooled in part because the material was so voluminous. After seeing page after page of fake writing, they began to have difficulty maintaining objectivity, because they had a preconception that the fakes were real.

Charles Hamilton (1980), the flamboyant Manhattanite, autograph dealer and auctioneer, tracks the lives of some of the most famous forgers in his book *Great Forgers and Famous Fakes*. Hamilton, who began his passion at age 12 after purchasing an autograph of Rudyard Kipling, begins his story with Henry Cleveland, who began forging Abraham Lincoln's signature shortly after the president's assassination in 1863. Because they were done so well and written around the time when Lincoln was alive, many of Cleveland's Lincoln fakes were wrongly authenticated.

Other bogus Lincoln signatures were created by a number of Depression-era forgers, such as Joseph Cosey, Eugene Field II, and Charles Weisberg. In the case of Cosey, he went so far as to forge the itinerary of the Lincoln–Douglas Debates in Lincoln's hand.

In the 1890s, Thomas Chancellor, a "carpetbagger," made his living in the deep South selling Bibles inscribed by Stonewall Jackson. This scam became so famous, it was covered in an article in the *New York Herald Tribune* in 1891.

Weisberg's fortés included his ability to capture the complex signature of Benjamin Franklin. The problem with the Weisberg fakes, however, was that he would date some of them at a time when Franklin was well into his 80s. By that time Franklin's handwriting had deteriorated, but the Weisberg copies remained in the style and vigor of the younger man. In 1935, Weisberg was caught and sent to jail, but his incarceration was short, and, when he got out, he resumed his illicit occupation. Cosey was also proficient in forging Franklin's signature. He was sent to San Quentin for passing bad checks in 1916, and imprisoned again in 1937 for a similar crime.

Figure 14.8. Two of the three George Washington spurious signatures (Weisberg and Cosey) are superb examples of what a master forger can do. The capital W and overall evenly thick line stroke of the Spring signature gives the fake away (adapted from Hamilton, 1980).

Most of these forgers were multi-talented. Field could do Walt Whitman, Mark Twain, Abraham Lincoln, Longfellow, and Teddy Roosevelt. Cosey's specialties included the fake signatures of George Washington, Aaron Burr, Patrick Henry, John Adams, James Madison, James Monroe, John Wilkes Booth, Grover Cleveland, Rudyard Kipling, Edgar Allen Poe, and Ulysses S. Grant. Cosey also drafted a beautiful rendition of the Declaration of Independence, which Charles Hamilton sold as an example of a good fake in 1969 to one Ernest Cook of Virginia Intermont College for $425. A few months later, another prominent Virginia college asked if Hamilton had verified a copy of the Declaration of Independence, which they were considering purchasing for $35,000! Hamilton set them straight.

In the case of Poe, Cosey concocted a letter to poet and critic N.P. Willis from Poe concerning his story "The Cask of Amontillado." The ingenious letter even had fake notes in the margins put in by Willis. This spurious document would show up every now and again, and Hamilton would have to let the owner know the unfortunate news.

While writing his very entertaining and informative book, Hamilton had contacted another dealer to ask if he had any fakes, and the dealer offered two of Poe, which were done by Cosey. "These," the dealer said, "were authenticated as fakes by A.S.W. Rosenback, a highly regarded rare book and manuscript dealer from Manhattan who had recently passed away." Hamilton was able to verify that in fact, these two documents were actually authentic! With the dealer's permission, Hamilton auctioned them off for several thousand dollars at his famous Charles Hamilton Galleries.

Other controversial cases include the Last Will and Testament of Howard Hughes, known as the Mormon Will, found in 1976, which gave 1/16th of his estate, or nearly $160 million dollars, to one Melvin Dummar, owner of a Utah filling station. In a highly publicized court battle, the will was eventually ruled a forgery, although there was much evidence presented by QD experts hired from Europe in support of the case that the will was indeed genuine. See Figure 14.3 and Rhoden's book *High Stakes*.

Twenty years later, at Christmastime 1996 in Boulder, Colorado, came the JonBenet Ramsey case, whereby a 6-year-old girl was found strangled to death in the basement of her family home. A ransom note written on a yellow legal pad and left on the staircase has many striking similarities to handwriting that appeared in the *National Enquirer* purported to be the writing of JonBenet's father, John Ramsey (*Tauton Gazette*, 1999). As a strange twist to the case, 10 years later, in 2006, an accused pedophile, John Mark Karr, admitted to killing JonBenet Ramsey, but his handwriting did not match the note, and his estranged wife also established that he was not in the state of Colorado when the little girl was murdered. DNA evidence excluded him as well, so the case is still unsolved.

Other cases where questioned documents have played an important role include the handwritten anthrax letters that killed several people in 2001; a letter purportedly signed in 2003 by Osama bin Laden, which came at a time when the world was questioning whether or not the terrorist was still alive (see Figure 8.10); and some documents about President Bush and the reasons why he lost his license to pilot a plane during the Vietnam War. This last case was presented by Dan Rather in 2005 on CBS news. The controversy had less to do with the content, and more to do with whether or not these military documents were written in the 1970s or created on a computer 30 years later and would therefore be forgeries. One issue concerned the "th" superscript (for example, 10th), which appeared in QD from the 1970s. Critics said that such a superscript could not be created with the old IBM selectric typewriter, but this was incorrect, and further there were genuine Bush documents from this era that did indeed carry the "th" superscript. The case became so contentious that Dan Rather was forced to resign from his anchor position even though he had been a well-respected newscaster for more than 40 years.

Questioned Documents and the 21st Century

In many ways, the field of questioned documents investigation has not changed from the time of Osborn, Quirke, or Harrison. The precepts they put forth hold true in most QD cases. However, as technology has advanced, there have also been many changes to the field. Most notably, the ability to generate quality reproductions has increased dramatically. In the case of mortgages and deeds registered in town halls, rarely are originals kept on file. Because of this advance technology, it has become much easier to create false documents and false signatures.

If Osborn were alive today, no doubt, he would devote additional chapters to such topics as digital signatures, machine-generated or Xerox copies, scanning machines, alterations caused by Wite-Out, cutting and pasting, and by graphic design programs such as Photoshop. He would also cover electrostatic machines that can detect handwriting impressions on sheets of paper that lie beneath the document in question, the use of light-boxes, microscopes, cameras, and computers to enhance, study, magnify, and reproduce questioned documents, facsimile machines and tti alterations, that is, the terminal transmission identification line at the top of the fax machine, and fax papers. Most fax machines today use normal typing paper. In the 1980s and 90s, many fax machines routinely used chemically treated rolls of paper that tended to fade over time. I had one case where the *copy* of the fax was better than the original fax, because the original had faded severely and became almost non-readable by the time the case came to court. Had we not made hard copies of the original faxes, the case would have fallen apart.

Retail outlets such as Home Depot, UPS, and many department stores now rely on signatures placed on computer screens. These are digitally stored and cataloged. As time progresses, the mechanics underlying these signature screens will become more sophisticated. Writing instruments are now being developed to provide data on such criteria as grip placement, pen pressure, and speed. Likewise, receiving screens are also being developed so that they can distinguish speed, letter design, and pressure. In the future, signatures created in this manner may replace inked hard copy originals because they have the advantage of being created by individuals who need not physically be in the same location when the documents are signed, and because the information recorded concerning the physical aspects of how the signatures were created would replace the traditional signatures that are recorded with ink on a page.

In this way, fraud can be reduced considerably. It may be fairly easy for some forgers to create a pattern that greatly resembles the signature being simulated, but a forger can never also produce that pattern with the same speed and pressure as the original author. It is reasonable to foresee a day when signatures created with special pens on sophisticated receiving pads may create a situation making it virtually impossible for a forger to simulate by free hand the writing of another person. In these instances, fraud would occur electronically by tampering with the parameters of the equipment recording said signatures.

It is now customary for banks to destroy original checks and store check signatures and endorsements on microfilm instead. This is a very dangerous practice for a variety of reasons. Even though documents signed digitally may eventually replace the traditional procedure of placing ink on a page to seal a contract, this is not the case today. Legislation should be enacted to prevent banks from destroying original checks. In my 35-plus years experience, I have had hundreds of cases where the signatures and endorsements on checks are paramount. Destroying these vital documents is bad business practice, akin to the absurd recent practice in elections of creating voting machines with no paper trail. It is a simple matter to maintain a tradition of keeping a paper trail, and one of the easiest ways is to insist to banks that they retain original checks, or mail them back upon request to the customer, and also insist on maintaining the longstanding practice of having original documents—that is, signed documents with ink on a page—held as sacrosanct.

Chapter 15
Disguise in Handwriting

Anyone who guarantees to penetrate the disguise of every specimen...is suffering from self-deception.

—Wilson Harrison, 1958, *Suspect Documents*

There are a number of reasons for disguise in handwriting. Most often an attempt is made by the writer to hide his identity. Sometimes, as with forgeries, there is a wish to make it seem that someone else is the author. Other times, a fictitious person is fabricated.

Harrison (1958) devotes a comprehensive chapter to this topic. He writes that "even the simplest consistent disguise is certain to present the document examiner with a stern task of skill" (349). He also makes it clear that not every case of disguise can be solved.

In support of this caveat, this examiner received a call from a company requesting the identity of a spurious signature. When presented with the signatures of the employees, one was singled out as a possibility, but it was clear that the evidence did not reach the stage of being "to a reasonable degree of scientific certainty." There was no distinguishing characteristic in the questioned document, which correlated with the standard. As we will see, there is also a difference between "knowing" something and "proving" it. I always use as a personal guide the baseline standard as to whether or not I could explain my findings to a jury. In some cases, the evidence for one's case may be demonstrable, but the subtleties involved may be such that the opposite view of the devil's advocate might carry the day. Other times findings are simply "inconclusive."

The most common means of disguise involves change in slant.

As we shall see, unraveling disguises involves complex procedures and advanced knowledge of the neurophysiology of handwriting, how the psychomotor pattern is created, what is easily changed, and which elements persist and why.

Harrison notes that the simple decision to change the slant creates profound differences in the rest of the writing. Note the alterations in size, rhythm, fluency, and letter design in Figure 15.1 when the subject was asked to write with a leftward slant. Would it be possible to prove in a court of law that both samples are written by the same hand?

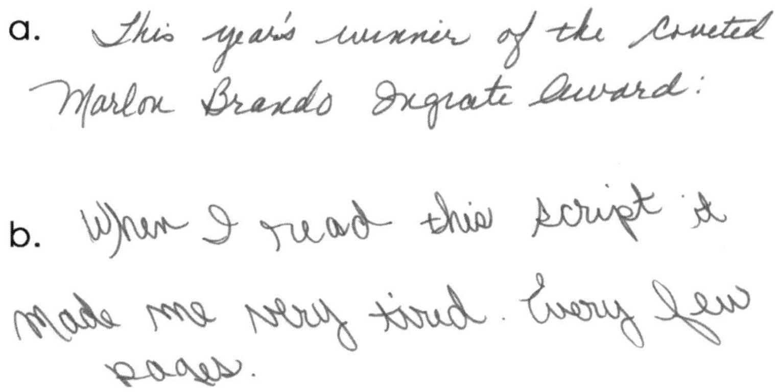

a. *This year's winner of the coveted Marlon Brando Ingrate Award:*

b. *When I read this script it made me very tired. Every few pages.*

Figure 15.1. Both writings are by the same person. The bottom script was a first attempt by the writer to change to a backward slant.

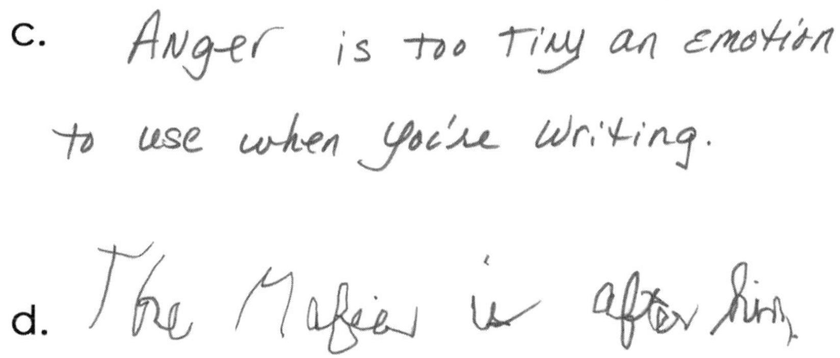

c. *Anger is too Tiny an emotion to use when you're Writing.*

d. *The Mafia is after him.*

Figure 15.2. Both scripts are written by the same person. The bottom script was written with the opposite (left) hand.

Based on his extensive files, Harrison has found that approximately 5 percent of disguised writings occur by penning the letter with the "unaccustomed hand" (usually the left). He also states that it can be a nearly impossible task to compare a disguised print script with a normal cursive one. Four different styles are presented in figures 15.1 and 15.2, yet all are written by the same person. Figure 15.1 was reduced 60% and Figure 15.2 was reduced 40 percent to further obfuscate the relationship between the two figures.

Change in any one characteristic feature (for example, size, handedness, slant, speed, letter design) can markedly change the rest of the script. Usually, if the writer makes one change, he or she does not feel the need to alter other aspects of the script because this simple procedure is so effective in disguising writing.

It takes an extreme effort of will to consistently change even one fundamental characteristic feature of a writing. As an exercise, Harrison suggests changing all vowels to a new design. The concentration required to maintain this alteration is extreme. After a few lines or at the ends of words, invariably, old patterns find themselves appearing.

Harrison therefore concludes that one cluster of features common to all disguised writing includes poorer quality of fluency and rhythm and slower speed as compared to the normal script. A writer with poor psychomotor coordination can never create a disguised writing of a high quality. Further, the greater the effort in changing the style, the more the departure from the original fluency. Exceptions to this general rule include the writings of a practiced forger (see George Washington forgeries, Figure 14.8) and calligraphers who by profession practice different styles.

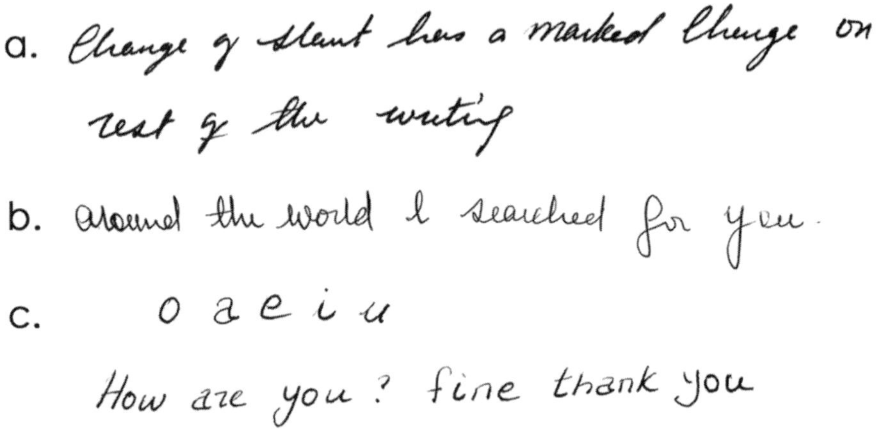

a. *Change of slant has a marked change on rest of the writing*

b. *around the world I searched for you.*

c. *o a e i u*

How are you? fine thank you

Figure 15.3. All three scripts are by the same writer. The top is the normal style, the middle with the left slant and the bottom with new vowels created and inserted at the request of the author.

Change of size is often used to disguise writing. Most often this results in disguised scripts that are much larger or much smaller than the normal writing. Envelopes and numbers on envelopes generally are less disguised as are numbers themselves and diacritics (i-dots, periods, semi-colons, t-bar placements). Suspect numbers in account books and idiosyncratic numbers, (7 with a bar through it), on the other hand, according to Harrison, are often written in a spurious manner.

In trying to ascertain the authorship of a disguised handwriting, the examiner must look beyond to such features that are independent of slant and letter design. These include type of pen used, quality of line stroke, legibility, size ratios of small to tall letters, initial strokes and endings, idiosyncrasies, connectedness, and space between letters and words. Features that Harrison says are almost never disguised include general arrangement of the words on the page, margins, line spacing, paragraph style (for example, indentations), and relationship of words to lines on a page when lined paper is used.

One way to compare overall layout is to reduce considerably the two blocks of writing.

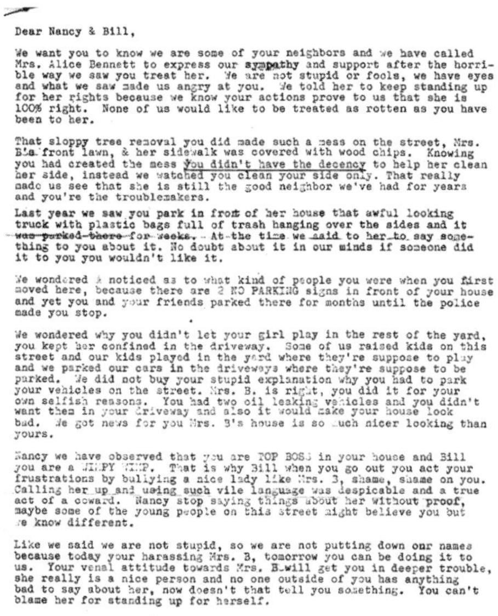

Dear Nancy & Bill,

We want you to know we are some of your neighbors and we have called Mrs. Alice Bennett to express our sympathy and support after the horrible way we saw you treat her. We are not stupid or fools, we have eyes and what we saw made us angry at you. We told her to keep standing up for her rights because we know your actions prove to us that she is 100% right. None of us would like to be treated as rotten as you have been to her.

That sloppy tree removal you did made such a mess on the street, Mrs. B's front lawn, & her sidewalk was covered with wood chips. Knowing you had created the mess you didn't have the decency to help her clean her side, instead we watched you clean your side only. That really made us see that she is still the good neighbor we've had for years and you're the troublemakers.

Last year we saw you park in front of her house that awful looking truck with plastic bags full of trash hanging over the sides and it ~~was parked there~~ for weeks. At the time we said to her to say something to you about it. No doubt about it in our minds if someone did it to you you wouldn't like it.

We wondered & noticed as to what kind of people you were when you first moved here, because there are 2 NO PARKING signs in front of your house and yet you and your friends parked there for months until the police made you stop.

We wondered why you didn't let your girl play in the rest of the yard, you kept her confined in the driveway. Some of us raised kids on this street and our kids played in the yard where they're suppose to play and we parked our cars in the driveways where they're suppose to be parked. We did not buy your stupid explanation why you had to park your vehicles on the street. Mrs. B. is right, you did it for your own selfish reasons. You had two oil leaking vehicles and you didn't want them in your driveway and also it would make your house look bad. We got news for you Mrs. B's house is so much nicer looking than yours.

Nancy we have observed that you are TOP BOSS in your house and Bill you are a WIMPY WIMP. That is why Bill when you go out you act your frustrations by bullying a nice lady like Mrs. B, shame, shame on you. Calling her up and using such vile language was despicable and a true act of a coward. Nancy stop saying things about her without proof, maybe some of the young people on this street might believe you but we know different.

Like we said we are not stupid, so we are not putting down our names because today your harassing Mrs. B, tomorrow you can be doing it to us. Your venal attitude towards Mrs. B will get you in deeper trouble, she really is a nice person and no one outside of you has anything bad to say about her, now doesn't that tell you something. You can't blame her for standing up for herself.

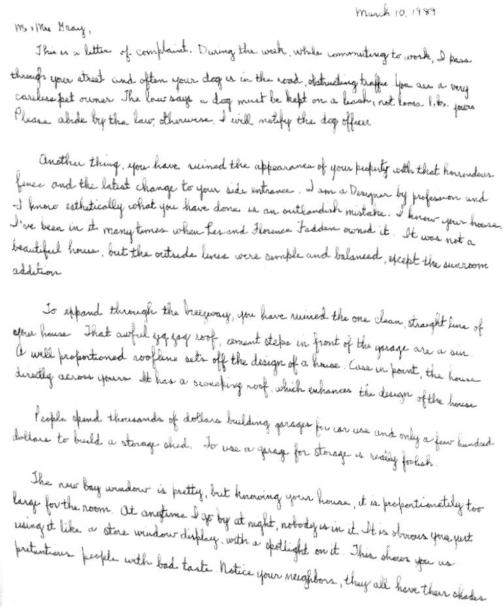

March 10, 1989

Mr & Mrs Gray,

This is a letter of complaint. During the week, while commuting to work, I pass through your street and often your dog is in the road, obstructing traffic. You are a very careless pet owner. The law says a dog must be kept on a leash, not loose like yours. Please abide by the law, otherwise, I will notify the dog officer.

Another thing, you have ruined the appearance of your property with that horrendous fence and the latest change to your side entrance. I am a Designer by profession and I know esthetically what you have done is an outlandish mistake. I know your house. I've been in it many times when Les and Florence Fadden owned it. It was not a beautiful house, but the outside lines were simple and balanced, except the sunroom addition.

To expand through the breezeway, you have ruined the one clean, straight line of your house. That awful zig zag roof, cement steps in front of the garage are a sin. A well proportioned roofline sets off the design of a house. Case in point, the house directly across yours. It has a sweeping roof, which enhances the design of the house.

People spend thousands of dollars building garages for car use and only a few hundred dollars to build a storage shed. To use a garage for storage is really foolish.

The new bay window is pretty, but knowing your house, it is proportionately too large for the room. At anytime I go by at night, nobody is in it. It is obvious you're just using it like a store window display, with a spotlight on it. This shows you as pretentious people with bad taste. Notice your neighbors, they all have their shades

Figure 15.4. These two anonymous notes were written by the same person. Even though one is typed and the other is in cursive, the overall layout is similar. By reducing the size, the overall pattern becomes easier to distinguish.

Whenever possible, the examiner should attempt to get the suspect to write the same words as those on the questioned document, even if it is in the normal hand.

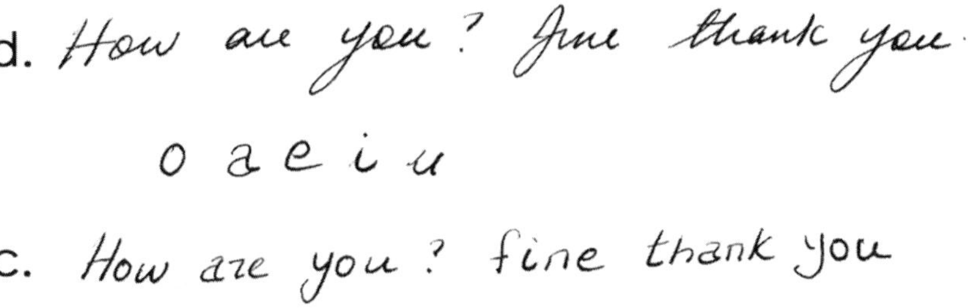
d. How are you? Fine thank you.
o a e i u
c. How are you? fine thank you

Figure 15.5. Note how, once the same words are used, the similarities become easier to identify. In this instance, we note the same size, spacing, slant, and general letter design for some letters such as the "how" and "you." Compare this to Figure 15.3, where, with different words, it is very difficult to make a case for common authorship.

In the case of disguised handwritings, wherever possible, it is suggested that the suspect provide the same words written under similar circumstances (for example, with the left hand, backward slant, as a print script). Oftentimes it is best to construct a series of sentences with similar words in similar sequences for the suspect to write. This is done for a variety of reasons. The idea is to get the writer in a comfortable situation so that his or her natural writing pattern will emerge. Frequently the suspect may try to disguise his natural handwriting. Naturally, one would want samples written from before the incident as well. If there are unpleasant statements or profane language in the anonymous note, it is often best to make necessary changes, so that curse words are eliminated and words with similar letter sequences put in their stead. The suspect should be required to **write *and* print** at least three or four pages of typed copy in his or her natural hand. If numbers are involved, the same numbers and other numbers should be listed as well.

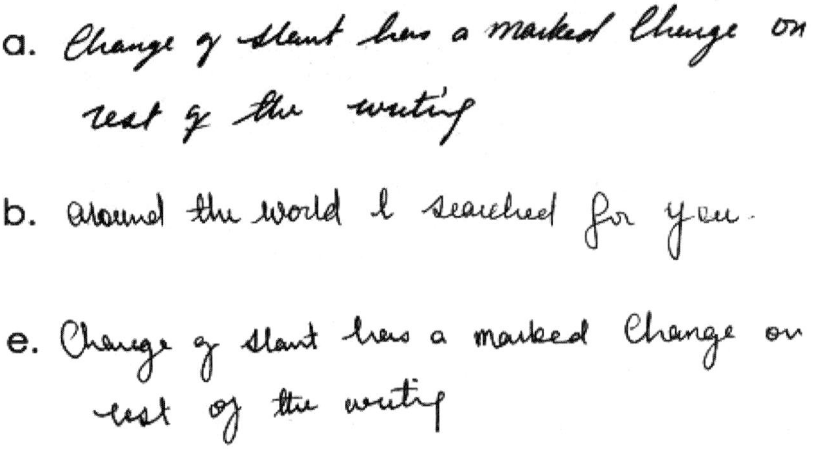

Figure 15.6. The writer was told simply to change the slant of the writing for the middle and bottom samples. Figures 15.2, 15.3, and 15.5 (samples a-e) were all written by the same individual.

In general, disguised handwritings are written more slowly and with less fluency than normal writings. Although certain general and even fundamental features can be altered, usually there are periods where concentration is relaxed and characteristic habitual patterns surface. Proof of common authorship in court may be difficult, because letter design may differ markedly, but other features such as margins, spacing, size ratios, and overall organization may remain unchanged.

This section adapted from "Disguise in Handwriting" by Marc J. Seifer, *Rhode Island Bar Journal*, December 1988, p. 23–24.

Plausible Deniability

The first time I heard the term *plausible deniability* was when Ollie North was testifying in the Iran Contra hearings, circa 1986. The idea was simply to carry out a covert operation in such a way that one's tracks could be covered. The following disguised signatures have used a variety of methods to accomplish plausible deniability. In most cases, the writer was aware ahead of time that he or she would cash a check and then later claim that the signature was not genuine. It was my task to uncover whether or not there were enough details of fundamental structure that were the same to establish cases for common authorship.

A signature is a habitual psychomotor pattern. The difficulty for **the forger of one's own signature** is to mask every ingrained feature and replace it with something else. In general, most disguises involved changing size, slant, and reverting to the Palmer model—that is, undoing the variety of changes that the writer had made as he or she matured. Wherever possible, names have been changed by dropping letters or changing spelling, but, in all instances, the pattern of the letters have remained the same.

Figure 15.7. A good close match. Note how similar the size, spacing, letter design, and placement of diacritics are. This comparison is your baseline, so we start with essentially a perfect match.

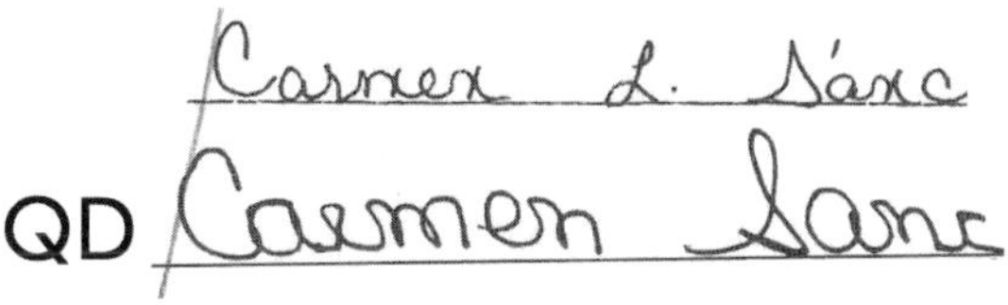

Figure 15.8. Disguise was attempted by increasing size and reverting to the Palmer model. Note that letter spacing, size ratios, and overall letter design remain the same. Thus we see

that, generally speaking, simple increase in size does not change the overall ingrained psychomotor pattern.

Figure 15.9. Decrease in size has not changed the overall spacing, size ratios, and letter design. Arrows point to essentially identical similarities in details of fundamental structure.

Figure 15.10. A rather poor attempt at a disguise achieved by changing size and slant and reverting to Palmer. Arrows point to the same secondary elaboration on the Greek E and ending o. One should also study all the other letters to see how they have been changed and why they are still similar. For instance, the a is similar in shape and in details except for the slant, and the c has a back-and-forth movement that has persisted but is not as elaborate. One can also begin to see where the subject got the idea of swinging back the ending o. Look at the o in the middle of the last name in both the known (at the top) and the QD. The swing-back movement appears in both.

Figure 15.11. Whenever possible, when dealing with disguised handwritings or suspect signatures, try also to obtain the printing of the writer. In this instance, the printed letters of the bottom signature help tie the QD to the writer. Note how the ca is connected, the overall spacing, and size ratios and the ending o.

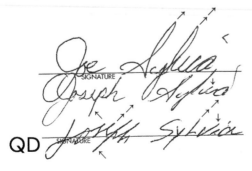

Figure 15.12. Disguise is achieved by reversing slant. In order to change slant, the wrist must be flipped roughly 90 degrees. Note that change in slant has affected letter pattern, but not overall design particularly in first word. This is a good close match for a reverse slant. The key, in general, is the spacing between letters, heights, and height ratios.

Figure 15.13. Disguise is achieved by reducing size, reversing slant in first name, and reverting to print script. Note which details of fundamental structure persist aside from the relative size, spacing, and height ratios: the small loop on the top of the o; the break between h and i, and unusual loose connection between the s and m in the last name.

Figure 15.14. Because the writer signed his exemplar with the word Joe, the bank teller requested that he use his proper name "Joseph." Note that once he did, the retraced bottom loop of the p becomes a telltale fundamental similarity. Disguise is achieved by essentially reducing the size of the upper zone and reverting to a combination of a Palmer and print script style. A key similarity in this instance is the slant.

Figure 15.15. An excellent disguise achieved by changing size and slant and reverting to a slow Palmer model. The few key similarities that remained include the separation of the cap M

from the e, the beginning stroke of the e, need to place an i-dot, the n moving into the o and the idiosyncratic open ending o. Even though the writer went to great lengths to alter her pattern, the final psychomotor movement was too deeply ingrained to be changed.

Figure 15.16. The disguise was achieved by increasing size of middle zone letters and reverting to print script. Nonetheless, many habitual

psychomotor patterns remain, particularly the size of most caps and size ratios as well as the following: the slight out-turn on the end stroke of the M, the flat top to the r, restricted first hump of an arcaded n, large full D taller than the G, and ending e that is taller than the s.

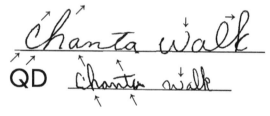

Figure 15.17. Disguise was achieved by reversing slant and decreasing size. Note the telltale 90 degree mirror-image quality of the slant reversal, overall similarity of the letter forms, idiosyncratic

decision to start the name with a lowercase capital C, and the same size ratios with C shorter than h and at the end, W shorter than l shorter than k.

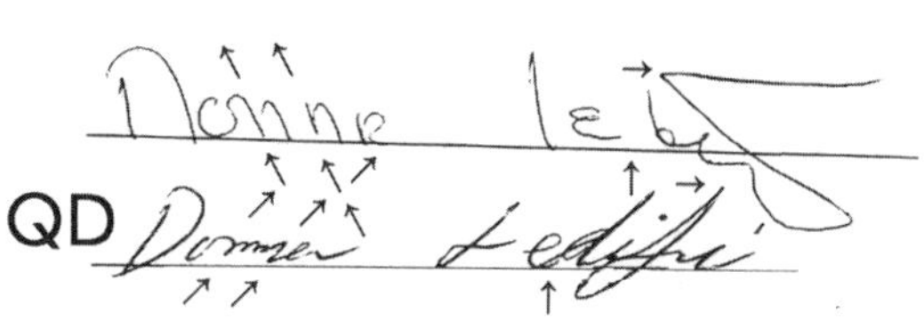

Figure 15.18. A very successful disguise achieved by reversing slant and reverting to a Palmer model when the exemplars were written with a print script. Nevertheless, we

again see the mirror-image slant reversal, particularly on the first name, and in the last name, the isolated e and size ratio tendency to emphasize the last part of the name with a rather tall near-the-end stroke. This case would be difficult to prove in court and, so I officially ruled it "inconclusive."

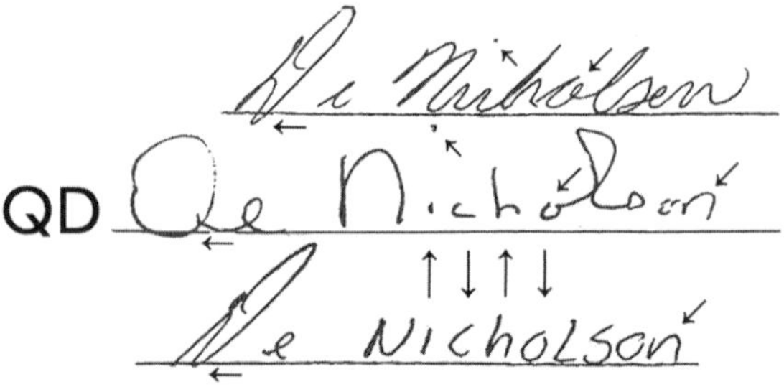

Figure 15.19. Another successful disguise achieved in the opposite manner as figure 15.18, in this instance, by printing the signature, increasing the size of the caps, decreasing the size of the lowercase letters, and changing the slant. In general, when obtaining exemplars, it is best to acquire both printing and cursive. In this instance, the printed *"icho"* exemplar letters are similar to the QD for the simpleness of design of the letters and spacing. Key similarities include, with the cursive exemplar, the high flying i-dot and the open o's. With the printing, the ending n is a very close match. Nevertheless, this case would be difficult to prove in court and so I officially ruled it *"inconclusive."*

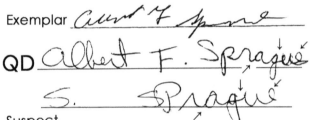

Exemplar

QD

Suspect

Figure 15.20. There is no similarity between the QD and the exemplar. Further, many letters of the last name match the handwriting of another suspect. Note in particular the overall size, ra connection, loose g-loop connection to the u and full ending e.

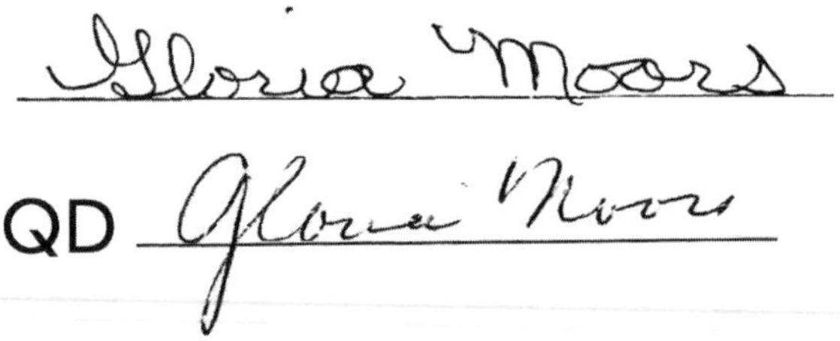

Figure 15.21. An example of a non-genuine signature. The QD does not match the exemplar in any way. Note the difference in size ratios with the l shorter than the G in the exemplar and taller than the G in the QD. The o's are closed in the exemplar and open in the QD, and, most importantly, the QD is written at a faster clip than the exemplar. In all, or almost all the cases, the QD is written in slower fashion, which is part of the evidence of the disguise. What is important about this example is that the QD is of a higher Form Level than the exemplar.

RULE: A person with a higher Form Level can create a disguised writing with a lower Form Level, but a person with a lower Form Level can not create a disguised writing with a higher Form Level.

Honolulu handwriting expert Reed Hayes (2006) suggests creating a worksheet with **two columns for the QD and the Known to compare** the following features:

Arrangement	Size	Size ratios	Pressure
Spacing for line	Within letters	Between letters	Word
Connecting stroke	Pauses	Pen lifts	Slant
Initial stroke	Terminal stroke	Embellishments	Simplification
Abbreviations	Slant	Puncutation	Signs/symbols

He also suggests noting **spelling idiosyncrasies** and to be aware of the issue of **natural variation**. Many handwriting cases involve the elderly and wills. Most often, if a good number of exemplars are provided, telltale habitual psychomotor patterns will be located that persist even through stroke, trauma, illness, and advanced age. Hayes therefore wisely suggests **obtaining contemporaneous writing samples**—that is, samples created at a date as close to the date of suspect document as possible (16, 132).

Case Study

One of the most difficult cases I received involved a lady who had the ability to write in a variety of styles with little similarity between some of them. See Figure 15.12 which compares one of her handwritings to a typed letter she also sent.

A couple on a block were being harassed, but they did not want to alert their suspects, which was everyone else on the block! We therefore obtained the voter registration cards from the suspects and based on that material I was able to identify the culprit. The writer turned out to be a "little old lady" who they never would have suspected. Once confronted, the lady actually moved out of town!

The first task was to tie all six letters together.

Figure 15.23 ties three of the letters together, and Figure 15.24 ties yet another letter, one in cursive, to a typed anonymous note. Referring to Figure 15.22 and looking at the two cursive samples, which begin "Hi Nancy," (HN) and "Mr. & Mrs. Gay," (MMG), we note the following key similarities:

a. Line 2 of HN, t of "at" with t of "pet", line 3.

b. Line 3, the "a" with its high end stroke with the t of street, line 2.

c. The word "and," line 2 of HN with "and," line 2 of MMG.

d. Very similar meager, light i-dots in both.

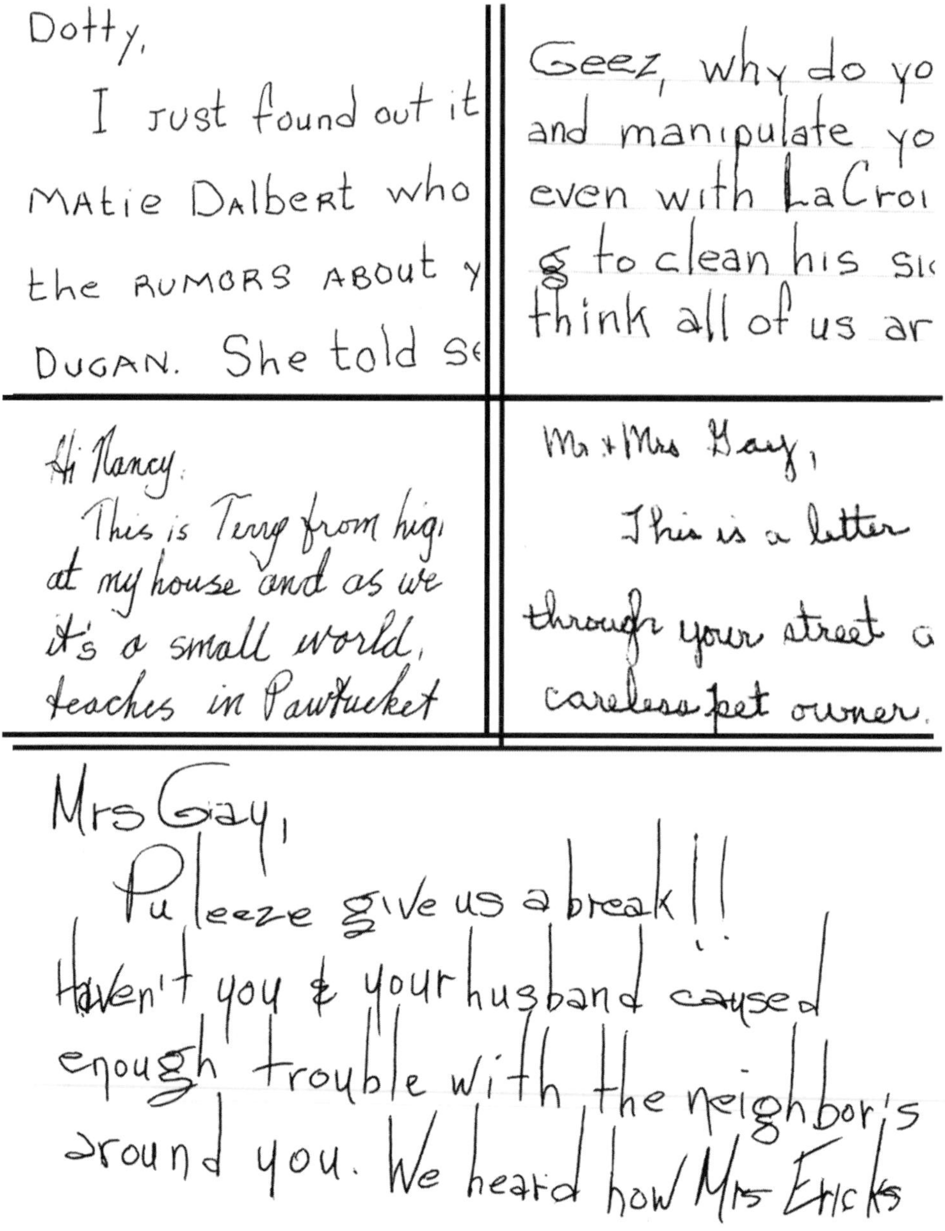

Dotty,

   I just found out it

Matie Dalbert who

the rumors about y

Dugan. She told se

Geez, why do yo

and manipulate yo

even with LaCroi

s to clean his si

think all of us ar

Hi Nancy,

This is Terry from high

at my house and as we

it's a small world,

teaches in Pawtucket

Mr + Mrs Gay,

   This is a letter

through your street a

careless pet owner.

Mrs Gay,

   Puleeze give us a break!!

Haven't you & your husband caused

enough trouble with the neighbor's

around you. We heard how Mrs Ericks

Figure 15.22. All five anonymous notes were written by the same person!

One letter that stood out in most of the notes was the G, written as a peculiar typewriter *g* in letters 3 and 4. Once the voter registration cards were obtained, I was able to find a key match with the word *March* with GE's handwriting. Further comparisons supported the case that GE was the culprit. Note that her name begins with the letter *G*.

	3	4	5
A	Gay,	Geez,	
B	neighbor	neighbor	
C	daught	taught	
D	ing	ing	
E	who	who stay	who SPREAd
F	the	the	the
G		look like	BACK

Figure 15.23. Columns 3, 4, and 5 correspond to words and letters taken from samples from 15.22 partially represented here.

By blowing up part of the word *March* (at bottom left), one begins to see how similar the two words really are. The *r* has a short flat top on both and is disconnected from the *c* in both. The loop of the *h* is almost an exact match including a slight ballooning out on the right side on both.

A careful study of disguise in handwriting gives the handwriting expert many clues as to how to separate genuine signatures from forgeries. In general, one must not make the mistake of thinking that a handwriting is a disguise when it is really a forgery. In general, when a person is attempting to disguise his or her signature, the goal is to make the QD look different than the exemplar. So, in this case, key similarities of details of fundamental structure (slant, size ratios, idiosyncratic letter designs, connecting strokes, endings, and end strokes) are good measures to build a case for common authorship.

On the other hand, when a second person is attempting to forge someone's signature, the goal is the opposite, namely to make the QD look like the exemplar. Thus, in this instance, one looks for key differences.

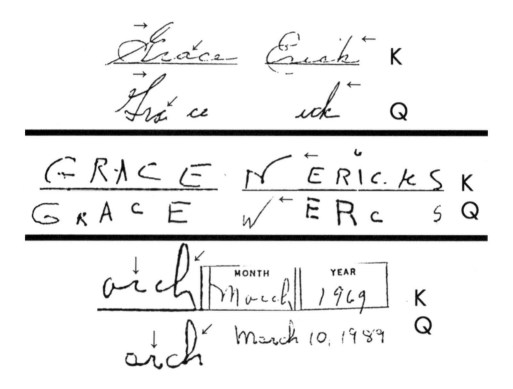

Figure 15.24. Note the following similarities:

a. Top loop of the G.

b. Overstroke on the a.

c. Extremely tall k-loop.

d. Same general letter design for the letters G R A C E R S.

e. Tall ending to the letter N.

f. Entire word March for size, spacing, slant, and letter design.

First and foremost, a handwriting expert must be objective. This means that oftentimes the expert may come to a finding in direct opposition to the one hoped for by the client. It is the duty of the expert to explain precisely what his or her findings are based upon. Most often, this achieved by matching up and enlarging the questioned document with various exemplars. Keep in mind that the opposition will most often come to the same results, so it is best for the client's attorney to have full access to precisely what the situation is. Obviously, try to obtain the originals or access to the originals whenever possible. The next best thing to an original is a color machine copy of the original, a color photograph (digital or otherwise), or a computer scan of the original.

When collecting exemplars, make sure to make a copy of the check if it is signed by the client or any suspects, and also save any handwriting samples, such as the envelope that the package is mailed in. I have solved a good number of cases by this simple method.

The most important tool that a handwriting expert has is his magnifying glass. It is best to have a variety of lens, so that different amounts of magnification can be achieved. I usually carry three lenses with me—a large one that magnifies 3x and two loops. These are lenses that you hold up to your eye and then bring the document to the lens. One magnifies 5X and another is a jeweler's loop, which can magnify 10X. You have to experiment, because sometimes only modest magnification of the handwriting is required. At other times, higher magnification is best.

Magnification can also be achieved with a good scanner and a computer. If you require very high magnification when scanning, increase the dots per inch from 300 to 500 or even 1,000. After the document is scanned into the computer, you can use Photoshop to enlarge to the appropriate size.

Many times you do not want to magnify too greatly, because sometimes under high magnification it actually becomes more difficult to undertake the assessment that is required.

Another important tool is a light-box. The light-box should also be taken to the documents if they are not released to your care. When using a light-box you are attempting to see if letters and letter combinations superimpose over each other. If you locate a spontaneous psychomotor sequence, such as a *th*, *gh*, or *ing* combination, or any other letter sequences such as in the signature, see if these parts superimpose over the questioned signature. If tracing has been ruled out, what you are looking for is a Gestalt rhythmic writing pattern that matches the knowns. Spend some time using a light-box. When the writing is of common authorship, oftentimes many letter sequences will fit over the exemplars in a "hand in glove" way.

When in court, you can also create transparencies of each handwriting and project the superimpositions by using an overhead projector, so that you can overlay a known signature to a questioned one. This can be a very effective way to visually present your case.

Figure 16.1. I took this photograph by hooking up my single lens reflex camera to the microscope.

I recently had a case whereby the opposition claimed that the signature was placed on a blank page and that the document was created afterward. This would mean that the typed portion of the writing should be on top of the ink on the page.

When looking at Figure 16.1, the photo clearly shows that the letters E and P superimpose over the inked signature, which are the diagonal lines going from bottom left to top right. The document had been placed on a light-box so it was underlit. I knew from looking at the original that the ink was on *top* of the print, not the reverse, and was astounded to see that the photo was a complete misrepresentation of the truth to the situation! The photo gave stunning support to the opposing view, even though it was flat out wrong.

Figure 16.2. Overlit with a lamp and natural light, this photograph more accurately reflects the situation. Arrows point to clear instances of the ink of the signature overlaying the line and typewritten portion of the document.

If you look at Figure 16.2, the black horizontal line is still bleeding through at the end of the first name above the printed *e*, but overall this technique more accurately reflects the true situation—namely that the signature was placed in the normal fashion on a pre-existing document. The lesson here is to make sure the lighting is correct for revealing the true situation, and to be aware that sometimes-excellent photographs or illustrations do not, in fact, reflect the true situation at hand. In other words, be wary of superb illustrations. Sometimes, they may be misleading or inaccurate.

A relatively new tool for the forger is Photoshop, which can create perfect forgeries, as signatures can be easily transferred from one document to another, and further, by changing magnification parameters, signatures can also be altered, or stretched in various ways, so that an original can be made to look slightly different. Letters can be enlarged or diminished, slant and even ink color can be changed, and clever adjustments can be added to alter letter designs.

The only solution for an expert is to ultimately insist on seeing the original. Keep in mind that spurious documents with today's technology can easily be created with Photoshop, a computer, and color copier. Such a spurious document can have multiple colors, for instance, a sheet typed with black ink, with a red seal, and signed in blue. It is also common practice to receive simulated original documents from such individuals as senators and presidents. Such personalized documents look like originals; however, they do not have pressure applied to the signature. There **must be indentations** corresponding to the natural pressure that happens when a real person holds a real pen and signs a page. The pressure will create a groove in the paper that can be seen, particularly under high magnification as through a microscope.

Turn the document over and feel it with your fingers. Study the underside with light held at an angle. If a document cannot be located with ink on the page, a handwriting expert can never be completely certain that it was not created by some other means. Insist on seeing the original.

Write your reports with the statement that your conclusions are based on the assumption that the documents studied "are fair representations of the originals." Always list which documents are originals and which are not. In this day, many cases are made using only machine copies. Try to avoid faxed copies. If it is hard to obtain originals, try to get first generation copies, color copies, or scanned copies of the originals that are mailed or e-mailed. Make sure that you mention that your analysis was based on the study of machine, faxed. or e-mailed copies, and that any conclusions drawn were based on the fact that the copies studied were assumed to be **fair representations of the originals**. End with the statement, "**This conclusion is based on a reasonable degree of scientific certainty.**"

There are different levels of certainty. The preponderance of evidence is only 51 percent. Beyond a reasonable doubt is above 75 percent. Personally, I like to be well over 90 percent certain. Your findings have to achieve a level of being self-evident, or, in Harrison's terms, "**demonstrable.**" I have often come up against a handwriting expert's report that has a conclusion drawn based on no demonstrable evidence. These reports can be very impressive to look at. They list all of the documents studied, they discuss a logical methodology, they include a weighty resume, but ultimately they say nothing. If a report cannot display a basis for a conclusion drawn, it is essentially useless, and the attorney has every right, and even the duty, to insist on explanations or illustrations, either verbally or in writing, which explain precisely why the expert has come to the conclusion he or she has come to.

I always think, can I make this case before a jury in a court of law? If I feel that I cannot make that case to a reasonable degree of scientific certainty, then I would rule inconclusive. You may know the truth, but proving it is something else.

One of the biggest mistakes novices make is settling for a meager amount of handwriting. Always insist on obtaining more samples. Stick to your guns.

Keep in mind that you are in independent expert and that more often than not, you will come to a finding that is *opposed* to what your client is hoping for. Let them know.

*In a burst of real-estate speculation in the heady 1980s,
Jonathan Googel, Benjamin Sisti, and Frank Shuch dazzled
Connecticut with their wealth, their flamboyance, and their
deals. As many as 6,000 people invested $350 million in
partnerships of their Colonial Realty Company that bought
shopping centers, apartment complexes, and office buildings.
The dealing stopped in September 1990, when banks forced
Colonial into bankruptcy.*

—*Investors Say Connecticut Empire Is Fraud*, George
Judson, *New York Times*, 1992

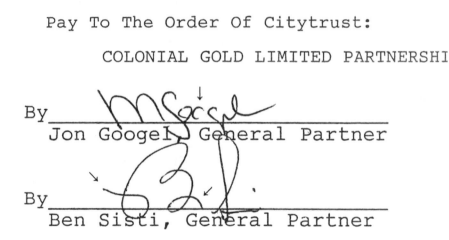

Figure 17.1 *These two real estate moguls were eventually arrested for bank
fraud. Arrows point to unusual graphics, such as a broken form on the open oval
in the top signature, and a counterstroke and evidence for unusual manual
dexterity in the bottom signature.*

Hopefully, you have learned a lot about the complexities of handwriting analysis and how to detect forgeries. The following are three case studies from the Colonial Bank scam, whereby Googel and Sisti sold real estate to investors and created promissory notes with various Hartford and Wall Street Banks. This was accepted business practice. However, at some point in their game, they decided to duplicate said notes by creating fraudulent signatures and then each note (the good one and the bad one) was sold to separate banks. The scheme involved a massive amount of handwriting forgeries.

In this way immediate net revenues would mushroom at an astounding rate. The recipients would gain the entire amount of the note doubled at once, rather than receive modest monthly revenues based on half that amount from the various holders of said notes. Googel and Sisti reaped in literally hundreds of millions of dollars in their Ponzi scheme.

In order to sort out the forgeries, the Connecticut Lawyer's Group was formed and a series of handwriting experts were hired. In my own case, because it was essential to see the original documents, I made a series of trips to banks in Connecticut and on Wall Street to study and reproduce the documents, so that I could sort out the genuine from the non-genuine signatures.

Take the Quiz: Find the Counterfeit

The following three figures are puzzles for the reader.

Study each of them carefully and see if you can locate the forgeries. There are four forgeries in all and one duplicate legitimate signature. Take your time. The answers will be provided at the end of the chapter. In all cases, the top signature is a genuine one. Try to locate the forgeries and list your reasons as to why you came to your conclusions.

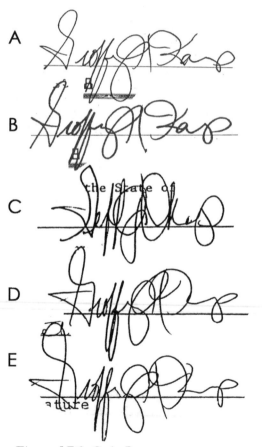

Figure 17.2. Quiz I.

Figure 17.3. Quiz II.

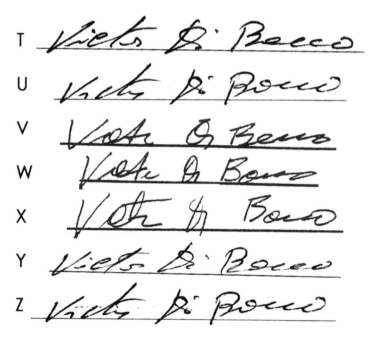

Figure 17.4. Quiz III.

Here are copies of the promissory notes used in the scam. For reasons of security and size limitations, the notes have been shortened.

NEGOTIABLE NOTE

$ 47,500.00	*East*	*Conn*	*March 6* 198
Principal Sum	Town	State	Date

FOR VALUE RECEIVED, the undersigned promise to pay to the order of COLONIAL GOLD LIMITED PARTNERSHIP ("Payee"), a Connecticut limited partnership at 65 K   Hartford, Connecticut April 1, 1987 at the rate of nine percent (9%) per annum, said interest and principal payable as set forth below, together with all taxes

Principal and interest shall be due and payable as follows:

Principal	Interest	Total Payment	Due Date
$ 1,000	$ 1,781	$ 2,781	September 1, 1987
$ 8,795	$ 2,441	$11,236	April 1, 1988
$ 8,519	$ 3,393	$11,912	April 1, 1989
$ 8,519	$ 2,627	$11,146	April 1, 1990
$ 8,519	$ 1,860	$10,379	April 1, 1991
$ 6,074	$ 1,093	$ 7,167	April 1, 1992
$ 6,074	547	$ 6,621	April 1, 1993
$47,500	$13,742	$61,242	

Each payment shall be applied first to late charges, if any, then to the payment of unpaid interest, and the balance applied to unpaid principal.

Default in the payment of interest and/or principal as provided herein for a period of ten (10) days after any of the same become due and payable, or the filing of a petition in bankruptcy filed by or

The undersigned agree to pay upon demand to the holder of this Note a "late charge" of five percent (5%) of the unpaid principal not received by the holder of this Note within ten (10) days after the same is due.

Presentment, protest and notice of dishonor are hereby waived.

This Note is governed by the laws of the State of Connecticut.

NEGOTIABLE NOTE

$ 47,500.00	*East*	*Conn*	*March 6* 198
Principal Sum	Town	State	Date

FOR VALUE RECEIVED, the undersigned promise to pay to the order of COLONIAL GOLD LIMITED PARTNERSHIP ("Payee"), a Connecticut limited partnership at 65 K   Hartford, Connecticut April 1, 1987 at the rate of nine percent (9%) per annum, said interest and principal payable as set forth below, together with all taxes

Principal and interest shall be due and payable as follows:

Principal	Interest	Total Payment	Due Date
$ 1,000	$ 1,781	$ 2,781	September 1, 1987
$ 8,795	$ 2,441	$11,236	April 1, 1988
$ 8,519	$ 3,393	$11,912	April 1, 1989
$ 8,519	$ 2,627	$11,146	April 1, 1990
$ 8,519	$ 1,860	$10,379	April 1, 1991
$ 6,074	$ 1,093	$ 7,167	April 1, 1992
$ 6,074	547	$ 6,621	April 1, 1993
$47,500	$13,742	$61,242	

Each payment shall be applied first to late charges, if any, then to the payment of unpaid interest, and the balance applied to unpaid principal.

Default in the payment of interest and/or principal as provided herein for a period of ten (10) days after any of the same become due and payable, or the filing of a petition in bankruptcy filed by or

The undersigned agree to pay upon demand to the holder of this Note a "late charge" of five percent (5%) of the unpaid principal not received by the holder of this Note within ten (10) days after the same is due.

Presentment, protest and notice of dishonor are hereby waived.

This Note is governed by the laws of the State of Connecticut.

Figure 17.5. One of these signatures is bogus.

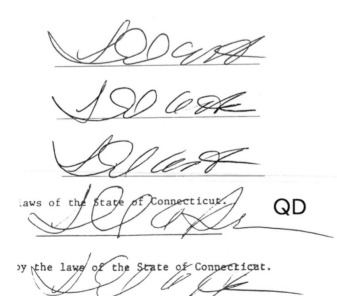

Figure 17.6. One can see that the QD is missing the E-like structure of the second letter, the capital letter of the last name (which looks like the letter S in the QD), and the long ending stroke of the QD are also different. Clearly, the QD is a non-genuine signature.

Colonial Reality was using freehand forgeries. They are not tracings, but rather, after a bit of practice, the forger takes a pen in hand and in a bold, rapid fashion tries to put down a signature that resembles the original.

In these cases, the forger had just one exemplar to work from, which was, of course, the genuine signature on the genuine promissory note. I obtained a half dozen or more additional genuine signatures from the injured parties and placed them on a page along with the genuine promissory note signature and the QD.

When trying to ascertain whether or not a signature is genuine, it is best to obtain as many exemplars as possible. In this way, the expert is able to familiarize himself with the various psychomotor patterns that are habitual to the writer. One looks at not only the obvious features such as the capital letters, slant, and general design, but also the **details of fundamental structure**, the least conscious aspects to the writing that still is created in a habitual way. The devil really is in the details!

Figurer 17.7 As you can see, the forger got the first letter D correct, but completely missed the essence of the capital P on the second name. The overall rhythm and angle are similar, but not the pattern that resembles an S rather than a P. Where the exemplars begin the P at the bottom loop by going down and then looping up to create the top loop, the QD does the reverse, starts at the top loop, goes around and then comes down to create the bottom loop.

Figure 17.8. (From Figure 17.2, the QD is letter C.)

Following the numbers, we note the following differences:

1. Top loop of *G* missing in QD.
2. Top of *f* has a loop in QD only.
3. Ending stroke comes from bottom loop in QD only.
4. This circle appears in QD only.
5. Right side of *K* very different from exemplars.
6. The *e* is made like an *e* in QD and made like an *r* in exemplars.

The forger got the overall pattern down pretty well, but completely missed all the details. The next two cases rested on the ability of expert to study the habitual pattern of the exemplars and sit with the QD's alongside of the originals. This was done on site at the banks where the notes were kept.

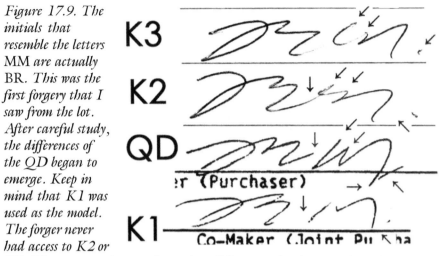

Figure 17.9. The initials that resemble the letters MM *are actually* BR. *This was the first forgery that I saw from the lot. After careful study, the differences of the* QD *began to emerge. Keep in mind that K1 was used as the model. The forger never had access to K2 or K3. The arrows point out the various differences. In the exemplars, there is an air-stroke between the two initials but not in the* QD. *The* QD *has a sharp middle angle in the second M-like capital, where that stroke is curved in the exemplars. The forger also misunderstood the endstroke. In K1 the writer is moving up with an air-stroke to create a dot. This was changed into a solid line in the* QD *only. The answer from the quiz was M from Figure 17.3.*

Figure 17.10. A well-performed freehand forgery. These signatures are enlarged about 140 percent, so when written actual size (at right), the differences are harder to determine. The key to unlocking this case was the ending o, *which is completely different in the* QD. *It is much flatter.*

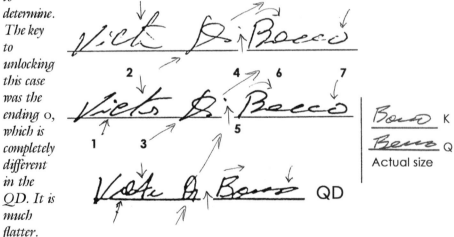

The B has a flat top on the QD *and on the model the forger used to create his simulation only (at right) whereas the true writer generally rounds the top of the B in all other exemplars. The t-bar is missing the air-stroke in the* QD *and executed differently, the dot is missing in the* QD, *and slant of middle initial is different as well.*

Referring back to the quiz, Figure 17.4, X was used as the model, as this was the signature on the original promissory note, V and W were the two QDs, and exemplar U was an identical copy of exemplar Z.

Note that there are scatter marks on Z that have been removed in U. This was done with Photoshop, and thus the two signatures look a little different, but they are essentially identical. On the famous Hitler diary forgeries, one mistake the QD examiner made was in using one of the forgeries as an exemplar. Thus, he was right in saying that both writings were written by the same hand; the only problem was, the hand wasn't Hitler's! In this instance, I included an extra exemplar to point out that handwritings can get confusing. Make sure that you carefully separate and label the exemplars from the QD's. Also, when dealing with complex cases, sometimes you may end up with multiple copies and thus several of the same exemplar can creep in as separate exemplars.

Another lesson here has to do with the problem of **natural variation**. The great difficulty that I encountered with this case was at the start. I drove down to the bank in Connecticut and the only exemplar I had was X from Figure 17.4 (or the small one labeled K in Figure 17.10). By coincidence, this was the only exemplar with a B made with a flat top, thus the main difference was just the ending o. The key to solving this case, as with any case, is to get as many exemplars as you can, and to work with originals whenever possible. Sometimes this means going on site. Once you sit down and compare original exemplars with the QD, the experience is very enlightening. It is just not the same thing to work from copies, color, scanned, or otherwise. Seeing originals allows you to study pressure patterns, stroke texture, and speed—three factors almost impossible to truly study from copies. Once originals are studied, cases are almost always solved. Any other course of action in difficult cases is a recipe for failure.

Keep in mind that oftentimes the original is a copy. I had a case several years ago that involved a document hand-stamped with an official red seal from a foreign government. The document was an original stamped document. The only problem was that all of the signatures were machine copies. The document I needed to see was held by the opposing side. It wasn't until I saw the true original document that I was able to render an opinion.

The same thing is true in America. Most deeds registered at the town hall are machine copies. These are official copies, and very often they are the only copies. There may be no original to be found that has ink on the page. Nevertheless, it is still of paramount importance to go to the town hall and see this first generation copy. Oftentimes there will be details that are lost in second- and third-generation copies (for example, key air strokes). In these instances, copy machines are not adequate. These documents must be photographed. I suggest a single lens reflex camera with close-up lenses. Take along a flashlight or other light source. Sunlight and natural light are also important tools for taking correct photographs on site. If a document has Wite-Out, for instance, a machine copy will not pick this up. Whenever possible, work with originals and obtain as many exemplars as you can. Try to get a range of dates, including, of course, documents from around the date as the QD.

> ## Rhode Island Murder Suspect Denies Being in State Where Crime Occurred, Witness Identifies Cranston Man
>
> Carl Stephen Rosati, 30, has been in the Adult Correctional Institution since his arrest Sept. 12 by state police on a fugitive warrant.... He was indicted, along with two other men, by a Florida grand jury, in connection with the slaying of Joseph Viscido Jr. of Deerfield Beach, on October 12, 1986.... Two witnesses to a 1986 Florida murder identified Carl Stephen Rosati of Cranston as one of the gunmen, from photographs presented to them.... One of the Florida men, Peter Dallas, last month pleaded guilty to second-degree murder and is expected to testify against Rosati if he is brought to trial in Florida.... Viscido was found shot to death on the floor of his apartment.... Rosati has been held without bail since his arrest.
>
> *—Providence Journal,* January 31, 1991

Without doubt, the most fulfilling case that I have had in my 35-plus year career as a handwriting expert was the Stephen Rosati extradition hearing, which was the longest extradition hearing in the state of Rhode Island. In September 1990, I was hired by Jack Cicilline, the well-known criminal attorney and later-day father of the mayor of Providence, to look at some documents alleged to have been signed by Stephen Rosati. He was being held for murder without bail at the ACI, which is the local jail in Rhode Island. At the start, I had no idea how I could be of service.

The Broward Sheriff's Office (BSO) in Florida had stated that on October 12, 1986, Stephen Rosati and Peter Dallas had entered Joe Viscido's apartment in Deerfield Beach at gunpoint to rob him of drugs, and as a result Viscido was killed in a scuffle. Six witnesses had ID'd Rosati, including two who were in the apartment, and Peter Dallas himself, who confessed. The third man accused was the alleged wheelman, Pete "the Greek" Roussonicolos.

All of this was in a series of newspaper articles covered predominantly in rhe *Providence Journal* and *Miami Herald*, but also in rhe *New York Times*, rhe *Sun-Sentinel* and elsewhere.

I drove over to the offices of the Rosati Group, which was in Warwick, Rhode Island, and met with Stephen's parents. The case was complicated, because the BSO was not just saying Rosati shot and killed Joe Viscido, they were also saying that in the autumn of 1986 Rosati was also *living* in southern Florida as several witnesses testified. Thus, if Rosati were signing documents in Rhode Island for the weeks and months around the time of Viscido's death, this would help greatly prove that BSO was wrong.

Mr. and Mrs. Rosati brought me into an office where there was a carton of documents that they said their son had signed. These included health club dispatches (in 1986, Stephen owned a Rhode Island health club), gasoline, and other credit card receipts and business checks signed by Stephen Rosati, who was the vice president of several companies associated with the Rosati Group. The handwritings were in several different styles.

"Are all of these Stephen's handwriting?" I asked incredulously.

"Yes," Carl, the father, said. "And if you find any that are not his, please remove them from the pile. We want to catalog every document he signed around this time to establish that indeed, my son was living and conducting business in Rhode Island in October of 1986, not in Florida."

After several other questions, I found out that Rosati, born and raised in Rhode Island, was a weight lifter who, with his father, purchased a health club in 1983, which he ran for two years. This was the same year that he won the body building championship to become Mr. Rhode Island. The following year, at age 24, leaving the club in other hands, he moved to Florida and lived there for the last few months of 1984 through most of 1985. For that period, Rosati was a male dancer. But this was a full year *before* the murder. From 1986 to 1988 he lived again in Rhode Island, where he continued to run and then sold the health club, and he also began to build houses. When the market dried up in 1989, which was three years after the murder, he moved back to Florida to try and sell real estate there, but by 1990, the year he was arrested, he was back working for the Rosati Group in Rhode Island. As a matter of record according to the Rosatis, during 1986, he had never been in Florida. "He was running his health club and building homes here in Rhode Island at that time, and we can prove it," Mrs. Rosati said.

After cataloging all of the documents, I was able to compile a time line. The murder was committed on Sunday night, October 12, 1986, which was a Columbus Day weekend. I had many key health club payroll checks that Rosati signed on Fridays, which he hand delivered to his employees, such as on Friday, October 3, October 10, October 17, October 24, and so on.

There was also a gasoline credit card receipt in Rhode Island for Saturday, October 11, and one in Connecticut, on October 15, three days after the murder. Also, there was a health club dispatch that was also dated October 11, the day before the murder. The problem I had was that these handwritings were in many different styles.

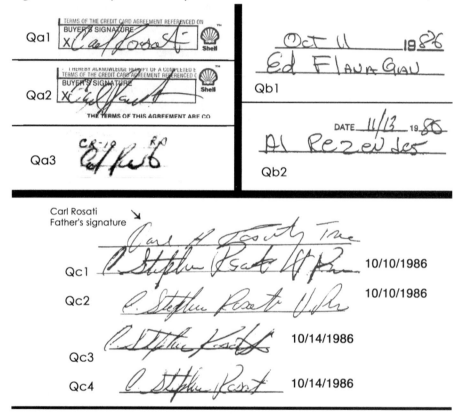

Figure 18.1. Three different groups of signatures and handwriting styles were presented to me as all being written in the Rhode Island area by Stephen Rosati. All dates are from October and November 1986. Viscido was killed October 12 in Florida. Qa 1,2, and 3 are gasoline credit card receipts signed in Rhode Island on 10/6 and 10/11, and in Stonington, Connecticut, on 10/15. The health club dispatches from Warwick, RI, Qb 1 and 2 were filled out October 11 and November 13. The payroll checks signed in front of a bookkeeper at the Rosati Group in Warwick, RI, on October 10, and the two from October 14 were signed at a bank.

As you can see, we have three distinct styles, two types of right slanted cursives, and a round upright print script. On top of that, the signatures say different things. The gasoline credit card receipts are signed Carl Rosati, and the checks are signed "C. Stephen Rosati, V. Pres." I grilled the parents.

"Are you sure Stephen signed all these documents?"

"Yes," Carl, the father said. "He has different styles."

"Why do the credit cards receipts say Carl Rosati?" I asked.

"Stephen's first name really is Carl," Carl the father said. "So since the credit card had the name Carl on it, Stephen thought it best to sign the credit cards with that name."

Naturally I was aware that people have different signatures for different types of documents. I, myself, tend to scribble my name on credit card receipts and even on checks, but when signing important documents or at book signings, I write much more legibly. Nevertheless, I remained skeptical that Stephen Rosati could have had all of these separate styles.

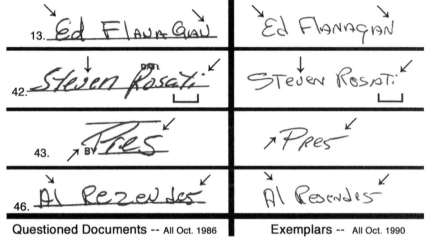

| Questioned Documents -- All Oct. 1986 | Exemplars -- All Oct. 1990 |

Figure 18.2. My first break in the case came when I discovered that Rosati made his s's like the number 5, which was seen in the health club dispatches as well. In my 20 years as a QD expert at that time, I had never seen this idiosyncrasy before. This, along with a gasoline credit card receipt signed the same day placed Rosati in Rhode Island on October 11, 1986, one day before the murder, a day Florida witnesses said he was in Florida.

My next step was to go to the ACI and obtain exemplars from the accused. I therefore typed out all of the information that I wanted, which were the key words that were in handwriting from these various documents. Naturally I did not want Rosati to see the actual documents, and of course I did not take them to the jail. Rosati would only see typed copy. I met with him on three separate occasions.

As I drove to the jail, I considered how these various documents might be signed if they were indeed all signed by Rosati. For instance, the writing of health club dispatches was in a print script. The signatures on the checks were in a style different than the style of the signatures from the credit cards. A good way to begin any case is to set out to try and prove the opposite finding that the client is seeking. In a sense, you play the devil's advocate. You do whatever you think an opposing expert would do. If you cannot disprove the case, this helps establish its validity. Many times, however, the expert ends up with a finding contrary to the hopes of the client. That's the way it goes. Your goal is always to find out the truth, no matter what it is.

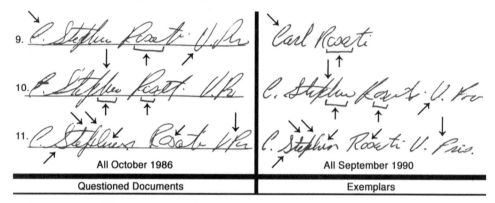

Figure 18.3. Various payroll checks witnessed by a bookkeeper and bank checks placed Rosati in Rhode Island on Friday, October 10, and Tuesday, October 14.

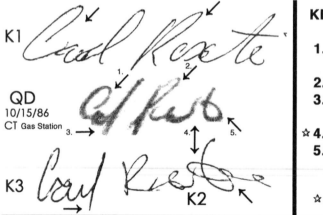

KEY COMPARISONS

1. **Long beginning loop on cap C.**
2. **Tall narrow cap R.**
3. **Abrupt ending I below baseline.**
☆ 4. **Thin upstroke to t.**
5. **Left tending curvearound t-bar.**

☆ *Extremely important similarity.*

Figure 18.4. Stephen had said that he drove down to New York with his mother and girlfriend on October 15. This was a trip that involved planning, and Stephen's mother, Esther Rosati, remembered that the trip was discussed that weekend. So, from her point of view, Stephen had to have been in Rhode Island that Sunday, which was the day of the murder, the following Monday, and of course Tuesday, the 15th, when they drove down.

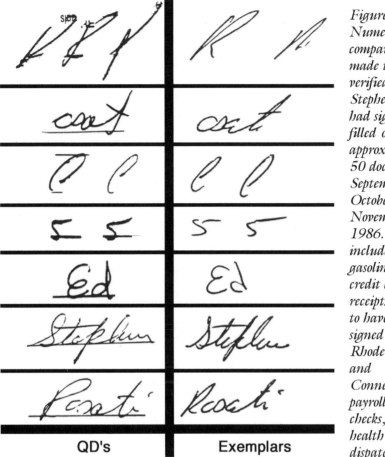

QD's	Exemplars

Figure 18.5. Numerous comparisons were made that verified that Stephen Rosati had signed or filled out approximately 50 documents in September, October, and November of 1986. These included gasoline and credit card receipts that had to have been signed on site in Rhode Island and Connecticut, payroll and bank checks, and health club dispatches.

I also wanted to see what Rosati's cursive and printing styles were. I assumed that checks would be signed on a table, whereas credit card receipts may have been signed on his lap, because in those days, an attendant filled up the gas tank while the driver sat in the car and the receipt was handed into the car to be signed. I also wanted to see examples of his writing with reversed slants, with eyes closed when writing and printing signatures, and also with his opposite hand.

Because I did not have any signed documents for Sunday, the day of the murder, and the following Monday, which was Columbus Day, I did not know whether or not Stephen Rosati was innocent. From my point of view, it was still possible that he could have flown down on Sunday, killed Joe Viscido, and been back on Monday. However, what was clear to me was that at least some of the witnesses had to be lying because they said Rosati was living in Florida during this time and that he was seen days and weeks before the murder—for instance, October 11, which, from my findings, could not have been true.

Once the judge saw my presentation, I could sense a shift take place in his thinking, because he now *knew for certain* that Stephen Rosati was indeed living and conducting business in Rhode Island at the time the Broward Sheriff's Office had six witnesses placing him in Florida.

Stephen, of course, had additional evidence to prove he was in Rhode Island the very day of the crime. This included phone records that verified calls he made from his office the Sunday of the murder and the following Monday to a second girlfriend that he had in Woonsocket, Rhode Island. No one else would have made these calls, and, further, this second girlfriend testified that she indeed had been with him that Sunday. She remembered because it was the day before Columbus Day.

Because of all of this evidence, Stephen's lawyer, Jack Cicilline, was able to block extradition to Florida for 10 months. If Stephen got to Florida, he would be facing a first-degree murder charge, and the punishment could have been the electric chair.

The judge ruled that Stephen Rosati had proven his case "beyond a reasonable doubt." However, because this was an extradition hearing and not a trial, any contradictory evidence would cause the judge to extradite. The reason was that ultimately a trial would have to sort out the truth.

The Broward Sheriff's Office flew up a drug dealer who was in the apartment when Viscido was murdered. Having made a deal for a reduced sentence, this individual pointed at Rosati and said, "He did it." And that was that. In late June of 1991, after being in jail in Rhode Island for 10 months, (this was a non-bailable offense) Stephen was extradited. BSO had a confession from Peter Dallas, and Dallas also said that he had killed Viscido with Rosati.

Miraculously, a separate investigation undertaken by Detective Michael Breece from the Florida Department of Law Enforcement located the real killers. Having been brow-beat by BSO, Dallas now admitted he had *never* met Stephen Rosati, didn't really know who he was, and didn't even know his name before he was told it! All of this had been fed to him during an interrogation. He recanted his confession. The governor of Florida appointed an independent prosecutor to review both cases, and in January 1992, Stephen Rosati, Peter Dallas, and Pete "the Greek" Roussonicolos were released as free men.

This was the most amazing case of my career, and it resulted in me writing a book about the entire affair, coauthored with Stephen Rosati, entitled *Framed!* I was gratified that my work as a handwriting expert helped save an innocent man. Without documentation, Rosati would have had a very weak case. As Stephen put it, "People lie; legitimate documents don't."

Analyzing handwriting
reveals business secrets

PHOTOS: DANIEL G. DUNN

LOOKING FOR CLUES

Handwriting expert Marc J. Seifer analyzes possible forged documents at his home Friday. The microscope and lighted box help him see details in each stroke of the pen, from a nervous hand to a retraced letter. Most of his work is done for lawyers and police departments

Wednesday, November 3, 1993 • The Narragansett Times

Graphological References Containing Validation Studies

A Chronological Bibliography

Many of the following handwriting studies were controlled scientific observations conducted in academic or medical settings by trained graphologists. Certain titles were adapted from the appropriate chapter of the text by the same author. This list is by no means exhaustive, but merely representative of the range of graphology studies performed during a century of inquiry. Refer to James H. Miller's (1982) *Bibliography of Handwriting Analysis*, which contains more than 2,300 references, the bibliography from Werner Wolff (1948/65), or Bob Backman's Handwriting Analysis Research Library (HARL) located in Greenfield Massachusetts, which has more than 86,000 entries.

(1867) Ogle, W. "Aphasia and Agraphia." *St. George's Hospital Reports*, 2, "Ogle created the word agraphia to specifically denote the loss of power of expression by means of writing" (Crepieux-Jamin, 1892).

(1892) Crepieux-Jamin, J. "Hysteria and Handwriting." *Handwriting and Expression*, London: Kegan, Trench and Trubner. "The examination of 45 handwritings of hysterical persons revealed...in 24 instances...marked agitation and the abnormally large movements of the pen." Excellent source text.

(1895) Preyer, W. *On the Physiology of Handwriting*. Preyer established that similar styles can be achieved when the pen was held by either right or left hand, foot, or mouth, thereby establishing that handwriting was centrally organized by the brain and not the appendage.

(1895) Freeman, F. "Preliminary Experiments in Writing Reactions." *Journal of Anatomy and Physiology*, 29. Motion picture equipment was utilized to record the act of writing, and components for changes of speed were noted.

(1900) McAllister, C.N. Research on movements used in writing studies. Yale Psychological Lab, vol. viii.

(1901) Meyer, G. *Die Wissenschaft-lichen Grundalgen der Grapholgie*, Berlin. A systematic study of factors of handwriting correlating with specific characterological features of identity was conducted, for example, artificiality, spontaneity, simplification, elaboration, slant, size, propensity toward roundedness, angularity, and so on.

(1907) Binet, Alfred. "Crucial Experiments in Graphology." *Philosophical Review*, 64, 22–40.

(1919) Downey, J. *Graphology and the Psychology of Handwriting*, Baltimore: Warwick and York. Bipolar expressive characteristics such as fluent or jerky, impulsive or deliberate were examined in 12 individuals in their handwriting, carriage, and expressive gestures, using 11 judges. Above chance correlations were achieved.

(1919) Hull, C., and R. Montgomery. "Experimental Investigation of Alleged Relations Between Character and Handwriting." *American Psychology Review*, 26, 63–74. A study of 17 fraternity brothers' inability to match graphological profiles with their own personality assessments.

(1926) Saudek, R. *Experiments With Handwriting*. London: George Allen & Unwin. Entire text devoted to the ascertaining of objective criteria in handwriting. For example, determining the relative speed of handwriting, developmental changes in the execution of the writing trail from childhood to adulthood, the role of the central nervous system, and so on. Footnotes and detailed bibliography included. Excellent source text.

(1929) Broom, M. E., B. Thompson, and M.T. Bouton. "Sex Differences in Handwriting." *Journal of Applied Psychology*, 13, 159–166.

(1933) Allport, G., and P. Vernon. *Studies in Expressive Movement*. New York, NY: Macmillan. This treatise contains numerous controlled experiments that discovered a congruence between expressive movements (handwriting, gestures, gait) and attitudes, traits, and values.

(1933) Seeman, E., and R. Saudek. "The Handwriting of Identical Twins." *Character & Personality*, 1, 22–40, 258–285.

(1934) Harvey, O. "Measurement of Handwriting Considered as a Form of Expressive Movement." *Character & Personality*, 2, 310–21. The author obtained significant correlations on 26 variables in handwriting analysis with the Thurstone personality schedule of 50 college females.

(1936) Roman, K. "Studies on the Variability of Handwriting: The development of writing speed and point pressure in school children." *Journal of Genetic Psychology*, 44, 139–60.

(1937) Reinhardt, J. "Heredity and Environment. A reexamination of some evidence from studies of twins with emphasis upon graphological method." *Character & Personality*, 5, 305–20.

(1939) Jacoby, H. "Uniqueness and handwriting," in *Analysis of Handwriting*. London: George Allen & Unwin. Two hundred samples were studies for the letter *i*. After careful analysis, no two strokes were found to be identical. The full 200 simples are provided. Excellent source text.

(**1944**) Lewinson, T.S., and J. Zubin. *Handwriting Analysis: A Series of Scales for Evaluating the Dynamic Aspects of Handwriting.* New York. Using objective criteria, the authors were successfully able to differentiate between the handwriting of delinquents and non-delinquents. Excellent source text.

(**1945**) Eysenck, H.J. "Graphological Analysis and Psychiatry: An Experimental Study." *British Journal of Psychology*, 35, 70–81.

(**1947**) Mendel, A. "The Left Slant in the Handwriting of Right-handed Individuals." *Personality in Handwriting*, London: Peter Own, Ltd. Seven right-handed, left-slanted writers "were asked to give a short history of their childhood" particularly with reference to their parents. These accounts were compared to the childhoods of six famous left slanted writers (for example, Longfellow, Thackery, Ibsen). In most cases, estrangement with the father was evident, 85–96. Excellent source text.

(**1948**) Wolff. W. *Diagrams of the Unconscious.* This masterwork explores a full range of experimental studies. The expressive movement in writing (especially the signature) is made chiefly in a state of "unawareness, automatically and impulsively.... These unconscious movements represent a reign of order, proportion and configuration, appearing in the same exact way as if they had been consciously calculated, measured and constructed..." (p.151) "[They] originate neither in change nor in conscious intention, but [rather]... they reflect unconscious principles of organization" (p.177). Included is a bibliography of 474 graphological studies from such journals as: *American Psychoanalytic Quarterly, Archives of Neurology & Psychology, British Journal of Psychology, Character & Personality, Experimental Psychology, Journal of: Abnormal & Social Psychology, Applied Psychology, Educational Research, Genetic Psychology, Social Psychology, Psychiatric Neurology, Clinical Psychopathology & Psychotherapy*, and *Journal of Psychology*. Excellent source text, a truly brilliant and unique work.

(**1948**) Hackbush, F. "Drawings By Children Before and After Epileptic Seizures." in Wolff (1948) 84–88. Increases in the sizes after seizures.

(**1948**) Muhl, Anita M. "Report on Twenty-three Years Research in Handwriting." *Medical Woman's Journal*, 55, 27–31, 60.

(**1950**) Sonnemann, Ulrich. "Longitudinal Study of the Handwriting of a Patient with a Brain Tumor." *Handwriting Analysis*, New York: Grune & Stratton. "Shivering of the ductus... [and] blotting [occurs and as the disease] progresses, difficulties in size control tend to become prominent," 31. Excellent source text based on the work of Klages.

(**1952**) Eliasberg, Wladimir. "Methods in Graphological Diagnostics." *Psychiatric Quarterly*, 26, 399–413.

(1958) Dennis, Wayne. "Handwriting conventions as determinants of human figure drawings." *Journal of Consulting Psychology*, 22, 293–5

(1958) Kanfer, A., and D. Casten. "Observations on Disturbances in Neuro-muscular Coordination in Patients with Malignant Disease." *New York Hospital for Joint Diseases*, 1–19. With the cooperation of fourteen doctors, including Casten, approximately 10,000 handwritings of cancer patients were studied for neuromuscular coordination for 12 years. Examination with a microscope revealed irregular pressure patterns and ink distributions in the handwriting of those afflicted. Corroboration was achieve by "three independent statisticians working at two of the major insurance companies in the New York area."

(1959/60) Hearns, Rudolph S. "Heredity of Psychological Types. A Study of the Handwriting of the Roosevelt Families over 200 Years." *World Analyst*, I, 3–9.

(1961) Fluckinger, Fritz A., Clarence A. Tripp, and George H. Weinberg. "Review of Experimental Research in Graphology: 1933–1960." *Perceptual and Motor Skills*, 12, 67–90.

(1962) Roman, Klara. Graphodyne recordings of muscle tension during the act of writing, in *Handwriting A Key to Personality*, New York: Noonday Press. The author invented a pen-like machine to measure the muscle tension in the writer. "Adequate muscle tone and a well-balanced interplay of tension and release are usually associated with general well-being and emotional stability…. Whereas disturbed tension-release patterns [objectively measure by the graphodyne] accompany emotional instability, neurotic conflict and poor adaptive capacity," (283). Excellent source text.

(1968) Stangohr, Gordon. "Opposite Hand Writings." *Journal of Forensic Sciences*, 13 (3), 376–89.

(1969) Marcuse, Irene. "The Handwriting of Suicides." *Guide to the Disturbed Personality*, NY: Arco Publ. Individual case studies are described. Graphics uncovered included downhill sloping and drooping of letters or letter connections below the baseline. Excellent source text.

(1969) Hearns, R. Dyslexia and Handwriting. *Journal of Learning Disabilities*, 2 (1), 39–44.

(1971) Beumont, P. "Small Handwriting in Some Patients with Anorexia Nervosa." *British Journal of Psychiatry*, 119, 349–50.

(1972) Swanson, B. and R. Price. "Signature Size and Status." *Journal of Social Psychology*, 19, 63–67.

(1972) Mullins, J. "A Handwriting Model of Children with Learning Disabilities." *Journal of Learning Disabilities*, 5, 306–11.

(1974) Pearl, R. A. "Value of Handwriting in the Neurological Examination." *Mount Sinai Journal of Medicine*, 41, 200–4.

(1974) Seifer, M., and D. Goode. "Handwriting: A Measure of Muscle Tension in Schizophrenics and Normals." *National Society for Graphology Newsletter*, Dec., 1–4. The author, a graphologist, under the direction of two medical doctors including D. Goode, isolated 10 variables from the Roman psychogram for measuring signs of muscle tension (for example, rhythm, pressure, speed, slant, and consistency) in a blind study of seven schizophrenic and 12 normal writers. The schizophrenic writers were found to be more tense, and significant differences between the two groups were achieved.

(1976) Lockowandte, Oskar. "Present Status of the Investigation of Handwriting Psychology as a Diagnostic Method." *Catalog of Selected Documents in Psychology*, 6, 4–5.

(1980) Luria, A. "Analysis of the Drawings of Patients with Severe Brain Damage." *Higher Cortical Functions in Man*, New York: Basic Books. A renowned Soviet neurologist, Luria analyzed the writings and drawings of individuals with severe damage to various lobes on the cerebral cortex. Luria found differences in the ability to write and copy pictures when the patient saw the drawings as compared to when they were described verbally, when they were allowed or not allowed to lip read, and when lines were superimposed over the target drawing to be copied. Excellent source text.

(1982) Levy, J. "Handwriting posture and cerebral organization: How Are the Two Related?" *Psychological Bulletin*, 91 (3), 589–608.

(1987, March) Vellutino, F. "Dyslexia." *Scientific American*, 34–41. "Mirror writing and similar problems are usually blamed on defects in visual perception, but in truth, dyslexia seems to be a complex linguistic deficiency" (p. 34). Dyslexics appear to have difficulty "relat[ing] stimuli perceived through one sensory system [e.g., seeing] to stimuli perceived through another system [e.g., hearing]," p. 38.

(1988) Sarah, C. "Handwriting as a Tool in the Diagnosis of the Hyperactive Child." in A. Carmi and S. Schneider (eds.), *Experiencing Graphology*, London: Freund Publishing House. A blind study of the handwritings of 24 children, all age 12 comprising one hyperactive group of eight and two control groups of eight, one group normal, and the other slightly retarded, were analyzed for 17 personality characteristics measured for four degrees of intensity. "Professional graphologists were able to differentiate clearly between normal and abnormal children, an to describe specifically the syndromes of both hyperactivity and retardation. The profiles obtained by graphological analysis match the appropriate clinical profiles" (p. 229). *Experiencing Graphology*. Excellent source text.

(1988, September) Tenhouten, W., M. Seifer, and P. Siegel. "Alexithymia and the Split Brain: Evidence From Graphological Signs." *Psychiatric Clinics of North America*, 331–338. Two graphologists, Seifer and Siegel, independently scored psychograms for the handwritings of eight epileptic split-brain writers and eight normal matched pairs. Both analysts achieved results that were significantly different between the two groups. Also, they achieved together compound reliability on form level scores and four specific variables under the emotional release sector of the psychogram. In general, the split-brain writers were found to have arrhythmic, fragmented and disconnected writings with perseverations, patching and missed or misplaced letters or words.

(1991) Wellingham-Jones, Patricia. "Characteristics of Handwriting Subjects with Multiple Sclerosis." *Perceptual and Motor Skills*, 73, 867–79.

(1993) Keinan, G. "Can Stress Be Measured by Handwriting Analysis?" The effectiveness of the analytic method; discusses theoretical implications and possible advantages of using handwriting parameters as an indication of acute stress. *Applied Psychology: An International Review*, 42 (2), 153–70.

(1992 Dec.) Maeland, A.F. "Handwriting and Perceptual Motor Skills in Clumsy, Dysgraphic, & Normal Children." *Perceptual and Motor Skills*, 75 (3), 1207–17.

(1995/96) Ward, Suzy. "Indicators of Sexual Abuse in Handwriting." *Journal of the American Society of Professional Graphologists*, IV, 35–56. "Through the study of 76 known survivors of sexual abuse, a representative graphological profile was created by using a bar chart" for 43 graphic variables.

(1995–96) Farmer, Jeanette. "Measuring Handwriting to Identify Thinking & Behavioral Styles in Four Quadrants of the Brain." *Journal of the American Society of Professional Graphologists*, IV, 69–97. Handwritings were correlated with the Hermann Brain Dominance Instrument "a forced choice, self-assessment questionnaire that identified four thinking styles...[to identify] not only the left and right hemisphere characteristics but also conscious and unconscious factors."

(1996 Dec.) Loewenthal, Hamid. "Inferring Gender from Handwriting in Urdu and English." *Journal of Social Psychology*, 136 (6), 778–83.

(2002) Seifer, Marc. "The Telltale Hand: How Writing Reveals the Damaged Brain." *Cerebrum: Dana Forum for Brain Science*, 4, 27–42. Covering a quarter-century of inquiry into the handwriting of brain damaged writers, the author presented examples of people who had aphasia, paralysis, and thus mouth writing, gun-shot wound to the head, brain tumors, multiple sclerosis, stroke, and a coma victim. In three cases, the studies were accompanied with MRI's, so that the reader could see the trauma in the writing trail as well as in the actual brain.

(2004) Griffiths, Renata. "The Wartegg Test: Its Use in Combination with Handwriting Analysis & the Tree Test." *Journal of the American Society of Professional Graphologists*, VI, 71–108.

Bibliography

Allport, Gordon and Phillip Vernon. *Studies in Expressive Movement*. N.Y.: Macmillan, 1933 and 1967.

Allport, Gordon. *Personality: A Psychological Interpretation*. N.Y.: Henry Holt, 1937.

Anthony, Daniel. *The Graphological Psychogram*. Newark, N.J.: 1969.

———. *Readings in Psychology Today*. Del Mar, Calif.: CRM Books, 1969.

Ave-Lallemant, Ursua. *The Star-Wave Test*. Munich: Ernst Reinhardt, 1978 and 1984.

———. "The Star-Wave Test: An Introduction & Test Guide." *Journal of the American Society of Professional Graphologists* 5 (1999): 103–20.

Backman, Bob. "Graphology in America." *min.ac.uk/marketingresearch/2169backeng.htm*, 2001.

Baldi, C. *Judging the Nature & Quality of a Writer from his Letters*. Bologna: 1644.

Baughan, Rosa. *Character Indicated by Handwriting*. London: L. Upcott Gill, 1890.

Bernard, Marie. *European Graphology*. National Society for Graphology, 1980.

———. *Pophal's Handwriting & Brainwriting*. New York: NSG, 1982.

Bettelheim, Bruno. *The Empty Fortress*, N.Y.: Free-Press, Collier-Macmillan, 1967.

Bowers, Ellen. "Dan Anthony: A Personal Interview." *Gold Nibs* (1989): 1–5.

Bradley, Nigel, ed. Oxford 1987: *First British Symposium of Graphological Research*, Derbyshire, Great Britain, 1987.

Brenner, Charles. *An Elementary Textbook of Psychoanalysis*. Garden City, N.Y.: Doubleday, 1957.

Brooks, C. Harry. *Your Character From Your Handwriting*. London: George Allen & Unwin, 1967.

Bryndon, L., N. Harrison, C. Walker, A. Steptoe, and H. Critchley. "Peripheral Inflammation is Associated with Altered Substantia Nigra Activity and Psychomotor Slowing in Humans." *Biol. Psychiatry*, Jan. 31, 2008.

Bunker, M.N. *Handwriting Analysis*. Chicago: Nelson Hall, 1966.

Byerley, T. *Characteristic Signatures*. London, 1823.

Cabanne, R.A. "Cannon on the Clifford Irving Hoax." *Journal of Forensic Sciences* 20 (1975): 5–15.

Camillo, Fanta. Remembrances of Max Pulver. Private Interview with M. Seifer. April 1981.

Cloniger, Susan. *Theories of Personality*, Englewood Cliffs, N.J.: Prentice Hall, 2004.

Crepieux-Jamin. *Handwriting & Expression*. London: Kegan, Trench & Trubner, 1892.

———. *The Psychology of the Movement of Handwriting*. London: George Routledge & Sons, 1926.

Deragna, S., R. Agostini, I. Coghi, G. Montanino, and M. Nicotra. "Psychosomatic Sterility. Search For a Hypothesis For Personality Structure Using Moretti's Graphology Method." *Minerva Ginecol*. 46 (1994): 31–40.

deSainte Colombe, Paul. *Grapho-Therapeutics*. Hollywood, Calif.: Laurinda Books, 1967.

DeSalamanca, Don Felix. *The Philosophy of Handwriting*. London: Chatto & Windus, 1879.

Dettweiler, Christian. *Disturbed Ego Development*. Translated by Hilda Halpern. New York, N.Y.: NSG, 1979.

Dines, Jess E. *Document Examiner Textbook*. Grand Cayman: Pantex International. 1998.

D'Israeli, Isaac. *Autographs in Curiosities of Literature*. Publisher Unknown, 1824.

Doremus, Laura. *Character in Handwriting*. New York: Charles Renard Co., 1925.

Downey, June. *Graphology & the Psychology of Handwriting*. Baltimore: Warwick & York, 1919.

Dresbold, M., with Kwalwasser, J. Sex, Lies, and Handwritin. New York: Free Press, 2006.

Eliasberg, Wladimir. "Graphology & Medicine." *Journal of Nervous & Mental Disease* 4 (1944): 381–401.

————. "Methods in Graphologic Diagnostics." *PsychiatricQuarterly* (1952): 2–15.

————. "Pen, Paper & Parkinsonism." *Geriatrics* 14 (1959): 705–08.

Eliasberg, Wladimir and H.O. Teltscher. "How Long was Roosevelt Ill before his Death?" *Diseases of the Nervous System*, 14 (1953): 322–28.

————. "Neuropsychiatry & Graphodiagnostics in Parkinson Research." *Acta Psychiaqtrica et Neurologica Scandinavica* 36 (1961): 387–406.

Emery, E. "Study Finds Graphologists Not Write about Personality." *Providence Journal* 1:5, 2:5 (1985).

Epstein, Lawrence, and Huntington Hartford. "Some Relationships of Beginning Strokes in Handwriting to Human Figure Drawing Test." *Perceptual & Motor Skills* 3 (1959).

Erikson, Erik. *Identity, Youth and Crisis*, New York: W.W. Norton, 1968.

Eysenck, H. "Graphological analysis and Psychiatry: An Experimental Study." *British Journal of Psychology* 35 (1945): 70–81.

Faideau, Pierre (ed.). *La Graphologie: Histoire, pratique, perspectives.* Paris: 1983.

Farmer, Jeanette. *Can Handwriting Exercises Be The Unrecognized Road to Developing Literacy?* Tucson, Ariz.: Mostly Books, 1997.

————. "Measuring Handwriting to Identify Thinking & Behavioral Styles in Four Quadrants of the Brain." *JASPG* IV (1995): 69–97.

Fay, S., L. Chester, and M. Linklater. *Hoax.* New York: Viking Press, 1972.

Fluckiger, Fritz and Tripp Clarence. "A Review of Experimental Research in Graphology." *Perceptual & Motor Skills*, Monograph 12 (1961).

French, William Henry. *The Psychology of Handwriting*. New York: G. Putnam's Sons, 1922.

Freud, Sigmund. *Wit & the Unconscious*. New York: Basic Books, 1938.

————. *Collected Works*. New York: Basic Books, 1938.

Gille-Maisani, J-G. *The Psychology of Handwriting*. London: Scriptor Publishers, 1991.

Graphique. *Your Character in Your Pen!* London: Frank Hollings Publishers, 1916.

Green, Jane Nugent. *You and Your Private I*. St. Paul, Minn.: Llewllyn, 1916.

Gross, Hans. *Criminal Investigation*. London: Sweet & Maxwell, 1924.

Hayes, Reed. *Forensic Handwriting Examination: A Definitive Guide*. Honolulu: ReedWrite Press, 2006.

Henze, Adolf. *Chirogrammatomantie*. Leipzig: Weber Publishers, 1863.

Hilton, Ordway. *Scientific Examination of Documents*. Chicago: Callaghan Co., 1956.

Hamilton, Charles. *Great Forgers & Famous Fakes*. New York: Crown Publishers, 1980.

Harrison, Wilson. *Suspect Documents*. New York: Frederick Praeger Publishers, 1958.

Hartford, Huntington. *You Are What You Write*: New York: MacMillan, 1973.

Hartmann, Heinz. *Ego Psychology & the Problems of Adaption*. New York: International University Press, 1952.

Harvey, O. "Measurement of Handwriting Considered as a Form of Expressive Movement." *Character and Personality*, 2 (1934): 310–21.

Hatfield Holmes, Iris. *History of Graphology*, Louisville, Ky.: HuVista Publishing, 2006.

———. *A Question of Honesty as Revealed in Handwriting*. Louisville, Ky., HuVista Publishing, 1988.

Hearns, Rudolph. *Handwriting: Analysis Through Its Symbolism*. New York: Vantage, 1973.

H.L.R. and M.L.R. *Talks on Graphology: The Art of Knowing Character Through Handwriting*. Boston: Lee & Shepard, 1897.

Howard, Clifford. *Graphology*. Philadelphia: Penn Publishing Co., 1911.

Hull, C. R. Montgomery. "Experimental Investigation of Alleged Relations between Character & Handwriting." *Psychology Review* 26 (1919): 63–74.

Jacoby, H.J. *Analysis of Handwriting*. London: George Allen & Unwin, 1939.

Kanfer, Alfred. "Cancer Detection & Handwriting." With Felix Klein and William Wolff, MD. Presentation to New York Chapter of American Graphology Society, Gene Steccone, Ed. April 13, 1965.

Kanfer, D. "Neuromuscular aberrations with developing malignancies." *The Bulletin of the Hospital for Joint Diseases*. (April 1958).

Kanfer, D. and R.S. Fischer. The *Proceedings of the American Association for Cancer Research* held in Philadelphia, Pennsylvania. (April 9–11, 1970)

Keehner, James. "Thea Stein-Lewinson." *ASPG* (2004): 22–223.

Keene, J. Harrington. "The Principles & Practices of Graphology, or Character Reading From Handwriting." Vermont. Original handwritten manuscript, 1887.

———. *The Mystery of Handwriting*. Boston: Lee & Shephard, 1896.

Kintzel-Thumm, Magdalene. *Psychology & Pathology of Handwriting*. New York: Fowler & Wells, 1905.

Klages, Ludwig. *A Discussion of Works*. Pebble Beach, Calif.: 1980.

————. *Handschrift and Charakter*. Leipzig: Verlig von Johann Publishers, 1929.

Klein, Felix. "Ludwig Klages Translations." *NSG Newsletter* 11 (1983): 3–6.

————. "The Guiding Image." in Oxford 1987: *First British Symposium of Graphological Research*, Nigel Bradley (ed.), Derbyshire, Great Britain (1986): 51–61.

Koestler, Arthur. *The Case of the Midwife Toad*. New York: Random House, 1972.

Koren, Anna. *The Typology of Rene Le Senne*. Haifa, Israel: Graphology Institute, 1984.

Le Senne, René. *Traité de caractérologie*. Paris: Presses Universitaires de France, 1945.

Levine, Alan. "Physical Aspects of Stroke Texture." *ASPG* (1993): 81–92.

Lewinson, Thea Stein. *Handwriting Analysis*. New York: Kings Crown Press, 1942.

Lewinson, T.S. "An Introduction to the Graphology of Ludwig Klages." *Character and Personality* 3 (1938): 163–176.

Lewinson, T.S., and J. Zubin. *Handwriting Analysis: A Series of Scales for Evaluating the Dynamic Aspects of Handwriting*. New York, 1942.

Luria, Alexander. *The Working Brain*. New York: Basic Books, 1973.

————. *Higher Cortical Functions in Man*. New York: Springer, 1970.

MacLean, P. "The Triune Brain." *American Scientist* 66 (1978): 101–13.

Marcuse, Irene. *Handwriting: Guide to the Disturbed Personality*. New York: Arco, 1969.

Marne, Patricia. *Crime & Sex in Handwriting*. London: Constable Publishing, 1981.

Marum, O. "Character Assessment from Handwriting." *Journal of Mental Science*, 91 (1945): 22–42.

Mendel, Alfred. *Personality in Handwriting*. London: Peter Owen Ltd., 1947.

Michon, Jean Hippolyte. *Systeme de Graphologie*. Paris: Publisher unknown, 1871.

Monte, Christopher. *Beneath the Mask*. New York: Holt, Rinehart & Winston, 1987.

Muhl, Anita. "Unreliability of Behavior as Evidenced in Handwriting." San Diego, Calif.: Lecture before American Woman's Assoc., September 1949.

Müller, W.H., and A. Enskat. *Graphologie Diagnostics: Their Basis, Possibilities & Borders*. Stuttgart, Germany: Hands Huber & Berne, 1961.

Naftali, Arie. Behavior Factors in *Handwriting Identification, Journal of Criminal Law* 56 (1965): 528–38.

Nezos, Renna. *Grapholog: The Interpretation of Handwriting*. London: Scriptor Books, 1992.

Odem, Israel. "Slant in Handwriting as a Means of Typology." *Abstracts*. Jerusalem: International Congress in Experiencing Graphology, 1985.

O'Neill, Edward. *Collected Translations of Crepieux-Jamin, Pierre Faideau, Max Pulver, Ania Telliard*. New York: NSG, 1983.

Olynova, Nadya. *Handwriting Tells*. Indianapolis, Ind.: Bobbs Merrill Co., 1969.

Osborne, Albert. *Questioned Documents*. Albany, New York: Boyd Printing Co., 1929.

Ploog, Helmut. "Bericht upber den Graphologiekongren in Mailand vom 21" in *Angewantde Graphollogie und Personlichkeits-diagnostik*, (2005): 51–55.

Poe, Edgar Allen. "Murders of the Rue Morgue." *Selected Poetry & Prose of Edgar Allan Poe*, 1961.

———. "Chapter on Autography in Eureka, Marginalia and the Literati." Boston, (1856/1884) 351–450.

Pokorny, Richard. *Handschrift als Gehirnschrift*, Berlin: Pub. unknown, 1949.

———. *Psychologie der Handschrift*, Berlin: Pub. unknown, 1973.

Preyer, William. *On the Physiology of Handwriting*. Hamburg: Pub. unknown, 1895.

Progoff, Ira. *Jung, Synchronicity & Human Destiny*. New York: Julian Press, 1959.

Providence Journal. R.I. "Murder suspect denies being in state where crime occurred." p. B3. (January 31, 1991)

Pulver, Max. *Symbolik der Handschrift*. Zurich: Orell Fussli, 1931.

———. *Symbolism in Handwriting*. Ed O'Neill (trans.)New York, 1980.

Quirke, Arthur J. *Forged, Anonymous & Suspect Documents*. London: George Routledge & Sons, 1930.

Rand, Henry. *Graphology: A Handbook*. Cambridge, Mass.: Sci-Art Publishing Co., 1961.

Rapaport, David. "Activity & Passivity of the Ego With Regards to Reality" in his *Collected Works*, New York: Basic Books, 1967.

Rexford J. *What Handwriting Indicates: An Analytical Graphology*. New York: G. Putnam & Sons, 1904.

Rhoden, Harold. *High Stakes: Gamble for Howard Hughes Will*. New York: Crown. 1983.

Rice, Louise. *Character Reading From Handwriting*. New York: F. Stoks & Co., 1927.

————. *Correspondence Course*. New York: Rice Institute of Graphology, 1924.

Riklan and Levitz. *Subcortical Correlates of Human Behavior*. Md.: Wilkins, 1969.

Roman, Klara. *Encyclopedia of the Written Word*. New York, 1962.

————. *Handwriting: A Key to Personality*. New York: Noonday Press, 1985.

Rubin, Roger. *The Influence of the Mother & The Father as Seen in Handwriting*. New York, 1985/2007.

Sands, R.C. "Thoughts on Hand-writing." *Knicker-Bocker* 12 (1838): 318–24.

Sara, Dorothy. *Handwriting Analysis for the Millions*. New York: Bell Publishers, 1967.

Saudek, Robert. *Psychology of Handwriting*. London: George Allen & Unwin, 1926.

————. *Experiments in Handwriting*. London: George Allen & Unwin, 1928.

Schuler, Carole. *Collected Lectures at the National Society for Graphology*. New York: *NSG*, 1975.

Sellers, Clark. "Albert S. Osborn: A Tribute." *Journal of Criminal Law and Criminology* 38 (1947): 75–78.

Seifer, Marc. "The Bin Laden Affair." *The Vanguard* (2002): 1–2.

————. "Brain Damage Seen In Handwriting." *Write-Up, NSG* 31 (2004): 6–10.

————. The Clifford Irving Forgery, *JASPG, III* (1993): 87–97.

————. "Conscious, Preconscious & Unconscious Determinants in Handwriting." *British Institute of Graphologists Tenth Anniversary Symposium Proceedings*. Cambridge, England: BIG Press, 1993.

————. "Creativity in Handwriting." *American Association of Handwriting Analysts* (1987) 1–2.

————. "Disguise in Handwriting." *Rhode Island Bar Journal* (1988): 23–24.

————. "Handwriting and Brain Functioning." A. Carmi & S. Schneider (Eds.) *Experience Graphology*. London: Freund Publishing House, 1988.

————. "Form Level." *Journal of the American Society of Professional Graphologists* VI (2004): 185–200.

————. "Forminveau Theoretische Betrachtungen." Munich: *Angewandte Graphologie Und Personlichkeits-Diagnostik* (2005): 29–47.

————. *Framed! Stephen Rosati Story*. Kingston, RI: Powerhouse Publishers, 2008.

————. "The Gamble of the Howard Hughes Mormon Will." *Lawyer's Weekly* 13 (1988): 1–3.

————. "Handwriting and MRI Correlations of Brain Damage."

————. "The Handwriting of Patty Hearst." *ESP Magazine* (1977): 32–34.

————. "The Handwriting of the Presidents." *ESP Magazine* 1 (1976): 40–42, 65–66.

————. "The Handwritings of Teddy Roosevelt, Benedict Arnold, Ralph Waldo Emerson & Elizabeth Cady Stanton." *Civilization Magazine* (2000): 36.

————. (1989) A History of Graphology. M. Westergaard (Ed.) *Directory of Handwriting Analysts*. Warren, MI: MW Press, pp. 1–14. (Also in 1982, 1983, 1986, 1988 editions.)

————. (1993) Letter from the Editor, *JASPG, III*, p. 3–4.

————. Letter from Editor-in Chief. The Founding of the Journal. *Journal of the American Society of Professional Graphologists*, V 1999: 3–4.

————. "A Longitudinal Study of the Handwriting of Nikola Tesla." Chapter 53 in *Nikola Tesla: Psychohistory of a Forgotten Inventor*. Ann Arbor, Mich.: University Microfilms, 1986.

————. "The Lost Wizard: A Longitudinal Study of the Handwriting of Nikola Tesla." *Tesla '84: Proceedings of the Tesla Centennial Symposium*. Colorado Springs, Colo.: ITS Press, 1984.

————. "Nikola Tesla & the House of Morgan." *The Many Faces of Psychohistory*. New York: Long Island University & International Psychohistory Society, 1984.

————. (1989, Fall) The Preconscious in Handwriting. JASPG, I, pp. 63-80.Graphology Institute, 1985. Haifa, Israel (translated into Hebrew.)

————. "The Preconscious in Handwriting." *NSG Newsletter*, (1975): 1–3.

————. "The Telltale Hand: How Writing Reveals the Damaged Brain." *Cerebrum: Dana Forum for Brain Science*, 4 (2002): 27–42.

————. "Uses of Graphology in Business." *Rhode Island Business Quarterly* (1972): 18–23.

Seifer, Marc, and David Goode, MD. "Handwriting: A Measure of Muscle Tension in Schizophrenics and Normals." *National Society for Graphology Newsletter* (1974): 1–3.

Seifer, Thelma, and Marc Seifer. "A Right Brain Approach to Handwriting Analysis." *JASPG* II (1991): 108–30.

Siegel, Patricia. "American Left-handed Writings" in *Abstracts*. Jerusalem: International Congress on Experiencing Graphology, 36.

————. "Integrity and Handwriting." *JASPG* 2 (1991): 55–71.

Singer, Eric. *A Manual of Graphology*. London: Gerald Duckworth & Co., 1969.

Stocker, Richard Dimsdale. *The Language of Handwriting*. New York: Bretano's Publishers, 1901.

Storey, Arthur. *A Manual of Graphology*. London: William Rider & Son, 1922.

Sonnemann, Ulrich. *Handwriting Analysis as a Diagnostic Tool*. New York: Grune & Stratton, 1950.

Szochet, Mel. *Determination of Male and Female in Handwriting*. Upper Saddle River, N.J.: 1981.

Taunton Gazette. "Reading Between the Lines: Monica Lewinsky and the Ramsey Ransom Note." Section D (1999):1–2.

Teillard, Ania. *The Soul of Handwriting*. Translated from the French by Ed O'Neill. N.Y.: circa 1980.

Teltscher, Herry O. *Handwriting: Revelation of Self*. New York: Hawthorne Books, 1971.

Tenhouten, Warren, Marc Seifer, and Patricia Siegel. "Alexithymia & the Split Brain." *Psychiatric Clinics of North America*, (1988): 331–8.

Vaisman, Lois and Virginia DiLeo. "Children in Distress: The Graphological Viewpoint," *JASPG* 2 (1991): 39–54.

Victor, Frank. *Handwriting: A Personality Projection*. Springfield, Ill.: Charles Thomas Publishers, 1952.

Von Hagen, Hugo. *Reading Character from Handwriting*. New York: RS Mighill & Co., 1902.

Ward, Suzy. "Sexual Abuse in Handwriting." *JASPG* IV (1995): 35–55.

Westergaard, Marjorie. *Directory of Handwriting Analysts*. Warren, Mich., 1988.

Wolff, Werner. *Diagrams of the Unconscious*. New York: Grune & Stratton, 1948 and 1963.

Wolfson, Rose. *Graphology*. *Projective Techniques*. Englewood Cliffs, N.J.: Prentice Hall, 1951.

Yalon, Dafna. *The Star Wave Test Across The Life-Span*. Quebec: International Graphological Society, 2004.

Index

MARC J. SEIFER studied all phases of handwriting investigation in post-graduate work for five semesters at the New School for Social Research in New York. Some of his graduate work was also on this topic. A graduate with a BS from the University of Rhode Island, an MA from the University of Chicago, and a PhD from Saybrook Institute, he worked for the Crime Laboratory at the University of Rhode Island, 1974–75, and throughout the 1990s, for the Rhode Island Fraud Unit of the Department of Human Services and the attorney general's office in handwriting fraud, where he worked on more than 8,000 cases. Other clients include police departments in Warwick, Central Falls, and South County, Public Defender's Office, UPS, insurance companies and banks, hundreds of local lawyers, Connecticut Lawyer's Group and the War Department Naval Undersea Warfare. With publications in *Psychiatric Clinics of North America, Rhode Island Bar Journal, Civilization, Cerebrum*, and *Lawyers' Weekly*, he was also editor-in-chief of *The Journal of the American Society of Professional Graphologists* for 10 years. *ASPG* is the only academic journal on the study of handwriting in America.

Dr. Seifer has testified in civil and criminal cases in state and federal courts in New York, Connecticut, Massachusetts, New Hampshire, Maine, and Rhode Island. He has lectured on all phases of handwriting investigation at Cambridge University and Oxford University in England, Israel, and Yugoslavia, at the University of Vancouver, Brandeis University, the Federal Reserve Bank in Boston, and for companies, insurance groups, and handwriting organizations throughout the United States. He has appeared as a QD Expert on the History Channel, WJAR TV News, Coast to Coast Radio, and on AP International TV. Feature articles on his work in the field have appeared in *The Economist, Rhode Island Monthly, Cosmopolitan, Narragansett Times, Taunton Gazette, New Bedford Standard Times, The Westerly Sun, The Providence Journal*, and *The Washington Post*. He has worked with medical doctors on handwriting and brain organization at Brown University, UCLA, and the University of Chicago. His results were published in the periodicals mentioned previously. His book *Wizard: The Life & Times of Nikola Tesla* is highly recommended by the American Association for the Advancement of Science. He teaches forensic graphology at Roger Williams University.